The Longer View

Paul A. Baran

The Longer View

Essays Toward a
Critique of
Political Economy

Edited and with an Introduction
by John O'Neill
Preface by Paul M. Sweezy

New York and London

Library of Congress Catalog Card Number: 68-13656
Standard Book Number: SBN 85345-113-3

. First Paperback Edition 1971
Second Printing

Monthly Review Press
62 West 14th Street, New York, N.Y. 10011
21 Theobalds Road, London, WCIX, 8SL

For what is, in my opinion, central to the Marxian position is the capacity and willingness to look beyond the immediately observable facts and to see the tree of the future in the tiny shoots barely perceptible in the present. It is the combination of historical vision and the courage to be utopian—with the vision sternly disciplined by an analysis of *tendencies* discernible at the present time, and with the utopia rendered concrete by the identification of the *social forces* that may be expected to further its realization.

— Paul A. Baran

Contents

IV

ON MONOPOLY CAPITALISM

V

ON THE POLITICAL ECONOMY OF GROWTH

VI

ON SOCIALISM

The Longer View

Preface

In his last letter before his death, Paul Baran wrote that the first thing he wanted to do during a forthcoming sabbatical leave was to "go over, change, and fix a bunch of different articles, reviews, etc., and make them into a book of essays." Among his papers I found two draft tables of contents, differing only in details and both bearing the overall title *The Longer View*. They both contained pieces he planned to write specially for the volume on which he had not yet begun work.

To carry out his intention as nearly as possible and to help with editorial tasks, I enlisted the cooperation of John O'Neill, now Professor of Sociology at York University in Toronto, who in the late 1950's had taken a doctorate under Baran's supervision in a special program combining economics and philosophy. Since the preliminary tables of contents with which we had to work contained unwritten essays, we had to make a few changes and we decided to add several pieces which we felt sure Baran would have agreed to include. (One of these, "Better Smaller But Better," had been written under the pseudonym Historicus, and I think it likely that he had forgotten it. Nevertheless, it remains among the most perceptive diagnoses of the socioeconomic condition of early Cold War America I know of.) On the whole, however, the book closely follows Baran's original conception, and I am confident brings together his most important, hitherto scattered, writings.

I accept full responsibility for the various circumstances which have delayed the publication of this volume until six years after its author's death. It would have been greatly preferable if it had been available sooner, especially to younger social scientists both here and abroad. And yet there may be something to be said in extenuation. Paul Baran's stature as a Marxist and political economist has been steadily rising since the publication in 1957 of his path-breaking book *The Political Economy of Growth.* That work was the beginning of what it is no exaggeration to call a revolution in the way Marxists, especially in the Third World, analyze the relations between advanced capitalist countries and their underdeveloped dependencies. It is sad that Baran did not live to see the effect of his work and to enjoy the recognition it has now attained. But one thing I think is reasonably clear: as a result of this recognition *The Longer View* will today reach a larger and even more appreciative audience than awaited it a few years ago.

I take this opportunity to thank John O'Neill for his cooperation and his patience.

—Paul M. Sweezy

March 1, 1970

Introduction:
Marxism and the
Sociological Imagination

Paul Baran is widely known as the author of *The Political Economy of Growth* and as co-author, with Paul M. Sweezy, of *Monopoly Capital: An Essay on the American Economic and Social Order*. Almost ten years separate these two major works, highlights of a life in the academic community which, despite setbacks, disappointments, loss, and loneliness, spoke clearly to men in every land where men are still willing and able to risk commitment to reason and a humane social order. The story of Baran's life in the United States and abroad, of his intellectual self-questioning, his moods of optimism and despair clarified by his own wit and charm, upon which so many friends came to rely, has been told elsewhere.[1] Here I propose to call attention to some of his most original and distinctive contributions to Marxian social thought.

The major themes of *The Political Economy of Growth* and *Monopoly Capital* were developed in a number of shorter essays which preserve much of the vigor and personal style of Baran's day-to-day reflections. These essays, which are presented here for the first time in a single collection, cover the whole range of Baran's talents and interests, from the technical analysis of the problems of economic planning to the brave rhetoric of his "Reflections on the Cuban Revolution." They display a breadth of sociological and economic analysis which represents a unique conquest of mind in its ability to situate itself in an environment where disorientation and abdication threaten many social thinkers. But it would be a distortion of Baran's own self-understanding to suggest that his achievement is simply that of a rare individual. For what was rare in him was the intellectual tradition in which he thought and for which it made sense to suffer. In Baran, Marxism and the exercise of sociological imagination were at once an exigency and a gift to be integrated into the human condition.[2] He conceived the Marxian legacy as properly a source of questions which seek to relate empirical findings in terms of a systematic and explicit awareness of their implications for individual biography and social history. In such a view there can be no mechanical relation between the exercise of the sociological imagination and its techniques. Moreover, the Marxian social scientist has history on his side only rarely. Meantime, the task of sociological analysis requires, as Baran himself expresses it, "the capacity and willingness to look beyond the immediately observable facts and to see the tree of the future in the tiny shoots barely perceptible in the present. It is the combination of historical vision and the courage to be utopian—with the vision sternly disciplined by an analysis of *tendencies* discernible at the present time, and with the utopia rendered concrete by the identification of the *social forces* that may be expected to further its realization." What is Marxian in this conception of sociological reason or imagination is the broad conviction (broad in the sense that it stems from the Enlightenment tradition and is now a world-revolutionary force) that human reason is a power in history and society, responsible for founding a social order which releases its potentialities both in the individual and the collective. In this task there are no historical guarantees. The vision of a rational social order represents an option to which men may commit themselves, but it is equally an option which they may refuse—not in the sense that it is only one value among others (for it is the matrix of all values), but in the sense that they may defend decaying partial truths against a conception of truth which is the birth of truth.

While working with Paul Sweezy on *Monopoly Capital*, Baran found it necessary to examine the core of philosophical and methodological assumptions which were the implicit foundations of the joint work. The result, so far as we possess it, is a series of essays on the situation of Marxism in the context of American monopoly capitalism. These essays are neither political manifestoes nor abstract methodological treatises. They are rather essays in self-understanding and orientation through an ideological perspective that is neither a flight into utopianism nor a submission to pessimism. Baran starts by putting Marxism itself into question.[3] That is to say, he raises the question of the historical relevance of Marxism in the absence of a vital proletarian consciousness in advanced industrial societies. Though not impressed by arguments about the growth and planning potentials of capitalism, he thought it imperative to reassess the nature of bourgeois ideology and its positive functions in the maintenance of the social order. The relation between social reality and ideological consciousness is far more complex than is presupposed by the critique of "false consciousness." Thus the ideology of competition, while objectively a misrepresentation of the business norms of monopoly capitalism, remains a powerful norm of individual socialization in the form of an "aggressive individualism." The consequence of such a norm is the subjectivization of objective chances for success and failure in abstraction from the social and political structure of monopoly capitalism. In accordance with the norms of bourgeois individualism, the tension between individual and social reality is privatized.[4] Conflict is artificially located in the individual psyche or else diagnosed as a "family problem." The rules of the game forbid the diagnosis of conflicts in terms of socioeconomic factors—a move dismissed as "projection"—and thus they prejudice the possibility of prescribing political remedies for individual malaise.[5]

The Marxian critique of the psychologistic reduction of the social process to individual behavior and its explanation in terms of the constants of a basic human nature is a permanent contribution to the methodological autonomy of the social sciences.[6] Indeed, it is now more usual for psychologism to appropriate some aspects of sociological theory and to appear in the form of "socio-psychologism," a mixture of Freudianism and a number of quasi-sociological concepts. Forced to recognize that the autonomy of the individual is structured in terms of social processes, exponents of socio-psychologism revert to an oversimplified view of the interaction between "environmental" factors and individual autonomy or alienation. But while psychologism and socio-psychologism both reveal important features of the human condition under capitalism, its desperate mentality and its impoverished culture, each fails to clarify our understanding of the historical potentiality of human nature for self-transformation in interaction with changes in social organization. "Thus a proper analysis of human motivations and conduct must refer to a time span shorter than that of psychologism but longer than that of socio-psychologism. It has to avoid the ahistorical frozenness of the former while escaping at the same time the newspaper headline orientation of the latter. And it must consider human development in its true context: the economic and social order determining the content and molding the profile of the relevant historical epoch."[7]

The latter observation points to the need for a more detailed analysis of the structure of the social order whose mode of self-comprehension, maintenance, and self-transformation raises doubts about the relevance of Marxian social

science. The primary characteristic of the capitalist industrial order is its unprecedented expansion of society's
productive resources, a reversal of the power of nature over
society achieved by means of a social transformation of the
economic and political basis of the power of a class of men
over the mass of men. It is, however, the interplay between
the dialectic of man and nature and the dialectic between
man and society which is crucial to the understanding of
the structure and genesis of the capitalist order. Here it was
that Marx located the conflict between the restless rationalization of the means of production, which characterizes
capitalism as an economic order, and the irrational moral and
political consequences of applying the same standard of
rationalization to the social relations of men. "The capitalist
order of production," Marx wrote, "is generally, despite all
its niggardliness, thoroughly wasteful as far as the human
material is concerned, just as, conversely, owing to its
method of distribution of products through commerce and
its manner of competition, it is very wasteful with regard to
its material means, and loses for society what it gains for the
individual capitalist."[8] From a historical standpoint, the
combination of the low productivity of labor and conditions
of general scarcity offered a rationale for a highly differential
participation in the consumption and investment processes
which determine the total flow of social goods. Indeed, it
might well be argued that the social injustices of the early
competitive phase of capitalism represented an unavoidable
phase of industrial growth, rather than expressions of the
absolute inhumanity of capitalism. However, once the technological basis of the capitalist industrial order reached the
degree of productive power possible today, the persistence of
social injustices and the impoverishment of large sectors of its
domestic and dependent populations raises the question of
the loss of any rationale for the social order of capitalism.
"In the earlier period, when scarcity was still inevitable, the

critical reaction of the discrepancy between the mode of functioning of the system as a whole and that of its parts was, and indeed could only be, a feeling of outrage at the *injustice* of capitalism. It is only in relatively recent times when plenty is within easy reach and its attainment is obviously prevented by the continued dominance of capitalism that the *irrationality* of the system moves into the forefront of critical thought."[9]

Marxian social science starts from the premise that the "confrontation of reality with reason"[10] is the fundamental norm of all thought, whatever the particular historical conception of the nature of reality or of the methods of reason. In actual practice there will always be a close relationship between reason and reality through the mediation of empirical research, of which a classical example is Marx's monumental analysis of the processes of the capitalist system. What has to be preserved in Marx's procedure is not merely his techniques of analysis and description. The techniques may vary with the growth of scientific knowledge in general, and with the specific requirements of problems to which Marx could hardly have addressed himself. It is the canon of *critical reason* which cannot be abandoned. The latter enjoins a critical awareness of the degree to which the capitalist system develops or obstructs human welfare and a careful scrutiny of the degree to which theoretical descriptions of the capitalist system illuminate or obscure the understanding of its implications for individual and social development. But under capitalism reason is divided against itself. Thus the corporate economy simultaneously promotes the most highly rationalized forms of production process, business administration, and market control, while undermining the culture and humanity of the social order which it professes to serve. It is only by means of a quite undialectical separation of the economic system from the social order of capitalism that it is possible to doubt the relevance of the socialist critique. On a casual view, monopoly capitalism may be considered to have solved its "production problem" and thereby to have defeated the socialist expectation that capitalism would founder on purely economic contradictions and inefficiencies. Certainly, this view has persuaded liberals in general and democratic socialists in particular to revise their tactics in the hope that "political" gains may be won within an economic order otherwise unchallengeable. When, however, the efficacy of the system of production under monopoly capitalism is measured by the standard of its ability to produce such basic ingredients of a humane society as a universal minimum standard of health, housing, education, and public conveniences, its performance is glaringly lopsided. What is called the strength of monopoly capitalism is its power to over-produce for consumption in the private sector for given levels of class income, while under-producing or mis-producing in the public sector, as determined by the liberal ideology and the power of corporate interests.[11] We are thus confronted with the spectacle of an increasing micro-rationality in the production sector, impelled by the expanding irrationality of the social forces which determine the composition of production. "Whereas the irrationality of the whole must be constantly maintained if exploitation, waste, and privilege, if—in one word—capitalism is to survive, the rationality of society's individual parts is enforced by the drive for profits and the competitive necessities of capitalist enterprise."[12]

The irrationality of capitalist society has been attributed to a variety of psychological and institutional factors ranging from "the conventional wisdom" to status-seeking and a level of industrialization so high as to render waste "inconsequential." Such descriptions never amount to a general theory and are even misleading when not related to the structure and behavior of the typical giant corporation

whose drive for profits, and its consequent production and
sales techniques, set the tone of economic life, which in
turn is an increasingly powerful determinant of the general
style of life. In an effort to provide just such an
understanding of the structure and working principles of
capitalism, Baran elaborated the Marxian concept of
economic surplus and its variants—potential and planned
surplus.[13] Baran departs from Marx by distinguishing between the *actual* economic surplus, the difference between
society's current output and current consumption, and *potential* economic surplus, "the difference between the output that *could* be produced in a given natural and technological environment with the help of employable productive
resources and what might be regarded as essential consumption."[14] Whereas the concept of actual surplus is a conventional notion derivable from economic statistics, the concept
of potential surplus embodies a critique of economic performance which is broader than conventional indicators of
economic efficiency. "Its realization presupposes a more or
less drastic reorganization of the production and distribution
of social output, and implies far-reaching changes in the
structure of society."[15] There are, of course, difficulties in
the concept of potential surplus since it has both quantitative
and qualitative dimensions. But these are more than outweighed by the usefulness of the concept of sensitizing the
analyst and social planner to the institutional processes which
determine the performance of the capitalist system, but are
taken as data when market behavior is relied upon as the sole
indicator of rational performance. The concept of potential
economic surplus directs attention to the structures of excess
consumption, output lost due to unproductive work, and the
irrational and wasteful organization of the productive apparatus, as well as to the loss of output due to the underutilization of plant and labor and the insufficiency of
effective demand. In each case, there is implied some stand-

ard of adequate, essential, and proper use of human, material, and social resources in terms of which disagreements over the nature of essential and non-essential consumption, productive and non-productive employment may be resolved. It is here that the Marxian social scientist encounters a combination of value relativism and value agnosticism which separates him from bourgeois social scientists who take the existing social and economic order for granted. Caught between the false dilemma of accepting the liberal ideology of consumer sovereignty and the phantasm of the socialist dictatorship of choice, the bourgeois economist overlooks the facts of molded choice and ignores the essential question, namely, the *nature of the social and economic order* which molds individual preferences.

The cancerous malaise of monopoly capitalism is not that it "happens" to squander a large part of its resources on the production of means of destruction, that it "happens" to allow corporations to engage in liminal and subliminal advertising, in peddling adulterated products, and inundating human life with moronizing entertainment, commercialized religion, and based "culture." The cancerous malaise of the system which renders it a formidable obstacle to human advancement, is that all this is not an assortment of fortuitously appearing attributes of the capitalist order, but the very basis of its existence and viability. And such being the case, bigger and better Food and Drug Administrations, a comprehensive network of Distinguished Citizens Committees, and the like, can merely spread a veil over the existing mess rather than clear up the mess itself. To use an earlier comparison once more: building sumptuous cemeteries and expensive monuments for the victims of war does not reduce their number. The best—and the worst—that such seemingly humanitarian efforts can accomplish is to dull people's sensitivity to brutality and cruelty, to reduce their horror of war.[16]

The conflict between the "micro-reason" demanded by the accumulation needs of the capitalist system and the "macro-madness" induced by the expansion of wants in order to realize expectations on given levels of investment is reflected in the individual's fractured experience as worker and consumer. The psychologistic assumptions of bourgeois social science ignore the nature of the socioeconomic processes which under specific historical circumstances define the individual's objective and subjective situation. Whatever historical necessity there may have been for the repression of human sensibilities in the production and consumption processes during the early stages of capitalist industrialization, the potential productivity of the modern industrial system now renders meaningless. However, in the absence of any alternative to the Protestant Ethic, the individual's non-work time (one can hardly speak of leisure) is invaded by a quantitative ethic of wants, which seduced him into cooperating with the alienation of his conscious sensibilities at work in order to satisfy a fantasy of wants conjured up in the "privacy" of the home. Thus the individual is torn in the conflict between the ideology of rationality and responsibility dictated in his working-life and the image of spontaneity and carefree living projected for his non-working hours.[17] Everywhere the individual finds himself upon a treadmill of *wants* which carries him further and further away from the satisfaction of his basic human *needs*. In an economy where the "service industries" are a major feature, the quest for self-identity and spontaneity is injured at the root by the processes of personality-molding aimed at controlling the contact points between producer and consumer. Self-alienation now assumes its most diabolical form as the individual struggles to fetishize aspects of himself as "selling-points" to which his total personality is subordinated until such time as it atrophies, or submits to any of a host of painkillers which are the equilibrators of the capitalist social order.

Baran could speak with great compassion of the fate of the alienated individual oppressed by the disordered culture of monopoly capitalism. But when he turned to consider the injustice and irrationality in the social structures of contemporary underdeveloped countries, he spoke in a voice vibrant with the power of rational criticism and the simple truths of freedom from hunger and want. It was because Baran refused to lose sight of the world scene that he never faltered in his sense of the relevance of Marxism to the understanding of the interdependencies between the fate of the individual under monopoly capitalism and the birth of the individual in countries lying in the shadow of Western imperialism. Much of Baran's stature derives from his ability to comprehend the history and morphology of capitalism in its encounter with relatively non-industrial societies and its effect upon the option of industrialization in those countries.

All the strength of Baran's vision is present in the early essay, "On the Political Economy of Backwardness." In the light of later experiences in Western growthmanship and the widening gap between the rich and poor nations of the world, Baran's analysis of the morphology of backwardness has the rare merit of having become increasingly relevant. What is true of capitalism at home is all the more true abroad: it creates a social order incompatible with the universalization of the material gains which it makes feasible from a technical point of view. The profound dislocation and permanent distortion of the social and political structure of countries which have experienced the intervention of European and North American capitalism is the major source of their industrial backwardness. The contact between advanced capitalism and the pre-capitalist economies of the underdeveloped countries did not produce the complementary revolutions in the agricultural and manufacturing sectors which characterized the classical "take-off" in Europe. The traditional economy merely suffered a sectoral juxtaposition of primary production for a world market and the importation of highly developed technology and communications systems necessary to the extraction and processing of raw materials. Caught between the feudal or semi-feudal monopoly of land and the foreign monopoly of industry, the indigenous bourgeoisie confined itself to the equally monopolistic gains of mercantile capitalism, characterized by rapid turnover, large but short-term risks, and correspondingly high rates of profits. Under these conditions, the mentality of the bourgeoisie is not such as to enter into the forms of large-scale investment which are necessitated by round-about processes of agricultural and industrial production guided by the rationale of high growth rates in the long run. There is even less chance of investment in the creation of the necessary forms of social overhead which provide the basic external economies necessary to induce business investment. However, these obstacles to indigenous, privately sponsored industrialization in the underdeveloped countries are in certain respects merely rationalizations of the prevailing social and political uncertainty which arises from the coalition of domestic and foreign property owners against a landless and unskilled laboring population. In this climate private capital goes abroad to seek more secure investments, while much of public investment takes the form of military and police expenditures to maintain the status quo. The underdeveloped economy differs from the advanced economy inasmuch as its *actual* economic surplus, although constituting a large proportion of total output, is nevertheless low in absolute terms. Yet this should not hide the fact that even in the underdeveloped countries there is a large potential economic surplus lost through the conspicuous consumption of the upper classes, capital flight, and the maintenance of government bureaucracies and military establishments. "There the difference is not, as in the advanced countries, between higher and lower degrees of development, between the now reachable final solution of the entire problem of want and the continuation of drudgery, poverty, and cultural degradation; there the difference is between abysmal squalor and decent existence, between the misery of hopelessness and the exhilaration of progress, between life and death for hundreds of millions of people."[18] The difference between the past history of capitalism and the future history of socialism in the underdeveloped countries is the only guarantee that they will not continue to stagnate under the weight of an oppressive social and political structure, aided and abetted by the reactionary world interests of the multinational corporation.[19] This is not, of course, to underestimate the technical difficulties of socialist planning, nor to overlook the ambiguity of history in which revolution and counterrevolution coexist. But neither is it to lose sight of what provides the ultimate justification of all genuine socialist effort—the vision of a humane social order rather than the scientistic fantasy of a "fail-safe" technology.

In the following pages the reader will find one man's vision becoming concrete with a wealth of historical and sociological fact, disciplined by critical analysis, chastened by the events of personal and world history, but never losing sight of the totality of human possibility which is man himself. What Baran asked from his fellow social scientists was not agreement so much as argument that was vital rather than neutral. For he sensed in the value-agnosticism of non-Marxian social science a deadly leveling of culture in which the sciences and the arts affect the same kind of appeal as the rest of the canned culture of monopoly capitalism, whose lack of content is thinly disguised by the effort and ingenuity involved in producing it. Baran was fond of quoting Hegel's remark from the *Phenomenology of Mind*, "the truth is the whole" (*das Wahre ist das Ganze*). The sense of that remark is that human knowledge is advanced by successive approximations in which truth emerges through a dialectic of persuasions, each of which illuminates some aspect of reality at the same time that its perspective casts a shadow on other aspects. But at no time is the progress of knowledge external to the history of man in the widest sense, namely, the dialectical alternation of freedom and alienation. The desire to escape the dilemma of the ideological roots of knowledge characterized the failure of positivist value-free social science. "The trouble with economics is not that it does not yet 'know enough,' as many of its practitioners love to repeat. Its fatal shortcoming is that it does not incorporate in its knowledge the understanding of what is necessary for the attainment of a better, more rational economic order. Hemingway's Old Man was a virtuoso fisherman. If he had a fault, it was his incapacity to realize the overwhelming destructive power of the sharks."[20] As Baran saw it, the obstacle to a more rational social order does not lie in our inability to devise logically impeccable welfare functions, or in any lack of moral will to improvement. What he labored to point out was the disjunction between the objective capacity for the creation of a more humane social order and the socio-political structure of monopoly capitalism which maintains itself as a system of social imbalance and irrationality. In the short run, Baran rejected both the utopianism of liberal reformers and the cynicism of intellectuals who permitted their capacity for action upon society and international politics to be crippled in a parody of rationality and self-effacement. In the longer view, Baran chose to struggle on behalf of those forces that make the desire for freedom and justice within a rational social order neither utopian nor romantic, but a plain commitment of the intellectual.

—*John O'Neill*

York University, Toronto

Notes

1. *Paul Baran: A Collective Portrait,* Paul M. Sweezy and Leo Huberman, eds. (New York and London: Monthly Review Press, 1965).
2. "The sociological imagination enables its possessor to understand the larger historical scene in terms of its meaning for the inner life and the external career of a variety of individuals. It enables him to take into account how individuals, in the welter of their daily experience, often become falsely conscious of their social positions. Within that welter, the framework of modern society is sought, and within that framework the psychologies of a variety of men and women are formulated. By such means the personal uneasiness of individuals is focussed upon explicit troubles and the indifference of publics is transformed into involvement with public issues." — C. Wright Mills, *The Sociological Imagination* (New York, 1961), p. 5.
3. "On the Nature of Marxism" in this volume.
4. John O'Neill, "Public and Private Space," in *Agenda 1970: Proposals for a Creative Politics,* T. Lloyd and J. McLeod, eds. (Toronto: University of Toronto Press, 1968).
5. It has been argued that the categories of Marxian social science are merely projections of Marx's own self-alienation. For a critical discussion, see John O'Neill, "Marxism and Mythology," *Ethics,* Vol. 77, No. 1 (October 1966), pp. 38-49.
6. Even so hostile a critic of Marxian social science as Professor Karl R. Popper makes clear the merits of Marx's refutation of psychologism. See "The Autonomy of Sociology" in *The Open Society and Its Enemies* (New York, 1963), Vol. II, Chapter 14.
7. "Marxism and Psychoanalysis" in this volume.
8. *Capital,* Vol. III, Chapter 5.
9. "Economics of Two Worlds" in this volume.
10. "On the Nature of Marxism" in this volume.
11. "Reflections on Underconsumption" in this volume.
12. "Marxism and Psychoanalysis" in this volume.
13. For a systematic study of the concept of economic surplus, see "Economic Progress and Economic Surplus," "Planning Under Socialism," and "Comments on *The Political Economy of Growth*" in this volume; *The Political Economy of Growth,* Chapter 2; and *Monopoly Capital,* Appendix by Joseph D. Phillips, "Estimating the Economic Surplus." For an elaboration and critical interpretation of Baran's concept of the economic surplus, see A. Nowicki, "Les contradictions de la croissance et le sous-développement d'après Paul A.

Baran," in *Tiers Monde,* tome IV, Nos. 13-14 (janvier-juin 1963), pp. 121-165.

14. *The Political Economy of Growth* (New York and London: Monthly Review Press, 1957), p. 23.

15. *Ibid.,* pp. 23-24. Compare "On the Political Economy of Backwardness" in this volume.

16. "Comments on *The Political Economy of Growth.*"

17. *Monopoly Capital* (New York and London: Monthly Review Press, 1966), Chapter 11.

18. *The Political Economy of Growth,* pp. 249-250.

19. *Monopoly Capital,* pp. 193-202.

20. Review of Joan Robinson, *Economic Philosophy* in *Amer. Econ. Rev.,* Vol. LIII, No. 3 (June 1963), pp. 455-458.

I

The Commitment
of the Intellectual

What is an intellectual? The most obvious answer would seem
to be: a person working with his intellect, relying for his
livelihood (or if he need not worry about such things, for the
gratification of his interests) on his brain rather than on his
brawn. Yet simple and straightforward as it is, this definition
would be generally considered to be quite inadequate. Fitting
everyone who is not engaged in physical labor, it clearly does
not jibe with the common understanding of the term
"intellectual." Indeed, the emergence of expressions such as
"long-haired professor" and "egghead" suggests that
somewhere in the public consciousness there exists a
different notion encompassing a certain category of people
who constitute a narrower stratum than those "working with
their brains."

This is not merely a terminological quibble. The existence
of these two different concepts rather reflects an actual social
condition, the understanding of which can take us a long way
toward a better appreciation of the place and the function of
the intellectual in society. For the first definition, broad as it
is, applies accurately to a large group of people forming an
important part of society: individuals working with their
minds rather than with their muscles, living off their wits
rather than off their hands. Let us call these people *intellect
workers*. They are businessmen and physicians, corporate

executives and purveyors of "culture," stockbrokers and university professors. There is nothing invidious in this aggregation, no more than there is in the notion "all Americans," or "all people who smoke a pipe." The steady proliferation of that group of intellect workers represents one of the most spectacular results of historical development thus far. It reflects a crucially important aspect of the social division of labor, beginning with the early crystallization of a professional clergy and reaching its acme under advanced capitalism—the separation of mental from manual activity, of white collar from blue collar.

Both the causes and the consequences of this separation are complex and all-pervasive. Rendered possible by, and contributing mightily to, the continual expansion of productivity, this separation has become at the same time one of the principal facets of the progressive disintegration of the individual, of what Marx referred to as the "alienation of man from himself." This alienation expresses itself not only in the crippling and distorting effect of this separation on the harmonious development and growth of the individual—an effect which is not mitigated but underscored by the intellect workers' getting some "exercise" and by the manual workers' occasional partaking of "culture"—but also in the radical polarization of society into two exclusive and all but unrelating camps. This polarization, cutting across the antagonism between social *classes*, generates a thick ideological fog obscuring the genuine challenges confronting society and creates issues as false and schisms as destructive as those resulting from racial prejudice or religious superstition. For all intellect workers have one obvious interest in common: not to be reduced to the more onerous, less remunerative, and—since they are the ones who set the norms of respectability—less respected manual labor. Driven by this interest, they tend to hypostatize their own position, to exaggerate the difficulty of their work and the complexity of the skills required for it, to inflate the importance of formal education, of academic degrees, etc. And in seeking to protect their position, they pitch themselves against manual labor, identify themselves with the intellect workers who comprise the ruling class, and side with the social order which has given rise to their status and which has created and protected their privileges.

Thus under capitalism the intellect worker is typically the faithful servant, the agent, the functionary, and the spokesman of the capitalist system. Typically, he takes the existing order of things for granted and questions the prevailing state of affairs solely within the limited area of his immediate preoccupation. This preoccupation is with the job in hand. He may not be satisfied with the level of costs in the factory which he owns, manages, or in which he is employed, and may seek to lower them. He may be given the task of "selling" public opinion on a new soap or a new political candidate, and he will carefully, scientifically attend to his assignment. He may not be content with the current knowledge of the structure of the atom, and hence will devote prodigious energies and talent to finding ways and means of expanding it. One might be tempted to call him a *technician*, but this could easily be misunderstood. As a president of a corporation, he may make weighty decisions affecting the national economy as well as the jobs and lives of thousands of people. As an important government official, he may greatly influence the course of world affairs. And as a head of a large foundation or scientific organization, he may determine the direction and the methods of research of a large number of scientists over a long period of time. All this is clearly not what is meant by the term "technician," which usually denotes individuals whose task it is not to formulate policies but to carry them out, not to set goals but to work out the means of their realization, not to provide the great designs but to look after the small details. And yet the designation "technician" comes closer to encompassing the nature of what I mean by "intellect worker" than the customary use of the word would suggest.

For, to repeat, the purpose of the intellect worker's work and thought is the particular job in hand. It is the rationalization, mastery, and manipulation of whatever branch of reality he is immediately concerned with. In this regard he differs little, if at all, from the manual worker who molds metal sheets, assembles parts of an engine, or lays bricks in constructing a wall. Putting it in negative terms, the intellect worker *as such* is not addressing himself to the meaning of his work, its significance, its place within the entire framework of social activity. In still other words, he is not concerned with the relation of the segment of human endeavor within which he happens to operate to other segments and to the totality of the historical process. His "natural" motto is to mind his own business, and, if he is conscientious and ambitious, to be as efficient and as successful at it as possible. For the rest, let others, too, attend to their business, whatever it may be. Accustomed to think in terms of training, experience, and competence, the intellect worker regards dealing with problems of that totality as one specialty among many. This is to him the "field" of philosophers, religious functionaries, or politicians, even as "culture" or "values" are the business of poets, artists, and sages.

Not that every intellect worker explicitly formulates and consciously holds this view. Yet he has, one might almost say, an instinctive affinity to theories incorporating and rationalizing it. One of them is Adam Smith's time-honored and well-known concept of the world in which everyone by cultivating his own garden contributes most to the flourishing of the gardens of all. In the light of this philosophy, the concern with the whole moves out of the center of the individual's preoccupation, and affects him, if at all, merely marginally, that is to say in his capacity as a citizen. And the strength and influence of this philosophy derive from the very important truth that it conveys: that under capitalism the whole confronts the individual as an overpowering objectified process irrationally propelled by obscure forces which he is incapable of comprehending, let alone of influencing.

The other theory which reflects the conditions and satisfies the requirements of the intellect worker is the notion of the separation of means from ends, of the divorce between science and technology on the one side and the formulation of goals and values on the other. This position, the ancestry of which is at least as distinguished as that of Adam Smith, has been aptly referred to by C.P. Snow as a "way to contract out." In Snow's words, those "who want to contract out say *we* produce the tools. *We* stop there. It is for *you*, the rest of the world, the politicians, to say how the tools are used. The tools may be used for purposes which most of us would regard as bad. If so, we are sorry. But as scientists, this is no concern of ours." And what applies to scientists applies with equal force to all other intellect workers.

Needless to say, "contracting out" leads in practice to the same attitude as the Smithian "minding one's own business"; it is indeed nothing but another name for it. And this attitude remains essentially unaffected by the now generally felt disposition to put one's faith in the government rather than in the principles of *laissez faire*, to substitute for God's invisible hand the more obvious if by no means necessarily more beneficent hand of the capitalist state. The result is the same: the concern with the whole becomes irrelevant to the individual, and by leaving this concern to others he *eo ipso* accepts the existing structure of the whole as a datum and subscribes to the prevailing criteria of rationality, to the dominant values, and to the socially enforced yardsticks of efficiency, achievement, and success.

Now I submit that it is in the relation to the issues presented by the *entire* historical process that we must seek the decisive watershed separating intellect workers from intellectuals.[1] For what marks the intellectual and distinguishes him from the intellect worker and indeed from all others is that his concern with the entire historical process is not a tangential interest but permeates his thought and significantly affects his work. To be sure, this does not imply that the intellectual in his daily activity is engaged in the study of all of historical development. This would be a manifest impossibility. But what it does mean is that the intellectual is systematically seeking to relate whatever specific area he may be working in to other aspects of human existence. Indeed, it is precisely this effort to *interconnect* things which, to intellect workers operating within the framework of capitalist institutions and steeped in bourgeois ideology and culture, necessarily appears to lie in strictly separate compartments of society's knowledge and society's labor—it is this effort to interconnect which constitutes one of the intellectual's outstanding characteristics. And it is likewise this effort which identifies one of the intellectual's principal functions in society: to serve as a symbol and as a reminder of the fundamental fact that the seemingly autonomous, disparate, and disjointed morsels of social existence under capitalism—literature, art, politics, the economic order, science, the cultural and psychic condition of people—can all be understood (and influenced) only if they are clearly visualized as parts of the comprehensive totality of the historical process.

This principle "the truth is the whole"—to use an expression of Hegel—carries with it, in turn, the inescapable necessity of refusing to accept as a datum or to treat as immune from analysis, any single part of the whole. Whether the investigation relates to unemployment in one country, to backwardness and squalor in another, to the state of education now, or to the development of science at some other time, no set of conditions prevailing in society can be taken for granted, none can be considered to be "extraterritorial." And it is wholly inadmissible to refrain from laying bare the complex relations between whatever phenomenon happens to be at issue and what is unquestionably the central core of the historical process: the dynamics and evolution of the social order itself.

Even more important is to realize the implications of the practice, studiously cultivated by bourgeois ideologists, of regarding the so-called values held by people as lying outside the purview of scientific scrutiny. For these "values" and "ethical judgments" which to the intellect workers are untouchable data, do not drop from heaven. They themselves constitute important aspects and results of the historical process and need not merely be taken cognizance of but must be examined with regard to their origin and to the part which they play in historical development. In fact, the de-fetishization of "values," "ethical judgments," and the like, the identification of the social, economic, psychic causes of their emergence, change, and disappearance, as well as the uncovering of the specific interests which they serve at any particular time, represent the greatest single contribution that an intellectual can make to the cause of human advancement.

And this raises a further issue. Interpreting their function as the application of the most efficient means to the attainment of some stipulated ends, the intellect workers take an agnostic view of the ends themselves. In their capacities as specialists, managers, and technicians, they believe they have nothing to do with the formulation of goals; nor do they feel qualified to express a preference for one goal over another. As mentioned above, they admit that they may have some predilections as citizens, with their predilections counting for no more and no less than those of other citizens. But as scientists, experts, scholars, they wish to refrain from endorsing one or another of these "value judgments." It should be perfectly clear that such abdication amounts in practice to the endorsement of the status quo, to lending a helping hand to those who are seeking to obstruct any change of the existing order of things in favor of a better one. It is this "ethical neutrality" which has led many an economist, sociologist, and anthropologist to declare that *qua* scientist he cannot express any opinion on whether it would be better or worse for the people of underdeveloped countries to enter the road to economic growth; and it is in the name of the same "ethical neutrality" that eminent scientists have been devoting their energies and talents to the invention and perfection of means of bacteriological warfare.

But it could be objected at this point that I am begging the question, that the issue arises precisely because of the impossibility of deducing by means of evidence and logic alone any statements concerning what is good or what is bad or what contributes to, rather than militates against, human welfare. Whatever force there may be in this argument, it is actually beside the point. It can be readily granted that there is no possibility of arriving at a judgment on what is good or bad for human advancement which would be *absolutely* valid regardless of time and space. But such an *absolute*, universally applicable judgment is what might be called a false target, and the insistence on its indispensability is an aspect of a reactionary ideology. The truth is that what constitutes an opportunity for human progress, for improvement in the lot of men and also what is conducive or inimical to its realization, differs in the course of history from one period to the next, and from one part of the world to another. The questions with regard to which judgments are required have never been *abstract,* speculative questions concerning "good" or "bad" in general; they have always been *concrete* problems placed on the agenda of society by the tensions, contradictions, and changing constellations of the historical process. And at no time has there been a possibility or, for that matter, a necessity to arrive at *absolutely* valid solutions; at all times there is a challenge to use mankind's accumulated wisdom, knowledge, and experience to attain as close as possible an *approximation* to what constitutes the best solution under the prevailing conditions.

But if we are to follow the "contractors-out," the "ethically neutral" minders of their own business, then we would bar precisely that stratum in society which has (or ought to have) the largest knowledge, the most comprehensive education, and the greatest possibility for exploring and assimilating historical experience, from providing society with such humane orientation and such intelligent guidance as may be obtainable at every concrete junction on its historical journey. If, as an eminent economist recently remarked, "all possible opinions count, no more and no less than my own," then what is, indeed, the contribution which scientists and intellect workers of all kinds are willing and able to make to society's welfare? The answer, that it is the "know-how" for the realization of whatever objectives society may elect, is completely unsatisfactory. For it should be obvious that society's "elections" do not come about by miracles, that society is guided into some "elections" by the ideology generated by the social order existing at any given time, and is cajoled, frightened, and forced into other "elections" by the interests which are in a position to do the cajoling, the frightening, and the forcing. The intellect worker's withdrawal from seeking to influence the outcome of those "elections" is far from leaving a vacuum in the area of "value" formation. It merely abandons this vital field to charlatans, crooks, and others whose intentions and designs are everything but humanitarian.

It may be well to mention one further argument which is advanced by some of the most consistent "ethical neutralists." They observe, sometimes haltingly and blushingly, that after all it is by no means establishable on grounds of evidence and logic that there is any virtue in being humanitarian. Why shouldn't some people starve if their suffering enables others to enjoy affluence, freedom, and happiness? Why should one seek a better life for the masses instead of taking good care of one's own interests? Why should one worry about the proverbial "milk for the Hottentots," if such worry causes discomfort or inconvenience to oneself? Isn't the humanitarian position in itself a "value judgment" for which there is no logical base? Some thirty years ago I was asked these questions in a public meeting by a Nazi student leader (who eventually became a prominent SS man and functionary of the Gestapo), and the best answer that I could think of then is still the best answer I can think of now: a meaningful discussion of human affairs can only be conducted with humans; one wastes one's time talking to beasts about matters related to people.

This is the issue on which the intellectual cannot compromise. Disagreements, arguments, and bitter struggles are unavoidable and, indeed, indispensable to ascertain the nature, and the means to the realization, of conditions necessary for the health, development, and happiness of men. But the adherence to humanism, the insistence on the principle that the quest for human advancement requires no scientific or logical justification, constitutes what might be called the axiomatic foundation of all meaningful intellectual effort, an axiomatic foundation without the acceptance of which an individual can neither consider himself nor be thought of as an intellectual.

Although the writings of C.P. Snow leave no doubt that he would unreservedly accept this point of departure, it would seem that he believes the commitment of the intellectual to be essentially reducible to the obligation to seek the truth. (It is worth noting here that there is also no basis in evidence or logic for the proposition that truth should be preferred to lies!) In fact, the principal reason for his admiration for scientists is their devotion to truth. Scientists—he says in the previously referred to address—"want to find what is *there*. Without that desire, there is no science. It is the driving force of the whole activity. It compels the scientist to have an overriding respect for truth, every stretch of the way. That is, if you're going to find what is *there*, you mustn't deceive yourself or anyone else. You mustn't lie to yourself. At the crudest level, you mustn't fake your experiments." (Italics in the original.) And yet, while this injunction goes a long way toward formulating the basic commitment of the intellectual, it falls short of taking care of the entire problem. For the problem is not merely whether truth is being told but also what *constitutes* truth in any given case as well as *about what* it is being told and *about what* it is being withheld. Even in the area of the natural sciences these are important issues, and there are powerful forces at work shunting the energies and abilities of scientists in certain directions and impeding or sterilizing the results of their work in others. When it comes to matters related to the structure and dynamics of society, the problem assumes central significance. For a true statement about a social fact can (and most likely will) turn into a lie if the fact referred to is torn out of the social whole of which it forms an integral part, if the fact is isolated from the historical process in which it is imbedded. Thus in this domain what constitutes truth is frequently (and can be safely) sought and said about things that do not matter, with the insistence on the pursuit and pronouncement of that kind of truth becoming a powerful ideological weapon of the defenders of the status quo. On the other hand, telling the truth about what *does* matter, seeking the truth about the whole, and uncovering the social and historical causes and interconnections of the different parts of the whole is decried as unscientific and speculative and is punished by professional discrimination, social ostracism, and outright intimidation.

The desire to tell the truth is therefore only *one* condition for being an intellectual. The other is courage, readiness to carry on rational inquiry to wherever it may lead, to undertake "ruthless criticism of everything that exists, ruthless in the sense that the criticism will not shrink either from its own conclusions or from conflict with the powers that be." (Marx) An intellectual is thus in essence a *social critic*, a person whose concern is to identify, to analyze, and in this way to help overcome the obstacles barring the way to the attainment of a better, more humane, and more rational social order. As such he becomes the conscience of society and the spokesman of such progressive forces as it contains in any given period of history. And as such he is inevitably considered a "troublemaker" and a "nuisance" by the ruling class seeking to preserve the status quo as well as by the intellect workers in its service who accuse the intellectual of being utopian or metaphysical at best, subversive or seditious at worst.

The more reactionary a ruling class, the more obvious it becomes that the social order over which it presides has turned into an impediment of human liberation, the more is ideology taken over by anti-intellectualism, irrationalism, and superstition. And by the same token, the more difficult it becomes for the intellectual to withstand the social pressures brought upon him, to avoid surrendering to the ruling ideology and succumbing to the intellect workers' comfortable and lucrative conformity. Under such conditions it becomes a matter of supreme importance and urgency to insist on the function and to stress the commitment of the intellectual. For it is under such conditions that it falls to his lot, both as a responsibility and as a privilege, to save from extinction the tradition of humanism, reason, and progress that constitutes our most valuable inheritance from the entire history of mankind.

It may be said that I am identifying being an intellectual with being a hero, that it is unreasonable to demand from people that they should withstand all the pressures of vested interests and brave all the dangers to their individual well-being for the sake of human advancement. I agree that it would be unreasonable to *demand* it. Nor do I. From history we know of many individuals who have been able even in its darkest ages and under the most trying conditions to transcend their private, selfish interests and to subordinate them to the interests of society as a whole. It always took much courage, much integrity, and much ability. All that can be hoped for now is that our country too will produce its "quota" of men and women who will defend the honor of the *intellectual* against all the fury of dominant interests and against all the assaults of agnosticism, obscurantism, and inhumanity.

Note

1. To avoid a possible misunderstanding: intellect workers can be (and sometimes are) intellectuals, and intellectuals are frequently intellect workers. I say frequently, because many an industrial worker, artisan, or farmer can be (and in some historical situations often has been) an intellectual without being an intellect worker.

II
On Marxism

On the Nature
of Marxism

Just as ample rainfall seldom fails to yield a large crop of mushrooms, so a period of sustained prosperity and high employment under capitalism produces almost inevitably a strong wave of confusion and uncertainty about the validity of the socialist cause, about the rationale of a socialist movement. Indeed, at the present time this vogue has swept not only large numbers of more or less distant sympathizers of socialism; even many of those who have been identified with the socialist movement have turned their backs on Marxism, rejecting it outright in favor of some variant of "New Dealism" and bourgeois liberalism or proclaiming the necessity for major revisions of what they take to be the Marxian doctrine. This raises two complex and closely interconnected questions: *First*, has the development of capitalism (in general, and in particular countries) taken such a turn as to obliterate the need for and the desirability of a socialist transformation of society? *Second*, has the development of capitalism taken such a turn as to so weaken the forces of socialism that a socialist transformation of society becomes impossible or highly improbable—even if it be most urgent and most desirable?

This essay originally appeared as two articles in the October and November 1958 issues of *Monthly Review*. Copyright © 1958 by Monthly Review, Inc.

In what follows, an attempt will be made to deal with these questions in "desperate brevity," not in the hope of being able to supply definitive answers but rather in order to suggest what might represent useful points of departure for further reflection and further discussion.

I

The first question must be examined in the light of American experience, for it is with reference to American capitalism that the matter is usually considered. Indeed, in the United States—the principal citadel of capitalism today—the structure of the capitalist order differs in many important respects from what was described by Engels in *The Condition of the Working Class in England* or even in the much later writings of Marx. The most conspicuous and farthest-reaching difference between American capitalism now and what may be regarded as the beginning of its modern era—the end of the third quarter of the nineteenth century—is the enormous advance made in the development of the forces of production. According to some estimates, productivity per man-hour in the American economy as a whole is now over five times as much as it was in 1880. Since these estimates are arrived at by taking into account the *entire* labor force employed in business, they obviously seriously understate the productivity increase per man-hour of *production* workers, i.e., of labor engaged in the process of production of goods and services, rather than in that of selling, advertising, etc. This underestimation is aggravated by the fact that even a goodly proportion of the production workers is actually engaged in *selling*: putting chrome and fins on automobiles, turning and twisting perfectly functional articles in order to create artificial obsolescence of earlier models, and the like. The importance of this productivity increase of production workers can hardly be exaggerated. In the first place, there is much evidence—if not yet systematically collated and analyzed—that the real wages of production workers have risen significantly less than their productivity. This means that the *economic surplus* produced by society has grown considerably larger, not only in absolute terms, but in the only relevant sense: as a share of aggregate output.

What is perhaps no less portentous: while this spectacular increase of output per man-hour was achieved to some extent by a marked improvement of health and efficiency of the working population, its mainspring was a vast expansion of the volume of productive equipment. The dimensions of this expansion can be at least partly assessed if it is considered that manufacturing establishments now use approximately ten horsepower of energy per production worker employed as compared with 1.25 horsepower in 1879. This sweeping mechanization was propelled by massive capital accumulation, by extensive exploitation of "economies of scale," and by a consequent general transition to mass production methods. And this in turn has led to the emergence and growth of large-scale industrial enterprises, and to a concentration of the bulk of industrial output in the hands of a relatively small number of giant concerns.

These concerns controlling large (and growing) shares of their industries' output are, as regards what is the principal, or rather the sole purpose of capitalist enterprise, returns on invested capital, in a position that is much more powerful than that of either their small competitive ancestors, or their small competitive contemporaries. Able to gauge the impact of their own business policies on the prices prevailing in their markets, they need not be content with the rates of profit that used to be earned in the competitive sectors of the present capitalist system. Far from being less single-minded in their pursuit of profits than capitalists used to be in the past—all assertions to the contrary on the part of the now so fashionable apologists of Big Business notwithstanding—the modern monopolistic and oligopolistic corporations find themselves in objective circumstances most favorable to highest returns, and in exploiting these circumstances to the hilt have developed what used to be the art of making a lot of money into what is rapidly becoming a science of long-run profit maximization.

Thus the increase of the productivity of labor (and the mechanism by which it is attained), combined with the mode of apportionment of its fruits as between wages of production workers and profits of capitalists, which is an inherent characteristic of the capitalist system, has a double-pronged effect: the economic surplus generated by the economy tends to become an ever-increasing proportion of aggregate output, and this economic surplus tends to be continually redistributed in favor of a steadily decreasing number of giant capitalist enterprises. If this were the end of the story, the capitalist system would be choking in the flood of economic surplus, for neither capitalists' consumption nor investment in capitalist enterprise would be able singly or jointly to absorb the rising tide. The former is not only physically limited—particularly since the bulk of the surplus accrues to a small number of giant corporations and big stockholders—but runs also counter to the captialists' basic urge to accumulate. The latter is circumscribed by the profit maximization requirements of monopolistic and oligopolistic business and tends under normal conditions to fall considerably short of the volume of the desired capital accumulation.[1] Under such circumstances chronic depression would be capitalism's permanent condition and increasing unemployment its permanent accompaniment.

Yet as most diseases of organic entities call forth some remedial forces, so are economic tendencies usually counteracted—at least to some extent—by opposing developments. Both the plethora of surplus and the ascent of monopolistic and oligopolistic enterprise have drastically changed the nature and strategy of modern business. Price-cutting which during the earlier, competitive phase of capitalism was the principal method by which individual firms sought to maintain and expand their sales, now ranks very low among the strategies of the competitive struggle. Its place has been taken over by tremendously expanded (and expensive) sales organizations, advertising campaigns, public relations programs, lobbying schemes, and by a continuous, relentless effort at product differentiation, model variation, and the invention and promotion of fancier, more elaborate, more sumptuous, and more expensive consumer goods.

But not even the resulting multiplication of waste and the rampant growth of the system's unproductive sector are able to provide sufficient drainage for the overflowing economic surplus. For a large part of the expenses of selling, advertising, model-changing, etc., become necessary costs of doing business under monopoly capitalism and are shifted on to the consumer, thus reducing his real income rather than absorbing economic surplus. At the same time an important share of the sizable income accruing to corporate executives, salesmen, admen, public relations experts, market researchers, and fashion designers is saved rather than spent by its recipients and gives rise to what might be called secondary accumulation of capital—another bracket in which the economic surplus makes its statistical appearance.

Nor are other, more or less automatically functioning mechanisms of surplus absorption—capital exports, corporate outlays on research and development, and the like—powerful enough to solve the problem. A conscious effort at utilization of the economic surplus is indispensable if its overflow is to be kept within tolerable limits, if depression and unemployment are not to be allowed to endanger the stability of the capitalist system. Such a conscious effort can only be undertaken by the government. The government in capitalist society is incapable, however, of purposeful employment of the economic surplus for the advancement of human welfare.

The powerful capitalist interests by which it is controlled, as well as its social and ideological make-up, render such a policy impossible. Unable to invest in productive enterprise—this would be manifestly in conflict with the dominant interests of monopolistic and oligopolistic business—and barred by the "values" and mores of a capitalist society from large-scale spending on welfare objectives (at home and abroad), even a so-called liberal government under monopoly capitalism sees in military spending about the only avenue to salvation, and thus adds deliberately organized waste in the government sector to automatically expanding waste in the business sector.

Waste, however, cannot expand smoothly and rapidly. For although the very survival of monopoly capitalism becomes increasingly dependent on squandering of resources and on acclerated preparation for war, *to the individual capitalist enterprise* waste represents a deplorable deduction from surplus to be resisted as strongly as possible. Thus no one firm, not even the largest, can squander more resources than is indicated by the prevailing business practices, so that increases in waste can only develop slowly and gradually, only as all the important firms enlarge their unproductive expenditures and thus set new standards for the economy as a whole. Similarly, the snowballing of governmentally organized waste and skyrocketing military budgets, indispensable as they are to monopoly capitalism, spell to individual congressmen and senators nothing but higher taxes or a heavier national debt burden and are permitted only reluctantly and only in an atmosphere of external danger (real or contrived).

Except during wars and their aftermaths, the interaction of all these forces creates a vast potential overflow of the economic surplus which means underproduction, under-consumption, and underinvestment, or—what is the same—underemployment of men, underutilization of productive capacity, and depression. The only remedy for this persistent malaise that is available to monopoly capitalism is further multiplication of waste in both private and public sectors of the economic system. The utter irrationality of this "cure" is just as obvious as it is clear that the only *rational* solution is social planning of production and distribution of goods and services. Such social planning is impossible, however, without social ownership of the means of production, without a socialist transformation of society. The *need* for this transformation was never more firmly established than it is now, for never was the gap between society's potentiality and society's performance so immense as it is in monopoly capitalism's present stage. Witnesses to this need are the squalid slums, the poverty and the illiteracy that are the lot of millions of families in the wealthiest country of the world; the moral, cultural, and intellectual decay gripping the entire advanced capitalist world; and—last but not least—the misery of hundreds of millions of people in the underdeveloped countries whose fate could be drastically changed if only a fraction of the resources continually wasted in the United States were to be used to help overcome their backwardness.

Nor can there be any doubt about the *urgency* of the replacement of monopoly capitalism by socialism. Indeed, every year lost means premature death and immeasureable suffering for millions of people in the entire world. Every year lost increases the mortal danger that capitalism may plunge into the last act of its dialectical drama and seek salvation in a thermonuclear holocaust.

II

But is not the case for the necessity and urgency of a socialist transformation of the world of monopoly capital nothing but an exercise in rationalism—of no historical relevance in view of the absence of a socialist movement in the United States and its weakness in most other advanced capitalist countries? For it must be clearly realized that the irrationality of a social order leads to a crisis and eventually to a breakdown of that social order only if and when the suffering which it imposes on the masses of the people who have to bear the burden of that irrationality provokes their resistance, arouses their wrath, and results in their determination to replace it by a new, by a better society. It is undoubtedly one of the most important insights of Marxism—an insight that probably more than any other sets Marxism apart from both utopian socialism and bourgeois rationalism—that the comprehension of the existence and nature of the irrationality of a social order, which may be attained by some isolated thinkers at an early stage of the historical process, is merely one, if by no means a negligible, aspect of the crisis of that social order. Comprehension does not become a historical force until and unless the masses' life under the irrational social order becomes intolerable and compels them to add their criticism through practical action to the intellectuals' theoretical criticism—thus raising both to the level of a revolutionary movement.

So we must ask: what if even the most pronounced irrationality of a social order does *not* result in insupportable suffering of the underlying population, or if the class ruling in society manages successfully to destroy people's awareness of their distress and/or to prevent the understanding of its causes, thus diverting the masses from opposing the existing social order? Marx and Engels—occasional remarks to the contrary notwithstanding—tended on the whole to discount both possibilities. Since it is the very essence of irrationality of a social organization that it inflicts, unnecessarily, pain and privation upon an underprivileged and exploited population (under capitalism, primarily the urban and rural proletariat), it was considered virtually certain that the life of the working masses would grow increasingly unbearable not necessarily only in the "knife and fork" sense of decreasing real income, but in the more general sense of worsening social existence. At the same time it was seen to be the historical peculiarity of the capitalist system that technological progress and the capitalists' need for literate and disciplined manpower would automatically create conditions for the emergence and development of a labor movement based on the workers' grasping both the causes of their misery and the necessity for the establishment of a more rational social order.

History did not proceed according to these expectations, which reflected the ardent faith in progress of the great century of enlightenment and rationalism. In countries of advanced capitalism such as the United States, Great Britain, Germany, and others, the two "hitches" just referred to have actually materialized. In these countries the general standard of living has risen considerably and the working population is now in a markedly better condition than it was, say, at the outset of capitalism's current, monopolistic phase. Not that the American, British, or German workers are actually well off. Far from it! Their wages are at best barely sufficient to provide a half-way decent livelihood for themselves and their families; their cultural standards are base and sordid; and their leisure hours are empty and frustrating. Persistent, sometimes receding and sometimes rising, waves of unemployment reduce significantly their skimpy average earnings and produce a perpetual state of indebtedness and job-insecurity. Recurring wars impose heavy blood tolls primarily on the working population.

And yet there has been a significant improvement of the workers' living and working conditions in the course of capitalist development. Since people are generally ignorant of the *potentialities* hidden in any given situation but are vivdily aware of the much worse conditions of the past, it is the comparison with what used to be rather than with what could be that determines their attitude toward the present.

Nor should it be overlooked that much of the suffering of the working class in a capitalist society affects different individuals with varying intensity. Unemployment, particularly noxious toil, loss of life and limb in wars—all confront people as *personal* disasters, as manifestations of *individual* misfortune rather than as the fate of a class exploited in a pernicious, irrational social order.

But what accounts decisively for the acceptance of the existing social and economic system by the underlying population is a process which is closely related to the developments just mentioned but has nevertheless a dynamic and a significance of its own. It is that the mentality of the dominant class has become undisputedly the dominant mentality, and that the systematically cultivated attitude of taking capitalism for granted, of considering it to be the obvious, the natural order of things, has become not merely the attitude of the bourgeoisie but the attitude of broad popular masses as well. Not that this permeation of society by the ideas, the ethics, and the social and political values of the ruling class represents something new or unexpected. On the contrary, the likelihood or even necessity of this were repeatedly stressed by Marx and Engels as early as the middle of the last century. Yet it would seem that their and other Marxists' view of the role of bourgeois ideology in the historical process needs to be broadened to take account of what has been happening in societies of monopoly capitalism.

In its classical concept, bourgeois ideology appears essentially as a comprehensive world outlook which, reflecting the class interests of the bourgeoisie, prevents society as a whole, but in particular its exploited classes, from understanding the irrationality of the capitalist system, and which, by *justifying* the existing social relations, protects these relations against the aspirations of the masses for whose basic human needs they fail to provide. As can be readily seen, this notion of bourgeois ideology is closely linked to the proposition that the irrationality of the capitalist system cannot but cause persistent (and increasing) suffering and privation to the underlying population. More specifically: while the frustration of basic human needs by the capitalist system was seen as the mainspring of a powerful and potentially overwhelming anti-capitalist movement, religious ideas and those of the sanctity of private property, of law and order, of equality and national interest, were visualized as shields of the capitalist order, as mighty taboos barring the underprivileged and exploited masses from seeking to abolish the exploitation of man by man and to establish a social organization more conducive to the satisfaction of human needs.

What prevents this essentially correct theory from fully coping with the problems presented by monopoly capitalism is that the role of bourgeois ideology has considerably expanded in the course of the last hundred years. In fact, bourgeois ideology was able not only to fulfill the functions discovered and analyzed by Marx and Engels but also to move on to new, even more ambitious tasks. It no longer serves merely as a brake on people's striving for a better society, it no longer represents merely a barbed wire entanglement keeping people from satisfying their basic needs and potentialities—it has now reached what might be called its ultimate target: it has crippled that striving itself, it has driven a powerful wedge between human *needs* and human *wants*. This "advance" has led to a far-reaching qualitative change of bourgeois thought. As long as the bourgeoisie was a progressive class, its ideology correctly reflected its class interests which, at least partly, were also the interests of society as a whole. This ideology had thus the character of a half-truth. It partook of truth without expressing all of it, it encompassed one aspect of the historical process—the rise of the bourgeoisie—without taking account of the other—the historical limitation and transitory character of the capitalist order. But as the bourgeoisie transformed itself into the ruling class under monopoly capitalism, as its interests have ceased to have anything in common with those of people at home and abroad, bourgeois ideology has "graduated" from being a half-truth to being a total lie. It now expresses merely the interests of the reactionary oligarchy and of its retainers, and even those interests it no longer expresses adequately. Not even the direct beneficiaries of the existing social order feel secure, satisfied, and comfortable under its reign. This can be studied with all the necessary concreteness in the breakdown of the bourgeois family and bourgeois education, in the collapse even of bourgeois moral standards, in the universally recognized vacuity of such principles as free competition, free trade, and equality of opportunity.

While it was thought earlier that people would be incensed by injustice, inequality, and exploitation but would be prevented temporarily from rising against them by fear of divine or civil opprobrium and punishment, under monopoly capitalism they actually do not understand and feel injustice, inequality, and exploitation *as such*, do not *want* to struggle against them but treat them as aspects of the natural order of things. While it used to be thought that bourgeois ideology would guard the existing social order from man's efforts to satisfy basic human needs—decent livelihood, knowledge, solidarity, and cooperation with fellow men, gratification in work and freedom from toil—the actual *wants* of men in the societies of advanced capitalism are determined by aggressive drives, are directed toward the attainment of individual privileges and the exploitation of others, toward frivolous consumption and barren entertainment. With bourgeois taboos and moral injunctions *internalized,* people steeped in the culture of monopoly capitalism do not want what they need and do not need what they want.

The classical understanding of the function of bourgeois ideology fails to encompass these profound changes for two reasons. In the first place, even Marx and Engels, much as they were aware of the plasticity and moldability of human nature, seriously underestimated the extent to which man's wants can be influenced and shaped by the social order within which he is enclosed. And, collaterally, giving capitalism only a relatively short life, they could not possibly anticipate the scope and the depth of *habit* formation resulting from centuries of capitalist development.

If the above considerations are valid, the societies of the advanced capitalist countries are ill. Just as protracted addiction to alcohol or to narcotics leads sooner or later to disaster, so a prolonged divergence between the *needs* of men and their *wants* cannot but result in catastrophe. The failure of an irrationally organized society to generate internal forces pressing toward and resulting in its abolition and replacement by more rational, more human social relations results necessarily in economic stagnation, cultural decay, and a widespread sense of despondency. Such a society—even if once the most advanced in the world—loses its position of leadership, slides into the backwaters of historical development, and turns into a breeding ground of reaction, inhumanity, and obscurantism.

It would be parochial and myopic, however, to judge the prospects of socialism in the world solely on the basis of the conditions prevailing in the countries of monopoly capitalism. Throughout world history those nations have led in a progress in which the irrationality of the social order gave rise to powerful counteracting movements. It was Lenin's genius to have recognized that in the age of monopoly capitalism and imperialism this function of leadership would be taken over by the nations inhabiting the colonial, dependent, and underdeveloped countries. Bearing the brunt of the irrationality of the capitalist system, not having been exposed to the same extent as the advanced capitalist countries to the debilitating and demoralizing impact of capitalist "culture" and bourgeois ideology, some of these nations have already revolted and others are revolting against the irrationality of the capitalist order and now march at the head of history's forward movement. Within an historically short time it will be in these countries that the tone of the world's further development will be set, while the countries of monopoly capital will first lag behind and then eventually be swayed by the force of example and by the slow but irresistible process of osmosis.

Although it cannot be denied that many aspects of this development as here sketched do not correspond to what is usually considered to be Marxian doctrine, nothing would be more fallacious than to conclude from it that they have rendered Marxism an obsolete or a misleading body of thought. Quite on the contrary, it is only with the help of Marxism that the momentous events of our time can be adequately studied and comprehended. What this calls for, however, is not thoughtless regurgitation of particular statements of Marx and Engels—torn out of time and context—but the consistent application of Marx' powerful analytical *method.*

III

Contrary to widespread opinion, Marxism is not and never was intended to be a "positive science," an assortment of statements about past and present facts, or a set of predictions about the shape or timing of future events. It was always an intellectual attitude, or a way of thought, a philisophical position the fundamental principle of which is continuous, systematic, and comprehensive *confrontation of reality with reason.* Not that this principle originated with Marx and Engels. Socrates' famous dictum "the unexamined life is not worth living" inspired progressive thought from its earliest beginnings and oriented a great philosophical tradition which centered on the critique of reality in the light of reason and whose aim and purpose was to seek out and to establish the prerequisites and the conditions for the growth and development of man. Yet it was left for Marx and Engels to take a decisive step forward in this centuries-old effort at confronting reality with reason. They translated the notions of both reality and reason from the metaphysical abstractions and idealistic assertions—the forms in which they appear in most pre-Marxian thought—into living, concrete categories of real, continuously moving, continually changing, human existence. Thus, while uncompromisingly committed to the principle of confronting reality with reason, while convinced that this confrontation represents the indispensable basis of all humanist thought and the only valid guidepost for meaningful human activity, Marxism by no means implies a dogmatic finding as to what defines reason or what constitutes reality at any given time.

To Marxism the meaning of reason and the nature of reality are closely interwoven, inseparable aspects of historical development. In terms of the *long run,* of the entire historical process, the content and the injunctions of reason are relative. They change with the changing forces of production, they enrich themselves with the expansion of our knowledge. William Blake grasped the essence of the matter with an artist's intuition: "Reason," he wrote nearly two hundred years ago, "or the ratio of all we have already known, is not the same that it shall be when we know more." This may be illustrated by an historical example referred to by Engels. Speaking of the origins of slavery, he remarked: "We are compelled to say—however contradictory and heretical it may sound—that the introduction of slavery under the conditions of that time was a great step forward. . . . It was an advance even for the slaves; the prisoners of war from whom the mass of the slaves was recruited, now at least kept their lives, instead of being killed as they had been before, or even roasted at a still earlier period." In other words, viewed against the background of cannibalism the institution of slavery was a *reasonable* arrangement, a step ahead in the evolution of reason.

Yet it is crucially important to realize that this relativity of the content of reason holds only in the longest run. In the *short run,* in any given historical period, what constitutes reason is *approximately* ascertainable. The determining factors are the level of social development, society's achieved fund of scientific insight, the accumulated wealth of practical human experience. To be sure, the qualification "approximately" can hardly be overstressed. For the intimate relation between reason and the continuously changing nature of reality makes it inevitable that what constitutes reason during any given historical period cannot be read off from a simple formula or encompassed by a neat definition.

This absence of a pat answer to the question as to what constitutes at any particular time the specific content of reason is invoked by contemporary bourgeois thought as an excuse for its own relativism and agnosticism. This excuse, however, is no more admissible than would be the contention that all efforts to cure disease ought to wait until medicine has reached its ultimate state of perfection. What the unavailability (and ineluctable impossibility) of *absolutely* valid statements about the meaning of reason actually points to is rather the perennial and all-important obligation of philosophical thought: the unremitting integration and re-integration, interpretation and re-interpretation of human knowledge and experience within a dynamic framework of reason. The fault of bourgeois thought today is *not* that it rejects the notion of eternal truth or denies the possibility of eternally valid definitions of reason. The fault, amounting to tragic failure, consists in "throwing out the baby with the bath," in using the inaccessibility of eternally applicable definitions of reason as an apology for abandoning the search for whatever meaning and content may be attributable to reason in any *concrete* historical situation. This leads not only to the complete abdication of philosophy in favor of opportunism and pragmatism, but also to obscurantism and the betrayal of reason itself.

What applies to reason applies also, with some modifications but with no less force, to our notions of reality. In the long run, the content of reality is also subject to perpetual change, partly because of continuous transformations in the real world itself, partly because of steady advances in our practical activity, in our empirical research, and in our theoretical understanding. Whether in the realm of social relations where historical development incessantly changes the structure of society or in regard to nature where scientific discoveries and human activity progressively modify what confronts us as "nature"—there is no eternal "reality." In the short run, on the other hand, in a concrete historical constellation, reality is subject to research and analysis; its structure can be comprehended with a degree of approximation sufficiently high to admit of purposeful and rational practice.

IV

The confrontation of reality with reason is by no means merely an abstract, intellectual undertaking. In every society that is split into classes, i.e., based on the exploitation of man by man, the exploiting class is vitally interested in the preservation of the existing pattern of social relations; and in administering the affairs of society it will seek to admit of only such change as will not endanger this pattern. The point is therefore unavoidably reached when the progress of reason and the expansion of our knowledge of reality are impeded, when existing and maturing possibilities for society's further advancement, for further growth and development of all its members, are sacrificed in favor of the interest of the dominant class in the continuation of the established social order—when, in other words, the particular interests of the ruling class come into conflict with the interests of society as a whole. At such historical junctures the confrontation of reality with reason reveals the irrationality of the existing social order, turns—in the words of Marx—into "ruthless criticism of everything that exists, ruthless in the sense that the criticism will not shrink either from its own conclusions or from conflict with the powers that be," and becomes the intellectual expression of the practical, existential needs of the entire society, and in particular of its overwhelming majority, the oppressed and exploited classes. It is precisely then that the confrontation of reality with reason is proscribed by the ruling class, is persecuted as subversive by its police, is condemned as sacrilegious by its priests, and is decried as metaphysical and unscientific by its ideologists. And it is precisely at such historical junctures that the criticism of reality in the light of reason, the unmasking of so-called common sense and practical intelligence—those caricatures of reason which the dominant ideology substitutes for reason itself—becomes at once one of the most responsible activities of the time and one of the most powerful engines of humanism and progress.

It was Marx's unprecedented and unsurpassed accomplishment to discover this law of historical development and to lay bare the part played in its operation by fruitful intellectual endeavor: to define and continuously redefine the meaning of reason, to assess and continuously reassess the structure of reality—confronting systematically the one with the other, pointing out the shortcomings of the concrete, specific reality in terms of equally concrete, equally specific standards of reason. Remaining realistic, because it derives its frame of reference from the study and observation of the attained stage of historical development, and retaining the courage to be utopian because it sets its sights on the not yet realized but already visible potentialities of the future, such intellectual effort performs an overridingly important function: it serves as a guidepost to the next steps in mankind's forward movement.

Marx did not stop, however, at the formulation of this general theory. He applied it to the contemporaneously all-important case of capitalism. To accomplish this he had to undertake a comprehensive analysis of the nature and laws of motion of capitalist society, evolving concomitantly a concrete and historically relevant notion of a more rational social order. This called for detailed empirical research into the historical roots, the institutions and working principles of capitalism—in a word, for a comprehensive study of economics, the anatomy of the capitalist order. To this undertaking Marx devoted the better part of his working life, and the resulting contributions to knowledge were truly prodigious. Indeed, so great were those achievements, so vast the energy which went into their attainment as to give rise to the view that Marx's chief concern was the advancement of *economics,* the creation of a new *economic theory* which would be superior to its antecedents by providing better explanations or more accurate forecasts in the realm of economic affairs.

That this view was given wide circulation by bourgeois writers is by no means fortuitous. For looking upon Marx as a "positive scientist," as a scholar engaged in the description and analysis of the economic process, made it possible to pick and choose among his individual statements, to accept or to reject them depending on the extent to which they happened to suit the commentators' own predilections, to treat him as "an economist among economists," designating him indeed—in the words of one of the most eminent American theorists—as "a minor post-Ricardian." And Marxists in the West, seeking consciously or unconsciously to retain a common ground of debate with their academic opponents, in effect lent their support to this interpretation of Marx; while the Soviet attitude of insisting dogmatically on the truth of every word in Marx's writings—although stemming from entirely different causes—had, paradoxically enough, the same result.

Yet this conception of Marx is in violent contradiction perhaps not always with the letter but always with the spirit of his entire work. For large as were his *positive* contributions to our understanding of capitalism, his paramount preoccupation was the *critical* appraisal of the capitalist order in the light of reason, that is to say in terms of its ability (or inability) to satisfy human needs, to provide for the growth and development of man. This involved in addition to a thorough study of the mode of functioning of the capitalist system, a *critical* scrutiny of dominant thought on capitalism with the purpose of establishing the extent to which it elucidates or obscures the prevailing divergencies between reality and reason. It is not accidental that the first (unpublished) version of Marx's principal work was titled "An Outline of a Critique of Political Economy," that his first major economic publication was called *A Contribution to the Critique of Political Economy* and that finally *Capital* carries a subtitle "Critique of Political Economy." In fact, all of Marx's and Engels' voluminous writing—after the broad statement of principle in *The Communist Manifesto*—was essentially a vast *critical* effort, a many-sided confrontation of reality with reason, an indefatigable onslaught on all ideological activity which attempted, consciously or unconsciously, to hide and to minimize the difference between the existing and a more rational society.

The critical effort yielded far-reaching results. In the midst of the first great capitalist celebration, at a time when hosanna cries to the victorious bourgeoisie set the tone of "public opinion" and of political economy, Marx demonstrated the contradictory, conflict-laden nature of the capitalist system. He showed that although the transition from feudalism to capitalism represented a tremendous advance toward a more rational condition of mankind, further progress would be warped, hamstrung, and ultimately blocked by the irrationality of the capitalist order. He proved furthermore that this irrationality is not a transitory or fortuitous characteristic of capitalism but is inherent in it, represents the inevitable outgrowth of its very foundation: the institution of private property in the means of production. And he was able to give specific content to the notion of rationality in the present state of historical development: a socialist planned society employing the socially owned means of production for the welfare of all of its members.

But what is most important, Marx went far beyond classical rationalism by recognizing clearly that it is the very essence of the irrationality of a social order to generate a social class which suffers from this irrationality, which bears the brunt of this social order's inadequacy, inhumanity, and injustice. In this class he saw the promise of progress, the social force which would do away with the irrational system and put in its place a better and more rational society. Marx identified this class as the proletariat, and he saw it exercising its historical power in the form of an expanding and maturing socialist movement. Not that he idealized the workers or believed in their heroism, unselfishness, or ardent dedication to human liberation. In his own words:

If the socialist writers assign to the proletariat this world-historical function, it is not because they consider the proletarians to be *gods*. Rather the opposite. Because the destruction of all humanity, even of the *appearance* of humanity, is empirically completed in the case of the fully developed proletariat; because all the existential conditions of the present society are concentrated in their entire inhuman extremity in the living conditions of the proletariat; because the human being has lost itself in the proletarian at the same time having not only won the theoretic awareness of this loss, but having been forced by inescapable, unvarnishable, imperative misery—that practical expression of *necessity*—to revolt against this entire inhumanity—this is why the proletariat can and must liberate itself. But it cannot liberate itself without abolishing its very condition of existence. And it cannot abolish its own condition of existence without abolishing all the inhuman conditions of the present society which find their concentrated expression in the situation of the proletariat.

V

None of Marx's conclusions have been vitiated, let alone refuted, by subsequent events. History never stands still, and capitalism has obviously undergone a number of important changes. But the more it changes, the more it remains the same—as the French saying has it—and while the basic irrationality of the system has altered some of its forms, that irrationality is now more pronounced than ever before. Nor has this irrationality proved to be a disease curable by assorted medications prescribed from time to time by social reformers of all kinds; it is today, as it was in the days of Marx, an integral component, a characteristic feature of the capitalist order itself. And that socialism represents the only rational exit from the impasse into which capitalism has driven mankind, that socialist planning is history's next and necessary step, has been demonstrated not only by theoretical reasoning but by vast historical experience.

Yet, as was pointed out earlier in this article, the proletariat in the advanced capitalist countries has not developed in the way anticipated by Marx. Bad as its condition has been, it was able to rise above the "inescapable, unvarnishable, imperative misery" which was observed by Marx, and which he expected would be accentuated with the passage of time. Although its social and cultural existence is in essence as inhuman as it was in Marx's time, it has largely failed to "win the theoretical awareness of its loss" and has tended to succumb to bourgeois ideology and to adjust itself to its degradation. What Marx misjudged in other words, is the intensity and speed with which the irrationality of capitalism would give rise to a movement powerful enough to carry out a socialist transformation of society. Yet serious as this miscalculation undoubtedly is, it should not even be mentioned in the same breath with the fallacy committed by those who consider the weakness or even absence of socialist movements in some countries to be a proof of the rationality, an argument for the desirability, or a sign of the progressiveness of the capitalist order. That position is no more defensible than would be the view that an inability of a human body to resist tuberculosis, however caused, furnishes a proof of the harmlessness or even usefulness of that illness. Both errors reflect essentially the wish being the father to the thought. The former, however, stems from insufficient appreciation of the obstacles barring the road to socialism, and— even if causing sometimes grave political errors—does no irreparable harm to the cause of reason. The latter, on the other hand, results inevitably in surrender to bourgeois ideology, in apologetics for the capitalist system, and in the abandonment of the struggle for a better society.

As long as capitalism lasts, as long as men live under an irrational social order, Marxism can neither be discarded nor refuted. For Marxism is nothing if not a powerful magnifying glass under which the irrationality of the capitalist system protrudes in all of its monstrous forms. Marxism will have outlived itself only when it has reached the end of its historical journey: when the confrontation of reality with reason has become redundant because reality will be governed by reason. Until then it remains the task of Marxian thought to carry on this confrontation under the concrete historical conditions of our time. What this specifically implies is the

necessity to comprehend as fully as possible the structure and the mode of functioning of monopoly capitalism—the present variant of the capitalist system. It calls,
moreover, for an effort to identify and to analyze that part
of society (nationally and internationally) which bears the
brunt of the irrationality of monopoly capitalism and which
sooner or later will provide the energies for its abolition. As
mentioned earlier, it was given only to Lenin to assimilate
fully the essence of the Marxian method. In analyzing
imperialism and in grasping the crucial role played in it by
the awakening of the peoples inhabiting the colonial, dependent, and underdeveloped countries, he brilliantly applied this
method to the reality of the twentieth century. The crisis of
Marxism will be overcome by further work in that tradition.

Notes

1. This is more fully explained in Chapter III of *The Political
Economy of Growth* (New York and London: Monthly Review Press,
1957).

2. Marx-Engels, *Gesamtausgabe,* Part I, Vol. 3 (Berlin, 1932), pp.
206 ff. (Translated from the German by the writer; italics in the
original.)

An Alternative
to Marxism

The rapidly spreading discussion of American economic growth suffers seriously from its unfortunate "take-off"—to use Professor Rostow's favorite expression. Inspired by the notion of the so-called Soviet challenge, it has been shunted into a blind alley by a particular interpretation of that ambiguous term which has been given wide currency in newspaper editorials and in the pronouncements of certain experts. There it has become customary to treat the expression "challenge" as a synonym of "threat," and thus to turn it into a new refrain in the dirge of the Cold War. Cited as the reason for the necessity to accelerate the growth of the American economy, it suggests that all that matters is a more pronounced expansion of our Gross National Product, or even only of the Gross National Product's military component.

This, in my view, is a distorted and biased understanding of the word challenge, and it is urgent that we realize the other, more important connotations of the term. For challenge implies not merely, nor even primarily, a threat. It is first and foremost an invitation to perform, an appeal to rise to a task, a call to live up to a standard of accomplishment. I am

This essay is a commentary on papers delivered by W.J. Fellner and W.W. Rostow at the annual meetings of the American Economic Association in 1959. It was first published in *Monthly Review*, March 1965. Copyright © 1965 by Monthly Review, Inc.

not arguing here a point in semantics, and whoever wishes to challenge my understanding of the word challenge is welcome to do so. What is at issue is rather the nature of the performance that is required if the United States is to demonstrate to the American nation and to the world at large the superiority of capitalism to socialism—a superiority not in "killing power" but in the capacity to provide a stable framework for the health, happiness, and development of people. Only if such superiority is established (and not simply taken for granted) is it possible to say with Professor Fellner that "rather general social interest attaches" to the preservation of "the essentials of a decentralized market economy and of its political institutions."

Yet when it comes to judging capitalism by this standard, the growth rate of GNP can be considered to provide only one of the relevant criteria. For, given the absolute volume of American national output, its sluggish and uneven rise may be less significant as such than as a reliable index of the underlying economic and social condition. To be sure, even this wealthiest society in the world is far from the state of affluence which is suggested by the title of a recent best seller. As pointed out by the late Professor Sumner Slichter in his March 20, 1959, statement before the Joint Economic Committee, in 1958 one-fifth of the spending units in this country had incomes of less than $1,890 before taxes and three-fifths had incomes of less than $5,139 before taxes. Only one out of five spending units had an income of $7,910 or more. Even if these numbers reflect a general standard of living much higher than that prevailing in the rest of the world, they hardly indicate the existence of merely "residual poverty" and the attainment of "freedom from want." This situation at home in conjunction with the state of starvation and disease endured by the majority of mankind living in the underdeveloped countries puts in sharp relief the callousness of the now-so-fashionable talk about the unimportance of further output increases and about the obsoleteness of the "conventional wisdom" as it relates to the husbandry of productive resources.

While there can thus be no doubt about the imperative need both at home and abroad for the largest possible increase of output, our economy has been keeping production markedly below the level which could have been attained with the human and material resources at our disposal. In approximately half of the exceptionally prosperous postwar years, unemployment in this country has been as high as six million and has reached disaster proportions in certain regions and for certain age, racial, and educational groups. It hardly needs to be added that this volume of unemployment, which is considerably in excess of what could be shrugged off as "frictional," has been accompanied at all times by an even larger proportion of underutilized productive capacity. Leon Keyserling estimated (in his testimony before the Joint Economic Committee on March 24, 1959) that in the six-year period 1953–1958 the loss of aggregate output reached over 150 billion 1957 dollars. This staggering sum is probably no more than half of what the loss amounts to for all the postwar years. It should be realized that this output foregone, if it had been produced and appropriately utilized, would have sufficed not only to solve some of the most burning national problems but also to lift over the hump the underdeveloped countries in whose welfare and development we profess such a strong interest. And it should not be forgotten that the agricultural commodities which our policy of production controls, administrative regulations, and bonus payments contrives to prevent from seeing the light of day are estimated at a quantity sufficient to eliminate the caloric deficiencies in the entire undernourished world.

This prodigious underutilization of productive resources in the midst of universal want is, however, only one aspect of the posture which this country displays in the face of the

Soviet challenge. The other side is the composition and the mode of utilization of such output as the economy does generate. It is open to serious question whether Keynes was right even with reference to Britain in 1935 when he wrote: "I see no reason to suppose that the existing system seriously misemploys the factors of production that are in use. . . . It is in determining the volume, not the direction of actual employment that the existing system has broken down."[1] But in any case, there surely can be no question about the inapplicability of this dictum to the United States of 1959. The relevant facts are well known and call for no elaboration. It is sufficient to recall some of the more striking statistics. In 1956, while automobile transportation absorbed 27 billion dollars, education (private and public) commanded 15 billion; while 3 billion worth of resources were used for recreational purposes of all kinds, 600 million were devoted to books; while basic scientific research was assigned 500 million, the services of stockbrokers and investment counselors were valued at 900 million; and the combined budgets of universities and colleges were a fraction of the outlays on advertising. Is it astonishing or incomprehensible that the cultural, moral, intellectual life of the country reflects to an ever increasing extent this state of affairs? Can one expect this propagation of truth, honesty, and a sense of national purpose among people exposed to an incessant barrage of advertising dedicated to the promotion of a remedy against "tired blood"—the concoction that made Charles Van Doren famous? Can one hope for the development and growth of reason and intellectual ability and integrity in a youth tutored by illiterate educators, brought up on violence and murder and crime on the TV screens, in the newspaper headlines, in the comic books, and facing on every side the irrationality, the destructiveness of the existing economic and social order? It surely is hard to face the Soviet challenge on this basis—to establish the superiority of capitalism to socialism on the strength to this cultural, moral, and intellectual achievement.

While not taking explicit cognizance of this general condition of the nation, the papers of Professors Fellner and Rostow address themselves to a search for remedies against the undeniably existing predicament. Professor Fellner, considering the growth rate of GNP to be "a pretty good 'proxy' " for what really matters, is concerned primarily with finding means to increase the rate of growth of GNP, and his solution of the problem is as simple as it is—to me, at any rate—unconvincing. His advice is to reduce markedly the corporate income tax, since "this would strengthen incentives, and much of the tax saving would go into capital formation (largely through reinvestment)." But are we justified in believing that such corporate tax savings would actually be employed in this way? I do not think that it could be demonstrated that corporate investment activity (housing apart) in the postwar period was stymied by lack of capital. What is more, Professor Fellner's expectation of an increase in corporate investment in response to larger corporate liquidity is wholly unrelated to his own finding of ubiquitous "noncompetitive forces on the supply side" of the economy, and to his own observation that "in retrospect the present period will generally be interpreted as one in which we have failed to fight a harmful concentration of market power. . . ." But since the investment policies of monopolistic enterprises are governed not only, and not even primarily, by possibilities for internal financing, one would think that the growth and proliferation of monopoly had something to do with the volume and direction of investment. This problem is, however, not even referred to in Professor Fellner's paper. Nor is there any attention given to another, perhaps even more worrisome, aspect of the matter: even if the device should work, and a larger volume of corporate investment could actually be induced by an appropriate taxation policy, is there any reason for supposing that this investment would flow into what might be considered socially desirable channels? Isn't there a larger probability that we would get "more of the same"—more sumptuous office buildings, more gadgets, more fins, more remedies against "tired blood" and "sour stomachs," and more Charlie Van Dorens to sell the stuff to a captive public?

As if to demonstrate the proverbial diversity of economic opinion, Professor Rostow takes a tranquil view of the slow growth of American national product but is disturbed over its allocation. The trouble with the latter, he feels, is that too large a share of Gross National Product remains in the private sector of the system, with, conversely, too small a share becoming available to the public sector. This view, which has been given much prominence by the writings of J. K. Galbraith, raises in my mind a number of important questions.

In the first place, it seems to be most doubtful whether the dichotomy between the private and the public sectors comes anywhere near to encompassing the complexity of the resource allocation problem. Indeed, I am by no means certain that an increase in the public sector at the expense of the private sector represents under all circumstances—and in particular in this country at the present time—a desirable reallocation of resources. This would depend not only on the method by which such a reallocation were to be accomplished but also, and decisively, on the use made of the resources available to the public sector. For the mere fact that there is very little to recommend the mode of resource utilization prevailing in the private sector does not constitute a blanket endorsement of whatever employment might be given to resources in the public sector. Thus it is a tragic truth that all the waste and all the destruction of human and material resources that take place in the private sector if such expansion were to be used for the building up of a larger military establishment and for supplying atomic weapons to irresponsible foreign governments—as is urged by many influential public figures. Nor can it be taken for granted that the extravagance of the private sector is much more deplorable than what has been happening in the name of American foreign aid to the Philippines and to Laos, Formosa, South Korea, South Vietnam, Pakistan, Iran, and Greece. And to take an altogether different example, it is by no means clear that even significant increases of appropriations to public education would not do more harm than good unless accompanied by a drastic reform of our educational system, with the latter hardly dependent on budgetary considerations. In other words, the insistence on the importance and urgency of resource transfers to the public sector is only justified if there is a strong basis for the conviction that they will be devoted there to socially desirable purposes.

But let us make the heroic assumption that the problem to which I have just referred did not exist, and that there is no room for doubt about the beneficent employment of such resources as come under the control of public authorities. The questions immediately arise as to what it is that keeps the public sector down to its present dimensions and as to what can be done to enlarge it at the expense of the private economy. It is Professor Rostow's method of dealing with these problems that I find most bewildering. If we shed our amiable academic terminology—stop talking about sectors, resource allocations, marginal adjustments and the like—and get down to brass tacks, what is at issue is a more or less significant increase of the share of the private product that is currently appropriated by the state. Such an enlargement of the government's take—unless wholly supported by a systematic, planned effort at an increase of aggregate output—can only be realized by the confiscation of an additional slice of private incomes. The bill would have to be paid by somebody, and while one could expect considerable and at least partly successful efforts to shift a large part of the costs upon the majority of the people, the profits of business and the revenues of the power elite could hardly escape being affected. There is, in other words, a pronounced and inevitable conflict between the expansion of the public sector and various, more or less powerful, private interests. Yet these interests are not even mentioned, let alone analyzed, in Professor Rostow's paper. We are told that we have to re-do our price structure, refashion our wages, redeploy our profits, revamp our entrepreneurship, reapportion our resources, with all of these categories being treated as if they referred to marbles which can be pushed around at pleasure. But a price is not only paid but also received; profit is not only an accounting concept but income; entrepreneurship not only a term most useful these days in drafting applications for research grants but the actual management of corporate business; and productive resources are not free gifts of nature but private property. All of these concrete elements and relations which constitute the basis of economic and social life appear in Professor Rostow's theorizing as disembodied entities obeying mysterious laws of movement. Although it is the outstanding characteristic of capitalism that people do not control the economic system but that the economic system controls people, Professor Rostow finds the "root cause" of our difficulties, not in the nature of our economic and social order, but in "certain American habits of mind." Accordingly the explanation of the way in which our productive resources are used is not sought in the prevailing system of ownership, not in the working principles of a market- and profit-determined economy, but in our "concepts," which in turn are produced by an "interplay of intellectual and political features of the American scene." Thus the impetus of the spirit takes over from the drive for profits, the interplay of concepts substitutes for the competition in the market, and habits of thought take the place of regularities of the historical process. This kind of social science from which society is abstracted and this kind of economic history in which there is no longer room for economic interests was recommended in one of Professor Rostow's recent publications as an alternative to Marxism and an alternative indeed it is. But not one which would tempt me to make the switch.

Note

1. J.M. Keynes, *The General Theory of Employment, Interest, and Money* (New York, 1936), p. 379.

A Non-Communist
Manifesto

On the jacket of W.W. Rostow's *The Stages of Economic Growth: A Non-Communist Manifesto,* the publisher advertises the product in these terms: "This book is a generalization from the whole span of modern history. It gives an account of economic growth based on a dynamic theory of production and interpreted in terms of actual societies. It helps to explain historical changes and to predict major political and economic trends; and it provides the significant links between economic and non-economic behavior which Karl Marx failed to discern." The author's own sales-pitch is equally strident: "The stages are not merely descriptions. They are not merely a way of generalizing certain factual observations about the sequence of development of modern societies. They have an inner logic and continuity. They have an analytical bone-structure rooted in a dynamic theory of production" (pp. 12f.). And the reason for this enthusiasm is not only the light which the new theory is supposed to shed upon the process of economic and social evolution but also its alleged power to dispose once and for all of the Marxian dragon with which so many others have done battle but failed to slay. The reader is urged to "note the similarities

---

Co-authored with E.J. Hobsbawm. This article was originally published as "The Stages of Economic Growth" in *Kyklos,* Vol. XIV, 1961, and is reprinted by permission of the publisher. Copyright © 1961 by Kyklos.

between his [Marx's] analysis and the stages of growth; and the differences between the two systems of thought, stage by stage."

We propose to accept this invitation and to carry out the comparison which Professor Rostow suggests. The first section will deal with the stages-of-growth scheme's contribution to the theory of economic development. The second section will attempt to answer the question whether Marxian thought is capable of surviving this newest assault.

I

Such attention as Professor Rostow's writings have hitherto been able to command in the literature on economic development has been based upon some of his earlier empirical studies. His theoretical contributions have been meager—in fact, largely confined to various types of classification. Does his latest effort significantly change this picture?

Professor Rostow advances three propositions. First, he insists that the problem of growth is a historical one which must be considered within a framework of a historical periodization. Second, he emphasizes—and this is perhaps his most notable point—that economic growth is not a continuous and smooth but a discontinuous and dialectical process which pivots on a sudden revolutionary transformation, the "take-off into self-sustained growth." Third, he stresses a particular aspect of this discontinuity of economic growth: that it proceeds not by a balanced development of all sectors of the economy, but by successive leaps forward of the economy's "leading sectors."

These are undoubtedly valuable insights, although it can hardly be said that they are new or that they originate with Professor Rostow. That theories of growth must be historical was perhaps the first discovery of political economy; it has merely been forgotten in the century or so in which econ-

omic growth was almost wholly neglected in academic economics, except for the Marxists and those who, like the Germans and Schumpeter, accepted much of the Marxist *Frage-
stellung* on the subject. The "take-off" is merely another
name for the "industrial revolution" which was the basic
analytic concept of modern economic history from the days
of Engels to those of Mantoux until smothered by the grad-
ualist criticism of Clapham, Ashton, and others between the
two wars. The argument for uneven development is equally
old. It was advanced by Marx, developed by Lenin, and
underlies the Schumpeter-Kondratiev analysis of nineteenth
century economic development.[1] To be sure, the rediscovery
of old truths is a most creditable accomplishment—
particularly in contemporary "behavioral sciences" where
apparently any nonsense goes as long as it has never been said
before—though not one calling in itself for a major ovation.

But when we come to consider Professor Rostow's other
achievements in the field of the theory of growth, the weaknesses are all too obvious. The first and most serious is that
his theory of "stages" actually tells us nothing except that
there are stages. The four other stages are implicit in the
"take-off," and add nothing to it. Given a "take-off," there
must obviously be a stage before it when the conditions for
economic growth are not present, another when the preconditions for the "take-off" exist, and yet another following it
when "an economy demonstrates that it has the technological and entrepreneurial skills to produce not everything,
but anything it wants" (which is Rostow's definition of the
stage of "maturity"), and yet another when it has acquired
the capacity to produce everything it wants (p. 10).[2] Indeed,
there is no departure ("take-off") of any kind—in the history
of nature, of societies, or of individuals—which cannot be
thought of as being preceded and followed by a number of
"stages." If one has a penchant for symmetry one only has to

make sure that the total number of stages—the "take-off" included—should be uneven.

Thus once we have one corner, we have the entire Pentagon. One weakness of this procedure is, of course, that analysis must remain confined to its area. Accordingly, the Rostovian stage theory, despite its comprehensive historic and sociological claims, reduces economic growth to a single pattern. Any and every country, whatever its other characteristics, is classifiable only in respect to its position on the stepladder, the middle rung of which is the "take-off." This gives the Rostovian stages an air of spurious generality—they appear to apply to any and all economies, to the USSR as to the USA, to China as to Brazil—which, as we shall see, is not without its ideological implications, though it overlooks the obvious fact that, however universal the technical problems of economic growth may be, different social types of economic organization can, or must, solve them in very different ways.

Yet even within its extremely narrow limits the Rostovian theory can neither explain nor predict without introducing considerations that are completely irrelevant to the stage schema. It simply fails to specify any mechanism of evolution which links the different stages. There is no particular reason why the "traditional" society should turn into a society breeding the "preconditions" of the "take-off." Rostow's account merely summarizes what these preconditions must be,[3] and repeats a version of that "classical answer," the inadequacy of which has long been evident: a combination of the "discovery and rediscovery of regions beyond Western Europe" and the "developing of modern scientific knowledge and attitudes" (p. 31). Here is the *deus cum machina*. Nor is there any reason within the Rostovian stages why the "preconditions" should lead to the "take-off" to maturity, as is indeed evidenced by Rostow's own difficulty in discovering, except long *ex post facto*, whether a "take-off" has taken place or not.[4] In fact, the Rostovian "take-off" concept has no predictive value. Similarly, when it comes to analyzing the "inner structure" (p. 46) of the take-off or of any other stage, the Rostovian theory subsides into statements of the type that "things can happen in any one of a very large number of different ways," which constitute a rather limited contribution to knowledge.[5]

Such explanations and predictions as Rostow attempts are therefore little more than verbiage having no connection with his stages theory or indeed with any theory of economic and social evolution, being generally based on what might be charitably called coffeehouse sociology and political speculation. The nearest he actually comes to an attempt at an explanation of *why* economic growth takes place is his emphasis on the importance of "reactive nationalism" and the crucial role of "an inherently competitive system of power" (pp. 109 and 151n) in which states are historically enmeshed.[6] The explanation tends to be circular—when a country has economic growth it is evidence of reactive nationalism[7]—as well as open-ended: when an obviously nationalist country does *not* initiate a take-off, it is because "nationalism can be turned in any one of several directions" (p. 29). Moreover, even this type of explanation is crippled by Rostow's refusal to admit the profit motive into his analysis, a refusal not concealed by an occasional parenthetical remark granting its existence.[8] Still, weak as it is, the explanation of economic growth by nationalism and the logic of international rivalry is the closest Rostow comes to an analysis of economic development as distinct from relabelling and classifying it.

And this is not very close. For in addition to an incapacity to answer relevant questions, Professor Rostow shows an astonishing lack of ability to recognize their existence or their import. Thus one of the crucial problems which faces

both the theorist and would-be planner of economic development under capitalist conditions is that "the criteria for
private profit-maximization do not necessarily converge with
the criteria for an optimum rate and pattern of growth in
various sectors" (p. 50), indeed, that under pre-industrial
conditions or in underdeveloped areas it can be shown that
they are more likely than not to diverge. The statesman or
economic administrator of a backward country knows that a
century of Western capitalism has failed to transfer any
country across the gap which separates the advanced from
the backward economies. He also knows that profit-oriented
private investment can be relied on to build his country's
tourist hotels but not its steelworks. Consequently he has
increasingly taken to imitating the Soviet method of achieving economic growth, which does not suffer from this disad-
vantage, rather than relying on the nineteenth century
European or American method which does. Rostow neither
explains any of these facts which determine the actual problem of economic development in underdeveloped areas, nor
does he even seem aware of them beyond the casual mention
already quoted. Conversely, the historian must explain why,
in spite of this divergence, or lack of convergence, a limited
number of countries around the North Atlantic in the eighteenth and nineteenth centuries actually managed to indus-
trialize on a capitalist basis. Rostow appears equally oblivious
of this problem.

This obtuseness is not accidental. Indeed, the nature of
Professor Rostow's approach makes it impossible for him to
solve such problems, and difficult even to realize their existence. For if we argue that the main motor of economic
change was at no time "profit-maximization (in the sense of)
economic advantage" (pp. 149ff.), we can hardly deal with,
let alone answer, questions which arise from the fact that all
economic development between the "traditional" society and
the appearance of the USSR was actually *capitalist* develop-

ment, which calls therefore for an analysis of the specific characteristics of *capitalism.* If we abstract from everything that separates "eighteenth century Britain and Khrushchev's Russia; Meiji Japan and Mao's China; Bismarck's Germany and Nasser's Egypt" (p. 1), we shall be unable to explain why Nasser's Egypt finds Khrushchev's Russia a more useful guide to economic development that eighteenth century Britain. If we are anxious to minimize the element of economic advantage in the relation between advanced and dependent (colonial) economies (pp. 108-112, 137-138, 156), we shall be unable to say anything useful about problems which arise out of the fact that dependent economies are dependent.

Why, it may be asked, should a man adopt a theoretical approach so obviously defective and indeed self-defeating? At least one plausible answer may be suggested. Professor Rostow, is, on his own admission, primarily concerned not with arriving at a theory of economic development, but with writing a "non-communist manifesto." Unlike other and wiser—we shall not say abler—scholars with similar objectives, he has chosen to abandon not merely Marx's conclusions and his arguments, but even the basic posing of the problem of economic development as Marx saw it. It was, as we have tried to show, an unwise decision, for the Marxian questions are fundamental to any attempt at an understanding of the process of economic development. What is required is at least an *understanding* of Marx's questions. To that level Professor Rostow has yet to rise.

II

An examination of the principal tenets of Rostow's theory of economic growth—if it can be said at all that such a *theory* is advanced in his book—thus reveals nothing that can be considered an addition to our knowledge of the history of economic development or an enrichment of our understanding of the processes involved. But Rostow offers something much more ambitious than "merely" a new theory of economic growth. He also proposes "a comprehensive, realistic and soundly based alternative to Marx's theory of how societies evolve." Let us examine this latest effort to put Marx into the waste basket. Since, however, it is neither possible nor would it be rewarding to trace all the misconceptions and misrepresentations of Marxian thought which Rostow has managed to compress in a few pages, we will have to limit ourselves to two problems which Rostow himself considers to be central to his manifesto.

The first relates to the nature of the engine which propels economic, social, and political evolution in the course of history. To this fundamental question, historical materialism provides a comprehensive and sophisticated answer. Far be it from us to seek to emulate Rostow in the claim that this answer supplies pat solutions to all problems raised by the complex events and patterns of history. What historical materialism does claim is to have discovered an indispensable *approach* to the understanding of historical constellations and to have focused attention on the nature of the principal energies responsible for their emergence, transformation, and disappearance. To put it in a nutshell: these energies are to be traced back to the always present tension between the degree of development of the forces of production on one side, and the prevailing relations of production on the other. To be sure, neither "forces of production" nor "relations of production" are simple notions. The former encompasses the existing state of rationality, science, and technology, the mode of organization of production and the degree of development of man himself, that "most important productive force of all" (Marx). The latter refers to the mode of appropriation of the products of human labor, the social condition under which production takes place, the principles of distribution, the modes of thought, the ideology, the *Welt-*

anschauung which constitute the "general ether" (Marx) within which society functions at any given time. The conflict between the two—sometimes dormant and sometimes active—is due to a fundamental difference in the "laws of motion" of forces and relations of production respectively. The forces of production tend to be highly dynamic. Driven by man's quest for a better life, by the growth and expansion of human knowledge and rationality, by increasing population, the forces of production tend continually to gain in strength, in depth, and in scope. The relations of production on the other hand tend to be sticky, conservative. Prevailing systems of appropriation and social organization, and political institutions favor some classes and discriminate against, frustrate, oppress other classes. They give rise to vested interests. Modes of thought freeze and display a tenacity and longevity giving rise to what is sometimes referred to as "cultural lags." When the forward movement of the forces of production becomes stymied by the deadweight of dominant interests and the shackles of dominant thought, one or the other has to yield. And since a dominant class never willingly relinquishes its time-honored privileges (partly for reasons of self-interest and partly because its own horizon is more or less narrowly circumscribed by the prevailing ideology sanctifying those very privileges), the clash tends to become violent. This is not to say that obsolete, retrograde relations of production are *always* burst asunder and swept away by revolutions. Depending on the circumstances prevailing in each individual case, the process unfolds in a wide variety of ways. Violent upheavals "from below" and relatively peaceful transformations "from above" are as much within the range of possibilities as periods of protracted stagnation in which the political, ideological, and social power of the ruling classes is strong enough to prevent the emergence of new forms of economic and social organization, to block or to slow a country's economic development.

Marx's historical materialism insists, however, that the development of the forces of production has thus far been *the* commanding aspect of the historical process. Whatever may have been its vicissitudes, whatever may have been the setbacks and interruptions that it has suffered in the course of history, in the long run it has tended to overcome all obstacles, and to conquer all political, social, and ideological structures subordinating them to its requirements. This struggle betweeen the forces of production and the relations of production proceeds unevenly. Dramatic conquests are less frequent than long periods of siege in which victories remain elusive, imperfect, and impermanent. Different countries display different patterns which depend on their size, location, the strength and cohesion of their ruling classes, the courage, determination and leadership of the underprivileged; on the measure of foreign influence and support to which both or either are exposed; on the pervasiveness and power of the dominant ideologies (e.g., religion). Moreover, the course taken by this struggle and its outcome differ greatly from period to period. Under conditions of capitalism's competitive youth they were different from what they have become in the age of imperialism; in the presence of a powerful socialist sector of the world, they are not the same as they were or would have been in its absence. No bloodless schema of five (or three or seven) "stages" can do justice to the multitude and variety of economic, technological, political, and ideological configurations generated by this never-ceasing battle between the forces and relations of production. What Marx and Engels and Lenin taught those whose ambition it was to learn rather than to make careers by "refuting" is that these historical configurations cannot be dealt with by "a generalization from the whole span of modern history," but have to be studied *concretely,* with full account taken of the wealth of factors and forces that participate in the shaping of any particular historical case.

To forestall a possible misunderstanding: the foregoing is not intended to advocate renunciation of theory in favor of plodding empiricism. Rather, it suggests the necessity of an interpenetration of theory and concrete observation, of empirical research illuminated by rational theory, of theoretical work which draws its life blood from historical study. Consider for instance any one of the many existing underdeveloped countries. Pigeonholing it in one of Rostow's "stages" does not bring us any closer to an understanding of the country's economic and social condition or give us a clue to the country's developmental possibilities and prospects. What is required for that is as accurate as possible an assessment of the social and political forces in the country pressing for change and for development: the economic condition and the stratification of the peasantry, its political traditions and its ideological make-up, the economic and social status, internal differentiation and political aspirations of the bourgeoisie, the extent of its tie-up with foreign interests and the degree of monopoly prevailing in its national business, the closeness of its connection with the landowning interests and the measure of its participation in the existing government; the living and working conditions and the level of class consciousness of labor and its political and organizational strength. Nor is this by any means the entire job. On the other side of the fence are the groups, institutions, relations, and ideologies seeking to preserve the status quo, obstructing efforts directed toward its overturn. There are wealthy landowners and/or rich peasants; there is a segment of the capitalist class firmly entrenched in monopolistic positions and allied with other privileged groups in society; there is a government bureaucracy interwoven with and resting upon the military establishment; there are foreign investors supported by their respective national governments and working hand in hand with their native retainers. Only a thorough historical-materialist analysis, piercing the ideological fog maintained by the dominant coalition of interests and destroying the fetishes continually produced and reproduced by those concerned with the preservation of the status quo, only such historical-materialist analysis can hope to disentangle the snarl of tendencies and countertendencies, forces, influences, convictions and opinions, drives and resistances which account for the pattern of economic and social development. And it is to this *Marxist* undertaking that Professor Rostow offers us his alternative: to assign the country in question to one of his "stages," and then to speculate on the "two possibilities" with which that country is confronted: it will either move on to the next "stage"—or it won't. And if it should move to the next "stage," it will again face two possibilities: it will either stay there for a while, or it will slide back again.

We may now turn briefly to Professor Rostow's other sally against Marx by which he seeks to provide "significant links between economic and non-economic behavior which Karl Marx failed to discern." This enterprise, he apparently feels, will deliver the "coup de grace" to Marxian thought, "for," he assures us, it is absolutely essential to Marxism that it is over property that men fight and die" (p. 151). What Karl Marx—"a lonely man, profoundly isolated from his fellows"—did not discern, but Professor Rostow does, is the following: "Man . . . seeks, not merely economic advantage, but also power, leisure, adventure, continuity of experience and security . . . in short, net human behavior is . . . not an act of maximization, but . . . an act of balancing alternative and often conflicting human objectives." "This notion of balance among alternatives," Professor Rostow observes, "is, of course, more complex and difficult than a simple maximization proposition; and it does not lead to a series of rigid, inevitable stages of history." We submit that this "notion" may well be "complex and difficult" but that it is also singularly devoid of any ascertainable content. It is remarkable how Professor Rostow, after having constructed a straw man bearing no resemblance to Marxism, finds it beyond his powers to vanquish even such a "hand-picked" enemy.

Indeed—to put it bluntly—the whole argument is too help-less to serve even as a starting point for a serious discussion. Even a passing acquaintance with the most important writings of Marx, Engels, and more recent Marxist writers is all that is required to realize the irrelevance of Rostow's carica-ture of Marxism. Far from asserting that "history is uniquely determined by economic forces," and far from ignoring the "significant links between economic and non-economic be-havior," the theory of historical materialism advanced by Marx and his followers is nothing if not a powerful effort to explore the manifold and historically changing connections between the development of the forces and relations of production and the evolution of the consciousness, emotions, and ideologies of men. So much so that the Marxian theory of ideology has served as the point of departure and as a guide to an entire discipline known under the name of "sociology of knowledge," with all analytical history of religion, literature, art, and science deriving its inspiration from the same source. Marx's theory of alienation, antici-pating much of the subsequent development of social psycho-logy, is in the center of modern study and criticism of culture. Marx's political theory has served as a conceptual basis for most that is valuable in modern European and American historical scholarship. And *The Eighteenth Bru-maire of Louis Bonaparte*—to name only one unsurpassed gem of historical and sociological study—still shines as a model of a comprehensive and penetrating analysis of the "significant links between economic and non-economic be-havior" in one particular historical case.

But all this escapes Mr. Rostow, who is not only incapable of contributing anything to the discussion of the relevant problems but even fails to comprehend the context within which they arise. For the problem of the "links between economic and non-economic behavior," or for that matter of the explanation of any human activity, economic or other, is not and never has been whether or not man "balances alternatives" or "adheres to the principle of maximization" (which terms, incidentally, if they mean anything at all, amount to exactly the same), no more than there is meaning to the question whether man does or does not have "freedom of will." No one in his right mind—Marxist, mechanical materialist, or idealist—has ever denied that men make choices, exercise their wills, balance alternatives, or, for that matter, move their legs when they walk. The problem is and always has been to discover what determines the nature of the alternatives that are available to men, what accounts for the nature of the goals which they set themselves in different periods of historical development, what makes them will what they will in various societies at various times. To this fundamental question there have been several answers. The theologian's solution has been that all human acts and decisions are governed by the omnipotent and inscrutable will of God. The idealist who substituted the human spirit for the Deity arrives at a very similar position, unable as he is to explain what accounts for the actions and transactions of the spirit. The adherents of "psychologism" view human activity as an emanation of the human psyche, itself an aspect of an eternally constant human nature. The historical materialist considers human actions and motivations to be complex results of a dialectical interaction of biotic and social processes, the latter continually propelled by the dynamism of the forces and relations of production as well as by the ideological evolutions deriving from them and influencing them in turn. Professor Rostow, however, has the simplest solution of all: he does not know what the answer is, nor does he appear to care. Anything can happen: man moves hither and thither, balancing alternatives, making choices, striving for power, engaged in maximization of who knows what. And this is the new, original, unprecedented "theory" which makes good what Karl Marx failed to discern.

We owe the reader an apology. Taken by itself Rostow's Manifesto does not call for a lengthy review. If we have undertaken to write one nevertheless, it is because of considerations from the realm of the sociology of knowledge. His is an important document. It demonstrates in a particularly striking way the low estate to which Western social thought has declined in the current era of the Cold War.

Notes

1. Cf. also A.F. Burns, *Production Trends in the United States Since 1870* (New York, 1934).

2. This stage Rostow misnames "the age of high mass consumption," for both by the logical requirements of his schema and by his own observations on the subject (pp. 73-74) what characterizes it is not fundamentally mass consumption (which is only one of the alternative uses to which resources can be put by society) but *abundance.* This error in nomenclature is by no means trivial; it is associated with Rostow's misleading treatment of the current stage of the United States' economic development, when *armaments* rather than mass consumption represent the economy's "leading sector."

3. And this not with any great perspicacity. Thus one would suppose that agricultural change creates the preconditions of industrialization not merely by supplying "expanded food, expanded markets, and an expanded supply of loanable funds to the modern sector" (p. 24) but also—and perhaps decisively—an expanded labor force for it.

4. Cf. the hesitations reflected in the footnotes to his table of "take-offs" (p. 38) and his inability to decide "whether the take-off period will, in fact, be successful in the six contemporary economies attempting take-off" (p. 44), as well as his failure to cope with the phenomenon of relapse after apparent take-offs. However, critics, and especially statisticians, should resist the easy temptation Rostow thus provides to reject the entire concept of economic development by industrial revolution.

5. For example: "Perhaps the most important thing to be said about the behavior of these variables in historical cases of take-off is that they have assumed many different forms. There is no single pattern. The rate and productivity of investment can rise, and the consequences of this rise can be diffused into a self-reinforcing general growth process by many different technical and economic routes, under the aegis of many different political, social and cultural settings, driven along by a wide variety of human motivations" (p. 46). Or, we may add, they may not rise, and may not be diffused.

6. "The general case is of a society modernizing itself in a nationalist reaction to intrusion or the threat of intrusion from more advanced powers abroad" (p. 34).

7. Cf. pp. 34-35 where the attempt is made, half-heartedly, to assimilate the pioneer industrialization of Britain to this pattern on no other grounds than that otherwise it would not fit the "general case." Admittedly, if a theory of economic evolution cannot explain the case which needs explaining most, namely the very first "take-off" in history, it is little more than scrap paper, though Professor Rostow does not seem too keenly aware of this. Cf. p. 27.

8. Cf. p. 28: "The merchant has always been present, seeking in modernization not only the removal of obstacles to enlarged markets and profits, but also the high status denied him," but especially the remarkably contorted pages on colonialism (pp. 108-112).

Economics
of Two Worlds

The upsurge of interest in mathematical economics and econometrics and the considerable effort lately devoted to their furtherance in the socialist countries have evoked strong reactions from both Marxist and bourgeois economists. Perhaps the most remarkable thing about the two sets of reactions is that they both tend to interpret this development in substantially the same way: the socialist camp's "conversion" to the mathematical method in economic theory and research is looked upon as a major concession or even as a surrender of Marxian economics to its bourgeois adversary. This appraisal seems to us to be mistaken. It undialectically treats economics as a discipline apart from the rest of social science and somehow concerned with an undifferentiated and unhistorical reality. And yet, as Engels correctly observed, "political economy is . . . essentially a *historical* science [and] cannot be the same for all countries and for all historical epochs."[1]

One of the principal results of Marx's scientific labors was the demonstration that capitalism, after constituting a tremendous advance in the growth of the forces of production

Co-authored with Paul M. Sweezy. This article was originally published by Panstwowe Wydawnictwo Naukowe (Warsaw) in a volume in honor of Oskar Lange, and is reprinted by permission. Copyright © 1964 by Panstwowe Wydawnicto Naukowe.

and in the evolution of a more rational society, turns into its own opposite and becomes an irrational and retrograde system. This transformation is a protracted and complex process. There is no one date at which the changeover can be thought of as having occurred, nor is there any particular aspect of capitalist development that can be looked upon as its unambiguous indicator. Whether the historical phase has been reached in which the system begins its qualitative change can only be established by considering it as a whole, in its manifold manifestations and in its global impact. Concentration on one brief time period, or on one country or geographical region, or on one set of quantitative measurements or qualitative observations is likely to produce misleading conclusions and distorted judgments. Such, for example, were the breakdown theories of writers like Rosa Luxemburg and Henryk Grossman which depicted the end of capitalism not as a lengthy process involving a worldwide socioeconomic order but rather as a single catastrophic event like an earthquake. And at the opposite extreme, but stemming from the same root, are the theories of capitalist stabilization recurrently put forward by Social Democratic writers who are as ready to generalize from the recent past of their own countries as they are to ignore the fact that capitalism is a global system.

It is one of the greatest strengths of Leninism that it has consistently avoided both of these errors. But this is not all. There is another fundamental tenet of Leninism which sharply differentiates it from other contemporary semi-Marxian or pseudo-Marxian currents of thought—that we, here and now, are actually living in the age of transition, the period in which capitalism is going through the process of decomposition, retreat, and displacement by a new, more rational economic and social order. The validity of this view is in no way refuted by the undoubted fact that there exist at the present time a number of capitalist countries in which the forces of production are expanding at a fairly rapid rate—for example, Germany, Italy, France, and Japan. For this expansion proves nothing in itself; it must be considered in conjunction with much else: with the factors which have brought it about (the vast destruction caused by, and the exceptional circumstances following, the Second World War); with the stagnation in the most advanced capitalist countries (the United States and Great Britain); with the condition of the vast majority of the people in the capitalist world who, far from moving forward on the road to economic and social development, are sliding back, either in relation to advanced countries, as is the case nearly everywhere in the underdeveloped areas, or absolutely as in most; and, last but not least, with the crucially important fact that a large number of societies are engaged in the construction of socialism. What is decisive for the validity of the Leninist thesis is that, as a world order, capitalism has ceased to be an instrumentality of advancement and has turned instead into the principal obstacle to the development of a more rationally integrated, more productive, less misery- and disease-ridden international society.

Likewise, if we seek to determine the role played in our time by the capitalist system within any particular country, it is futile to use as a yardstick the state of individual units of production or even of entire branches of the economy. There are many components of a capitalist economy—even a very undeveloped one—which become progressively more rational, more efficient, and more productive. Many a giant corporation has grown into a scientifically organized, superbly managed, and efficiently operated center of production; and many of the technical functions of the capitalist economy, be they in the field of finance and insurance or of retail distribution and transportation, have come to be discharged effectively and efficiently.

But just as it would be a fatal mistake to judge the state of an underdeveloped country by the quality and efficiency of its tourist hotels, gambling casinos, or sometimes even railroads, so it is impossible to infer anything about the total rationality of a system from whatever level of rationality may have been reached in its individual parts. For it is an outstanding characteristic of capitalism, indeed one of its distinguishing features, that the rationalization of its parts which it undoubtedly promotes is not accompanied by an increase in the rationality of the economic and social order as a whole. As Marx noted in a different connection, "the capitalist order of production is generally, despite all it niggardliness, thoroughly wasteful as far as the human material is concerned, just as, conversely, owing to its method of distribution of products through commerce and its manner of competition, it is very wasteful with regard to its material means, and loses for society what it gains for the individual capitalist."[2]

It might be objected that the very fact that Marx observed (rather than predicted) this phenomenon more than a hundred years ago shows that there is nothing new about it and that it can therefore hardly be regarded as specific to the current epoch of the general crisis of capitalism. Actually, what this fact illustrates is merely the continuity of the process which transforms capitalism and turns it from a promoter into an inhibitor of progress. This continuity exists and is important, but it should not be allowed to obscure the qualitative change which has set in during the century since Marx wrote *Capital*. When the level of development was so low that universal scarcity was still inevitable, and capitalism was, however wastefully and anarchically, creating the conditions for a mighty upsurge in the forces of production, the contrast between the partial rationality of the enterprise and the total irrationality of the system could still be treated as one of the necessary costs of progress. Compare this with the situation today when science and technology have advanced to the point that scarcity and the human suffering resulting from it could easily be done away within the lifetime of one generation—if only the roadblocks put in the way of the rational utilization of available resources and knowledge by a retrograde capitalist system could be removed. In the earlier period, when scarcity was still inevitable, the critical reaction to the discrepancy between the mode of functioning of the system as a whole and that of its parts was, and indeed could only be, a feeling of outrage at the *injustice* of capitalism. It is only in relatively recent times when plenty is within easy reach and its attainment is obviously prevented by the continued dominance of capitalism that the *irrationality* of the system moves into the forefront of critical thought.

Nor is this all. The widening gap between the rationality of the parts and the irrationality of the whole, between the senselessness or even destructiveness of the purpose to which human activity is devoted and the efficiency of that activity itself, results of necessity in a distorted development of the forces of production and in particular of the most important force of production of all: man himself. To quote Marx again: "More than any other mode of production, [capitalism] squanders human lives, or living labor, and not only blood and flesh, but also nerve and brain. Indeed it is only through the most enormous waste of the individual development that the development of mankind is at all preserved and maintained in the epoch of history immediately preceding the conscious reorganization of society."[3] The tremendous expansion and refinement of resources devoted to the augmentation of killing power; the direction of the highest available skills to such fields as law, advertising, salesmanship, and financial manipulation; the shunting of vast amounts of energy and talent from socially vital tasks to what happens to be profitable in a shifting market—all this bears eloquent testimony to the far-reaching smothering of partial rationality under the deadweight of total irrationality.

It is against this background of ever growing tensions— within the separate parts of the system and between them and the whole—that it is necessary to consider the development of bourgeois economics in the current epoch. Reflecting these tensions, current work in bourgeois economics can be divided into two parts. The first, often referred to nowadays as microeconomics, deals with the parts; the second, or macroeconomics, deals with the whole. In both, we can see clearly how developing contradictions in the economy itself call forth corresponding contradictions in the realm of theory.

It seems safe to say that most current work in microeconomics aims at exploring the conditions for raising the efficiency and improving the performance of the capitalist enterprise. Its specific content is therefore determined by the needs of the capitalist enterprise and by the standards of efficiency and performance under which it operates. These in turn depend on the nature of the enterprise itself, which is today the giant monopolistic (or oligopolistic) corporation. These economic units have evolved everywhere in the capitalist world during the past seven or eight decades and now occupy a dominant position in all of the more advanced capitalist countries. The problems engendered by this kind of enterprise differ markedly from those associated with its predecessor in the era of competitive capitalism.

At the risk of oversimplification, these differences can be described as follows. The competitive firm was small relative to the size of the industry of which it was a member. It bought its factors of production and sold its standardized product at prices over which it had no control. In these circumstances, it could strive for maximum profits only by improving its techniques or its organization—in other words, by actions which were necessarily confined to its own production process. Maximum profits and optimum methods of production thus went together.[4] The ideal competitive capitalist has therefore been traditionally conceived of as an inventor and organizer, always interested in making a better product at lower costs. Insofar as he studied at all, the subjects which attracted him were technological and managerial in nature—engineering and what the Germans call *Betriebswirtschaftslehre*. He could expect little benefit from studying the outside world, except for such knowledge (very limited at the time) which it might provide him about general business fluctuations and the ups and downs in the market for his own product. Within the limitations imposed upon him by the relatively narrow scope of his operations and by the anarchy of social production as a whole, the competitive capitalist was induced to promote partial rationality both by the hope of profit and by the threat of extinction if he should fall too far behind his rivals.

When it comes to the monopolistic corporation of today, the situation is very different. The firm is large not only in terms of the industry to which it may be considered to belong,[5] but also in terms of the nation's or even the world's economy; what it produces is often strongly identified with its name so that, in the eyes of buyers, there may be no close substitutes available. Commanding a significant degree of monopoly power, the giant corporation confronts the prices at which it sells its output and buys its inputs not as objective market data but as magnitudes which depend on its own operations and on those of a small number of other similarly situated concerns. As a vast enterprise not necessarily identified with any particular group of individuals but rather thought of by its owners and managers as an everlasting entity, it seeks to maximize the flow of profits over a much longer planning horizon than the small competitive capitalist can afford to take account of. Its drive for maximum attainable profits under such circumstances no longer involves merely finding the best ways to reduce the costs of production of a given commodity or group of commodities. It has to keep under continuous review the problem of what commodities to produce—their physical attributes, their outward appearance, brand names, etc. Durability and quality have to be determined in the light of the firm's other lines of production and traditional practices, as well as of the behavior of other suppliers of related or possibly related products. In arriving at decisions, it is necessary to weigh advertising and other marketing costs; and in fixing the quantities of the various commodities to be produced as well as the prices to be charged, the shape of all relevant demand and marginal revenue curves has to be explored and taken into account. The outside world which the competitive capitalist has to take for granted not only directly influences the monopolistic corporation's production process but is subject to deliberate manipulation on its part.

It can be readily seen that the identification of the firm's path to maximum profits when all these factors—plus many others relating to taxes, tariffs, foreign exchange rates, etc.[6]—are duly considered calls for a calculatory effort that is vastly more complex than that required by a small competitive business. The commonsense prescriptions of the intuitive entrepreneur of old, the time-tested devices made familiar in *Betriebswirtschaftslehre* are no longer capable of coping with the task in hand. Recourse must be had to a more powerful apparatus of what has come to be called "decision-making"; a new "management science" using mathematical techniques able to encompass a large number of variables (and constraints) has to be developed. It is therefore by no means accidental or due solely to the immanent evolution of pure thought that advanced mathematical studies of behavior patterns, the exploration of the properties of more complex constellations of uncertainty, the development of mathematical techniques of programming, and the perfection of techniques of statistical measurement have moved to the center of bourgeois microeconomic thought.

It must not be thought, however, that the development of all these sophisticated and often genuinely scientific methods for guiding the behavior of a monopolistic or oligopolistic corporation has anything in common with a search for the optimal allocation and utilization of society's productive resources, or for that matter even with the partial rationality standards which were relevant to the process of commodity production under a regime of competitive enterprise. The nature and volume of output, the technology employed, the investment undertaken, the raw materials used, the prices charged—none of these, no matter how rational the methods by which they were arrived at, can be thought of as corresponding to the needs of society as a whole or even as reflecting the growth of the forces of production in one of its component parts. It is as if a superbly skillful typist operating a perfectly faultless electric typewriter were to set to work, enjoined to avoid a single typographical error because one hundred typewritten pages proofread and free of mistakes have to be ready promptly at 4 p.m. for delivery to the janitor for removal to the dump.

What applies to the parts of the system applies with equal if not greater force to the whole. There the prevailing irrationality is even more drastic and obvious than that obtaining within the confines of the individual enterprise.

At a sufficiently high level of abstraction, the conditions for a rational economic organization are almost self-evident. Given a certain input of social labor and an output of goods and services corresponding to the degree of development of the forces of production and the productivity of labor, society can either consume or accumulate what it produces. If we assume a closed system, these two categories— consumption and accumulation—obviously exhaust society's total current output. And if we abstract from the possibility of consuming what was produced in an earlier period, it is clear that society must consume and accumulate exactly what it produces, neither more nor less. Should aggregate output exceed society's combined desire to consume and accumulate, labor input must be curtailed and the amount of leisure correspondingly increased. If aggregate output falls short of society's desire to consume and to accumulate, labor input has to be increased (if this is possible), or the productivity of labor has to be raised (if this is feasible). If neither alternative is open, a diversion of resources from consumption to investment with a view to augmenting society's future productivity is the only other possible course.

Just as it is necessary to allocate productive resources (human labor, living and congealed) to the satisfaction of current consumption and accumulation needs, so it is indispensable to decide on the specific apportionment of total effort to the production of different items entering into consumption and investment respectively. Marx put the matter concisely: "Given social production, the allocation of time naturally remains of the essence. The less time society requires to produce wheat, cattle, etc., the more time it gains for other production, material or intellectual. Just as in the case of a single individual, the all-sidedness of society's development, of its enjoyment, and of its activity depends on the saving of time. The economy of time, this is what all economy dissolves itself into—in the last analysis. Society must purposefully apportion its time to realize an output corresponding to its total needs, just as an individual must properly apportion his time to acquire knowledge in appropriate proportions or to satisfy different demands on his energy. Economy of time as well as planned allocation of working time to different branches of production thus constitutes the first economic law under conditions of social production."[7]

To be sure, this statment of the "first economic law" leaves open a number of important questions which need to be answered if the rationality of society's economic organization is to be assured. To mention only two: First, how are the needs and preferences of society's members for various possible combinations of goods and services (including leisure) to be ascertained? The age-old problem of the relation of the individual to society is obviously not automatically solved by the overall rationality of the social organization. The second question concerns the distribution of social income: equal shares for all? To each according to his contribution to social output? Or to each according to his needs? Although the problem will lose much of its present urgency when the development and organization of the forces of production have advanced to the point where scarcity has been overcome, and when the new society has succeeded in radically restructuring human wants, nevertheless for a considerable time to come it is bound to remain an important part of the task of rationally planning social existence. From our present point of view, the thing that needs to be stressed is that it is only when the "first economic law" has been consciously made the organizational principle of society that the rational solution of other problems moves into the realm of the feasible. It is only at this stage that many of the now known technical devices will be able to serve their proper purposes: referenda and opinion polls, democratic elections, and genuine free choice by individuals.

Comparing the elementary principles of rational economic organization with the *modus operandi* of the capitalist system puts into sharp relief the irrationality of the latter. Under capitalism neither the total amount of labor performed nor the output produced is determined by the existing level of productivity and by society's wants and needs, nor are these variables influenced by any social scale of preferences (however arrived at) with regard to labor and leisure. It is one of the most striking aspects of the irrationality of the capitalist process that all these things, which ought to be so closely intermeshed, are in fact governed by the separate, disconnected, and often conflicting forces which generate both the aggregate and the composition of effective demand. Thus the distribution of income, largely determined by the pattern of ownership of means of production, accounts in the main for both aggregate demand for consumer goods and aggregate individual saving. The profit-maximization policies of monopolistic corporations decide the share of social income going into surplus. The same profit objectives call forth investment outlays the magnitude of which is unrelated to the size of the extracted surplus, the amount of individual saving, or society's need for investment. Accordingly, fluctuations in the amount of work performed (regular employment, part-time employment, overtime work) are in no way governed by changes in society's desire or need for more or less output and do not take place according to any rational scheme intended to serve the best interests of society as a whole (for example, an across-the-board lengthening or shortening of the work week, advancement or postponement of the retirement age, shortening or lengthening of the time devoted to education, and so forth). The adjustment of the aggregate amount of social labor to changes in market demand takes place rather through changes in the volume of unemployment, which affects the members of the capitalist class and other privileged strata in society hardly at all but imposes untold suffering, insecurity, and degradation on the underlying population which depends for for its livelihood on the sale of its labor power.[8]

The irrationality of the process which determines the level of employment and the volume of output is matched by the irrationality of that which determines the composition and distribution of what is produced. This is not the place to present the amply available evidence;[9] suffice it to point out that while poverty and severe privation affect more than one-third of the population of the United States, "in 1960, the highest five percent of all consumer units received about 20 percent of total disposable income, or very much more than the 15.5 percent of income received by the lowest 40 percent of all consumer units."[10] At the same time, the resources at the disposal of the country's entire educational establishment (public and private) are smaller than what is spent on the sales effort (advertising, direct selling, automobile model changes, etc., etc.).

This situation is necessarily reflected in bourgeois economics. As long as the productivity of human labor was so low as to render inevitable a general state of scarcity, it was possible to treat poverty and privation on one hand and wealth and luxury on the other as Hegel's "cunning of reason." Necessitating hard work on the part of the poor and providing the rich with the wherewithal and incentives to invest, the existing economic and social order could be regarded as history's devious but highly successful stratagem for the attainment of general progress. The apparent irrationality of the capitalist system could be depicted as merely a facade hiding the profound rationality of the process as a whole. Under these circumstances, it was seen as the task of economics to teach the uninstructed man in the street to believe in the beneficial design of the structure hidden behind the uninviting appearance of the scaffolding.

After the First World War, and in particular in the years of and following the Great Depression, this traditional justification of the increasingly manifest irrationality of the capitalist order became less and less plausible. Most of those who continue to defend the system no longer do so on grounds of rationality but instead rely on appeals to tradition, "human nature," religion, "true" versus "false" reason, and so on.[11] Others rest their case on the assertion that only capitalism guarantees individual freedom—defining the latter so as to make it synonymous with the preservation of existing inequality and privileges, which, in turn, are "explained" as emanations of the God-given order of nature.[12]

Dominant economic thought, however, has taken a different course. It has accepted, however grudgingly and reluctantly, the principal tenet of the Marxian critique of the capitalist order: its anarchy and deeply rooted irrationality. At the same time, bourgeois economics refuses to draw the logical conclusions from that irrefutable finding.[13] The strategy adopted has been rather to try to steal the Marxian thunder by devising schemes to make the system work without interfering with the basic features of capitalism: private enterprise and production for maximum profits. It is this strategy that has inspired the bulk of thought and research in the area of macroeconomics, and it is in the requirements of this strategy that one finds much of the reason for the emergence and development of advanced mathematical techniques of theoretical reasoning and statistical work.

The characteristic focus of this intellectual effort is the elaboration and refinement of one of Marx's favorite analytic devices: the bisectoral model of simple and expanded reproduction.[14] In Marx's work, to be sure, this model had no independent standing. Its purpose was rather to illustrate the anarchy and irrationality of the capitalist mode of production. By the specification of the conditions necessary for the harmonious expansion of the economy he sought to demonstrate the stringency of the requirements that would have to be fulfilled,[15] and tried to show how small was the likelihood of such a harmony being achieved under capitalism. This, it cannot be overemphasized, is the very opposite of the use to which Marx's model has been put by bourgeois writers who, following in the footsteps of Tugan-Baranowski, see in it a proof of the capacity of the capitalist system to expand harmoniously *ad infinitum*.

For such harmony to prevail and for the economy to expand on the basis of a full utilization of available human and material resources, the strategic variables determining the mode of functioning of the system as a whole would have to be controlled. Since the classical and neoclassical view—that the necessary controls are efficiently, albeit indirectly, exercised by the price mechanism and the rate of interest—has been exploded, the question of the nature and availability of alternative controls within the framework of the advanced capitalist system has become the central issue facing bourgeois economics. So far, however, it has carefully avoided facing up to this issue and instead has sought to deal with the problem by assuming it away. Either the relevant magnitudes and relations (volume of investment, proportion of income consumed, rate of technological advance, etc.) are assumed to turn out correctly as a result of the working of the competitive mechanism—although the incapacity of the mechanism to produce such a result has been amply proven; or else these variables are treated as though they were determined by a social plan—although the absence, and, as we believe, the impossibility, of such a plan under capitalism is one of the system's outstanding characteristics.[16] Much ingenuity has been devoted to elaborating these growth models, but in view of their failure to provide any concrete indications of the processes which determine the relevant magnitudes and functional relations, the significance of the results achieved is, to say the least, somewhat dubious.

This is not to deny that to the extent to which they contribute to the clarification of the requirements for the maintenance of correct proportions and balanced growth in *any* economy based upon division of labor and involving technological change, models of this kind are essential to the furtherance of the theory of economic planning. By leading to improved knowledge of the variables and relations that need to be controlled to assure a rational utilization of resources, they not only can help to indicate the nature of the informational material which is essential to the planning authority but also to identify the strategic leverages that can be successfully employed for the attainment of the plan's goals. Where functional relations are concerned, they may direct attention to the need to study behavior patterns which were previously neglected. In these ways, they can enrich the toolbox needed for the rational, socialist administration of society's resources.

But the situation appears in quite a different light when these constructs are viewed as elements of a theory of capitalist reality. We have then to ask which aspects of that reality are taken into account and which are abstracted from. If, as we believe to be the case, what is abstracted from includes essential characteristics of capitalism, the models involved not only fail to advance our understanding of the working principles of the system but actually help to obscure them. For by postulating the existence of adequate direct or indirect controls over the behavior of key variables when in fact none exist; by assuming the absence of monopoly when in fact it is ubiquitous and far-reaching in its effects; by supposing full employment in the long run when in fact it is rather an exception than a rule—in all these ways, the currently fashionable models abstract not from secondary features of the process that they seek to explain but from its most essential characteristics. Thus they substitute for the capitalist economy an imaginary rational system which has nothing in common with capitalism but the name. The result, it need hardly be said, is an apologetic defense of the status quo—and this quite apart from the subjective intentions of the model-builders.

The apologetic role played by this type of theorizing is by no means reduced by the apparent precision attained through the use of mathematics. In fact, it is the other way round. Both mathematical language and mathematical reasoning can be particularly treacherous in that they permit the drawing of logically impeccable conclusions from inadequate premises and create the appearance of a coordinated and cohesive system when in reality no such system exists. Just as, in the microeconomic case, the glittering efficiency of the modern corporation covers up the meaninglessness of the purpose which it serves, so in the macroeconomic case the elaborate mathematical model serves to conceal the irrationality of the economic organization which it purports to illuminate.

The tasks of Marxian political economy are different under different economic and social orders, in different countries, and in different historical periods. It is an error to believe, as some Marxist writers have, that political economy, being the science of capitalism *par excellence*, becomes superfluous under socialism.[17] While under socialism both the object and objectives of political economy undergo a profound change, its responsibilities actually increase.

On the macro level, it becomes the theoretical guardian of the rationality and socialist orientation of the system as a whole, as well as the chief instrumentality for the formulation of society's economic goals and the general strategy for attaining them. To the fulfillment of these tasks, only Marxian political economy brings the great intellectual tradition of socialist thought and the theoretical lessons learned from the accumulated experience of socialist construction. It alone possesses the theoretical tools needed for the analysis of the economic institutions, scientific possibilities, and social relations that are decisive in the elaboration and carrying out of society's economic plans.

But while on the macro level, it is only Marxian political economy that can serve as a guide to a socialist society, it has no such "comparative advantage" when it comes to the micro level, to the problems of the rationality and efficiency in the individual sectors and units of a socialist economy. Indeed, Marxian political economy has never addressed itself to the problems of optimization that arise in the separate parts of the economy, neither to the minimization of costs of production of a given output nor to the maximization of profits on a given amount of invested capital. Concerned with the totality of the capitalist process and with the developmental tendencies inherent in it, Marxian political economy has never sought to compete with *Betriebswirtschaftslehre* and its more modern variants, any more than it has attempted to develop a theory of consumer's choice or of investor's behavior under conditions of uncertainty. It has been content to leave the exploration of the conditions for optimizing the capitalist's position within the capitalist order to bourgeois economics which quite naturally responded to *that* challenge with alacrity and ability.

As a result, on the micro level, bourgeois economics has been able to evolve a body of theoretical reasoning and techniques of empirical observation which now turn out to be of considerable value to the economic administration of a socialist society. Not that *all* the results of bourgeois microeconomics can be included in this category. For example, the (often highly subtle) analysis of the interacting strategies of oligopolistic corporations, or the analysis of the interrelations between inventory policies and market fluctuations, is obviously "dated." Their relevance is confined to the capitalist system. At the same time, the techniques developed in the solution of these and similar problems may well be usable for different purposes by socialist economic planners. Lenin put the essential point concisely when he wrote: "Large banks constitute the 'state apparatus' which we *need* for the realization of socialism and which *we take ready-made* from capitalism. Our task is only to *cut off* what are *capitalist perversions* of this excellent apparatus, to make it still larger, still more democratic, still more comprehensive."[18] And a few months later, after the Revolution, he repeatedly stressed that "if we correctly understand our tasks we must learn to build socialism from the managers and organizers of capitalist trusts." He might have added that there is something to be learned from the capitalist economists as well.

Thus from the viewpoint of the political economy of socialism, there is everything to be said for the adoption of all the advanced, mathematical and non-mathematical, techniques of observation and analysis developed by bourgeois economics. So long as care is taken to "cut off the capitalist perversions," much of what has been established in bourgeois economics—but constitutes under capitalism a manifestation of naive, ahistorical rationalism and turns inevitably into apologetics for the status quo—can be effectively used under socialist planning. To take one example among many: the theory of consumer's behavior conveys under capitalism the false, ideological notion that the "autonomous" consumer is the sovereign ruler of the economy, while in fact it is the capitalist system itself that determines the nature of his wants, tastes, standards, spending habits, and so forth. The very same theory of consumer's behavior, however, can be employed (and developed) under socialism as a powerful means for ascertaining needs and wants of consumers within an entirely different social setting. Such adoption and adaptation of elements of bourgeois economic research and theorizing to the needs of socialist planning not only do not constitute "concessions" by Marxian political economy to bourgeois economics; they do not even bear any relation to its subject matter and its interests.

Under capitalism, in advanced and underdeveloped countries alike, Marxian political economy has a twofold task. One is to continue exploring the *modus operandi* of capitalism with a view to ascertaining the changing forms in which the irrationality of the system manifests itself, and to assessing its capacity to survive despite the fact that it has already turned into an impediment to the further development and progress of society. In this connection, bourgeois economics can be of some help. What it has to offer is primarily the analytical techniques for studying the short-term determinants of income and employment developed by Keynes and some of his followers. Even here, however, it is important to distinguish between those contributions which really advance our understanding of the capitalist mechanism and those which depict capitalism as an essentially rational system which needs only a few reforms to make it viable and beneficent.

The second task of Marxian political economy was aptly defined by Engels: "The task of economic science is to demonstrate the newly emerging ills in society as the necessary consequences of the existing mode of production, but also as indications of its impending dissolution, and to uncover within the dissolving economic structure the elements of the future, new organization of production and distribution under which those ills will be abolished."[19] For obvious reasons, bourgeois economics is no help here. In fact, far from being interested in showing the relation between prevailing social ills and the underlying mode of production, it can be said that present-day bourgeois economics devotes all its ingenuity to obscuring this connection.

It is not that the existence of these ills can be denied. They are too obvious and have even inspired an extensive popular literature of the Vance Packard type.[20] Nor can they be brushed off as of no importance: there has probably never been a period in United States history when the responsible leaders of ruling-class opinion have been so outspokenly alarmed about the state of the nation's morals and manners. What they cannot admit, however, is that these conditions are the direct outcome of the capitalist social order itself. They must be attributed to some external or universal malaise—to the weaknesses of "human nature," to the deadening effect of "industrialization," to the unchecked propensity of people to procreate—to anything but the profoundly irrational and anti-human nature of an economic system based on private property and exploitation. And the elaborate apparatus of modern economic theorizing is placed unreservedly at the service of these hard-pressed defenders of the status quo.

The leading economists of the English neoclassical school— from John Stuart Mill through Marshall and Pigou to Keynes

—were all outspoken, even if relatively moderate, reformers. They knew that many grave social ills such as extreme poverty, maldistribution of wealth and income, and unemployment were directly caused by the working principle of the economic system, and they did not hesitate to advocate remedial reforms. There is hardly a trace of this honorable tradition in bourgeois economics of today: even the most "radical" wing, represented by Galbraith's works, *American Capitalism* and *The Affluent Society*, turns out on careful inspection to be the most enthusiastic apologist for a society dominated by *big* business. And if the neoclassical concern for reform has been jettisoned, how much more complete has been the abandonment of the older classical economists' passion to discover in the present the shape of the future, and to single out for intensive analysis whatever forces seemed to hold promise of new and better times to come. Anti-historical to the core, present-day bourgeois economics scorns any effort to investigate the nature of the changes that are taking place or where they are leading. The great question *Quo Vadis?*, which occupied not only Adam Smith and David Ricardo and John Stuart Mill but also in our time Joseph Schumpeter, has simply disappeared from the agenda of the bourgeois economics, yielding its place of honor to a species of what has come to be called "operations research"—the quest for appropriate means to achieve predetermined ends, regardless of the nature or the historical significance of the ends in view. Thus economics in the age of monopoly capitalism becomes a kind of scientifically refined tool for the manipulation of society and its members by the dominant interests. And, ironically, it is precisely this scientific refinement which so successfully obscures the all-important fact that thereby reason is being put into the service of unreason. If, before the advent of capitalism, science had to pose as magic to gain recognition, nowadays magic can only achieve acceptance by posing as science.

As against this development in bourgeois economics, Marxian political economy must maintain its traditional critical position. It must indefatigably confront the society of monopoly capitalism and its ideological embellishments with the mirror of unadorned reality. It must abide by its age-old commitment to treat society as a whole and to lay bare the connection between the misery prevailing in different aspects of human existence under capitalism and the irrationality of the entire system, an irrationality which cannot be assumed away but rather must occupy a central place in all genuinely scientific endeavor. Taking from the bourgeois science everything that can be useful to the construction of a new society, it must combat everything that is being used for the preservation of the old. As a variant of Marx's last thesis on Feuerbach might state: At the present time science is creating the conditions for changing the world; what matters, however, is the *nature* of the change for which it is used.

Notes

1. *Anti-Dühring*, Part II, Chapter 1.
2. *Capital*, Vol. III, Chapter 5.
3. *Ibid.*
4. Needless to say, there is no implication that the attainment of a production optimum by the individual firm means a socially optimal utilization of society's productive resources. For one thing, the firm's optimum depends on the relative prices of the various inputs, including labor. But there is no reason to suppose that wages under capitalism bear any relation to what is socially desirable—quite the contrary, especially in the earlier stages of capitalist development when forced migration from the countryside, dire poverty, and abysmal ignorance conspired to depress wages often below even a bare subsistence minimum. And for another thing, the kinds and quantities of commodities produced depend, even under ideal competitive conditions, on the distribution of income which is affected not only by

the factors just noted but also by the pattern of ownership of the means of production.

5. Many, if not most, giant corporations form parts of different industries which are not even necessarily related.

6. It should be noted in this connection that the most important capitalist corporations today typically operate on a worldwide scale. See the essay by the present authors, *Notes on the Theory of Imperialism* in *Problems of Economic Dynamics and Planning: Essays in Honor of Michal Kalecki.*

7. *Grundrisse der Kritik der Politischen Oekonomie* (Rohentwurf) 1857-1858 (Berlin, 1953), p. 89.

8. In at least one-half of the seventeen years of unprecedented prosperity following the Second World War in the United States, government-reported unemployment was in the neighborhood of five million, and according to trade-union sources at least six million. The corresponding loss of aggregate output during the postwar period has been estimated at a minimum of $500 billion; for the years 1958 to 1962 alone, the cumulative excess of potential over actual output has been calculated by the President's Council of Economic Advisors at $170 billion. (*The Economic Report of the President,* January 1963, p. 28.)

9. Some of it is assembled in *Monopoly Capital* (New York and London: Monthly Review Press, 1966) and appeared in part in *Monthly Review* (July-August 1962). Much pertinent material can be found in Michael Harrington, *The Other America: Poverty in the United States* (New York, 1962); Gabriel Kolko, *Wealth and Power in America* (New York, 1962); and numerous other monographs.

10. Conference on Economic Progress, *Poverty and Deprivation in the United States: The Plight of Two-Fifths of a Nation* (Washington, D.C., 1962), p. 4.

11. Cf. Friedrich A. Hayek, *Individualism and Economic Order* (London, 1949), in particular the first essay, "Individualism: True and False."

12. Thus Professor Milton Friedman attributes the existing distribution of wealth and income to a rule of chance such as governs a lottery, and by appeal to highly questionable eugenics supposedly responsible for differences in individual endowments. See his *Capitalism and Freedom* (Chicago, 1962), pp. 163 ff.

13. The following two statements by Keynes are highly characteristic of this attitude: "When the capital development of a country becomes a by-product of the activities of a casino, the job is

likely to be ill-done." And "a somewhat comprehensive socialization of investment will prove the only means of securing an approximation to full employment; *though this need not exclude all manner of compromises and of devices by which public authority will co-operate with private initiative.*" *The General Theory of Employment, Interest, and Money* (New York, 1936), pp. 159, 378 (italics added).

14. It is amusing that the parentage of contemporary model building in bourgeois economics is generally treated as strictly "classified information," with Walras (whose entire system has very little to do with the aggregative method employed) being substituted for Marx as a more respectable ancestor.

15. In fact, as has emerged from subsequent research, the requirements formulated by Marx were not even sufficient and need to be supplemented both by disaggregation of the two sectors which underlay his model as well as by a specification of technological relations.

16. The settlement of all the basic problems stemming from the irrationality of the capitalist process by means of suitable assumptions is well illustrated in Nicholas Kaldor and James A. Mirrlees, "A New Model of Economic Growth," *The Review of Economic Studies,* Vol. XXIX, No. 3.

17. See N. Bukharin, *Oekonomik der Transformationsperiode* (Hamburg, 1922), p. 2.

18. *Can the Bolsheviks Maintain State Power?* (October 1917). Italics in the original.

19. *Anti-Dühring*, Part II, Section 1.

20. Packard's books include: *The Hidden Persuaders* (1957); *The Status Seekers* (1959); *The Waste Makers* (1960).

Marxism
and Psychoanalysis

My topic tonight is one which by profession I am hardly qualified to discuss. I am an economist, and my concern with psychoanalysis is only marginal. If nevertheless I am going to speak about "Marxism and Psychoanalysis," it is because as a social scientist and as a Marxist I have to consider the social process as a whole; I have to study the phenomena which play a major role in the social life of our time. And it is a fact which we should face squarely: psychoanalysis today exercises an influence which is probably more pervasive than that of any other doctrine or school of thought which contributes to the formation of our "collective mind." It would be instructive to poll this large audience and to find out how many came here tonight because Marxism appears in the announcement and how many because of their interest in psychoanalysis.

Ever since Marxism stepped upon the intellectual stage as a powerful effort to understand historical development, its most important bourgeois adversary has been what I may call "psychologism." Although appearing in different forms, assuming different guises, and presented in different terms, psychologism has always rested on two main pillars: first, the

This essay is the reworked transcript of a lecture given at the Tenth Anniversary meeting of *Monthly Review* in New York on May 19, 1959. It was first published in *Monthly Review,* October 1959. Copyright © 1959 by Monthly Review, Inc.

reduction of the social process to the behavior of the individual; and second, the treatment of the individual as governed by psychic forces deriving their strength from instincts which are considered to be deeply imbedded in "human nature," with "human nature" in turn constituting an essentially stable, biotically determined structure.

Gradually, in the light of far-reaching changes in the real world and of accumulating historical and anthropological knowledge, these concepts became increasingly untenable, and traditional psychologism was forced into the background. What took its place is a new version of psychologism: an amalgam of Freudian psychoanalysis and some quasi-Marxian, sociological notions—a doctrine which I propose to call "socio-psychologism." This new arrival on the ideological scene distinguishes itself from its defunct predecessor by recognizing freely that the individual is not entirely a man for himself but is influenced by society, is somehow affected by the social setting within which he grows up. What is crucial, however, is that society in socio-psychologism is viewed as "environment": family, occupational stratum, inter-racial relations, residential community, and the like.

We must realize the implications of both positions. In the first, if it is "human nature" that determines the historical process, and if this "human nature" is unalterable, then all attempts to achieve a radical transformation of the human character and of the foundations of the social order are necessarily doomed to failure. In that case we might as well give up all hope for a society without exploitation of men by men, without injustice, without war, because all these things—exploitation, injustice, war—are the ineluctable result of the everlasting properties of the human animal. Encapsulated in his perennial "nature," man is eternally condemned to live down his original sin; he can never aspire to a free development in a society governed by humanism and reason. It hardly needs adding that what follows from these premises is a conservative or indeed a reactionary attitude toward all the burning issues of our time, an attitude close to the heart of the most "old-fashioned" elements of the ruling class.

Different conclusions emerge from socio-psychologism. For the proposition that human development is determined by the social "milieu" and depends on the nature of inter-personal relations—on conditions obtaining within the family and so forth—leads obviously to the conclusion that significant changes (improvements) in human existence can be brought about by suitable "adjustments" in the prevailing environment. More togetherness and love, more schools and hospitals, and more co-ops and family counseling services then become the appropriate response to the human predicament in our society.

As in the case of all ideologies, neither psychologism nor socio-psychologism is a mere hallucination wholly unrelated to the real world. Each reflects, albeit in a distorted, ideological manner, an aspect of the actual, existential condition of man in capitalist society. By enunciating a manifest lie—the sovereign power of the individual in our society—psychologism points unmistakably to the loneliness, unrelatedness, and impotence of men under capitalism, and thus comes nearer the truth than the shallow liberal claptrap treating "us" as controlling and shaping our lives, or pontificating about national or even international "communities" determining their own destinies. Similarly, in raising the principle *homo homini lupus* to the status of an eternal verity, in considering man to be by nature a selfish, aggressive monad fighting ruthlessly for a place in the market, psychologism captures more of the capitalist reality than those doctrines which would have us believe that the character of the capitalist man can be changed by sanctimonious incantations concerning love, productivity, and the brotherhood of men. For, with exploitation, injustice, and war having molded for centuries the character of men, treating the existing human species as a formidable rock not easily displaced or transformed is undoubtedly more appropriate than the view of the superficial meliorist who would reshape human attitudes by intensified preaching, by larger federal grants-in-aid to education, by strengthening the Pure Food and Drug Administration, or by electing a Democratic President.

Socio-psychologism, too, mirrors important aspects of our society. By uncovering the horrors of our culture—the dismal state of our educational system, the misery of our cities, the abominable "climate" in which Negroes, Puerto Ricans, Mexicans, and unemployed whites live in this country—socio-psychologism is nearer the realities of capitalism than the enthusiastic celebrators of free and unhampered private enterprise. At the same time, by attributing this social condition to "our" lack of enlightenment, to "our" incapacity for purposeful action, to the power of "conventional wisdom," and to similar psychic "facts," it expresses the refusal to see the fundamental causes of the existing malaise, a refusal that constitutes the characteristic and indeed decisive element of the ruling ideology. Moreover, the insistence of socio-psychologism on the curability of all of these ills by means of various and sundry "adjustments" is part and parcel of the spirit of manipulation in which the Big Business executive "fixes" the problems confronting his corporation by such methods as establishing recreation facilities for his workers, or appropriating more money for market research or advertising, or by initiating some fancy product variation. Thus socio-psychologism becomes one of the most important components—if not *the* most important component—of the ideology of monopoly capitalism which seeks to find ways of eliminating the most crying irrationalities, the most conspicuous injustices of the capitalist system in order to preserve and strengthen its basic institutions.

But to realize and to unveil the ideological nature of both psychologism and socio-psychologism is only one part of what needs to be done. Even this job can be adequately performed only if the differences between the two doctrines are clearly understood, and if this ideological development is carefully analyzed as a reflection (and an aspect) of the transformation of the underlying economic, social, and political reality itself. Yet, as in the case of most problems posed by the emergence and evolution of monopoly capitalism, Marxism has been seriously remiss in coping with this matter. Failing to distinguish between old-fashioned psychologism and its modern, more sophisticated offshoot, Marxism, both in the West and in the U.S.S.R., have been seeking to refute the latter by employing arguments applicable only to the former. This has been particularly tempting since marshalling the arguments called for little effort: all of them are readily available in the works of Marx and Engels, as well as in the writings of later Marxists.

Even more serious is that another equally important part of the Marxist commitment has been left unattended to. This is the separation of the wheat from the chaff, the distillation of whatever genuine scientific insights may be submerged in the ideological flood of socio-psychologism. For to the development of Marxism nothing is more essential than the systematic identification and absorption of such scientific advances as are attained by bourgeois scholarship—accompanied by relentless unmasking and debunking of its manifold ideological ingredients.

Thus in dealing with psychoanalysis—a doctrine which is the mainstay of socio-psychologism and which differs significantly from earlier theories underlying psychologism—Marxists have taken the position that all of it is nothing but ideology void of scientific content. This attitude has been based to a large extent on the notion that Freud's abiding concern with the irrational underpinnings of the conduct of men is tantamount to glorification of irrationality, to its elevation to the status of the ultimate, inexplicable, irreducible determinant of human activity. If such had been Freud's view, there would be little indeed to distinguish him from all and sundry philosphers of romanticism and existentialism. Yet although Freud undoubtedly had strong tendencies in that direction—particularly apparent in some of his later writings—the bulk of his work is inspired by a different intention. Having recognized what is indisputable—that irrationality governs a large part of human behavior—Freud directed most of his life's effort to an attempt at a *rational* understanding of irrational motivations. Far from considering irrationality to be an elemental phenomenon inaccessible to scientific analysis, Freud sought to develop a comprehensive theory providing a *rational* explanation of irrational drives.

To be sure, this ambitious goal remained beyond Freud's reach. Nevertheless, he took the matter further than anyone before him, and—I might add—anyone after him, even if he did fail to arrive at a satisfactory concept of human conduct. And just as Marxism has been the heir and the guardian of what is most valuable and progressive in bourgeois culture, so it is incumbent upon Marxism today to take up Freud's work where Freud left it, and to turn his insights to good use in the elaboration of a rational theory of human activity.

I submit that only Marxism is able to fulfill this task. For the Marxian theory of social dynamics sheds penetrating light on the factors principally determining human behavior. What is needed is to revive some of the central—albeit neglected—strands in Marxian thought, and to focus them on the problem at hand. While this claim of mine cannot be fully substantiated in a short lecture, I would like to attempt a "telegram-style" outline of the relevant considerations.

It is fundamental to the Marxian approach to the study of

man that there is no such thing as an external, invariant "human nature." With due regard for what can be considered biotic constants, the character of man is the product of the social order in which he is born, in which he grows up, and the air of which he inhales throughout his life; it is its result and indeed one of its most significant aspects. Yet it is of the utmost importance to understand that what is meant by "social order" in Marxian theory is at most only a distant cousin of the notion of "society" as employed in socio-psychologism. The latter, it will be recalled, refers to "environment," to "inter-personal relations," and to similar aspects of what constitutes the *surface* of social existence. The former, on the other hand, encompasses the attained stage of the development of productive forces, the mode and relations of production, the form of social domination prevailing at any given time, all together constituting the *basic* structure of the existing social organization. Changes of the social order (in the Marxian understanding of that term), radical and shattering as they always are, have taken centuries to mature and have occurred only a few times in the course of history. Correspondingly, changes in the nature of man have also proceeded at a glacial pace; while assuming tremendous proportions if looked at in full historical perspective, they have been all but imperceptible in the lifespan of entire generations. Still it is a fallacy to mistake the slowness of change in the character of man for its absence. This error leads to psychologism and to the belief in the everlasting sameness of the human species. And it is no less fallacious to deduce from the existence of change its rapidity. This error in turn leads to socio-psychologism and to the illusion that human beings can be "remodeled" by persuasion or by some repair jobs within the existing social order, that they can be manipulated into something different from what the social order has made them.

Thus a proper analysis of human motivations and conduct

must refer to a timespan shorter than that of psychologism but longer than that of socio-psychologism. It has to avoid the a-historical frozenness of the former while escaping at the same time the newspaper-headline orientation of the latter. And it must consider human development in its true context: the economic and social order determining the content and molding the profile of the relevant historical epoch. Accordingly the exploration of the human character can neither rely on empty abstractions such as "man in general" nor gain much insight from an ever-so-careful examination of spurious concretes such as the "other-directed personality," the "trade-union man," the "chamber of commerce man," or the "man in the gray flannel suit." At the present time and in this country, the object of the investigation is the human being born with certain inherited characteristics and reared as a member of a class in capitalist society or—more specifically —in capitalist society's most advanced stage, the reign of monopoly capital.

This suggests that—leaving biology aside—the first step of such an investigation has to be directed toward the understanding of the basic factors determining human existence under the prevailing social order. Outstanding among these factors is the vast expansion of society's productive resources. Based on a spectacular intensification of the subjugation of nature (including human nature) by society, this growth of productivity has promoted (and has been promoted by) a tremendous increase of rationality in the productive process as well as in the mental habits of men. Yet it is inherent in the capitalist order, and indeed its most striking characteristic, that this advance in rationality has proceeded in a complex and contradictory fashion. It has been primarily an advance of *partial* rationality and has remained essentially confined to segments of the social fabric, to its particular units and aspects. Thus the efficiency of industrial and agricultural enterprises, the rationality of their administration, of their cost and price and profit calculations, as well as of their efforts to manipulate the market, have reached unprecedented dimensions. But this increase in *partial* rationality has not been accompanied by a corresponding growth of *total* rationality, of rationality in the overall organization and functioning of society. In fact, the total rationality of the social order has declined; the disparity between partial and total rationality has been growing increasingly pronounced. This can be fully realized if one thinks of the contrast between the automated, electronically controlled factory and the economy as a whole with its millions of unemployed and other millions of uselessly employed people; if one considers the efficiency with which redundant chrome and fins are being affixed to unfunctional automobiles; or if one contemplates the palatial office towers, planned and equipped according to the last word of science, in which highly skilled employees devise the most effective methods for the promotion of a new soap, standing.next to squalid slums in which families of five vegetate in one dilapidated filthy room. But the abyss dividing the parts from the whole is most horrifying if one places next to each other the breathtaking productive power harnessed in the energy of the atom, and the death, the misery, the human degradation, that mark the existence of the great majority of mankind subsisting in the under-developed countries.

The basic reason for this glaring cleavage between partial and total rationality, between the rising "know how," and the declining "know what," is the alienation of man from his means of production, an alienation that has become increasingly marked throughout the history of capitalism and is strongly accentuated in its current monopolistic phase. Indeed, the concentration of the means of production in the hands of a small group of oligarchs—responsible to no one but themselves and to their everlasting commitment to keep increasing their profits—who smoothly and rationally preside over their corporate empires has completed the fixation of the productive apparatus as a power outside and above the individual, a power dominating his existence but entirely inaccessible to his control. And at no time in history has this power over the vast and growing productive forces been to such an extent power over life and death of millions of men, women, and children everywhere.

But the most insidious, and at the same time the most portentous, aspect of this overwhelming power of the objectified productive relations over the life of the individual is their capacity to determine decisively his psychic structure. For the conflict between total and partial rationality not only sets the tone of the entire capitalist culture; it also sinks deeply into the mentality of the human being brought up in and molded by the all-pervasive institutions, values, and habits of thought which make up that culture. The exigencies of the productive process call for the development of an increasingly well-trained, literate, and intelligent manpower. Earning a livelihood at the conveyer belt, in the office, or in the sales force of the modern corporation depends on the possession of rational attitudes and aptitudes greatly superior to what was required at an earlier, less advanced stage of capitalist development. Much of the work that used to be guided by authority, tradition, and intuition is now based on scientifically established procedures and accurate measurements. Yet, as stressed above, this highly rationalized effort is directed toward largely irrational ends; the individual worker is not only unconcerned with the outcome of the productive process in which he plays an infinitesimal part but this outcome has no meaning and no purpose; it cannot inform his activity with the knowledge of aim or with the pride of accomplishment.

This incessantly reproduced clash between what might be called "micro-sense" and "macro-madness" is, however, only one part of the story. The other, even more important, aspect is the profound impact of the lack of total rationality upon the dynamics and nature of partial rationality itself. I must therefore amend what I said above about the achievements in regard to partial rationality. For reason is indivisible, and the irrationality of the whole cannot coexist harmoniously with the rationality of the parts. The one continually threatens the other, and their antagonism expresses one of the profound contradictions of the capitalist system. Whereas the irrationality of the whole must be constantly maintained if exploitation, waste, and privilege, if—in one word—capitalism is to survive, the rationality of society's individual parts is enforced by the drive for profits and the competitive necessities of capitalist enterprise. Thus this partial rationality continually edges forward—albeit jerkily and unevenly—but the advance takes place at the cost of its being warped, perverted, and corrupted by the irrationality of the surrounding social order. As a result, such a progress as has been attained is far from uniform. Some of it constitutes genuine steps forward in the rational comprehension of the world and in the development of the forces of production. This applies to much of what has been accomplished in such areas as mathematics and natural sciences, as well as in certain branches of historical research. Elsewhere, however, what parades as an increase in rationality is frequently nothing but the amplification and propagation of business "know how," of the rationality of the capitalist market. There the intellectual effort which takes market relations for granted is exclusively directed toward manipulation in the interest of corporate enterprise. What it promotes is "practical intelligence," the capacity to make the best of a given market constellation, to maximize one's advantages in the struggle of all against all. Thus, important parts of physics and chemistry have been pressed into the service of war and destruction; much mathematical and statistical ingenuity has been turned into an auxiliary of monopolistic market control and profit maximization; psychology has become a prostitute of "motivation research" and personnel management; biology is made into a handmaiden of pharmaceutical rackets; and art, language, color, and sound have been degraded into instrumentalities of advertising.

Under such circumstances human rationality inevitably becomes crippled, and its advance is pushed into a direction that bears no relation to the prerequisites for, and the needs of, human health, happiness, and development. If the compulsion to take *anything* for granted is a fetter on the expansion and perfection of men's capacity to reason and to understand, the oppressive and stifling function of that fetter grows in proportion to the irrationality of what men are brought up not to question but to accept as a datum. True, taking capitalism for granted when it was an essentially progressive social order interfered relatively little with (or even promoted) the development of partial rationality. By the same token, however, the necessity not to scrutinize but to treat as part of the natural order of things the regime of monopoly capital, along with all the waste and all the destruction that go with it, constitutes a straitjacket within which reason cannot but suffocate. Thus the clash between partial and total rationality becomes complicated and aggravated by the no less violent conflict between reason and the debasement of reason which dominates the sphere of partial rationality itself.

This condition has manifold psychological ramifications to only two of which I can now attempt to draw your attention. First, such rationality as prevails solidifies itself into a system of rules, procedures, and habits of thought that not only does not further the satisfaction of human needs but becomes a formidable obstacle to human development and, indeed, survival. As bourgeois rationality turns increasingly into the rationality of domination, exploitation, and war, the ordinary man revolts against this obstruction to his aspirations for peace, happiness, and freedom. Yet, afflicted with "common sense" that is studiously nurtured by all the agencies of bourgeois culture and the principal injunction of which is to take capitalist rationality for granted, he can hardly avoid identifying the rationality of buying, selling, and profit-making with reason itself. His revolt against capitalist rationality, against the rationality of markets and profits, thus becomes a revolt against reason itself, turns into anti-intellectualism, and promotes aggressiveness toward those who manage to capitalize on the rules of the capitalist game to their advantage and advancement. It renders him an easy prey of irrationality.

Irrationality and aggressiveness in our time are, therefore, not emanations of some unalterable human instincts. Nor do they express simply the supposedly "natural" rejection of *reason.* Irrationality and aggressiveness in our time reflect primarily the refusal to accept as sacrosanct the rationality of capitalism. They testify to the protest against the mutilation and degradation of reason for the sake of capitalist domination. This outcry against bourgeois rationality, as well as its identification with reason as such, is magnificently depicted in Dostoevsky's Underground Man who "vomits up reason" and who scornfully rejects the commandment to accept the proposition that two times two equals four. While this strikingly exemplifies the posture of irrationalism, an important aspect of the Underground Man's attitude should not be lost sight of. It is that the Underground Man, irrational, and "crazy" as he is, is actually profoundly *right* in "vomiting up reason," in refusing to bow to the logic of two times two equals four. For this logic *is* the logic of the capitalist market, of the exploitation of man by man, of privileges, insecurity, and war. To be sure, his contempt for *this* rationality, his uprising against the "common sense" of human misery, is an irrational reaction to a pernicious social order. But it is the only reaction available to the isolated and helpless individual who, incapable of comprehending the forces by which he is being crushed, is unable to struggle effectively against them. This reaction is neurosis.

Secondly, as I mentioned earlier in passing, the development of the forces of production and the advance of rationality with which it has been associated were based on a tremendous intensification of human domination over nature. The result of this harnessing of natural resources to the needs of men has been a momentous rise in the output of goods, services, health, and literacy—combined with a spectacular lightening of the burden of human toil. Yet this advance was achieved not merely by the expansion of human control over the objects and energies of the outside world; it was based on a perhaps even more radical subjugation of the nature of man himself. This subjugation has two separate, if closely interconnected, aspects. In the pre-capitalist era, it involved the emergence and development of the domination and exploitation of man by man. Extracting from the underlying population varying quantities of economic surplus, the dominating and exploiting classes used this economic surplus to assure their privileged positions in society, at the same time directing larger or smaller shares of the surplus to investment in productive facilities or to the maintenance of military, religious, and cultural establishments. Applied to those days, however, the expression "surplus" is a euphemism. With productivity and output rising only very slowly, the condition had not yet been attained in which the consumption of the ruling class and its outlays on productive investment and on religious and military and other purposes could be based upon a genuine sufficiency of goods and services for the people. Sheer violence and elaborate systems of political enforcement always played a major role in the process of extraction of the requisite sources. Yet neither would have been able to fulfill this task had it not been for the development and propagation of religious, legal, moral—in one word:

ideological—notions which sanctified the ruling classes' claims to their appropriations and which were turned in the course of centuries into a comprehensive network of internalized thoughts, beliefs, fears, and hopes, compelling the people to recognize the rights and to heed the demands of their rulers.

A new chapter was opened by the advent of the capitalist order. Now the human being had to go through a further process of "adjustment." To the qualities cultivated in the wood-hewers and water-carriers of old had to be added a new and all-important characteristic, that of rationality. For now it was no longer sufficient to be an obedient and selfless serf or a cruel and rapacious squire; what was required henceforth was a diligent, docile, efficient, and reliable worker in a rationalized, streamlined, profit-maximizing capitalist enterprise. This enforced what is probably one of the most far-reaching transformations of "human nature" experienced thus far. If in the course of preceding history man had been made submissive by exploitation and domination, the working principles of the capitalist order demanded that he should acquire the ability to calculate and the habit of acting with forethought and deliberation. What was left of his elemental emotionality, of his spontaneity, after having been disciplined for centuries by the whip of his titled overlords, came now under the much more systematic, much more comprehensive pressure of the callously and accurately calculating market.

As deliberateness in the business of earning a living—and in all other aspects of life as well—became the prerequisite for survival in capitalist society, spontaneity came to be disdained and feared not only as a source of disruption of the production routine but as a threat to the stability of the class-dominated and exploitative social order. From the very beginning of the capitalist era it was accordingly exposed to a withering fire of economic sanctions and social opprobrium, and the assault against it was mounted simultaneously by the entire apparatus of bourgeois ideology and culture, including such divergent components as Christian religion and the utilitarian philosphy. And in capitalism's current, monopolistic phase this attack has multiplied in scope and intensity. Just as human relations in corporate empires came by necessity to be attuned to "making friends and influencing people," so has love been "streamlined" into a scientifically approved means of securing medically indicated sexual gratification, while beauty is identified with the precise measurements of Miss America, and nature, music, literature, and art are valued in exact proportion to their serving as purveyors of "relaxation." Not that the campaign against spontaneity was ever decided upon or directed by some executive committee of capitalist elders, although attributing to Marxism such a view of the matter has long been the stock in trade of professional Marx-refuters whose ignorance of Marxism is exceeded only by their incapacity to understand it. The implacable hostility toward spontaneity and the powerful tendency toward its suppression are rather the inherent characteristics of a mode of production based on commodity exchange and unfolding within a system of relations of production, domination, and exploitation. Far from being a premeditated, well-planned strategem of the ruling class, calculated to repress the drives and aspirations of the underlying population, both the ascent of deliberateness and the decay of spontaneity affected the members of the ruling class itself and turned them in the course of time into unhappy beneficiaries of an unhappy society.

The crux of the matter, it seems to me, is that market-oriented deliberateness and market-induced suppression of spontaneity, "adjusting" the privileged and the underprivileged alike to the requirements of the capitalist system, fatally damage what Freud, and before him Marx and Engels, identified as the sources of human happiness: freedom of individual development and the capacity to experience sensual gratification. Putting a severe tabu on the individual's emotionality and channeling what is left of it into an aggressiveness which is disciplined and directed toward the attainment of success and the elimination of rivals in the competitive struggle, they produce "affect-crippledness"—to use an expression of Freud—and generate the phenomenon which was put into its proper theoretical context by Marx in his concept of the alienation of man from himself. This alienation of man from himself—the maiming of the individual, the subjugation of his nature to the needs of capitalist enterprise, the mortal wounding of his spontaneity, and the molding of his personality into a self-seeking, deliberate, calculating, and circumspect participant in (and object of) the capitalist process—represents the basic framework within which the psychic condition of man evolves in capitalist society.

It is only within this framework that I can see a promise of a genuine understanding of psychic disturbances in our time. As I mentioned earlier, achieving such an understanding was not given to psychoanalysis. To be sure, Freud's identification of sexual malfunctioning as the principal source of psychic disorder represented a major advance in psychological thought. But what Freud's theoretical structure fails to provide—all assurances and appearances to the contrary notwithstanding—is a satisfactory explanation of the sexual malfunctioning itself. Not that Freud was unaware of this weakness of his doctrine, but it was in attempting to fill this crucially important gap that his efforts were least successful. It was here that he sought to find refuge either in psychologism or in socio-psychologism: either in a concept of a biotically unchanging human nature with equally unchanging intra-family relations as symbolized in the ancient Oedipus legend; or in surface observations referring to habits of child rearing and of sexual enlightenment. Neither of these approaches enabled him to solve the central issue confronting psychology at the present time: the specification of the part played by more or less invariant biological factors in the determination of the psychic structure of man, and the analysis of the profound impact upon the human psyche exercised by the alienation of man from himself in the society of monopoly capitalism.

Marxists, impressed by the momentous accomplishments of Pavlov and his school, have focused attention on the former aspect of the matter and have tended—paradoxically enough —to sidestep Marx's revolutionary contribution to psychology: the sociology of the psyche. Still, while there can be no dispute about the importance of physiological factors in governing human behavior, it is indispensable to recognize the vast extent to which the economic and social order of capitalism and the process of alienation which it generates mold the psychic and, indeed, the physical functioning of men in the capitalist era. For it is impossible to understand sexual malfunctioning apart from the capitalism-caused atrophy of spontaneity; it is impossible to understand the shrinking capacity to experience sensual gratifications of any kind apart from the capitalism-generated proliferation of deliberateness, selfishness, and aggressiveness. I would go further and say that it is impossible to comprehend human activity in our society except as an outcome of a dialectic interaction of biotic forces and the working principles of monopoly capitalism, with the latter dominating, subjugating, and directing the former. And it is crucially important to recognize the nature of this interaction of the determinants of human existence under capitalism, because it is the powerful dynamism of the social and economic order which points to the location of the strategic leverage which in fullness of time will shift the historical gears and orient the development of man toward a fuller realization of his physical, emotional, and rational capacities. This leverage is to be found neither in tranquilizing pills nor in "social adjustments," nor in the preaching of love of productivity and of "meeting of minds." This leverage must be found in the establishment of a more rational, more human society, and conversely in the abolition of a social order based upon the domination and exploitation of man by man. Not that socialism would change the situation "overnight." Expecting the liquidation of the centuries-old legacy of capitalism within a relatively short—if ever so eventful—period of transition reflects the attitude of socio-psychologism, which is as fallacious in this case as it is in others. Thus it is by no means an accident that those who hold the views of socio-psychologism are among the severest critics of the existing socialist societies: censuring sharply the Soviet Union or even China for not having abolished the alienation of man, and for not having yet created the socialist individual. It hardly needs stressing that demanding such impossible changes amounts to demanding no changes at all; that stipulating the immediate realization of what can develop only slowly on the basis of vast institutional transformations as a condition for the participation in the struggle for a better society is tantamount to deserting this struggle altogether.

A few concluding remarks: what I have said so far is not meant to suggest that there may be no possibility of individuals who are ill finding a measure of relief through currently available means of psychiatric treatment. The frequently reiterated observation that the degree of success attained in psychotherapy is largely independent of the school of psychological thought to which the therapist adheres, but is rather determined by the skill and personality of the physician and the amount of attention given by him to the patient, suggests the absence of any well-founded theory underlying psychotherapeutic practice. Moreover, psychotherapy's relative success in dealing with isolated symptoms of nervous disorder and the generally admitted failure of its efforts at curing character neurosis would tend to confirm the earlier expressed view that the phenomena underlying character neurosis are inaccessible to treatment on the individual plane. Indeed, the insistence on the possibility of altering character structures on the individual plane, of "producing" a healthy, well-functioning and happy individual in our society is in itself an ideology. It tears asunder individual and society, it ignores the alienation of man under capitalism, and it represents a capitulation to socio-psychologism. It obscures the painful but ineluctable truth that the limits to the cure of man's soul are set by the illness of the society in which he lives.

III
On Planning

National Economic Planning

The two decades that constitute the proximate frame of reference of the present—necessarily sketchy—survey have witnessed a truly spectacular growth of practical and theoretical endeavors in the field of economic planning.

In the socialist sector of the world—the U.S.S.R., the countries of eastern and southeastern Europe and China—economic planning has developed (or is developing) into the effectively controlling principle of economic organization. In the advanced capitalist West, doctrines of economic planning have largely displaced earlier concepts of economic liberalism and exercise a powerful influence upon economic policies and economic thought. In backward capitalist areas, planning is increasingly accepted as the indispensable tool of economic progress.

Tempting as it would be to examine the causes and ramifications of this far-reaching social and intellectual development, the present account must confine itself to a brief report on a few of its salient features—leaving aside many important aspects of the planning problem as well as foregoing the discussion of the profound crisis of the capitalist order to which the ascendance of economic planning appears to be the historical response.

This article first appeared in *A Survey of Contemporary Economics*, B.F. Haley, ed. (Homewood, Ill.: Richard D. Irwin, Inc., 1952), and is reprinted by permission. Copyright © 1962 by Richard D. Irwin, Inc.

In what follows, Part I will consider planning for full employment under advanced capitalism; Part II, planning for economic growth under backward capitalism; and Part III, planning under socialism.

I. PLANNING UNDER ADVANCED CAPITALISM

A. The Background

1. *The Neoclassical Dilemma.* Although "from the time of the physiocrats and Adam Smith there has never been absent from the main body of economic literature the feeling that in some sense perfect competition represented the optimum solution,"[1] serious doubts about the reliability of the "invisible hand" have disturbed not only John Stuart Mill, but even the more complacent Marshall, Wicksell, and Pigou (to name only the most outstanding).

One deep discomfort arose from the realization that the distribution of wealth was such that even if earnings were in accordance with the marginal productivity theory, perfect competition would yield anything but an optimum distribution of income (and optimum allocation of resources). The other was caused by the divergence of social and private utilities, or—using the apt formulation of Max Weber—by the discrepancy between private and social rationalities that characterizes even the construct of perfect competition.

Troublesome as these faults were, matters were even worse in the real world with which "perfect competition" had never had much in common. There the growth of monopoly, immobilities and indivisibilities of factors, inequalities of bargaining positions and opportunities, political and economic privileges of all sorts, accounted for economic (and social) results that were greatly at variance with what one might have expected on the basis of a study of the mirage of perfect competition.

The way out of this perplexity was seen by the neoclassical

writers in a moderate amount of government intervention. To quote Samuelson again " . . . [they] recognized [d] that in these circumstances any interference (a la Robin Hood) with perfect competition which transfers income from rich to poor would be beneficial."[2] Also, interference that would aim at the elimination or reduction of monopoly or at some rectification of the neglect of social rationality by the private enterprise system, such as building of public schools, hospitals, and the like, would have been regarded by the neoclassical economists as, on the whole, desirable.

Yet their professed sympathy for social reform and public regulation was essentially alien to the main body of their thought. Resting upon the assumption of full employment of resources, the reasoning of the neoclassical school left little room for changes in prevailing institutions. The only way in which the poor could become better off was through increased productivity that under competitive conditions would raise real wages. Otherwise there was little or nothing that could be done to improve their wretched position. Unless benefits for the poor were to be obtained by a redistribution of income *among the poor themselves* (which would be patently beside the point and possibly even detrimental by disturbing wage differentials that were assigned an important function in the allocation of resources), such benefits could only be secured by reducing the share of total real income accruing to the rich in form of profits, rent, and interest. Since the propensity of the rich to plow back their earnings into productive enterprise was regarded as sufficiently bolstered by the forces of competition and the puritan injunction to thrift, any reduction of the income going to them was expected to cause a diminution of the "surplus" available for investment, as well as of the incentives to invest on the part of the capitalist class. As a result, economic progress would necessarily slow down, and the picayune improvements of the lot of the poor that possibly could be secured by redistributive measures would be more than offset by the subsequent retardation of the growth of output and real income.

Placed against the background of this "iron law" of basic economic interrelationships, the advocacy of governmental intervention had inevitably a hollow sound.[3] It reflected the anxieties of the small businessman helplessly watching the rise of his large-scale rival, it expressed the bewilderment of the common man whose daily experiences hardly tallied with the optimism of a Bastiat or a J.B. Clark, it served as an indication of the noble sentiments and high ethical standards of its protagonists—but also as a testimonial of their starry-eyed disregard for the elementary principles of sound economics.[4] This is where the matter rested for a number of relatively harmonious decades that witnessed an unprecedented economic growth of the Western world. The advances attained overshadowed the stupendous price that had to be paid for progress[5]—the criticisms of the competitive process could be countered by pointing to its readily observable triumphs.

Yet toward the end of this exceptional epoch an old malignant disease began assuming major proportions. To be sure, large unemployment had existed in earlier phases of the capitalist age; it was not until the twenties of our century, however, that in conjunction with other social and political developments it became a powerful threat to the continuity of the existing social order.

2. *"The New Economics."*[6] It was in an attempt to face the urgent issue of unemployment that The New Economics of J. M. Keynes laid the foundations for planning for full employment under capitalism. Its central insight is actually very simple. It repudiates Say's Law, and recognizes as the outstanding characteristic of the capitalist process—as Karl Marx did, some eighty years earlier—the absence in the market automatism of a "built-in" mechanism keeping aggre-

gate effective demand on a level requisite for the maintenance of full employment.

In the absence of any such mechanism, the state has to assume responsibility, when unemployment develops, for measures calculated to raise aggregate effective demand to a level compatible with full utilization of human resources. Should private investment under full employment conditions (once they are reached) decline below the level of intended savings, the state should stand ready to take such steps as may be called for to offset the deficiency in private spending.

That is, however, where the role of the state (and economic planning under capitalism) ends. Once the necessary steps are taken to assure the attainment and the maintenance of full employment, traditional economics comes back into its own. Only to the extent to which great inequalities of income and misallocation of resources stand in the way of promoting high levels of income and employment, should governmental economic planning be concerned with income distribution and resource allocation. Keynes sees "no reason to suppose that the existing system seriously misemploys the factors of production which are in use.... It is in determining the volume, not the direction of actual employment that the existing system has broken down."[7]

B. The Tool Box

The state can attempt to fulfill its functions in a number of alternative ways. Yet, whichever way is chosen, the indispensable prerequisite of an active participation of the government in the process of determination of the level of income and employment is the ability to prognosticate more or less accurately the behavior of various economic aggregates exercising an important influence on the level of business activity in a capitalist economy. The analytical tools provided by Keynes and the economists following his lead appeared to render such prognostication feasible.

The most important among them is the concept of the consumption function relating aggregate spending on consumers' goods and services to national income. This relationship was treated as fairly stable, thus permitting the isolation of the volume of currently intended savings.[8] Such confidence as there was in the stability of the consumption function was, however, severely shaken during the last decade. The postwar experience has drawn attention to the level of accumulation or decumulation of assets as a powerful determinant of the volume of consumers' expenditure.[9]

An even more trenchant argument questions the usefulness of the entire concept. It was pointed out that the "community's propensity to consume" has little to do with the choice as between consumption and saving.[10] The overwhelming majority of the population, even in countries as rich as the United States, save a negligible part of their income, and—what is even more important—of total savings accumulated by the nation.[11] Thus under conditions of full employment *all* personal savings constitute only a small part of total savings, and savings from what some tax laws define as "earned income" an almost negligible part.[12] The bulk of the savings that has to be offset by intended investment if full employment is to be maintained consists of *business savings* and of such savings as are directly influenced by corporate profits and corporate decisions concerning dividends.[13] In other words—even if it were established that the "propensity to consume" schedule is stable enough to yield a predictable relationship of consumption to disposable income—this relationship would account only for a fraction of total savings.[14] The remainder depends on the depreciation-reserves-dividends-spending decisions of boards of directors, decisions that cannot be very well attributed to the working of some general psychological laws—in any case very "unreliable customers in economics," to use Schumpeter's expression.[15]

Yet there is very little light that The New Economics sheds on what determines business expenditures. Accounting for investment goods (including construction) as well as for inventories and gross exports, this sector of aggregate demand is treated as an independent rather than dependent force in the process of income generation.[16] A certain, presumably small, part of it is regarded as "induced" by changes in income, but the bulk of it is looked upon in Keynesian writings as "autonomous," i.e., as motivated not by *actual* variations in income and demand but by *anticipations* of future changes in aggregate demand, in the demand for particular products, or expected changes in the relation between prices and costs.

Although some progress has been achieved by government agencies (Securities and Exchange Commission, and U.S. Department of Commerce) as well as by some private organizations in polling business about its investment plans, not much reliance can yet be placed upon such surveys. "To a great extent we still rely today largely on hunches and anticipation of other people's behavior, just as the forecasters did before Keynes' writing."[17]

With the predictions concerning personal and business expenditures based thus on highly tenuous estimates, the decisions concerning governmental revenues and outlays are derived from little more than "enlightened guesses." The fiscal authorities are not even able to gauge reliably the impact of their own actions (more or less spending or taxing) on aggregate income since the magnitude of the multiplier obviously depends on the relationships just referred to.

The foregoing may be fully accepted by an advocate of governmental planning for full employment. Granting that the government's ability to prognosticate adequately the behavior of the relevant economic aggregates is deficient, and that therefore planning for government intervention cannot go beyond groping for the right set of measures at any given time, he may abandon the ambition to "plan" for periods longer than a few months and take the position that a "flexible" fiscal policy accompanied by other "flexible" arrangements is all that is needed to achieve the substance of the desired result. As suggested by the authors of *National and International Measures for Full Employment,*[18] whenever unemployment should reach certain predetermined magnitudes, inflationary measures would be called for; whenever the price index rises to some agreed-upon level, deflationary measures would be in order. It is held that with sufficiently rapid reactions on the part of the authorities, in particular if such rapid reactions could be presumed by the public on the basis of experience, employment could be maintained on a stable and satisfactory level.

C. The Application

Yet the acceptance of this principle or, for that matter, even the availability of a sufficiently powerful forecasting apparatus in the hands of the government does not *per se* indicate the specific policies that may be adopted to promote and sustain full employment. Recognizing that aggregate demand tends to be insufficient to provide a market for full employment output (at given prices), the government can embark upon a variety of programs for the expansion of investment, consumption, or both.

1. While certain nonfiscal measures may be taken in order to improve business conditions, governmental planning for full employment is associated primarily with fiscal policy. The government may seek to expand aggregate effective demand by a reduction of taxes. The effectiveness of this procedure, occasionally dubbed "deficit without spending," is predicated upon the condition that the governmental deficit thus incurred be large enough to make up, in conjunction with the multiplier effect, the deficiency in aggregate effective demand.

If the marginal propensity to spend should prove to be low, the requisite deficit may assume major proportions—may in fact exceed the entire normal expenditure budget of the government.[19]

2. The disposable income in the hands of individuals and businesses may be expanded by an *increase of government expenditures*. Such an increase may be financed through higher taxes, through governmental borrowing, or through printing of new money.[20]

a. *"Leaf-Raking."* This kind of expenditure is by definition not associated with any purchase of useful objects on the part of the government. Digging ditches or building pyramids are the examples of this kind of governmental outlay used by Keynes, and they illustrate adequately the nature of the spending involved.

b. *"Social Service Investment."* In this case the government acquires for the amounts spent *useful objects* such as schools, hospitals, parks, and roads. Their distinguishing feature is that the services that they render either do not enter the market at all, or if they so enter do not normally compete in the market with goods and services produced by private business. An important limitation of spending programs (a) and (b) is that their scope is limited by the potential of the construction (and related) industries. To be sure, this potential may be expanded, but such expansion may be difficult in the short run in view of the immobility of various factors, and moreover, may be irrational in terms of social priorities.

c. *Foreign Aid.* In their effect on *domestic* real income, direct governmental purchases of goods and services for shipment abroad or giving money to foreigners for purchases of domestic products are identical with the type of spending under (a).

d. *Military Spending.* While obvious political arguments may justify it, it combines the negative features of both "routes" (a) and (b).

e. *Investment in Productive Enterprise.* Of all forms of governmental spending, this one would involve governmental economic planning that goes far beyond attempts at anticipation and compensation of short-run aggregate demand deficiencies. It would call for active participation of government in the determination not only of the volume of new investment but of its direction as well. Accordingly, it would require governmental operation of productive plant and facilities. For successful implementation of such economic policy, the government would have to possess advance information on the specific investment plans of private business so as to be able to arrive at appropriate decisions in regard to its own investment projects. It would have to be guided in its investment policies by its own knowledge of existing or potential technological improvements, as well as by its own estimates of future demand.[21] It frequently would have to "invade" fields in which investment is curbed by prevailing monopolistic controls, and would have to operate in other fields in which investment is lacking in view of insufficient attractiveness of profit prospects to private interests (low-cost housing, for example).

The "complementarity" of this approach undoubtedly entails considerable difficulties. The government's decision to invest in a certain industry could not properly be made without certainty about private undertakings in that area. Private investors in their turn would have to weigh possible governmental operations as one of the major factors determining the profitability of a departure. If expectations of monopolistic profits—at least for a certain period—constitute a propelling force of new private investment, the ever present danger of governmental engagement in the same line of output may well become an important deterrent to private venture. If plowing back of profits by existing firms is predicated upon their ability to maintain certain market and price structures, the threat of governmental "undercutting" may well paralyze the expansion or maintenance of privately owned facilities.

The resulting decay of the "capitalist climate" and of the capitalists' willingness to invest may progressively increase the aggregate investment deficiency and force a corresponding expansion of government investment, if full employment is to be preserved. Not that the only way of offsetting a lack of private investment is governmental *investment*. As pointed out by Kalecki, "both public and private investment should be carried out only to the extent to which they are considered useful. If the effective demand thus generated fails to provide full employment, the gap should be filled by increasing consumption and not by piling up unwanted public or private capital equipment."[22] Yet it is not unlikely that in the foreseeable future in most capitalist countries, the alternative to insufficient private investment would have to be expanded governmental investment rather than increased consumption. In that case an "investment strike" on the part of business, accompanied possibly by a shrinkage even of existing productive enterprises, may force the government to nationalize the declining industries in order to maintain or to expand them according to requirements.

f. *Spending on Consumption.* "Investment dollars are high-powered dollars. Consumption dollars are, too."[23] An expansion of income and employment can also be secured by governmental sponsorship of private or collective consumption. The only requirement for this kind of spending to result in a relatively large increase in total income and employment is that the initial beneficiaries should be people with a high marginal propensity to spend. Schemes such as food stamp plans and free school lunches for children aim at the fulfillment of this requirement. If satisfaction of collective rather than individual wants is to be preferred, this approach may partly merge with the one outlined under (b).

This type of spending is clearly preferable to public works

of the (a) variety. It may even be more advantageous than financing of productive investment, if—as mentioned above—such investment should be considered redundant. Wherever urgent investment remains unattended to because of its insufficient appeal to private business, this type of spending on current consumption may be a luxury that a nation attempting to utilize its resources rationally could ill afford.

D. The Obstacles

The methods thus briefly listed differ among one another in their short-run efficiency and in their impact on long-run economic development. The goal of full employment may be attainable at some cost by each and all of them. It should be borne in mind, however, that the approach outlined in the preceding sections applies only to advanced capitalist countries where unemployment of manpower caused by insufficiency of aggregate demand is accompanied by underutilization of plant and equipment. Where this is not the case, as in less developed countries, where the human unemployment is not "Keynesian" but "structural" or "disguised," the planning authorities face altogether different problems. We shall come to this aspect of the matter in Part II.

But even with respect to highly industrialized countries, fiscal policy does not represent a simple cure of underemployment. The difficulty, if not impossibility, of prognostication of the measure of the aggregate demand deficiency is an obvious cause of possible excessive governmental spending—and of inflationary effects of a full-employment policy. Also, shortages of certain products, as well as increases in monopoly power appearing under full-employment conditions (or even before full employment is reached) are likely to generate inflationary pressures. The resulting rises in the cost of living and trade union demands for higher money wages are bound to give new turns to the inflationary spiral. Needless to say, full employment accompanied by inflation is neither a stable nor a tolerable state of affairs. Undermining the possibility of rational calculation, generating a state of permanent uncertainty, progressively depleting the working capital stocks of enterprises, continuous inflation endangers the entire elaborate credit structure of the capitalist economy and creates a dangerous cleavage between debtors and creditors.

The inflationary concomitants of a fiscal policy directed toward the attainment and *maintenance* of full employment thus present the planner for full employment with a rather unpleasant dilemma: either giving up the full-employment goal and being content with considerably less than full employment or else adopting appropriate fiscal policy measures and supplementing them with a battery of physical controls and governmental administrative interventions.

This indeed is a Hobson's choice. The former course implies the abandonment by the protagonists of planning for full employment of their basic claim that *full* employment can be attained and maintained within the capitalist system. The latter alternative involves political and social problems that are crucial to the entire concept of planning for full employment—that are, however, largely neglected in the literature of The New Economics.

What is at issue is the theory of the state. As mentioned above, the Keynesian concept of economic planning is based on the identification of the state with "society as a whole," of governmental action with *volunté générale*. In this thinking—developed perhaps most explicitly by A. P. Lerner—the government is seen as an essentially neutral *instrumentality* that can be employed for the furthering of the interests of the "public," the "community," or whatever other term may be used to designate the rather undifferentiated sum total of inhabitants of a given country that constitutes "society" in the liberal frame of reference.[24]

The only hurdles that are to be overcome are stupidity and

ignorance. "The effects that the government should consider are primarily the effects on the *public* in whose interests the government is supposed to be acting . . . ."[25]

This abstract notion of the role of the state in the socioeconomic process is, however, hardly a fruitful hypothesis for adequate comprehension and prediction of actual behavior of government. This attitude, treating all social and political matters as a "frightful muddle" (J. M. Keynes), ignores the paramount importance of the *interests* of the class exercising a controlling influence in society, excluding thus from consideration of social and economic development all its essence and all its propelling forces.

To be sure, class interests in general and the interests of the ruling class in particular do not prescribe unique courses of action in every given situation. Nor are the contents and precise definition of these interests always certain.[26] Still, to use Robbins' apt distinction, the "objective" interests are on the whole ascertainable, even if the "subjective" interests are frequently moot.[27] The dissolution of this dichotomy, the raising of the subjective appraisals of interests to the level of comprehension of their objective contents, may be all the "amplitude of freedom" that is left to rational argument in social and economic matters. That this "amplitude of freedom" is very narrow and that it is *without* rather than *within* its confines where the causes of all important economic and political departures are to be sought, is perhaps *the* most important insight gained thus far by social science.[28]

One need not go far in the acceptance of any particular theory of the state to recognize that various schemes of government planning and action for full employment under capitalism must be considered with regard to their compatibility with the controlling interests in a capitalist society.[29] From the point of view of the short run, the important question may be the relationship of the necessary measures to the "subjective" interests involved. As far as the long run is concerned, it is the extent to which the government's economic plans and activities serve or hamper the "objective" interests of the capitalist class that will decide their fate within the capitalist order. The former problem, urgent as it is in day-to-day political decisions, need not detain us any longer. Not only is it possible to assume, it is even possible empirically to observe that where subjective *misapprehensions* about the nature and implications of full-employment measures blocked their acceptance by the dominating interests, such misapprehensions were eventually disspelled by rational argument and actual experience. Yet where resistance to governmental intervention in economic affairs stems from *correctly* assessed objective interests of the capitalist class, the vigor and tenacity of the opposition become overwhelming, and policies that are in conflict with those interests are doomed.[30]

Examined in this light, however, only a few of the "routes" to full employment briefly referred to above appear to be realistic within the capitalist system, while others are either (in the long run) inconsistent with the maintenance of a private enterprise economy or else presupposed political changes that would be tantamount to a fascization of the political order of capitalism.

The approach closest to the heart of business interests is what was classified above as "nonfiscal measures" as well as "deficit without spending." The former, if properly undertaken, may be conducive to an improvement of the "business atmosphere," while the latter, not interfering with the freedom of action of business, and not resulting in any expansion of governmental participation in economic affairs, is acceptable as "countercyclical planning" even to those who are decidedly opposed to all economic planning on the part of the government.[31]

Matters are much more complex with respect to fiscal measures involving increases in governmental spending.[32]

Clearly, the "balanced budget" or "unit multiplier" method are altogether out of question as far as the business class is concerned. Requiring, as it does, a level of taxation that would "nationalize" and redistribute the bulk of national income (and accordingly destroy the value of a large part of privately owned assets) it " . . . implies nothing less than a social revolution."[33] Equally distasteful would be a full-employment strategy referred to above as "investment in productive enterprise." Such a policy would progressively push the government into extensive participation in business activities and would, in all likelihood, create conditions necessitating a further expansion of the governmental sector of the economy. Only little foresight is needed to envisage a more or less complete nationalization of private enterprise as the end of this process, and even less insight to see the unacceptability of this course to the business class and to a government operating within the framework of a capitalist society.

Nor are large-scale subsidies to consumption consistent with the functioning of a healthy capitalist order. Not only could such subsidies raise the floor under the wage level, providing the wage earner with a subsistence minimum regardless of employment and thus changing his relative valuation of income and leisure, but what is perhaps more important, such unearned payments, if they assumed major proportions, would be alien to the fundamental system of ethics and values associated with the capitalist system.[34] The compulsion of "earning one's bread in the sweat of one's brow" is cement and mortar of a social order the cohesion and functioning of which are predicated upon monetary incentives. Reducing the necessity to work for a living, the distribution of a *large volume* of free goods and services would shatter the social discipline of the capitalist society and weaken the positions of social prestige and social controls crowning its hierarchical pyramid.

Not much choice is thus left to the planner for full employment in a capitalist society—with all available alternatives hardly conducive to a rational utilization of resources and to long-term growth of welfare and productivity. "Leaf-raking," the most wasteful of them, may actually meet with the least opposition on the part of the controlling interests. Building schools, hospitals, and roads may readily at an early stage violate overriding social priorities, and constitute thus a manifest misallocation of resources. Foreign investment and armaments are obviously readily expandable outlets of spending—yet the exploration of their implications would lead us far beyond the scope of the present essay and into the realm of the theory of imperialism.

E. Alternatives

Confronted with a battery of formidable obstacles, planning for full employment under capitalism can thus hardly live up to the expectations of its protagonists.

1. *Abandonment of Full Employment*. They may—as mentioned above—abandon their goal of *full* employment and resign themselves to a countercyclical governmental policy designed to smooth cyclical fluctuations and maintain employment and income at some "adequate" level—markedly below what could be termed complete utilization of available human resources.

In this way, inflationary pressures and their undesirable concomitants could be avoided. The continuous existence of an "industrial reserve army" (Marx) would keep labor "in its place," would assure the maintenance of work discipline in the capitalist enterprise, would preserve the social "command position" of the entrepreneur by safeguarding his fundamental source of social power: the ability to hire and fire.

It is highly questionable, however, whether this arrangement offers a workable solution of the "liberal dilemma." In the first place, only rich countries may be in a position to forego a large share of potential output, to waste another portion of it on unproductive purposes, and to reduce the income of the working members of society by what would be needed to prevent destitution of the unemployed. In countries where the per capita national product is less lavish such a policy may constitute an obvious and unbearable irrationality.

Even more serious may be the consideration that the workability of the "industrial reserve army" device is much less certain now than it would seem to have been in the heyday of capitalist efflorescence. Now that the trade unions have attained a powerful position, *large-scale* unemployment may periodically be necessary if the bargaining power of labor is to be sufficiently reduced for the social conditions briefly outlined above to be achieved.[35] Large-scale unemployment, involving seven to eight million "statistically" unemployed may well be beyond what could be called the "margin of political tolerance." The economically "necessary" reserve army may be very much larger than the politically possible one.

If the political impossibility of tolerating unemployment large enough to assure prevention of inflation and the maintenance of the capitalist "climate" should *force* the government to transcend the goal of only "adequate" employment and push it into larger expenditures needed for the maintenance of full or nearly full employment, all the perplexities that were to be avoided would be with us once more.

2. *Fascism*. To be sure, there is a way of disposing of them. Instead of relying on an "industrial reserve army" to make the trade unions "reasonable," labor can be *forced* to be reasonable. Instead of counting on the normal contractual relations of the capitalist market to generate the necessary labor discipline, such discipline can be *imposed* by administrative means.[36]

The requisite set of compulsory measures could not be adequately administered, however, by a constitutional, democratic government under normal "nonemergency" conditions—"perhaps only a totalitarian state could muster sufficient economic (and political) power to enforce a solution upon the contending parties possibly by eliminating one of them as an organized force."[37] Should there be any doubt which of the "contending parties" would be eliminated as an organized force, A. P. Lerner helps to dispel it: "If we are to enjoy very high levels of full employment without inflation, it may be necessary to give up the determination of wages by collective bargaining,"[38] and rely upon " . . . compulsory arbitration for wage determination in which both the worker and the employer get a fair deal."[39]

We return thus once more to elementary notions of the theory of the state. With all the basic institutions of the capitalist society left intact, with all its essential property relations unaffected, with the economic and political status of the business class, if anything, enhanced, it would be nothing short of fatuous to assume that a government resting upon such a socioeconomic foundation could be a "neutral" entity acting *not* in the interests of the economically dominant class in society but on behalf of the general "public." Such "neutrality" was always claimed by fascist governments and their spokesmen; it would seem to be redundant at this time to provide an elaborate proof of the mendacious nature of that pretense.[40]

In fact, on few matters is there so much consensus, among all competent students of fascism, as well as documentary evidence (accumulated in war crimes trials in Nuremberg and elsewhere) as on the finding that big business dominated the policies of Germany's fascist state. Nor was this a purely German phenomenon. Matters were no different in Italy,[41] or in Japan where a dozen so-called Zaibatsu families controlled exclusively the economic (and not only economic) policies of the fascist-militarist government.[42]

There is no reason to assume that all these and similar cases were purely fortuitous, and that "strong" governments in other capitalist countries that would seek to solve the problems attendant upon full-employment policies by a destruction of trade unions and by an authoritarian fixing of the share of national income going to labor would not also be fascist regimes dominated by the most influential and powerful class in society. Yet the nature of the regime is bound to influence decisively the choice of "routes" that it adopts in order to provide for full employment. Controlled by capitalist interests, it cannot engage in "spending on productive enterprise" since such spending is essentially inimical to capitalist institutions. All the more is it inclined to use the "military expenditures" route toward full employment. Not only is this device highly acceptable to big business, it is also fully in keeping with the fascist ideology prone to consider domestic economic problems in terms of "living space," "co-prosperity zones," and "national power."[43]

The machinery of regulation that has been developed by fascist governments, and that embraced more or less closely coordinated controls over wages, prices, investment, credit, foreign trade, etc., has been amply described in the literature.[44] After a lengthy period of groping it evolved into a set of measures directed toward three interrelated objectives: (1) maximization of total output by means of full employment and highest exertion on the part of the working members of society; (2) maximization of the volume of resources extractable for armaments and related (political) purposes by rigorous controls of mass consumption; (3) avoidance of inflation by an authoritarian division of real income among the social classes.

At hardly any time—not even during the war—did these objectives lead to an adoption of what may be termed a coordinated, consistent plan. In the main they were approached by *ad hoc* measures that added up, as time went on, to a maze of rules and regulations covering all aspects of economic and social life. Inefficient as it was, this system of controls was developed to its bureaucratic perfection in Germany, and represents still the greatest experiment of peacetime economic planning under capitalism.[45]

3. *Laborism.* There has been suggested, however, another formula that could represent a possible solution of our dilemma. The "contending party" to be sacrificed on the altar of full-employment equilibrium would not be labor but the capitalist class. Under this arrangement, which one could call with Schumpeter the rule of "laborism," the government would no longer be dominated by business interests but by the other party to the contest—the trade unions.

A trade union administration determined to abolish bargaining over the distribution of the social product by eliminating one of the two decisive claimants would have to be a much stronger government than a regime sponsored and supported by the business class, since its task would be considerably more complex. Indeed, the claimant whom it would wish to "abolish" would be the economically and socially ruling class in society, entrenched in traditional positions of property and power, resting upon an elaborate structure of custom, habit, and prevailing social values. Compared with the magnitude of this undertaking, the task of fascism was easy. Outlawing the unions, or still better "taking them over," and suppressing their political mouthpieces was actually all that was needed to destroy them as an "organized force." To be sure, such an action militated against the political institutions of democracy, violated such notions as freedom of assembly, organization, and speech. It did not disturb, however, the basic socioeconomic structure of the capitalist order. It was in other words a *political* revolution neither accompanied nor followed by what could be termed a social transformation.[46]

What is envisaged in "laborism's" advent to power is, however, precisely the opposite: with the continuity of political institutions maintained, with the structure of social values and ideologies unaffected, the prevailing *economic* and *social* system is expected to be radically altered. To make matters still less realistic, this drastic overturn in the basic economic order of a capitalist society is expected to be carried out by an organization that by its very nature constitutes an integral part of that society. Set up not to abolish collective bargaining but to secure it, brought up not to flout the market mechanism but to gain a place in it, educated not to combat the institutions of capitalist society but to grow into one of them—the trade union movements in advanced capitalist countries such as the United States or Great Britain are constitutionally and ideologically unable to assume dictatorial political powers needed to undertake revolutionary changes in the economic and social structures of their societies.

Where in extraordinary political constellations they achieve political power they become frustrated by the very circumstances to which they owe their political success, and assimilate themselves to the conventional functions of a government in a capitalist society, wholly unable to adapt that government to their original plans and purposes. Nor could it be different. The nature of any particular government depends in the last analysis not on the individuals that happen to hold official positions; it is crucially determined by the socioeconomic structure of the society over which it presides.[47]

Yet, assuming that a "laborist" administration were to succeed in squaring the circle, in "suppressing" the capitalist class in a capitalist society, the contradictory nature of the resulting situation is easily visualized. In attempting to serve the interests of its supporters, it would seek to counter possible aggregate demand deficiencies by efforts to increase consumption, be it through outright spending on consumption benefits (food subsidies, etc.) or through appropriate tax policies accompanied by transfer expenditures.

The "laborist" government would have to deal with inflationary pressures that would appear once full employment is reached (or approached), by freezing wages on some level agreed upon with the trade unions and by the enactment of suitable measures to enforce stable prices.

On the basis of available experience there can be little doubt that such a policy would have a highly discouraging effect upon private investment. Compelled to pay high wages, exposed to trade union demands concerning working conditions, unable to increase prices to allow for increased costs, subject to rigorous controls of a hostile administration, the businessman would find it rational not only to refrain from new investment but possibly to abstain from maintaining his enterprise in working order.

As far as the employment aspect of the matter is concerned, the "laborist" government may have no strong reasons for worry. The deficiency in aggregate demand caused by the growing inadequacy of private investment could be made up by further expansion of governmental spending on consumption, social services, and the like. Yet such a policy would imply neglecting the maintenance and necessary expansion of the nation's productive plant and would obviously be unacceptable to any responsible government. In other words: confronted with an "investment strike" on the part of the capitalist class, the laborist administration would find itself compelled either to retreat and to grant such concessions to the business community as may be needed to restore the confidence of the investor or else to undertake on an ever expanding scale investment and operation in the field of productive enterprise.[48]

In the former case the rule of "laborism" would rapidly draw to a close; a policy of yielding to "economic necessities" would deprive it of its original mass support without endearing it to its capitalist opponents. Should the latter course be adopted, "laborism" would begin transcending the framework of a capitalist society and enter the road to all-out socialization.

II. PLANNING UNDER BACKWARD CAPITALISM

A. The Issues

The burning issue confronting underdeveloped countries[49] is not that there is at times insufficient employment of available men *and* available capital equipment but that the existing quantity of capital goods (and land) is inadequate to assure a level of productivity that would provide the backward countries with tolerable standards of livelihood.[50] The only way to prevent a continuous deterioration of living standards (apart from mass emigration unacceptable to other countries, or a slowing down of population growth that cannot be expected under prevailing conditions) is to assure a steady increase of total output at least large enough to offset the rapid expansion of the population.[51]

An obvious source of such an increase is the vast multitude of entirely unemployed or ineffectively employed manpower.[52] There is no way of employing it usefully in agriculture, where the marginal productivity of labor tends to zero. It could be provided with opportunities for productive work only by transfer to industrial pursuits.[53] For this to be feasible, large investments in industrial plant and facilities have to be undertaken. Under the conditions obtaining in underdeveloped countries such investments are not forthcoming for a number of important and interrelated reasons.

Disregarding capital imports, the only source from which investment can be provided is the "economic surplus" currently generated by the economic system. There are no hard and fast rules by which its magnitude can be established. It represents the difference between Gross National Product and aggregate *essential* consumption, and is therefore usually larger than voluntary saving. The definition of what constitutes "essential consumption" is clearly elastic and would greatly depend on the country and period under consideration.

The crucial hurdle obstructing the development of underdeveloped countries is that even such meager "economic surplus" as could be mobilized from their small aggregate incomes is usually frittered away on unproductive purposes. With a very uneven distribution of income, large individual incomes exceeding significantly what could be regarded as "reasonable" requirements for current consumption accrue, as a rule, to a relatively small group. Many of them are large landowners maintaining a "feudal" style of life with large outlays on housing, servants, travel, and other luxuries. Their "requirements" for consumption are so high that there is little room for saving.

Other members of the "upper crust" receiving incomes markedly surpassing "reasonable" levels of consumption are wealthy businessmen. Yet their drive to accumulate capital and to expand their enterprises is continuously counteracted by the urgent desire (or social compulsion) to imitate in their living habits the socially dominant "old families," to prove by their conspicuous outlays that they are socially (and therefore also politically) not inferior to their aristocratic partners in the socially ruling coalition.

But if the social structure existing in the underdeveloped countries and the values held by their upper income groups depress saving markedly below some hypothetical magnitude of available "economic surplus," the will to reinvest funds in productive enterprise is effectively curbed by other factors. One of these is a strong reluctance on the part of the businessmen to damage their carefully erected monopolistic positions by creation of additional productive capacity.[54]

More important, however, is the absence of suitable investment opportunities, paradoxical as this may sound with reference to backward areas.

The shortage of investible funds and the lack of investment opportunities represent two aspects of the same problem. A great number of investment projects, unprofitable under prevailing conditions, could be most promising in a general environment of economic expansion. Large-scale investment is predicated upon large-scale investment. Roads, electric power stations, railroads, and houses have to be built *before* businessmen find it profitable to erect factories and to invest their funds in new enterprises.[55]

Nor is there usually land going to waste in backward areas that is fit for agricultural purposes and at the same time readily accessible.[56] The expansion and improvement of agricultural production would normally require considerable investment. In underdeveloped countries such investment is just as unattractive to private interests for agricultural as for industrial purposes.

Approached thus via agriculture, an expansion of total output would also seem to be attainable only through the development of industry. Only through increase of industrial productivity could agricultural machinery, fertilizers, electric power, etc., be brought within the reach of the agricultural producer. Only through an increased demand for labor could agricultural wages be raised and a stimulus provided for a modernization of the agricultural economy. Only through the growth of industrial production could agricultural labor displaced by the machine be absorbed in productive employment.

If and when investment projects are undertaken in spite of all adversities, the "economic surplus" required to support them is frequently provided not by an intended contraction of resource utilization elsewhere in the economy, but by inflation. It is clear that the quantity of resources withdrawn from the lower income groups through the mechanism of inflation is considerably larger than what would correspond to the amount of spending that initially ignited the inflationary development. In advanced countries the resulting redistribution of real income in favor of the business class—socially undesirable as it may be—has the possibly redeeming effect of leading to an accelerated formation of physical capital.[57] In underdeveloped countries, however, waste accompanies iniquity. The customs and spirit of their high-income receivers being what they are, increasing profits and windfall gains resulting from inflationary price movements produce a higher propensity to embark on unproductive expenditures on the part of the monied groups of the population.[58]

All the domestic obstacles standing in the way of economic development in backward capitalist countries, as well as the hurdles resulting from the international setting of the underdeveloped economies, find their expression in the balance-of-payments difficulties continuously experienced by backward areas. Their discussion would take us, however, beyond the scope of the present account.[59]

B. The Remedies

Left to itself, the situation appears as a "system not only of vicious circles, but of vicious circles within vicious circles, and of interlocking vicious circles."[60] Not that in the course of time some progress might not be attained by the normal functioning of the price and profit mechanism, by international capital movements, and the like. Whether such progress would be rapid enough to prevent major human catastrophes in many underdeveloped countries is highly conjectural. It is undeniable, however, that not much time is left for the transformation of the economies of the backward areas.

True, this is not the first time the population of the underdeveloped countries has experienced misery. But it is the first time that hundreds of millions of human beings have become convinced that because of new scientific knowledge and new technical skills their misery is not necessary. In Asia, in Africa, in Latin America, that conviction is growing. And the people of these lands are determined to solve their economic problem.[61]

In an effort to overcome backwardness, the government could undertake a variety of planning measures. A fiscal policy of capital levies and highly progressive taxation could syphon off surplus purchasing power, and eliminate nonessential consumption. The savings thus enforced could enable the government to step in and make the requisite investment wherever the private capital refrains from undertaking required industrial projects or wherever monopolistic controls block the necessary expansion of plant and facilities.

In addition, an entire arsenal of "preventive" devices is at the disposal of the authorities. Inflationary pressures resulting from developmental activities (private and public) could be reduced or even eliminated if outlays on investment projects could be offset by a taxation system providing for a corresponding and simultaneous contraction of spending elsewhere in the economic system.

In the interim, speculation in scarce goods and excessive profiteering in essential commodities could be suppressed by rigorous price controls. An equitable distribution of mass consumption goods in short supply could be assured by rationing. Diversion of resources in high demand to nonessential purposes could be prevented by allocation and priorities schemes. Strict supervision of transactions involving foreign exchanges could render impossible capital flight, expenditure of limited foreign funds on luxury imports, pleasure trips abroad, and the like.

The combination of these measures could accomplish a radical change in the structure of effective demand in the underdeveloped country and a reallocation of productive resources to satisfy society's need for economic development.

C. The Obstacles

The mere listing of the steps that would have to be taken in order to assure an expansion of output and income in an underdeveloped country reveals the implausibility of the view that they could be carried out by the governments existing in most backward capitalist countries. The reason for this impossibility is only to a negligible extent the absence of a competent and honest civil service needed for the administration of the program. A symptom itself of the political and social marasmus prevailing in underdeveloped countries, this lack cannot be remedied without an attack on the underlying causes. Nor does it go near the roots of the matter to lament the lack of satisfactory tax policies in backward countries or to deplore the absence of tax "morale" and "discipline" among the civic virtues of their population.

The crucial fact rendering the realization of a developmental program illusory is the political and social structure of the governments in power.

In our judgement, there are a number of under-developed countries where the concentration of economic and political power in the hands of a small class, whose main interest is the preservation of its own wealth and privileges, rules out the prospect of much economic progress until a social revolution has effected a shift in the distribution of income and power.[62]

If to appease the restive public, blueprints of progressive measures such as agrarian reform, equitable tax legislation, etc., are officially announced, their enforcement is willfully sabotaged. The government, representing a political compromise between landed and business interests, cannot suppress the wasteful management of landed estates and the conspicuous consumption on the part of the aristocracy, cannot suppress monopolistic abuses, profiteering, capital flights, and extravagant living on the part of the businessmen.

III. PLANNING UNDER SOCIALISM

A. "Socialist Economics"

Although the social and political structure of the country where planning is to become the guiding principle of economic organization appears basic to all discussion of its contents and direction, most of the literature on socialist economics pays hardly any attention to this aspect of its subject matter. Wholly in the tradition of all utopian thought on the subject of "good society," this literature escapes into a painstaking discussion of the economic organization of an "established" socialist order characterized primarily by "consumers' sovereignty." It would be redundant to attempt here a summary of its "notably abstract" contents. Not only was such a survey recently presented,[63] but the material involved bears only a tenuous relation to realistically conceived problems of economic planning.

The writings in question could perhaps be interpreted as a normative endeavor to elaborate rules for an "ideal" economic organization and conduct, compliance with which would yield an economic "optimum." They "might be considered as providing a theoretic basis for the work of a central planning board seeking to rationalize the planning system of a socialist state."[64] Yet this claim can hardly be sustained. As Bergson has pointed out in his celebrated contribution to welfare economics,[65] the contents of any "optimum" are determined by the values adopted in its formulation; the stipulation of the means by which such an "optimum" could be attained is therefore evidently meaningless without reference to those basic ends—in particular, since " 'means' are also 'ends.' "[66] This observation, true as it is in its incontrovertible generality, constitutes undoubtedly an advance from the transparently ideological doctrine identifying "welfare" under the specific existential conditions of a capitalist society with human "welfare" at large.[67] It represents, however, only the first "critical" (in both senses of this word) step toward a concrete, historically relevant doctrine of welfare and of economic planning for welfare.

Indeed, "ends" and "values" taken as "given" in economic analysis (in keeping with the practice advocated notably by Lionel Robbins)[68] do not fall from heaven but constitute themselves moving forces and important outcomes of the concrete socioeconomic process. The range of values, objectives, and means within which the relevant choices are to be made is thus fairly closely delineated by the essential characteristics of the stage of social and economic development, as well as by the interests of the class ruling at any particular time. Not much useful purpose is therefore served by considering planning in a socialist society as directed toward the attainment of "optima," the contents of which are borrowed from the individualistic value system of the capitalist world or from some personal predilections of the writers.

After all, one of the crucial *raisons d'être* of a socialist society would seem to be the pivotal function accorded in it to *social organs of control* carrying out measures the social merits and implications of which could not be properly assessed by individuals. What is more, it is presumably the purpose of whatever political action is taken to establish a socialist system to create such social organs of control that would limit consumers' sovereignty (*and mold consumers' preferences*) in the interests of the community as a whole in preference to an arrangement in which it is the capitalist enterprise which performs this function for the benefit of private interests.[69]

This does not by any means imply that the central planning

board would "sovereignly" or "arbitrarily" brush aside the preferences of the public and be guided by the whims of its members. On the contrary, the board's policies may be fully compatible with " . . . a principle likely to be accepted by socialists . . . of giving people what they want where there is no good reason for a contrary policy."[70]

However, it is precisely the *meaning* of this maxim that is at issue. The actual process of determination of the nature and direction of economic activity, of the share of output devoted to consumption or investment, of the assortment and quality of various products placed on the market may well represent a historical *novum* defying categories inherent in our conventional frame of reference. The planning board would be obviously subject to strains and stresses of its rapidly changing social environment and would have to respond to the wishes and needs of a society involved in a revolutionary transition. It would thus neither substitute its own preferences for those of the people nor efface itself by merely executing the desires of the consumers—desires expressing a value scheme representing a holdover from a social structure of an earlier historical phase. It would strive to promote an attitude on the part of the population that would be conducive to the attainment of some new "optimum."[71]

It is the inability to perceive this interaction that bars a realistic approach to the problems of socialist planning on the part of liberal economists interested in the problem of socialism. *"Liberalism takes the individual as given* and views the social problem as one of right relations between given individuals."[72] Is it astonishing that from such a position one cannot visualize a social system the entire concept of which is built upon the recognition of the decisive influence of the social structure upon the nature, values, volitions, and actions of the individual?

It must be stressed that a radical reorientation of all aspects of social existence could not unfold under the rein of unfettered individual freedom. Nor would it be reasonable to assume that perfect social consensus would support the revolutionary measures involved. Directed as they would have to be against vital interests of previously privileged classes, violating many short-run preferences of others, such a revamping of the socioeconomic structure would necessarily involve compulsion. The extent of such compulsion would vary from country to country depending on prevailing conditions—it is hardly conceivable that it could be altogether absent anywhere. "It is highly doubtful whether the achievements of the Industrial Revolution would have been permitted if the franchise had been universal. It is very doubtful because a great deal of the capital aggregations that we are at present enjoying are the result of the wages that our fathers went without."[73]

In advanced and backward countries alike, the problem facing the board would be not slow adjustments to small changes—the main prerequisite for the applicability of the rules derived from static analysis—but choice among few technological alternatives involving large indivisibilities and "fixed coefficients." Attempting to cope with such perplexities, the board would look in vain for guidance to the literature of socialist economics.[74]

To be sure, those rules can be and have been reformulated in a way sufficiently general for them to refer to all situations in which a rational allocation of resources is accepted as a desirable objective. "If we so order the economic activity of the society that no commodity is produced unless its *importance* is greater than that of the alternative that is sacrificed, we shall have completely achieved the ideal that the economic calculus of a socialist state sets before itself."[75] It is clear, however, that such a general principle, common sense though it is, offers no help whatever to the planning board confronted with actual choices. The decision concerning the relative *importance* of various alternatives would have to be made without the assistance of the welfare economists.

Not that the planning board could not make such decisions rationally. In making them, however, it could not rely on any ready-to-use prescription of economics but would have to perform a duty essentially germane to its function in a dynamic society. It would have to engage in the task of "social engineering," i.e., formulate social *priorities* in the light of economic, political, and possibly defense requirements of any given situation. In this endeavor it would constitute, actually, only a part of the "brain trust" of a socialist society—executing social decisions and participating at the same time in formulating them by providing indispensable information on "what is possible."[76]

At the peril of some oversimplification it may be said that the board would permit consumers' preferences to determine the composition of output *within* the board's relevant "priority classes." On the other hand, the desire of some consumers to have resources transferred from a higher "priority class" to a lower (e.g., from the production of work clothes to the production of fancy neckwear) may be resisted by the planning board.

It goes without saying that most of these problems disappear or lose much of their urgency as soon as the board's "autonomous program" has accomplished its purpose and significantly raised the country's total output, or attained whatever other objectives appeared urgent during the transition from capitalism to socialism. Loosening the board's priorities schedules, this development would, at the same time, widen its "priority classes"—in other words, increase the area of the board's indifference with respect to the allocation of resources. In the meantime, the redistribution of income will have fully affected the structure of consumers' demand, and the "taste-molding" activities of the planning board will have resulted in a new pattern of consumers' preferences.

Where the board's "autonomous program" was small from the very beginning, where in other words developmental requirements loomed less large in the early stages of economic planning, the transitional period would be accordingly shorter and simpler. In such conditions the interference of the board with the preferences of the consumers would be necessitated merely by shortages resulting from the change in the social structure, and by the "taste-molding" endeavors of the board. It is clear that the sacrifices and discomforts resulting from such disregard of consumers' preferences would be less stringent than those springing from severe scarcities.

B. The Soviet Experience

It is perhaps the very limited extent to which economic theory can offer help to a central planning board engaged in the administration of a system in the throes of economic development and in transition from capitalism to socialism that accounts for the conspicuous paucity of theoretical publications on economic planning on the part of Soviet economists. Indeed, as was suggested above, an economic science that has drawn its inspiration from the study of the "coordinating operation of the market and at times the failure of the market to achieve a coordination of decisions" is not geared to deal with problems confronting an economy in which the "coordination of decisions" is a function of a central political body.[77] Nor are possibly other branches of social sciences which are designed to study the processes taking place in capitalist (and precapitalist) societies as yet in the position to provide insight as to the regularities characterizing the behavior of such an authority.[78]

It could hardly be otherwise. Although the basic philosophy of the central authority may determine the goal of its activities, its concrete policies are shaped by the specific circumstances prevailing at any given time.

Even if it were possible to establish some regular pattern of the authority's reaction to any set of specifiable economic and political conditions, an attempt at a general theory of its policies would be necessarily jeopardized by the impossibility of anticipating adequately domestic and international developments determining, and *themselves determined by*, its actions.

Thus the experience of Soviet planning has lent itself very little to theoretical summaries; and most useful writing on the subject has been by necessity of a historical character.[79] Whether in monographs dealing with relatively short periods and with special aspects of the Russian planning effort or in larger treatises seeking to encompass the entire period since the Revolution, students of Soviet planning have had to analyze the policies of the Russian government as caused by, or themselves causing, specific economic and political constellations. It is by no means fortuitous, therefore, that efforts at a comprehension of Soviet economic reality in terms of conventional economic theory reached their apex in the years of the New Economic Policy, i.e., at a time when the "coordination of economic decisions" was still largely entrusted to the market mechanism, and have become increasingly rare and unrewarding in the ensuing two decades, in the years in which economic planning has become the effectively governing principle of Soviet economic life.

A brief consideration of the problems that the Soviet planners are called upon to solve may serve to render the foregoing more explicit.

1. *The Determination of the Long-run Goal of Economic and Social Development.* It goes without saying that decisions under this heading represent the bases of all plans and policies pursued by the Soviet government. Although strongly affected by the ideology (and social basis) of the ruling party—and to that extent explicable in its terms—they are powerfully influenced by the specific conditions under which

they have to be made. The tasks confronting the Soviet government have turned out to be quite different from what was anticipated in earlier Marxist thought. Indeed, although political developments in Russia permitted the seizure of political power by a socialist party, the economic and social prerequisites for a socialist order were entirely absent. Fully aware of this contradiction, the Bolsheviks had no intention of immediately establishing socialism (and comprehensive economic planning) in their hungry and devastated country.[80]

Their plan was rather to resist all internal and external attempts to overthrow the socialist regime and to preserve political power until the victory of socialism in Europe's leading industrial nations. All economic measures in the years immediately following the Revolution were subordinated to this basic purpose.[81] Once socialism had prevailed in the advanced countries of the world, the fortress of Russia's economic and social backwardness was expected not to be stormed by a frontal assault but to succumb to a carefully planned flanking operation. Aided by highly developed socialist countries such as Germany and Great Britain, socialist Russia was to approach slowly, although much faster than before, the levels of productivity and welfare attained in the Western world. "The achievement of socialism was . . . thought of by Lenin at this time primarily in terms of world revolution."[82]

The New Economic Policy that followed the phase of War Communism was still merely a set of temporary measures, designed to promote a recovery of the national economy from the catastrophic depths into which it had been plunged by war, foreign intervention, and revolution. The purpose of those policies was not, any more than that of the earlier ones, the introduction of a socialist economic system, but the creation of transitional conditions that would permit the socialist government to retain political power until the triumph of socialism in the West.

The picture changed drastically in 1924. The failure of the last revolutionary attempt on Germany (the Hamburg uprising in the fall of 1923) placed the Soviet government face to face with an essentially new situation. It had become clear that the expectation of an early victory of Western socialism was erroneous, that socialism in Russia was isolated. This implied, however, that the Soviet regime in Russia, considered earlier as an essentially provisional arrangement for the duration of the "holding out" phase, had to stabilize itself for an indefinite period separating it from the world revolution, and to build "socialism in one country."[83]

Such stabilization was predicated upon a number of crucial conditions. First, the regime had to be able to meet Russia's urgent need for economic development—without any significant foreign assistance;[84] secondly, the economic growth of the country had to be so directed as to render it as immune as possible to economic blockade or outright military aggression deemed probable under conditions of "capitalist encirclement"; and third, the living standards of the population had to be improved and the internal political and economic basis of the socialist regime strengthened and broadened.

These objectives became the guiding principles of the Five Year Plans of which the first was enacted in the spring of 1929.[85]

2. *The Determination of the Speed of Attainment.* The policies followed at any given time are only partly determined by long-term goals. The other coordinate is provided by the decision concerning the *tempo* at which the realization of these ends is sought. To be sure, the speed with which the long-term goals are to be attained is far from independent of the nature of the goals themselves. Indeed, the development of an integrated economy independent of foreign markets and able to support technically no less than econo-

mically its own further growth calls primarily for expansion of basic industries. This in itself necessitates certain minimum rates of advance. In the absence of an already existing elaborate framework of an industrial economy, every major industrial project requires outlays far in excess of its own cost. These outlays have to be synchronized if waste is to be avoided; plants consuming electric power have to be built at the same time as power stations are erected, coal mining has to be expanded simultaneously with the construction of blast furnaces, and dwellings for workers have to built where new factories are established.[86]

What is more, prevailing technological standards impose indivisibilities that have to be taken into account in the determination of the investment program of any given year. Neither automobile factories nor hydroelectric plants can be acquired piecemeal or in such sizes as might be convenient. Even if adoption of units smaller than technologically optimal, or of a technology less capital intensive than the most advanced should appear rational at any particular moment, such policy might prove to have been myopic in the longer run.

At the same time, the nature and rate of investment decided upon for the initial period of the program exercises a powerful influence upon the speed of expansion in ensuing periods. The basic industries constructed during the first period produce the investment goods to be used in the next; the volume of saving needed in the next period is thus greatly influenced by investment decisions made earlier.[87]

If the goal of expansion of basic industries necessarily implied rather high rates of speed in the execution of the development program, the Soviet government's appraisal of the international situation and of the dangers threatening Russia's external security suggested even higher *tempo* of growth.[88]

To some extent the accelerated preparation for defense coincided with the general industrialization program. Calling for emphasis on basic industries and mining as the essential prerequisites for current and potential expansion of military output, it reinforced the reasoning underlying the Soviet broad plan of economic development. On the other hand, suggesting dispersal of industry, erection of parallel plants, and the industrialization of the more distant areas of the Soviet Union, it prevented full utilization of available "external economies" and thus increased the magnitude of the required investment. It stimulated, however, the development of the backward regions of the U.S.S.R.—highly desirable on its own account.

No such harmony, tentative as it may have been, existed with regard to the third fundamental objective: strengthening of the internal basis of the regime and improvement of the standard of life. That goal would have pointed to an altogether different strategy and to altogether different rates of development.

What is necessary in such a situation is a decision on the magnitude of the "economic surplus" that can be used for investment (and defense) purposes in any given period. If great urgency is attached to the attainment of the developmental (and/or defense) goals, consumption standards may be fixed at "rock bottom." This "rock bottom" is indicated by the need to preserve health and productive efficiency of the population and to maintain political stability.

It goes without saying that the reduction of current consumption to such "rock-bottom" levels is highly undesirable. Under conditions of strain that would inevitably result from such "belt tightening," even small hitches in production, let alone crop failures, may easily give rise to major difficulties.[89] Moreover, the political and economic costs of mobilizing the marginal amount of the "surplus" may be entirely out of proportion to the advantages that can be derived from it for the developmental program. Thus the first Five Year Plan, although programming extremely high rates of expansion, was very far from scheduling a reduction of consumption to "rock-bottom" levels. In actual fact it anticipated an increase of consumption by as much as 40 percent over the quinquennium.[90]

The decision on the magnitude of the "economic surplus" extractable from the economy for investment purposes is thus of an eminently political and socio-psychological nature. It has to take into account not only the "margin of social and political tolerance" but also the effect of any level of consumption on incentives and efficiency. It has to depend, moreover, on the possibility and the cost of securing control over the "economic surplus" by the governmental authorities.[91]

3. *The Mobilization of the "Economic Surplus."* The authorities can secure the resources needed for investment, defense, social services, administration, and the like in a number of alternative ways. Some of the criteria by which the choice has to be made are purely technical—the reliability, convenience, and cost of various procedures. Where the resources involved represent a large share of an absolutely low aggregate income, as is the case in the Soviet Union, political considerations assume prime importance. The mobilization of the "surplus" has to be so organized as to minimize the political resistance to what is bound to be an unpopular policy. At the same time the distribution of the burden of the program among various social groups and classes has to be calculated so as to strengthen the social and political basis of the regime. Much of the controversy in Russia in the late twenties and earlier thirties centered around this issue.

The best procedure for withdrawing from the population the share of its money income which is required to meet the government's outlay is an income tax. Under the conditions prevailing in the Soviet Union prior to the industrialization period this method of raising revenue was beset with considerable difficulties. As far as the urban population was concerned, the tax could be readily assessed and collected. Matters were much less simple with regard to the rural sector of the economy. Neither the assessment of income accruing in agriculture nor the collection of the tax from subsistence farmers appeared to be a manageable task. The fiscal authorities were confronted with strong resistance on the part of the peasants—only recently freed of the tax and rent burdens of the Czarist days—and measures of enforcement of the tax assessments, such as removal of produce in kind or confiscation of livestock, were bound to provoke profound hostility against the government and were politically intolerable.

Another method of securing the resources needed for the realization of the governmental program is the expansion of the earnings of the government-owned and operated sector of the economy (industry, transportation, trade, etc.). This could be accomplished by keeping industrial prices low in relation to prices of agricultural products—combining, however, such a price policy with a wage policy leaving large profits in the hands of the nationalized enterprises. Such a course, favoring the agricultural population, would place the burden of the program upon the shoulders of industrial workers. Even if it could have been made to yield sufficient revenue—a doubtful assumption in view of the relative smallness of the government sector of the economy prior to its expansion under the Five Year Plans—it would have been politically wholly unacceptable.

The accumulation of profits in the governmental sector of the economy could be brought about not merely by an appropriate wage policy but also by raising the prices charged for its output. The obvious advantage of this procedure as compared with relying on industrial wage policy alone is that it distributes the burden of the accumulation process between the urban and the rural sectors of the population.[92]

Yet this strategy, involving the "opening of the scissors," i.e., a shift in relative prices in favor of industry, could be and was effectively counteracted by the "kulaks," i.e., peasants in possession of marketable surpluses, who refused to exchange on terms proposed by the government. While rural demand for some products of the nationalized sector was sufficiently inelastic to enable the government to obtain for them certain quantities of agricultural produce, the general tendency of those agricultural producers that mattered was either to reduce their output or to increase their own consumption of agricultural produce, rather than to trade on terms below what they considered to be a "parity" ratio.

At the peril of overemphasizing one aspect of the problem at the expense of others, it may be said that the collectivization of Soviet agriculture was motivated to a large extent by the necessity of overcoming this crucial hurdle. To be sure, expansion of agricultural output and release of agricultural manpower for industrial employment—possible only through transition to large-scale farming and through mechanization of agricultural production—were by themselves objectives of tremendous importance. However, without a reorganization of the agricultural economy assuring the possibility of "syphoning off" agricultural surpluses, progress in agricultural production would have only slowly affected the volume of agricultural output available for nonrural consumption.

By transferring the disposal of agricultural output from individual peasants to government-supervised collective farm managements, collectivization destroyed the basis for the peasants' resistance to the accumulation policy. From now on the share of agricultural output consumed on the farm could be fixed by direct apportionment to collective farm members, while farm consumption of nonagricultural commodities could be regulated by fixing the prices paid by the government for the marketed share of agricultural output and charged by the urban sector of the economy for goods supplied to the farm population.

The way was thus open for wage and price policies to become the main instruments for mobilization of the "economic surplus" of the entire economy. The total of wages paid (including the apportionment in kind to collective farm members) is calculated to absorb the share of total product allotted to consumption, while the government secures control over the part of national income to be devoted to investment, defense, social services, administration, etc., through the profits of the government-controlled enterprises.

These profits could be transferred in their entirety to the government, which could use them to defray its planned outlays. In actual fact a more complicated procedure is employed. A large share óf the profits is paid over to the government in the form of an "advance." This "advance," called "turnover tax," is contributed to the state budget immediately following the marketing of the factory's products, *independent of cost accounting.*[93] The balance of the profits—the difference between the wholesale price net of turnover tax and cost—appears as profits *sensu strictu.* A share of these profits is paid to the government at the end of the accounting period as "deduction from profits," while the remainder is left with the enterprises for various stipulated purposes.[94]

There are a number of reasons for the employment of the cumbersome device. One is that "the State cannot wait for periodical balance sheets to be issued in order to determine how much a given establishment has accumulated."[95] Payment (or nonpayment) of the turnover tax serves thus as a rapidly reacting indicator of the extent to which productive plans are fulfilled by the individual enterprise. Equally important perhaps is the consideration that "flooding" of individual enterprises with vast profits not to be surrendered until the end of an accounting period would generate an atmosphere of "quasi-prosperity" in their managerial offices and exercise an adverse effect upon the effort to assure economical conduct of plant operations. Moreover, this arrangement prevents accumulation of "artificial" profits generated *within* the industrial system and not representing a withdrawal of "economic surplus." " . . . Since a very large part of what is produced by heavy industry is consumed by State-owned industry . . . prices of industrial equipment either do not include the turnover tax or only at a very low rate . . . ."[96]

This is not the place for a detailed description of the Soviet financial system.[97] Suffice it to add that the "turnover tax" and the "deductions from profits" account for the bulk of the "economic surplus" generated in the country. The balance appears in the form of small amounts of profits reinvested locally, the even less significant income taxes, various minor business taxes, loans from the public and the like.

4. *The Allocation of the "Economic Surplus."* Most of the "economic surplus" is channeled through the government budget into a variety of purposes. While a share of it serves to support the military establishment, governmental administration, and social and cultural undertakings, the balance is used to carry out the investment program.

Two types of problems have to be solved in determining the use of these investment funds. The *total* must be divided among different industries, and a choice has to be made concerning the technical form that investment should take in any particular case.[98] The former issue is to a large extent prejudged by the decisions concerning the goal and tempo of the developmental program. Once these decisions are made, "the problems of economic planning seem to acquire a resemblance to the problems of military strategy, where in practice the choice lies between a relatively small number of plans, which have in the main to be treated and chosen between as organic wholes, and which for a variety of reasons do not easily permit of intermediate combinations."[99]

This choice between "a relatively small number of plans" seems to be made by an appraisal of the feasibilities and implications of the available alternatives. Certain specific bottlenecks—shortages of steel or machine tools or transportation facilities—may dictate the selection of a plan calling for the least quantity of the critical item. The need to concentrate scarce managerial or technical talent on one construction project rather than dissipating it on a number of undertakings may dictate the preference for a certain technological process.

Such a preference, in turn, may temporarily preclude investment even of relatively small quantities of resources to other branches of the economy, although the advantages that such investment may promise could be large. "The economic plan singles out each time the leading branches of the national economy, the crucial links that have to be grasped for the entire chain of economic development to be pulled up."[100]

The consecutive plans are thus characterized by the nature of the "link" singled out. "The crucial link of the first Five Year Plan was the heavy industry with its heart piece— machine building. The decisive links in the second and third Five Year Plans were the leading branches of the heavy industry—metallurgy, machine building, fuel, energetics, chemistry. Under the conditions of the Patriotic War the crucial link in the plan was military production."[101] It is this concentration upon the highest priority tasks that gives the Soviet economy the character of a "target economy." At any particular time certain highest priority objectives command exceptional attention. This frequently results in transitory "disproportionalities." The fulfillment of one target is accompanied by lags in the attainment of others. The next period witnesses, then, a shift of emphasis to the backward "links" that have to be pulled up for the "chain" to be straightened out.

This strategy of local advances followed by a subsequent consolidation of the conquered terrain is dictated, however, by the specific conditions of the Russian economy, and may well represent a particularly effective method for a rapid development of underdeveloped countries. Where slow growth rather than urgent structural change should constitute the guiding principle of the economic effort, the pattern of "campaigns" and "targets" may be inappropriate, and investment could be allocated in relatively small portions among different branches of the economy with a view to equating their productivities on the margin.

However, the decision about the production targets and the distribution of the investment funds among different *branches* of the economy leaves unanswered the question how to choose between different *modes* of producing the desired output. The solution of this problem suggested by conventional theory (the ratios of costs of factors to their respective marginal value products should be the same for all factors) would provide no succor to the planning authority. Even if sufficient continuity of substitution could be assumed, the planning board would have to consider not only the *social* costs involved in the employment of an additional quantity of a factor, but also—and this is most important—take into account the impact of its own activities on the future relative scarcities of factors.

Thus the existence of a large rural surplus population may have suggested (and still suggests) that in Russia strong preference should be given to techniques employing much labor and little capital. Yet such advice would overlook the large social cost of transferring a man from the village into industrial occupation. The additional industrial worker must be provided with urban dwelling space. Paid the going industrial wage, he must be assured of the quantity of food, clothing, etc., that is usually consumed by industrial workers.[102] Even if his product in the new occupation should exceed the cost of his sustenance in the city, it may be impossible for technical and/or political reasons to extract the requisite additional food from agriculture. True, the "disguised unemployed" had contributed previously nothing or little to total agricultural output while consuming a certain quantity of food. That food came, however, from his family's table and constituted no drain on the sparse "marketed share" of agricultural output.

Since the expansion of agricultural output and the increase of agricultural supplies available to the cities require not only large-scale investment but also a considerable amount of time, the physical limitations on the amount of food that could be placed at the disposal of the urban population may by themselves call for the selection of capital-intensive rather than labor-intensive techniques of production.

The same conclusion may be arrived at if it is considered that the abundance and "cheapness" of currently available labor is only a temporary condition *preceding* the realization of any given stretch of the developmental program. The planning board, aware of the aggregate demand for labor entailed by its own plans, has to bear in mind therefore that relatively soon, during the life-span of the equipment that is to be installed, labor may turn from a relatively ample to a relatively scarce factor.

These very general considerations may suffice in the present context. A lively and extensive discussion of possible formal criteria to be followed in making specific investment decisions has been taking place in the recent Soviet literature; it would exceed by far the available space to present here a detailed account of its contents.[103] The planning board itself has not yet stated, to my knowledge, what principles it follows in making the relevant decisions. It is most likely, however, that the Soviet economist Chernomordik expresses the official view.

Our advocates of the employment of a coefficient of

effectiveness to solve the problem of comparing alternatives try to equip themselves with some kind of a slide rule to mechanize the labor of project-making. This mathematical method only serves, in the last analysis, to divert attention from the real problem: the comprehensive study of the basic processes of the economy; ascertainment of the effect on the national economy of any particular capital construction.[104]

5. *The Balance Sheet.* The investment decisions of the central authority as well as of managements on lower (plant and regional) levels are combined with the estimates of the magnitude and composition of consumers' goods supply and checked for mutual consistency in the so-called national-economic balance sheets. To describe the procedure involved, it may be best to present an extensive quotation from the work of a Soviet economist:

> The balance sheets and distribution plans as drawn up at the present time include: firstly, material balance sheets (in kind) showing the proportions of the material elements of reproduction; secondly, value (price) balance sheets showing the proportions in the distribution of financial resources and ensuring proper proportion in the distribution of the social product in respect of its material form and its value; thirdly, balance sheets for labor power.
>
> Material balance sheets (in kind) consist of the following: (1) balance sheets of industrial products which, considering the main purpose for which they are to be used, represent the elements of the fixed funds of the national economy that ensure fulfillment of the construction program of the national economic plan (equipment and building materials), (2) balance sheets of industrial and agricultural products, which, considering the main purpose for which they are to be used, represent the elements of the circulating funds of the national economy that ensure fulfillment of the production program of the national-economic plan (metals, fuel, electric power, chemicals, agricultural raw materials), (3) balance sheets of industrial and agricultural products which,

considering the main purpose for which they are to be used, represent articles of individual consumption.

The material balance sheets and distribution plans, which are approved by the Government, cover products of national-economic importance as well as products which require centralized distribution because of their shortage. During the war the number of items of funded products, i.e., products distributed by the center, had to be considerably enlarged.

Value balance sheets consist of the following: (1) balance sheet of the population's money income and expenditure, (2) the State Bank's cash plan, and (3) the state budget.

The income side of the balance sheet of the population's money income and expenditures covers the wage fund of the workers and office employees and other incomes of the urban population; the expenditure side covers expenditure by the population in buying goods at state and cooperative stores, paying for services and other money expenditures. The chief purpose of this balance sheet of the population's money income and expenditure is to ensure proper proportion in planning the volume of trade, the wage fund and the money income of collective farmers. This balance sheet serves as a basis for drafting the trade plan and also for planning the wage fund in the national economy.

The State Bank's cash plan serves as an important means for planning money circulation. The income side accounts for money received by the State Bank from trade turnover and payments by state organization; the expenditure side accounts for payments made against the wage fund and other money expenditures. The State Bank's cash plan makes it possible to determine the volume of currency emissions required for the ensuing period.

The state budget is a most important financial balance sheet which determines the distribution of the bulk of the national income. The main items of revenue in the state budget are accumulations of the socialist economy in the form of profits and turnover tax, and money received from the population in payment of taxes, subscriptions to state loans, etc. The expenditure side of the state budget consists of disbursements made in financing the national economy (production and capital construction), social and cultural development, administrative expenses and expenditures on defense. The function of the state budget is to ensure the financing without deficit of the national economy with the aid of the country's internal financial resources.

The labor power balance sheets include: (1) the balance sheet for labor power in the state economy, which determines the demand for labor power and skilled personnel in the various branches of the national economy, and the principal sources for recruiting labor for it (training the state labor reserve schools, organized hiring of labor), (2) the balance sheet of labor power in the collective farms, which determines the utilization of collective-farm labor resources for carrying out the plan of agricultural production and for work in industry.

The balance sheets system in the national-economic plan makes it possible correctly to solve the problem of planning resources, consumption and distribution in the national economy.[105]

The method thus briefly sketched represents a merely formal solution of the task of maintaining a general dynamic equilibrium of the Soviet economy. Whether it assures a smooth functioning of the economic system depends obviously on the magnitudes that are entered in that generalized "input-output" matrix.[106] The degree of accuracy that is attained in the estimation of the shape of the technological transformation functions, of the volume of actual production in individual plants, and of consumption of various goods by the consumers, determine the extent to which the plan is able to avoid disproportionalities and waste.

There can be no doubt that both have characterized the working of Soviet planning—particularly in its earlier phases. Yet the causes of these deficiencies may have been primarily associated with the historical setting of the Russian planning effort rather than with the principles underlying it. The breakneck speed of the "target-economy" calling for the "leading links" strategy accounted for continuous occurrence and recurrence of major successes in some parts of the economy and equally serious "gaps" in others; the poverty of the country made it impossible until the late thirties to accumulate sufficient reserves to permit a rapid plugging of those "gaps"; and the lack of personnel scientifically trained for planning work on all levels caused avoidable mistakes in the preparation of the estimates determining the relationships embodied in the plan.

The "hitches" that occur in the functioning of the system become less frequent and less costly as their causes gradually disappear. Slowing down the speed of industrialization, filling the "pipelines" of the economy with the indispensable stocks of food, raw materials, fuel, etc., the availability of adequately prepared planning officials, combined with growing levels of literacy and civic responsibility on the part of the population, lead to a progressive improvement of the actual performance of the economic system.[107]

As Maurice Dobb points out, " . . . the notion that successful development from one economic situation, with its given combination of resources and configuration of demand, to another might be a more crucial test of the contribution made by an economic system to human welfare than the attainment of perfect equilibrium in any given situation seldom commanded attention."[108] Such attention on the part of social scientists is, however, urgently called for by the problems faced by many relatively advanced nations, but faced especially by the multitudes living in the world's underdeveloped countries.

Very little of what constitutes the main body of our customary economic theorizing would seem to be of much help in solving these perplexities. What the Soviet experience strongly suggests is the need for concrete historical research into the social and political prerequisites for economic growth and development. The "standards of perfection" evolved in the writings on "economics of socialism" offer no guidance in the effort to conquer backwardness, squalor, and oppression. "The advocacy of impossible changes is advocacy of no changes at all." The contribution that economic science can make to the solution of the problems of a planned economy is more likely to be found on the lines suggested by Wassily Leontief and "linear programming" than in the refinements of "optimum conditions" pertaining to an imaginary world. This contribution would be amply rewarded—by the continuous "feedback" linking realistic economics with the demands and issues of reality. What this implies, however, is that in a rationally organized society the economist of our days would be one of the "disguised unemployed" to be transferred to the position of "social engineer" helping to understand and to create the conditions for economic and social progress.

Notes

1. P.A. Samuelson, *Foundations of Economic Analysis* (Cambridge, Mass., 1947), p. 203.

2. *Ibid.,* p. 206. However: "It is the part of responsible men to proceed cautiously and tentatively in abrogating or modifying even such rights as may seem to be inappropriate to the ideal conditions of social life." – Alfred Marshall, *Principles of Economics* (London, 1890; 8th ed., 1921), p. 48.

3. Cf. A.C. Pigou, "Some Aspects of Welfare Economics," *Am. Econ. Rev.,* XLI (June 1951), in particular pp. 301-302.

4. Even so, it represented a threat to dominant interests by supplying ammunition to social reform movements and by encouraging the development of trade unions. It was left to Pareto, who was contemplating social reality not through the looking glass of English moral philosophy but from the more austere position of a "disinterested" aristocratic observer, to formalize an attitude that expressed adequately the monopolistic answer to the

Mill-Marshall-Pigou "revolt of the middle classes." By repudiating the validity of interpersonal comparisons of utility, Pareto purged political economy of all the reform implications disturbing the British (and German) economists. As it was impossible (in his opinion) to make any scientific statements concerning cardinal utility, any judgment on distribution of wealth and income became to him an ethical value proposition beyond the realm of economic science. Taking from the rich and giving to the poor became nothing that could be recommended by economics, since even the notion "rich" and "poor" lost meaning in the Pareto frame of reference. What appeared as common sense to Smith, Ricardo, Mill, Marshall, Pigou—not to speak of the uninstructed man in the street—turned out to be a non-scientific ethical preference, with the economist's preference counting no more than anyone else's. Schumpeter completed the structure by rationalizing and glorifying monopoly.

5. Cf. Paul Mantoux, *The Industrial Revolution in the Eighteenth Century* (London, 1928), as well as Friedrich Engels, *The Condition of the Working Class in England* (London, 1920).

6. This is the title of a useful collection of papers related to Keynesian economics edited by S.E. Harris (New York, 1947).

7. J.M. Keynes, *The General Theory of Employment, Interest, and Money* (New York, 1936), p. 379. Cf., however, on p. 157: "There is no clear evidence from experience that the investment policy which is socially advantageous coincides with that which is most profitable."

8. From the original $C = C(Y)$ the expression changed to $C = C(Y - B - W)$ where B stands for withholdings of income payments to individuals on the part of business, while W represents the net withdrawings of income on the part of the government (tax collection less transfer payments). Should both B and W be regarded themselves as functions of the size of GNP and the above relationship accordingly rewritten $C = C[Y - B(Y) - W(Y)]$ the original concept of the consumption function would be restored—although deprived of its original simplicity. It is questionable, however, whether B and W can be properly regarded as functions of GNP or whether their behavior is more or less independent of changes in GNP. Cf. P.A. Samuelson, "Simple Mathematics of Income Determination," *Income, Employment, and Public Policy: Essays in Honor of Alvin H. Hansen* (New York, 1948), pp. 133-155.

9. Cf. E.E. Hagen, "The Reconversion Period: Reflections of a Forecaster," *Rev. Econ. Stat.*, XXLX (May 1947), pp. 95 ff., as well as the literature referred to therein.

10. This is, in itself, a rather misleading notion inasmuch as it places the "responsibility" for any given allocation of income as between consumption and saving (and therefore indirectly for any given level of employment) on society at large rather than on that class in society that is in the position to make decisions in regard to saving or consumption.

11. Cf. Moses Abramovitz, "Savings and Investment: Profits *vs.* Prosperity," *Am. Econ. Rev.,* XXXII (June 1942, Suppl.), p. 56; for the postwar period: Council of Economic Advisors, "The Annual Economic Review," *The Economic Report of the President* (Washington, 1951), App. B, p. 223; and J.N. Morgan, "The Structure of Aggregate Personal Saving," *Jour. Pol. Econ.,* LIX (Dec. 1951), pp. 528 ff.

12. This is even more pertinent if the analysis refers not to the United States or Great Britain but to the rest of the world where the savings of the "public" are altogether negligible, where virtually all the savings are accumulated by business, and possibly landowning, interests.

13. This point is stressed in an unpublished paper, "An Analysis of Retained Business Receipts," by Lorie Tarshis. Cf. *Surv. Curr. Bus.,* XXX (July 1950), p. 10, Table 5—making due allowance, of course, for the years of the war when special conditions boosted individual savings.

14. It is interesting that the most outstanding recent work on the consumption function—*Income, Saving, and the Theory of Consumer Behavior* by J.S. Duesenberry (Cambridge, Mass., 1949)—nowhere even mentions that what it is dealing with is nothing but this small share of what has to be offset by investment if full employment is to be maintained.

15. Schumpeter goes too far when he maintains that ". . . of course, practically all business savings which in turn, constitute the greater part of total savings—is done with a specific investment purpose in view," since some of it may be done for speculative purposes or in order to assure a steady flow of dividend payments. J.A. Schumpeter, *Capitalism, Socialism, and Democracy* (New York and London, 1942; 3rd ed., 1947), p. 395.

16. "The 'blade' of investment carves out economic fortune; the 'blade' of the propensity to consume remains stationary while the carving is done."—A.F. Burns, "Keynesian Economics Once Again," *Rev. Econ. Stat.,* XXIX (Nov. 1947), in particular p. 262.

17. Gerhard Colm, "Fiscal Policy," *The New Economics,* p. 461. Needless to say, the part of business demand that is linked to foreign trade is, if anything, even less predictable, dependent as it is not on domestic conditions but on the still less tractable developments in

foreign countries.

18. United Nations Group of Experts (Lake Success, 1949).

19. For a brief and simple presentation of this and other variants of fiscal policy see A.H. Hansen, "Three Methods of Expansion through Fiscal Policy," *Am. Econ. Rev.,* XXXV (June 1945), pp. 382-387. For a masterful analysis of the implications of the alternative methods see Michal Kalecki, "Three Ways to Full Employment," *Economics of Full Employment* (Oxford, 1944), pp. 39 ff., as well as Nicholas Kaldor's App. B to William Beveridge, *Full Employment in a Free Society* (New York, 1945).

20. The "balanced budget" or the "unit multiplier" methods are of almost exclusively theoretical interest. If the deficiency in aggregate demand that is to be offset is at all large, the adoption of this strategy would require an exorbitant level of taxation. See the excellent summary of the argument in Samuelson, "Simple Mathematics. . .," as well as the literature cited therein.

21. This is not to suggest that such demand would have to be exclusively "guessed"; the government's plans of its own future activities may influence the nature of further demand.

22. "Three Ways to Full Employment," p. 53.

23. Samuelson, "Simple Mathematics. . .," p. 137.

24. To be sure, this view of the state is fully compatible with the recognition of the existence of so-called pressure groups that play such a prominent role in political science literature. Yet the very notion of the pressure group presupposes the existence of some neutral entity upon which the pressure is being exerted.

25. A.P. Lerner, "An Integrated Full Employment Policy," in *Planning and Paying for Full Employment,* A.P. Lerner and F.D. Graham, eds. (Princeton, 1946), p. 164. Or ". . . private enterprise and public enterprise are both useful instruments for serving the public welfare, and . . . the issue between them is best resolved in each particular instance by the pragmatic economic test of which is able to operate more efficiently."—A.P. Lerner, "Foreign Economic Relations of the United States," *Saving American Capitalism,* S.E. Harris, ed. (New York, 1948), p. 279—as if both private and public enterprise were engaged in a contest of performance with an impartial and disinterested arbiter handing down the verdict. While the naive rationalism of this writer was neither fully shared by J.M. Keynes nor is entirely acceptable to the more responsible representatives of the Keynesian school, it expresses adequately the basic attitude underlying the entire approach.

26. The usually striking divergence of long-run and short-run interests may by itself give rise to considerable doubts as to what *actually* promotes the best interests of a social class in a concrete historical constellation.

27. Lionel Robbins, *The Economic Basis of Class Conflict* (London, 1939), p. 4.

28. A somewhat similar conclusion arrived at from altogether different premises is expressed by F.H. Knight: ". . . it is a . . . pernicious idea that by education a society can lift itself by its bootstraps."—"Principles in Economics and Politics," *Am. Econ. Rev.,* XLI (March 1951), p. 23.

29. "In all societies—from societies that are very meagerly developed and have barely attained the dawnings of civilization, down to the most advanced and powerful societies—two classes of people appear: a class that rules and a class that is ruled. The first class, always the less numerous, performs all political functions, monopolizes power and enjoys the advantages that power brings, whereas the second, the more numerous class, is directed in a manner that is now more or less legal, now more or less arbitrary and violent. . . ."—Gaetano Mosca, *The Ruling Class* (New York, 1939), p. 50.

30. What would seem to be in contradiction with the above thesis is only apparently so. Such infringements upon the objective interests of British capitalism as have occurred from 1940 to 1950 and that were laid at the door of the Labour government are much more attributable to special circumstances or to the emergencies of the war and postwar period than to specific policies of the Labour administration. They were therefore accepted without much ado by the representatives of the British business classes. ". . . with the partial exceptions of transport and steel, all of the nationalization, or semi-nationalization programs were based squarely on findings, and in large part on recommendations, which had been made by Conservative-dominated fact-finding and special investigating committees. . . . Even the nationalization of the iron and steel industry seems to have been mainly the realization of a plan for reorganizing the industry which had been advanced by the Iron and Steel Federation itself. . . . To cap it all, the top planning machinery evolved by the Labour government represents a relatively minor adaptation of wartime controls to somewhat altered peacetime circumstances."—R.A. Brady, *Crisis in Britain* (Berkeley and Los Angeles, 1950), p. 41.

31. Cf. Milton Friedman, "A Monetary and Fiscal Framework for Economic Stability," *Am. Econ. Rev.,* XXXVIII (June 1948), pp. 245 ff.

32. For an interesting discussion of business attitudes toward deficit spending see Sir S. Alexander, "Opposition to Deficit Spending for the Prevention of Unemployment," *Income, Employment, and Public Policy*, pp. 177-198.

33. P.M. Sweezy, "Duesenberry on Economic Development," *Explorations in Entrepreneurial History* (Feb. 1951), pp. 182 ff.

34. Schemes could conceivably be devised, however, under which consumption subsidies would be paid not to unemployed but to employed persons and made proportional to their wages.

35. "On an average of good and bad years [statistical] unemployment should be higher than five to six million—seven to eight perhaps. This is nothing to be horrified about because . . . adequate provisions can be made for the unemployed."—Schumpeter, *Capitalism, Socialism, and Democracy*, p. 383; cf. also John Jewkes, *Ordeal by Planning* (New York, 1948), pp. 78 ff., for similar views and estimates.

36. "The Nazis succeeded in overcoming the problems created by full employment because they had first broken the labour movement. Discipline in industry was ensured by substituting terror, along with a mystical propaganda appeal, for the fear of unemployment. The vicious spiral was cut at the root by fixing wages."—Joan Robinson, *The Problem of Full Employment* (London, 1943), p. 36.

37. M.W. Reder, "Problems of a National Wage-Price Policy," *Can. Jour. Econ. Pol. Sci.*, XIV (Feb. 1948), p. 58.

38. A.P. Lerner, "Rising Prices," *Rev. Econ. Stat.*, XXX (Feb. 1948), p. 26.

39. A.P. Lerner, "Money as a Creature of the State," *Am. Econ. Rev.*, XXXVII (May 1947), p. 316.

40. "The freedom from doctrines and dogmas . . . results in the fact that economic policy in the national socialist state is determined by considerations of expediency and, without prejudice applies such measures as are necessary in any given case for the economic welfare of the people."—Eberhard Barth, *Wesen und Aufgaben der Organisation der gewerblichen Wirtschaft* (Hamburg, 1939), p. 9, as quoted by Franz Neumann, *Behemoth, the Structure and Practice of National Socialism 1933-1944* (Toronto-New York-London, 1944), p. 233.

41. ". . . the middle-class composition of the fascist party determined the *form* of the fascist action; the forces that gave the action of the fascist leadership direction and content was all the time the big bourgeoisie."—Ignazio Silone, *Der Faschismus, seine Entstehung und seine Entwicklung* (Zurich, 1934), p. 166. Translated from the

German by the writer.

42. "The predominance of the business group in Japan's ruling coalition has not been established during the course of the war. It was, in fact, already fully expressed in the cabinets which both preceded and followed the Manchurian invasion of September 18, 1931 . . . all the way down to Pearl Harbor. . . . Thereafter the forced growth of heavy industry and the still greater concentration of vested monopoly interests in the furtherance of which the authority of government was liberally drawn upon, merely confirmed and extended the dominant position occupied by the Zaibatsu in the Japanese regime."—T.A. Bisson, *Japan's War Economy* (New York, 1945), p. 203 f.

43. The pursuit of military might as the most important "route" to full employment does not preclude—in fact calls for—a marked improvement in the living conditions of the population. Stemming from the mere existence of full employment, such an improvement represents the indispensable condition for the political stability of the fascist-militarist regime. Under certain circumstances it may even result in a far-reaching identification of popular ideologies with those of the fascist rulers. Cf. Oscar Lange's review of Paul M. Sweezy, *The Theory of Capitalist Development,* in the *Jour. of Philosophy*, XL (July 1943), pp. 378-384, as well as Sweezy's reply in his Preface to the second printing of *The Theory of Capitalist Development.*

44. In addition to the already cited work by Franz Neumann, cf. K.E. Poole, *German Financial Policies, 1932-1939* (Cambridge, Mass., 1939); Maxine Y. Sweezy, *The Structure of the Nazi Economy* (Cambridge, Mass., 1941); Otto Nathan, *The Nazi Economy* (Durham, 1944); Thomas Balogh, "The National Economy of Germany," *Econ. Jour.,* XLVIII (Sept. 1938), pp. 461 ff.

45. The mode of operation and the efficiency of the German economic organization are discussed in detail in United States Strategic Bombing Survey, *The Effects of Strategic Bombing on the German War Economy* (Washington, D.C., 1946). Cf. also Emile Despres' review of this report in *Rev. Econ. Stat.,* XXVIII (Nov. 1946), pp. 253 ff., and the reply by P.A. Baran and J.K. Galbraith, *ibid.,* XXIX (May 1947), pp. 132 ff. Cf. also B.H. Klein, "Germany's Preparation for War: A Re-examination," *Am. Econ. Rev.,* XXXVIII (Mar. 1948), pp. 56 ff.

46. The speed and ease with which the societies of Western Germany, Italy, and Japan reverted after the war to a pre-fascist *political* order, this reverse calling for no changes in their social and economic structure, offers an excellent historical illustration of the distinction made above.

47. To adapt Schumpeter's brilliant analysis of a social class to the very similar problem of government "for the duration of its collective life, or the time during which its identity may be assumed each [regime] resembles a hotel or an omnibus, always full, but always of different people."–J.A. Schumpeter, *Imperialism and Social Classes* (New York, 1951), p. 165.

48. The British experience is succinctly summed up by Aneurin Bevan: "There is no way in which it is possible for anybody to carry out a plan in the modern state involving stability of employment, involving the proper dispersal of industry, involving all the things that we mean by effective control over economic life, unless the power has passed from the hands of the oligarchs into the hands of democrats. . . . Parliament is made responsible for the government of the nation and for overriding social policies, but private property has all the levers."–*Democratic Values,* Fabian Tract No. 282 (London, 1950), pp. 7, 9.

49. For a somewhat more extensive discussion of what follows in this section, cf. the essay "On the Political Economy of Backwardness."

50. There is no simple definition of what is to be considered a backward area. P.N. Rosenstein-Rodan suggested to this writer that all countries where the per capita annual income is lower than some $150 to $200 should be regarded as "underdeveloped." *Partners in Progress: A Report to the President by the International Development Advisory Board* (Washington, 1951), presents (pp. 102 ff.) a listing of underdeveloped areas the population of which is estimated at 1,075,273,000 (for midyear 1949). This list does *not* include continental China or the countries of Eastern and Southeastern Europe. If those countries are taken into account, the estimate of the population living under conditions of economic backwardness would reach approximately 1.8 billion people, i.e., nearly three-quarters of the world's total.

51. A decline in the growth of population ". . . will require a tremendous increase in production, an increase that . . . can bring rising standards of living and new vistas of health and individual welfare to the world's most poverty stricken peoples."–F.W. Notestein, "Population, the Long View," in *Food for the World,* T.W. Schultz, ed. (Chicago, 1945), p. 52 and *passim.*

52. The majority of this manpower is "disguised unemployed," i.e., "persons who work on their own account and who are so numerous, relatively to the resources with which they work, that if a number of them were withdrawn for work in other sectors of the economy, the

total output of the sector from which they were withdrawn would not be diminished even though no significant reorganization occurred in this sector, and no significant substitution of capital."–United Nations Group of Experts, *Measures for the Economic Development of Underdeveloped Countries* (New York, 1951), par. 17.

53. "The economic case for the industrialization of densely populated backward countries rests upon [the] mass phenomenon of disguised rural unemployment."–Kurt Mandelbaum, *The Industrialization of Backward Areas* (Oxford, 1945), p. 2.

54. *Measures for the Economic Development. . .*, par. 35.

55. "An underdeveloped country is poor because it has no industry, and an underdeveloped country has no industry because it is poor."–H.W. Singer, "Economic Progress in Underdeveloped Countries," *Soc. Research*, XVI (Mar. 1949), pp. 1-11.

56. ". . . in most countries where under-employment is acute, nearly all the cultivable land is already cultivated."–*Measures for the Economic Development. . .*, par. 21.

57. The German inflation following the end of the First World War is a case in point.

58. The usefulness of the "ideal-type" model presented above, which is not meant to depict accurately the situation in any one particular underdeveloped country but attempts to bring into relief the problem faced by all of them, is confirmed by various empirical studies referring to specific countries. See for instance the *Report to the President of the United States by the Economic Survey Mission to the Philippines* (Washington, D.C., 1950), p. 2.

59. The reader will find an interesting treatment of the problems related to the balance of payments of underdeveloped countries in: J.H. Adler, *The Underdeveloped Countries: Their Industrialization* (New Haven, 1949); J.J. Polak, "Balance of Payments Problems of Countries Reconstructing with the Help of Foreign Loans," *Quart. Jour. Econ.*, LVII (Feb. 1943), pp. 208-240, reprinted in *Readings in the Theory of International Trade*, H.S. Ellis and L.A. Metzler, eds. (Philadelphia, 1949).

60. Singer, "Economic Progress in Underdeveloped Countries," p. 5.

61. Stringfellow Barr, *Let's Join the Human Race* (Chicago, 1950), p. 5.

62. *Measures for the Economic Development. . .*, par. 37: "The landowners in the higher middle class hold the balance of power in Parliament and in the main political parties, there being few Egyptians of prominence who are not owners of land. This common interest in

land results in great solidarity among the well-to-do who influence the Government and make the passage of progressive legislation very difficult whenever it threatens their interest."—A.M. Galatoli, *Egypt in Midpassage* (Cairo, 1950), p. 86.

63. Abram Bergson, "Socialist Economics," *A Survey of Contemporary Economics,* H.S. Ellis, ed. (Philadelphia, 1948), Volume I, Chapter 12.

64. *Ibid.,* p. 412.

65. "A Reformulation of Certain Aspects of Welfare Economics," *Quart. Jour. Econ.,* LII (Feb. 1938), pp. 310-334; reprinted in *Readings in Economic Analysis,* R.V. Clemence, ed. (Cambridge, Mass., 1950), Vol. I, pp. 61-85; and briefly restated by the author in "Socialist Economics."

66. "Socialist Economics," p. 413.

67. An identification implicitly assumed by Marshall and Pigou. It is worth noting that Bergson, who was the first to insist on the relationship between value judgments and "optima" concepts, has also "fallen into the trap" of implicitly accepting individualistic behavior as supplying the value judgment underlying his "welfare function." This was shown in the brilliant essay by K.J. Arrow, *Social Choice and Individual Values* (New York, 1951), *passim* but in particular p. 72.

68. *An Essay on the Nature and Significance of Economic Science* (London, 1932).

69. Thus the notion of "consumers' sovereignty" is misleading under capitalism, where it is not "the consumer is king" but where the producer holds firmly the reins of power in his hands. Cf. Maurice Dobb, "Economic Theory and Socialist Economy—A Reply," *Rev. Econ. Stud.,* II (Oct. 1934), pp. 144 ff., and Alfred Sherrard, "Advertising, Product Variation, and the Limits of Economics," *Jour. Pol. Econ.,* LIX (Apr. 1951), pp. 126-142.

70. A.P. Lerner, "Economic Theory and Socialist Economy," *Rev. Econ. Stud.,* II (Oct. 1934), p. 53.

71. Whether this would be done indirectly by influencing social values or more directly by staging advertising campaigns for some commodities, by suspending the production of others or by manipulating prices of still others is a matter of technical detail that would have to be settled on grounds of expediency. Cf. Maurice Dobb, "Economic Theory and Socialist Economy," pp. 144 ff.

72. F.H. Knight, *Freedom and Reform* (New York and London, 1947), p. 69.

73. Bevan, *Democratic Values*, p. 12.

74. "Thus the proposition that the marginal value productivity of a factor must be the same in every use—it being understood that values are proportional to the marginal rates of substitution of the individual households—clearly obtains only if the principle of consumers' sovereignty prevails as an end."—Bergson, "Socialist Economics," p. 430. Cf. also Eduard Heimann, "Developmental Schemes, Planning, and Full Employment," *Planning and Paying for Full Employment*, A.P. Lerner and F.D. Graham, eds. (Princeton, 1946).

75. A.P. Lerner, "Statics and Dynamics in Socialist Economics," *Econ. Jour.*, XLVII (June 1937), pp. 253 ff. (italics supplied).

76. It may be worth pointing out that the foregoing in no way supports the contention of Max Weber, Mises, Hayek, Brutzkus, and others, that a rational calculation would be impossible in a socialist society. Under static assumptions with "consumers' sovereignty" determining the allocation of resources it is just as possible under socialism as under competition. So much is fully established by Barone, Lange, and others. Under dynamic assumptions, in particular under conditions of rapid change in all "data," no mechanical devices can assure such rationality, either under capitalism or under socialism. In the former system, it is the entrepreneur who decides what is "rational"; in the latter, the planning board. The advantages of the discretional powers of the entrepreneurs, frequently seen in the fact that owing to large numbers their errors may cancel out, are greatly reduced under conditions of large-scale business and considerable uniformity of business opinion, and are anyway decisively outweighed by the superior knowledge, disinterestedness, and ability to encompass the needs of society as a whole on the part of the planning board.

77. Oscar Lange, "The Scope and Method of Economics," *Rev. Econ. Stud.*, XIII (1945-1946), p. 26.

78. See, however, Nathan Leites, *The Operational Code of the Politburo* (New York, 1951), for an attempt to establish a pattern of *political* conduct of the Soviet leadership, an attempt that illustrates, if anything, the sterility of the generalizing formalism characteristic of much of modern social sciences.

79. "La méthodologie soviétique de planification a grandi avec la pratique de l'administration de l'économie socialisée. Cette discipline scientifique n'était enseignée dans aucune chaire universitaire au monde. On ne pouvait l'étudier dans aucun manuel. Les oraticiens soviétiques ont été obligé d'apprendre la science de planification par

l'expérience de leurs propres erreurs et lacunes qu'ils ont dû découvrir et rectifier."—Stanislas Stroumiline, *La Planification en U.R.S.S.* (Paris, 1947), p. 29.

80. "Not 'introduction' of socialism is our *immediate* task, but *immediate* transition merely to control by the Soviets of Workers' Deputies over the social production and distribution of products."—Lenin, "On the Tasks of the Proletariat in the Present Revolution" (April 7, 1917), as translated in E.H. Carr, *The Bolshevik Revolution 1917-1923* (London, 1950), p. 80.

81. "The Party proclaimed the country an armed camp and placed its economic, cultural and political life on a war footing. . . . It took under its control the middle-sized and small industries in addition to large-scale industry, so as to accumulate goods for the supply of the army and the agricultural population. It introduced a state monopoly of the grain trade, prohibited private trading in grain and established the surplus-appropriation system under which all surplus produce in the hands of the peasants was to be registered and acquired by the state at fixed prices, so as to accumulate stores of grain for the provisioning of the army and workers. Lastly it introduced universal labor service for all classes. . . . All these measures which were necessitated by the exceptionally difficult conditions of national defense and bore a temporary character were in their entirety known as War Communism."—*History of the Communist Party of the Soviet Union (Bolsheviks), Short Course* (Moscow, 1949), pp. 282 ff.

82. Carr, *The Bolshevik Revolution,* p. 107.

83. Cf. Stalin's *Report to the XVIII-th Congress of the CPSU* on March 10, 1939, where he developed also his modification of the theory of the "withering away" of the state under socialism. The meaning of that new orientation is frequently misunderstood. As Rudolf Schlesinger points out, "What was really discussed was not whether it was possible to build an ideal type of Socialism in one country but whether what could be built in one country should be supported or opposed."—*The Spirit of Postwar Russia, Soviet Ideology 1916-1946* (London, 1947), p. 103.

84. For a short review of the foreign economic relations of the U.S.S.R. cf. P.A. Baran, "The U.S.S.R. in the World Economy," *Foreign Economic Policy for the United States,* S.E. Harris, ed. (Cambridge, Mass., 1948).

85. For the history of the planning effort at that time see Friedrich Pollock, *Die Planwirtschaftlichen Versuche in der Sowjetunion,*

1917-1927 (Leipzig, 1929), *passim*, and Maurice Dobb, *Soviet Economic Development Since 1917* (London, 1948), pp. 230 ff.

86. Cf. Dobb, *loc. cit.*

87. Correspondingly, a program directed toward economic development via consumers' goods industries implies automatically not only smaller initial investment but also much lower rates of subsequent growth.

88. "We are 50-100 years behind the advanced countries. We have to traverse this distance in ten years. We will either accomplish it or else we will be crushed."—Joseph Stalin, *Problems of Leninism* (11th ed., Moscow, 1939), p. 329 (translated from the Russian by the writer). It is interesting to note that this statement was made on February 4, 1931, exactly ten years prior to Germany's invasion of Russia.

89. This is the reason for the stress placed by the Soviet authorities on the accumulation of sizeable reserves of all important consumers' goods. Cf. G. Sorokin, *Sotsialisticheskoie Planirovanie Narodnogo Khosiaistva SSSR* [Socialist Planning of the National Economy of the U.S.S.R.] (Moscow, 1946), p. 24.

90. Dobb, *Soviet Economic Development Since 1917,* p. 235. This increase did not materialize in view of unexpected difficulties associated mainly with the peasants' resistance to collectivization.

91. On the share of national product devoted to investment, cf. Abram Bergson, "Soviet National Income and Product in 1937," *Quart. Jour. Econ.,* LXIV (May and Aug. 1950), pp. 208-241, 408-441; also P.A. Baran, "National Income and Product of the U.S.S.R. in 1940," *Rev. Econ. Stat.,* XXIX (Nov. 1947), pp. 226-234.

92. This policy could be and was—actually not according to plan—reinforced by inflationary developments accompanying almost the entire period of the first two Five Year Plans.

93. M.I. Bogolepov, *The Soviet Financial System* (London, 1945), p. 9 (italics supplied).

94. Approved local investment, payment of bonuses to employees, erection of welfare establishments (work canteens, rest homes, etc.).

95. Bogolepov, *The Soviet Financial System.*

96. *Ibid.,* p. 10.

97. Good treatments of the subject will be found in Bogolepov, *The Soviet Financial System;* Dobb, *Soviet Economic Development;* Alexander Baykov, *Soviet Economic System* (Cambridge-New York, 1947); and in the Russian language in K.N. Plotnikov, *Budzet Sotsialisticheskogo Gosudarstva* [The Budget of the Socialist State]

(Moscow, 1948), and N.N. Rovinski, *Gosudarstvenny Budzet SSSR* [The State Budget of the U.S.S.R.] (Moscow, 1949).

98. Maurice Dobb, "A Note on the Discussion of the Problem of Choice Between Alternative Investment Projects," *Soviet Studies,* II (Jan. 1951), p. 291.

99. Dobb, *Soviet Economic Development,* p. 6. "Much substitution in production arises through shifts in the extent to which alternative processes are used, rather than through variation in factor combinations in the individual process."—T.C. Koopmans, "Efficient Allocation of Resources," *Econometrica,* XIX (Oct. 1951), pp. 455 ff.

100. Sorokin, *Sotsialisticheskoie Planirovanie,* p. 22 (translated from the Russian by the writer).

101. *Ibid.,* p. 23.

102. This quantity itself is largely influenced by political considerations!

103. Condensed translations of the relevant articles are published in *Soviet Studies* as well as in the *Current Digest of the Soviet Press.* Norman Kaplan has presented an excellent summary and analysis of the debate in "Investment Alternatives in Soviet Economic Theory," *Jour. Pol. Econ.,* LX (April 1952), pp. 133-144.

104. D.I. Chernomordik, "Effectiveness of Capital Investment and the Theory of Reproduction: Toward a Statement of the Problem," *Voprosy Ekonomiki* (June 1949), pp. 78-95, translated in *Soviet Studies,* I (April 1950), pp. 359-363.

105. A.D. Kursky, *The Planning of the National Economy of the U.S.S.R.* (Moscow, 1949), pp. 129 ff. The remainder of the chapter from which the above is cited contains additional valuable information on the methodology of Soviet planning. Cf. also Sorokin, *Sotsialisticheskoie Planirovanie, passim.*

106. The problems involved in elaborating such a matrix are akin to those discussed in W.W. Leontief, *The Structure of the American Economy, 1919-1929* (Cambridge, Mass., 1941), in particular p. 34, although the difficulties that have to be overcome in the planning practice may not be quite as stupendous as suggested by Leontief's analysis. It may be sufficient for the "central" matrix to include only the "leading links" of the economy, leaving a great deal to the functioning of the decentralized economic units.

107. An impressive testimonial of efficiency was the rapid conversion and reallocation of the Russian industry during the war, as well as its reconversion and growth during the postwar years. On the

latter, cf. Abram Bergson, J.H. Blackman, and Alexander Erlich, "Postwar Economic Reconstruction and Development in the U.S.S.R.," *Annals Am. Acad. Pol. Soc. Sci.,* CCLXIV (May 1949), pp. 52 ff., as well as the more recent statements on the "Results of the Fourth (Postwar) Five Year Plan," *New Times,* XVII (April 25, 1951), Suppl.

108. *Soviet Economic Development,* p. 3.

IV
On Monopoly Capitalism

Reflections
on Underconsumption

At a time when many distinguished writers in the fields of economics and social comment are devoting increasing attention to waste and excessive consumption in our society, theorizing in terms of underconsumption may be deemed bizarre and anachronistic.[1] Yet, without attempting to review the extensive literature on underconsumption, it will be argued in what follows not only that the basic concepts developed in underconsumption theory are of paramount importance to any attempt to understand the working principles of the capitalist system, but that ignoring them constitutes an insuperable obstacle to the comprehension of the very phenomena of waste and excessive consumption that have been moving into the center of current preoccupation.

This essay originally appeared in *The Allocation of Economic Resources* by Moses Abramovitz and others. It is reprinted with the permission of the publishers, Stanford University Press. Copyright © 1959 by the Board of Trustees of the Leland Stanford Junior University.

When the essay was first published, Baran noted: "This essay reflects work carried on jointly with Paul M. Sweezy, the preliminary results of which we hope to submit in the none too distant future in a book on American capitalism [*Monopoly Capital,* Monthly Review Press, 1966]. The responsibility for the specific formulations contained in this paper, however, is mine."

To be sure, the theory of underconsumption has never had much standing among reputable economists. The reasons— apart from those that need to be dealt with in terms of sociology and knowledge—for this conspicuous lack of esteem for a theoretical position that dates back to the very beginnings of modern economics are twofold. In the first place, there has been a general sense, best expressed perhaps by Professor Gottfried Haberler, that the scientific standard of the underconsumption theories is unduly low.[2] Secondly, it has been held that the actual course of capitalist development was to such an extent at variance with what was taken to be the factual presuppositions of the underconsumption theory as to render that theory baseless.

The first objection undoubtedly has some force; even the expression "underconsumption" has been used very loosely, with different writers attaching widely different meanings to it. Although it is self-evident that for this expression to be usefully employed it is necessary to state unambiguously *with regard to what* consumption is considered to be deficient, this elementary rule has by no means always been observed. Thus, to a number of writers "underconsumption" spelled simply an insufficiency of consumption for the maintenance of health and efficiency of the population. Others, in speaking of underconsumption, have referred to an apportionment of aggregate output between consumption and investment (or between consumption and other "nonconsumption" purposes, such as construction of fortifications or of monuments) which they considered to be inadequate in terms of what they took to be the proper allocation of resources either in the present or as between the present and the future. Still others treated underconsumption as a condition in which the share of output absorbed by current consumption is such as to give rise to a volume of investment exceeding that which would be warranted by the prevailing level of output (and income), with the result that aggregate effective demand would be insufficient for the maintenance of full employment of resources.

While the first mentioned variants of the underconsumption concept are hardly useful for analytical purposes, the last one represents a most promising point of departure for further inquiry. In fact, all that is required to turn it into a powerful tool for the study of capitalist development is its refinement and reformation. The needed refinement calls primarily for a qualitative and quantitative differentiation of consumption into its *useful* and *wasteful* components, for it is only along these lines that we can hope to clarify both the dynamic of consumption itself and its impact on socioeconomic development as a whole. The required reformulation should state clearly that "underconsumption" is not necessarily a description of achieved results but, rather, refers to an important *tendency* operative in the capitalist process and co-determining its outcome at any given time. This tendency obviously is neither the *only* tendency at work, nor even necessarily the dominant one. In any particular situation, its effect may be modified and indeed completely offset by other tendencies, with the resulting parallelogram of forces responsible for the actually evolving historical constellation.

These considerations must be taken into account when we turn to the second objection to the underconsumption theory: its alleged lack of correspondence with observed historical events. This point, frequently made, was reiterated most recently by Nicholas Kaldor, who dismisses the proposition that as a result of increasing monopoly "the share of profits would go on rising beyond the point where it covers investment needs and the consumption of capitalists" and, therefore, that "the system will cease to be capable of generating sufficient purchasing power to keep the mechanism of growth in operation" with the flat statement: "the plain answer to this is so far, at any rate, this has not happened."[3] It should be obvious, however, that this argument, far from disposing of the problem, fails even to reach the theoretical level on which it arises. What would we think of a theorist in the field of international economics who would deal with the issue of balance of payments' disequilibrium by enunciating the profound wisdom that international payments "so far, at any rate" have always been in balance? It surely does not require prolonged reflection to realize that what matters with regard to international payments is not the surface phenomenon of their always being in balance, but the truly significant questions concerning the structure of output, the level of income, and the volume of employment with which any given balance is associated, and the process by which such balance as may exist is actually attained. Similarly, in a theoretical analysis of the generation of "sufficient purchasing power to keep the mechanism of growth in operation," little is gained by registering whatever volume of purchasing power happened to enter the market resulting in such a level of income and employment (and unemployment) as happened to prevail, if no effort is made to pierce the obvious and to comprehend the forces which gave rise to that volume of purchasing power and which determined the nature and the rate of growth of the output related thereto.

Nor is it necessary in this particular case to depart far from the immediately observable, measurable *fact* that Moloch which is always seeking to devour analytic thought in contemporary social science. For, if the available and currently forthcoming statistical evidence were based on categories calculated to reveal rather than conceal what might be called the basal metabolism of the capitalist system, the relevant relations would become apparent even to the naked eye. While the confines of this essay preclude anything like a comprehensive discussion of this problem, its barest outline may be drawn with reference to American experience.

The most conspicuous feature of the evolution of American

capitalism, particularly since about 1870, is the enormous growth of the forces of production. Between 1869 and 1956, output per man-hour in the commodity-producing industries (agriculture, mining, and manufacturing) multiplied approximately eight times.[4] There is to my knowledge no estimate of the per man-hour productivity increase during the same period of *production workers*, i.e., of labor engaged in the process of *production*, rather than in that of administration, selling, financing, advertising, etc.[5] That increase must have been very much larger, since the proportion of production workers in the total labor force has markedly declined, and since the growth of "productivity" of the nonproduction workers has proceeded very slowly.[6] The importance of the magnitude of the productivity increase of production workers can hardly be exaggerated. The relation between the productivity of production workers and their real wages has not been studied systematically for a period comparable to that covered by Professor Barger's investigation of distribution. Yet, according to statistics available for the years 1909 to 1956, there has been a considerable gap between the growth of productivity and the rise of real wages of production workers. While the output per man-hour of production workers has risen in the course of that half-century by 277.1 percent, their real average hourly earnings increased by 230.0 percent so that the real earnings of production workers per unit of output declined by 13.5 percent.[7] As a result, the *economic surplus* produced by society has grown considerably larger, not merely in absolute terms, but in the only relevant sense: as a share of aggregate output.

What is perhaps even more significant is that, while this spectacular increase of output per man-hour of production workers was achieved to some extent by a marked improvement of health and efficiency of the working population, its mainspring was a vast expansion of the volume of capital equipment. The dimensions of this expansion are suggested by a comparison over time of capital (except land and improvements) employed per worker. Measured in 1929 prices and adjusted for standard hours, it increased from \$1,860 in 1879 to \$3,760 in 1909, and to \$6,260 in 1944.[8] Since these statistics are calculated by taking into account the *entire* labor force, they undoubtedly underestimate the extent of the mechanization of the work of production workers. This may be more adequately assessed if it is considered that manufacturing establishments use now approximately 10 horsepower of energy per production worker as compared with 1.25 horsepower in 1879. This sweeping mechanization was propelled by massive capital accumulation, by extensive exploitation of "economies of scale," and by a consequent general transition to mass production methods; and this in turn has led to the emergence and growth of large scale industrial enterprise and to a concentration of the bulk of industrial output in the hands of a relatively small number of giant concerns. These concerns, controlling large (and growing) shares of their industries' output, are, as regards the purpose of capitalist enterprise (i.e., returns on invested capital) in a position that is much more powerful than that of either their small competitive ancestors or their small competitive contemporaries.[10] Able to gauge the impact of their own business policies on the prices prevailing in their markets, they need not be content with the rates of profit that used to be earned in the competitive markets of old and that are still being earned in the competitive sectors of the present capitalist system. Far from being less single-minded in their pursuit of profits than capitalists used to be in the past—all assertions to the contrary on the part of the now so fashionable apologists of Big Business notwithstanding—the modern monopolistic and oligopolistic corporations find themselves in objective circumstances most favorable to highest returns, and, in exploiting these circumstances to the hilt, have developed what used to be the art of making a lot of money into what is rapidly becoming a science of profit maximization in the long run.[11]

Thus the increase of the productivity of labor (and the mechanism by which it is attained), combined with the mode of apportionment of its fruits as between wages of production workers and profits of capitalists, which is an inherent characteristic of the capitalist system,[12] has a double-pronged effect; the economic surplus generated by the economy *tends* to become an ever-increasing proportion of aggregate output, and this economic surplus *tends* to be continually redistributed in favor of a steadily decreasing number of giant capitalist enterprises.[13]

If these were the only tendencies operating in the capitalist system, there would be no need to argue the theoretic relevance of the underconsumption concept as previously formulated. The capitalist system would be choking in a flood of economic surplus, for neither capitalists' consumption nor investment in capitalist enterprise would be able singly or jointly to absorb the rising tide. The former is not only physically limited—particularly since the bulk of the surplus accrues to a small number of giant corporations and wealthy stockholders—but also runs counter to the capitalists' basic urge to accumulate. The latter is circumscribed by the profit maximization requirements of monopolistic and oligopolistic business and tends under normal conditions to fall considerably short of the volume of the desired capital accumulation.[14] Under such circumstances, chronic depression would be capitalism's permanent condition, and increasing unemployment its permanent accompaniment.

Yet, as most diseases of organic entities call forth some remedial forces, so economic tendencies are usually counteracted—at least to some extent—by opposing developments. Both the plethora of surplus and the ascent of monopolistic and oligopolistic enterprise have drastically changed the nature and strategy of modern business. Price-cutting, which during the earlier, competitive phase of capitalism was the principal method by which individual firms sought to maintain and to expand their sales, now ranks very low among the strategies of the competitive struggle.[15] Its place has been taken over by tremendously expanded (and expensive) sales organizations, advertising campaigns, public relations programs, lobbying schemes, and by a continuous, relentless effort at product differentiation, model variation, and the invention and promotion of fancier, more elaborate, more sumptuous, and more expensive consumer goods. In the euphemistic words of Professor Arthur F. Burns: "The rivalries of the business world are nowadays as keen or keener than ever. Competition with respect to the quality of products and the services associated with them has increased. However, less stress is being placed by many of our larger businesses on price competition."[16]

The results of this development are a rampant growth of the system's unproductive sector and a striking multiplication of waste. The proportion of nonproductive workers in the labor force of manufacturing industries has increased from 19.4 percent in 1919 to 23.1 percent in 1957.[17] To be sure, a part of this increase is attributable to the expansion of research activities on the part of industrial concerns. It should be clear, however, that in areas other than those related to the production of armaments much of what goes under the name of research is merely a glorified form of merchandising.[18] At the same time these statistics fail to reflect the full extent of the increase of the unproductive component in manufacturing. For, as pointed out earlier, the definitions of the Bureau of Labor Statistics referred to above classify as production workers those whose assignment is actually undistinguishable from that of salesmen, advertising men, and the like. This category of labor affixing chrome and fins on automobiles, producing different wrappings for identical products, turning and twisting perfectly functional articles in order to create artificial obsolescence of earlier models, all merely with the view to sales promotion, belongs undoubtedly to the unproductive segment of the labor force. Not that the boundaries of this group are readily drawn or that its size is easily measured. Yet the difficulties of definition and measurement should not be allowed to obscure the existence of a phenomenon or to serve as an excuse for the refusal to exercise rational judgment in its analysis. While taking this into account may well bring up the estimate of the unproductive part of the manufacturing labor force to as much as one-third of the total, this is by no means the end of the story. A not insignificant part of the construction industry engaged in the erection of luxurious office buildings—the castles of the feudal barons of today—and of even more sumptuous hotels and golf clubs supported by the expense accounts of corporate executives, much of the catering trade owing its existence to the same source, and many other similar activities, all represent an important drain of the overflowing economic surplus.

But as the economic surplus grows and the process of its unproductive absorption assumes an increasing importance, activities providing for such relief tend to separate themselves from production proper and to become organized in establishments of their own. The pride of place in this group—which includes among others legal practice, finance, real estate, and insurance—belongs indisputably to monopoly capitalism's very own creation: the sprawling and still briskly expanding advertising industry. The economic importance of advertising is not even approximately measured by the volume of resources which it directly absorbs, although this is by no means negligible.[19] Its significance stems from its promoting a continual enlargement of the economy's unproductive sector, from its constituting one of the most powerful devices for the propagation of artificial obsolescence and irrational differentiation of consumer goods, from its representing an indispensable mechanism for the systematic molding of consumers' wants to suit the requirements of monopolistic and oligopolistic business.

Still the growth of the economic surplus tends to surpass the possibilities of its utilization, for a large part of the expenses of selling, advertising, model-changing, etc., etc., become necessary costs of doing business under monopoly capitalism and are shifted on to the consumer, thus replenishing the economic surplus. At the same time a large share of the sizable income accruing to corporate executives, salesmen, admen, public relations experts, market researchers, and fashion designers is *saved* rather than spent by their recipients and gives rise to what might be called "secondary accumulation of capital"—another category in which the economic surplus makes its statistical appearance.[20]

Nor are other more or less automatically functioning mechanisms of surplus absorption—capital exports, corporate outlays on research and development, and the like—powerful enough to solve the problem. A conscious effort at utilization of the economic surplus is indispensable if its congesting effects are to be kept within tolerable limits, if depression and unemployment are not to be allowed to assume major proportions and thus to endanger the stability of the economic and social order. Such a conscious effort can be undertaken only by the government. The government in capitalist society, however, is not constituted in a way to promote the purposeful and sustained employment of the economic surplus for the advancement of human welfare.[21] The powerful capitalist interests by which it is controlled, as well as its social and ideological make-up, render such a policy most difficult if not entirely impossible. It is unable to control the practices of Big Business, let alone invest directly in productive enterprise, since this would be manifestly in conflict with the dominant interests of monopolistic and oligopolistic corporations.[22] It is barred by the values and mores of a capitalist society from large-scale spending on welfare objectives (at home and abroad). Thus even a liberal, progressive administration tends to seek salvation in military spending, adding in this way deliberately organized waste in the government sector to automatically expanding waste in the business sector.

Waste, however, cannot expand smoothly and rapidly. For, although the very survival of monopoly capitalism becomes increasingly dependent on squandering of resources, *to the individual capitalist enterprise* waste represents a deplorable deduction from surplus, to be resisted as strongly as possible. Thus, no one firm, not even the largest, can squander more resources than is necessitated by prevailing business practices, so that increases in waste can only develop slowly and gradually, only as all the important firms enlarge their unproductive expenditures and thereby set new standards for the economy as a whole. Similarly, the snowballing of governmentally organized waste and skyrocketing military budgets, indispensable as they are to monopoly capitalism, spell to individual Congressmen and Senators (and to the majority of their constituents) nothing but higher taxes or a heavier national debt burden, and are permitted only reluctantly and only in an atmosphere of external danger (real or contrived).

Except during wars and their aftermaths, the interaction of all these forces creates a vast potential excess of economic surplus, which means underproduction, underconsumption, and underinvestment, or—what is the same—underemployment of men, underutilization of productive capacity, and depression.[23] The only remedy for this persistent malaise that is available to the capitalist system is further multiplication of waste both in the private and the public sectors of the economy.

The process thus briefly sketched cannot be comprehended

by even the most painstaking observation or statistical measurement of the economic and social surface, for that surface itself is not an elemental datum but is at any particular time the *outcome* of the interacting and interlocking tendencies which in their dynamic totality constitute historical development. This can be seen clearly in the case of the two categories that matter most in the present context. The magnitude of profits in any given year as reported by statistical agencies reflects only partly and tenuously the size of the economic surplus generated by the system during that period. Leaving aside taxation, there is an entire group of important factors accounting for the gap between the volume of reported profits and the amount of the economic surplus. The components of that gap can be readily identified, impossible as it may be to measure them even approximately with the help of the available statistical information. It includes land rent and interest and a large part of executive salaries and expense accounts. It comprises a considerable share of depreciation and depletion allowances and of the firms' nonproduction expenditures: on advertising, public relations, lobbying, legal departments, market studies, model changes, and the like. Thus the magnitude of profits that actually rises to the statistical surface is determined not only by the size of the economic surplus but also by the mode of its utilization, both of which depend in turn on the character of industrial organization, on the prevailing degree of monopoly, on the extent to which taxes, selling costs, etc., are shifted to the consumer, and so forth.

It could be objected that all of this is unimportant and that what is relevant is exclusively the *actual* share of statistically reported profits in national income, or even merely the relation of the proportion of the profit share which the profit recipients desire to accumulate to the volume of aggregate intended investment. From the viewpoint of short-run business analysis and forecasting this objection is undoubtedly justified; but if the problem be considered in terms of economic and social development in the longer run, or in terms of human welfare even in the short run, this objection falls to the ground. For surely both the present condition of society and its prospects in the future are greatly influenced by the mode of utilization not only of the statistically recorded part of the economic surplus (profits and individual saving) but also of its probably larger unrecorded part. It is surely not a negligible question how large that unrecorded part is, whether it finds its way into education, urban renewal, or aid to poverty-stricken peoples, or whether it is absorbed by advertising, merchandising, or the military establishment. In other words, even if Mr. Kaldor's earlier referred-to contention were true that the share of profits does *not* "go on rising beyond the point where it covers the investment needs and the consumption of capitalists,"[24] it would still remain decisively important, whether the absence of that rise has been caused by the constancy or decline of the share of economic surplus in aggregate output, or whether that rise has been merely hidden by the procedures of statistical reporting or the intricacies of tax regulations, or, finally, whether that rise has been prevented by the diversion of an increasing proportion of the economic surplus to some governmentally determined purposes. In the latter case, clearly, the nature of those purposes is of the utmost relevance.

Looking at the matter from the other side: what applies to profits also applies, *mutatis mutandis,* but with no less force, to consumption. The statistically recorded consumers' expenditure obviously covers *all* consumption, regardless of whether it is consumption of productive workers or of non-productive workers, whether it is consumption of teachers or consumption of soldiers. It includes, in other words, not merely useful consumption but also consumption which merely wastes part of the economic surplus. Again, these distinctions may not matter much for the determination of the immediate business outlook, but they matter a great deal if what is at issue is the welfare of society, its economic, moral, and cultural condition. To the present and future of the American people (and of the world as a whole) it matters a great deal that (in 1956) $42 billion were spent on military purposes while $1.5 billion were found for economic aid to underdeveloped countries; that automobile transportation absorbed $27 billion, while education (private and public) commanded $15 billion; that $3 billion worth of resources were used for recreation goods of all kinds, while $.6 billion were devoted to books; that basic research was assigned $.5 billion, while the services of stockbrokers and investment counselors were valued at $.9 billion.

Once more, even if it were true (which it is not) that there has been no actual decline of consumption as a share of aggregate output, it would remain a problem of overriding importance what economic and social forces are keeping consumption on whatever level it happens to maintain, what are its composition and its distribution. Just as in the earlier-mentioned case of the balance of international payments, so also in regard to consumption: what is decisive is the nature of the *balancing factor*, the morphology of the difference between what consumption would be in a rational social order and what it is under the impact of Madison Avenue, of the value and mores of monopoly capitalism. Without an analysis of that morphology there can be neither an understanding of the present nor a meaningful assessment of the developmental probabilities in the future.

As Marx remarked, "all science would be superfluous if the appearance of things coincided directly with their essence."[25] Ignoring this basic principle results inevitably in the descent of economics into shallow empiricism and in the abandonment of the great tradition of social thought in favor of what goes nowadays under the name of "behavioral sciences."

Notes

1. Cf. *Problems of United States Economic Development* (New York: Committee for Economic Development, 1958), Vol. I, in particular the contributions of Moses Abramovitz, Roy F. Harrod, Ralph Hawtrey, David Riesman. See also J.K. Galbraith, *The Affluent Society* (Boston, 1958).

2. Gottfried Haberler, *Prosperity and Depression* (Geneva, 1939), p. 119.

3. Nicholas Kaldor, "A Model of Economic Growth," *Economic Journal* (December 1957), p. 621.

4. For the increase of man-hour productivity from 1869 to 1949, cf. Harold Barger, *Distribution's Place in the American Economy Since 1869* (Princeton, N.J., 1955). The change from 1949 to 1956 is estimated on the basis of *Economic Growth in the United States, Its Past and Future* (New York: Committee for Economic Development, 1958), p. 31.

5. "The Bureau of Labor Statistics includes in its definition of *production workers* all nonsupervisory workers (including working foremen) engaged in fabricating, processing, assembling, inspecting, receiving, storing, handling, packing, warehousing, and shipping; also workers engaged in maintenance, repair, janitorial and watchman services, product development and auxiliary production for a plant's own use (e.g., powerplant) and record-keeping, and other services immediately associated with these production operations. In this group is found the bulk of all factory machinists, mechanics, toolmakers and other craftsmen, welders, filers, grinders, and other operatives, janitors, charwomen, guards, and similar service workers (except, for example, plant cafeteria personnel), and most of the unskilled laborers employed in manufacturing. *Non-production workers,* defined by process of exclusion from the production worker category, are those engaged in executive, purchasing, finance, accounting, legal, personnel, cafeteria, medical, professional, and technical activities; sales delivery, advertising, credit, collection, installation and servicing of the firm's own products; routine office functions, factory supervision, and force-account construction. The bulk of factory management and personnel employees, engineers, scientists, bookkeepers, typists, clerks, salesmen, payroll workers, and employees engaged in similar activities are included in this group."—"Non-production Workers in Factories, 1919-1956," *Monthly Labor Review* (April 1957), pp. 435 ff. (italics added). To be sure, the distinction made by the Bureau of Labor Statistics is not the same as the distinction suggested by our analysis, i.e., between those engaged in contributing to the creation of useful

goods and services, the production and distribution of which would be required also in a more rational social order and those whose activities are determined by the composition of output enforced by the capitalist system and by selling operations characteristic of the capitalist market. The BLS distinction is useful, nevertheless, since it provides at least an idea of orders of magnitudes and trends which aggregative data entirely obscure.

6. Barger, *Distribution's Place in the American Economy*, p. 39.

7. *Productivity, Price, and Incomes* (Washington, D.C.: Joint Economic Committee, Committee Staff, 85th Congress, 1st Session, 1957), Table 54, p. 148, and Table 57, p. 151.

8. Simon S. Kuznets, "Long-Term Changes in the National Income of the United States of America Since 1870" in *Income and Wealth in the United States, Trends and Structure*, Simon S. Kuznets, ed. (Cambridge, Mass., 1952), p. 78, *Income and Wealth Series II*.

9. *Economic Growth in the United States*, p. 32.

10. The advance of concentration between 1909 and 1947 is shown in Paolo Sylos Labini, *Oligopolio e Progresso Tecnico* (Milan, 1957), Appendix to Chapter I. On the development during the postwar decade information is provided in the following table:

Share of Total Value Added by Manufacture Accounted for by Largest Companies in 1954 Compared with 1947

	Percent of value added in 1954	Percent of value added in 1947
Largest 50 companies	23	17
Largest 100 companies	30	23
Largest 150 companies	34	27
Largest 200 companies	37	30

Source: 85th Congress, 1st Session, *Concentration in American Industry*, Report of the Subcommittee on Antitrust and Monopoly to the Committee on the Judiciary, U.S. Senate (Washington, D.C., 1957), p. 11.

11. See James S. Earley, "Marginal Policies of 'Excellently Managed' Companies," *Amer. Econ. Rev.* (March 1956).

12. It has been well observed by Harold M. Levinson that: "The potentialities of redistribution out of profits are very slight as long as producers remain free to adjust their prices, techniques and employment so as to protect their profit position." See "Collective Bargaining and Income Distribution," *Amer. Econ. Rev.* (May 1954), p. 316.

13. Some statistics illustrating this process of profit redistribution are presented in *The Political Economy of Growth.*

14. This is more fully explained in Chapter III of *The Political Economy of Growth.*

15. *Business Week* (June 15, 1957) characterized this change succinctly by referring to the existing price system as one "that works only one way—up."

16. Arthur F. Burns, *Prosperity Without Inflation* (New York, 1957), p. 83.

17. See "Non-production Workers in Factories, 1919-1956," p. 436, and *Fortune* (April 1958), p. 215. It is most important to realize that this ratio had declined in 1942-1944 to around 14 percent when wartime exigencies reduced the need for sales promotion and enforced a measure of rationalization in the conduct of capitalist enterprise.

18. See Eric Hodgins, "The Strange State of American Research," *Fortune* (April 1955).

19. By 1880 advertising had increased threefold since the Civil War period. By 1900 it stood at $95 million a year, which marked a tenfold increase over the amount in 1865. By 1919 it exceeded half a billion dollars, by 1929 it reached $1.12 billion, and in 1957 it is estimated to have climbed to no less than $10.5 billion. It rose from .59 percent of national income in 1890 to 1.27 percent in 1929 and to 3.14 percent in 1957. See Neil H. Borden, *The Economic Effects of Advertising* (Chicago, 1942), p. 48; David M. Potter, *People of Plenty* (Chicago, 1954), p. 169; and the 1957 estimate presented in *Printer's Ink* (February 8, 1957). If activities kindred to advertising are taken into account—public relations and market research—the size of the aggregate "influence" business would be in the neighborhood of $15 billion or over 4 percent of national income.

20. One of the foremost functions of advertising is to "fight" this "secondary accumulation of capital" by shaping the wants of the upper- and middle-income groups and thus raising their propensity to consume. This is illustrated by a recently undertaken survey of the market for new automobiles: "Nearly two-thirds of the new-car buyers hold executive, professional or semi-professional positions. Much less than a third of the purchases are made by people in non-supervisory jobs. And probably only a fraction of these are in factory work."—"New Cars: Who Buys Them; How They're Paid For," *U.S. News and World Report*, March 14, 1958.

21. Hence the striking inadequacy of public services in the wealthiest country in the world, deplored but not explained by J.K. Galbraith in *The Affluent Society.*

22. "It [the public utility concept] originated as a system of public restraint designed primarily, or at least ostensibly, to protect consumers from the aggressions of monopolists, it has ended as a device to protect the property, i.e., the capitalized expectancy, of these monopolists from the just demands of society, and to obstruct the development of socially superior institutions. This perversion of the public utility concept from its original purpose was perhaps inevitable under capitalism. Here, as in other areas of our economic and social life, the compelling sanctions of private property and private profit, working within a framework of special privilege, determined the direction and outlook of public policy. Just as in the days of the Empire all roads led to Rome so in a capitalistic society all forms of social control lead ultimately to state protection of the dominant interests, i.e., property. The public utility concept has thus merely gone the way of all flesh."—Horace M. Gray, "The Passing of the Public Utility Concept," *Journal of Land and Public Utility Economics* (February 1940). Reprinted in E.M. Hoover, Jr., and Joel Dean, eds., *Readings in the Social Control of Industry* (Philadelphia, 1942), p. 294.

23. As Professor Arthur F. Burns remarks: "Every sustained spending wave that occurred between 1939 and 1954 was heavily influenced, if not dominated, by war finance or its sequelae."—*Prosperity Without Inflation,* p. 12. This applies, however, not merely to the Second World War and the subsequent twelve years, but to nearly the entire life-span of monopoly capitalism.

24. Kaldor, "A Model of Economic Growth."

25. Karl Marx, *Das Kapital* (6th ed.; Hamburg, 1922), Vol. III, Part 2. Cited and translated by Paul A. Baran.

Better Smaller
But Better

The editors of MR should be congratulated on their admirable paper on "Cooperation on the Left." It is a message of hope to those members and sympathizers of the Left, who, lonely in their bewilderment, desperate in their anxiety, stifled by their doubts and uncertainties, long for nothing more than cooperation, unification, solidarity.

And yet there is something illusionary about this eloquent appeal. Needless to say, there can be no disagreement about the desirability, even urgency, of cooperation among all progressive elements of American society. Needless to stress that never before have the potential role and responsibilities of the Left been so great as they are today. It is equally obvious, however, that the chances that the Left will be able to rise to its tasks and opportunities are unfortunately worse than poor.

In what follows, an attempt is made to sketch briefly the reasons for this rather bleak conclusion.

For a number of historical reasons, some of which are well known while others are in need of further elucidation, American capitalism is uniquely stable at the present time. This stability is impressive in the economic field; it is even more

This essay originally appeared in the July 1950 issue of *Monthly Review* under the penname Historicus. Copyright © 1950 by Monthly Review, Inc.

spectacular in the realm of ideology. What in a different ideological climate would constitute a crisis can be taken with comparative equanimity in the American setting. For example: 3 million unemployed in Italy force De Gasperi's Catholic government to rely on the police as its main pillar of support; 13 percent unemployed in Western Germany rocks the foundations of the Bonn regime; a comparable volume and percentage of unemployment in the United States hardly enters into political calculations at the present time. In other words, economic stability has to be considered with due allowance for the "margin of political tolerance." This margin is wider in the United States than in any other part of the capitalist world.

It is not that the inherent nature of the capitalist economy has changed. In spite of many stabilizing factors (a large federal budget being the most important) the economy is on the whole as "depression-prone" as it ever was. Bust is just as likely to follow boom as in any other period of capitalist history. What is new about the current phase of American capitalism, however, is what may be called the "manipulative ability" acquired by the ruling classes and their government —a manipulative ability that has greatly increased in the last couple of decades, that has received valuable laboratory testing during the war, and that in itself is one of the most important aspects of the increasing monopolization of the socioeconomic structure of our society. Big Business relies less and less on the proverbial "invisible hand"—the hand belongs with ever increasing obviousness to its own representatives in the federal government. (A cynical illustration was provided in the March 20th issue of *Life*. In an article devoted to describing and praising Mr. Acheson's "total diplomacy," the reader was informed that the Secretary of State, before announcing this new policy of the American "people," had discussed it thoroughly with ten "business leaders" whose names are listed in the story.)

Big business and its strategists have learned much more thoroughly than is frequently believed (and frequently suggested by old-fashioned holdover ideologists from the liberal age) the lessons of the Great Depression, the devices elaborated by Keynes and his school, and the implications of the war experience. They know perfectly well that employment can be "made," that its level can be pre-determined within fairly narrow limits, and that keeping it somewhere not too far from full employment—the meaning of "not too far" depending on the width of the margin of tolerance mentioned above—is the only course compatible with political security and good profits. The issue of financing the government's "full-employment" policies is by now largely a red herring. Nowadays, neither budget deficits nor the resulting increases in the public debt frighten any one who matters. What does remain a major, indeed a crucial, issue is to find suitable ways of spending the amounts of money that may be required to maintain, say, the present "comfortable" level of underemployment. All outlets that would be rational in the sense that they would contribute to the increase of human welfare, are more or less incompatible with the vested interests of the ruling classes. Payment of doles tends to raise the wage level; government investment in steel, chemicals, public utilities, etc., tends to destroy carefully erected monopolistic fortresses. And so it goes. If the problem were to spend one or two billion a year, a solution could be found at the expense of less powerful interests. But with anything from $15 to $25 billion to be pressed into the income stream, the difficulties are well-nigh insuperable.

Or rather they would be if it weren't for the Cold War.

The Cold War seems to solve this problem in a most admirable way. No interests that matter are violated as long as the money is spent on armaments and foreign operations. The short-run effect on employment and profits is the same as if the expenditures were of a "rational" type, and the long-run effect is even better since no new productive equipment is created to compete with existing facilities.

This "economic" solution must be supported by a suitable political structure. This political structure is the systematically incited psychosis of the Cold War.

The Cold War is thus by no means irrational from the point of view of the American ruling classes. Everything synthesizes beautifully in its general effects. It provides the political climate in which an agreement can be extracted from the American people to spend $20 billion annually for military purposes. It sets the stage for the complete destruction of an independent labor movement: at the present time the CIO and the AFL are vying for the distinction of being accepted as the most faithful servant of American capitalism. It has reshuffled domestic political forces in such a way that openly fascist organizations and individuals, only a few years ago hiding in the underworld of American politics, are able to operate in the center of the political stage—witness the current McCarthy affair. And, last but not least, it provides the grand strategy for expanding and protecting American investments abroad, investments that are very close to the hearts of the biggest American business interests. In one word: it furnishes the political formula for the concerted struggle for preservation of capitalism abroad and for its strengthening and, if necessary, fascization at home.

The stability and durability of this arrangement appear to depend on three factors: (1) How long can the Cold War be maintained in view of the increasingly obvious disappearance of specific objects of contest? No reasonable person in the American government believes seriously that China or Poland, Romania or Bulgaria, Hungary or Czechoslovakia, can be brought back into the capitalist fold. (2) How long can playing with guns be continued without their commencing to "fire by themselves"? In other words, are there forces within the military establishment that press toward a conflict as the establishment grows larger and politically more important? (3) How long will the country be willing to accept the proposition that the interests of American capitalism briefly outlined above are identical with the interests of the American people?

Unfortunately, it would seem that in view of the "manipulative ability" of the American ruling classes, and in view of the all-pervasive machinery of public opinion formation, the Cold War can be prolonged for many years to come. Likewise—but more fortunately—it seems likely that its transformation into a shooting war can be avoided for a long time. The third question thus takes on crucial importance. It is the problem of the "subjective factor" in the total situation.

There is no doubt that the present weakness of the subjective factor is adequately characterized in the article of the editors. To a certain extent, this weakness is the result of relatively prosperous economic conditions. They are not as good as they could be, given a rational husbandry of American resources, but they are very good in comparison with the thirties. Nevertheless, economic conditions are not the decisive factor. The boom of the last decade—all the hosannas of the press and politicians to the contrary notwithstanding—has affected the broad masses of the American people much less than one is commonly led to believe. For example, in 1948, the year of record-breaking prosperity, about one-third of all households in the United States had incomes of less than $2000. While real wages of well-organized groups of workers have held their own or even increased, there is ample evidence that the real wages of poorly organized workers, of white-collar employees, and of racial minority groups have declined since the war and are in absolute terms on a miserable level. With taxes at their present oppressive level, with sky-rocketing monopoly prices in some fields, with strong government-supported measures against organized labor, etc., etc., there ought at least to be incentive for the development of a powerful subjective factor of the British Labour Party type. We should not forget that most of the talk about the "welfare state" is—at least so far—nothing but eyewash. Social security benefits are little better than poor relief; health insurance is still far away; and industrial pensions affect only workers in the leading, most strongly organized industries.

The real rub, in other words, is not in economic conditions. The weakness of the subjective factor in America, the impotence of the American Left, cannot be understood without a full appreciation of the *ideological* stability of American capitalism. We have to understand the ideologically overpowering impact of bourgeois, fetishistic consciousness on the broad masses of the working population. The still-vigorous belief in the possibilities of individual advancement within the framework of capitalist society. The deep-seated acceptance of bourgeois values, especially the desirability of reaching the status of the next-higher group. The supremely streamlined, multi-pronged manipulation of the public mind. The heart-breaking emptiness and cynicism of the commercial, competitive, capitalist culture. The systematic cultivation of devastatingly neurotic reaction to most social phenomena (through the movies, the "funnies," etc.). The effective destruction in schools, churches, press, everywhere, of everything that smacks of *solidarity* in the consciousness of the man in the street. And finally, the utterly paralyzing feeling of solitude which must overcome any one who does not want to conform, the feeling that there is no movement, no camp, no group to which one can turn.

Is this going to last forever? Social psychology and political experience alike suggest that the prospects are bleak. Quite possibly major changes will come only as the result of shocks; in the humdrum of slow evolution the status quo reproduces itself continuously with only such changes as the manipulative machine wishes to induce. The outcome may be fascism, but there seems to be hardly a chance of anything progressive growing in such soil. The ruling class knows this.

It is aware of the fact that it does not face any serious dangers in the absence of shocks. It knows that the result of shocks is unpredictable. It will do everything within its power to avoid them—unless the military machine runs away with the bomb! This may be the strongest factor making for peace rather than the "fundamentally peaceful and democratic inclinations of the average American."

Where does the Left and its cooperation come in? Not very much, not very broadly, not very obviously. The main avenue of activity is to attack the ideological front—by clarifying the issues, by trying to cut through the cultural fog of capitalist society, by trying to break the notion of the "identity of interests" of the ruling classes with those of the working masses. This is not a program of mass politics, nor should it be the program of a sect. It is a blueprint of intellectual activity, of enlightened economic, ideological, political thinking and discussion that should be free of dogmatic fetters and petty political considerations. It is a program of building cadres, of what Marx used to call *Selbstverständigung*.

There is hardly any room for political cooperation on the Left at the present time because there are no politics of the Left. The time will perhaps come, possibly sooner than we think. But just now the issues are ideological, and ideological problems cannot be solved by organizational makeshifts. To the extent that so-called liberals are themselves fully and unreservedly subject to the prevailing obfuscation, to the extent that they serve as faithful soldiers of the Cold War army, to the extent that they debase themselves to the function of informers and stool-pigeons, to that extent "cooperation" with them can only be of the same nature as "cooperation" between the murderer and his victim. Nor is such cooperation desirable. What is needed—let us say it again and again—is clarity, courage, patience, faith in the spontaneity of rational and socialist tendencies in society. At the present historical moment in our country—"better smaller but better."

The Theory
of the Leisure Class

The Theory of the Leisure Class is Thorstein Veblen's first and certainly his most popular major work. It not only contains nearly all the notions that are now commonly associated with his name, it also foreshadows much of what appears in a more developed form in his subsequent writings. The scope of the present attempt to undertake a brief evaluation of that book must therefore be both narrow and general. It must be narrow because it has to consider the core of *The Theory of the Leisure Class*: the concepts of pecuniary emulation, conspicuous leisure, and conspicuous consumption. It must be general because it has to essay an at least tentative assessment of what might be regarded as the central scaffolding of Veblen's thought: his methodological approach and his principal results.

The greatest obstacle to a proper appreciation of the theory of pecuniary emulation, conspicuous leisure, and conspicuous consumption is its tantalizing lack of precision. At the risk of gross misapprehension which Veblen's mode of presentation so stubbornly invites, and at the cost of sacrificing the rich and frequently overwhelming orchestration with which the main themes are habitually introduced, the principal tenets of the doctrine may be outlined approximately as follows: at

---

the dawn of human history, under conditions of "primitive savagery" or of a "peaceful habit of life," productivity of labor was barely adequate to provide for the most elementary level of subsistence. Consequently there was no surplus available for appropriation and accordingly no possibility for exploitation of man by man. Thus immune to crystallization of social classes and to emergence of hierarchies of wealth and status, society lived under the benign reign of Saturn, so eloquently and nostalgically eulogized by Virgil:

> No fences parted fields, nor marks nor bounds
> Divided acres of litigious grounds,
> But all was common.

At some point in time, this state of primitive communism yields to the next historical phase to which Veblen refers as "barbarism" or "consistently warlike habit of life." In that period the development of productive resources is sufficiently advanced not only to sustain the working population but also to permit its subjugation and exploitation by an emerging upper class whose livelihood is henceforth derived from the appropriation of the fruits of the labor of others, whose members are henceforth exempt from the burden of toil and are enabled to enjoy ever higher standards of living. Indeed, ample leisure and ample consumption become now the main characteristic of those belonging to the upper stratum, and the public display of the ability to work little and to consume much assumes paramount importance as indicating an individual's (or a group's) commanding position in society. Becoming thus vehicles of the competitive striving for prestige and status, both consumption and leisure tend to expand in scope and to gain conspicuousness in form.

Yet although it is the state of society in which this happens that attracts Veblen's abiding interest, its contours and contents remain distressingly hazy. Not merely is it left open what processes account for the transition from "primitive savagery" to "barbarism," but what is much more serious, no clear indication is given as to the particular historical era to which the latter designation is supposed to apply. There are numerous statements, in fact, suggesting that Veblen thought of it as extending to his very days. To be sure, there is much to be said for the view that ever since the disintegration of the early communes barbarism and a consistently warlike habit of life marked all of human history. It hardly needs stressing, however, that this very applicability of the notions of "barbarism" and "consistently warlike habit of life" to nearly all of recorded history renders them singularly useless as principles of periodization, let alone as keys to the understanding of the actual historical process.

And this points directly to what I consider to be Veblen's fundamental weakness. While talking about history more than most other writers in the field of social sciences, while most persistently and most conspicuously flirting with what in his days was called the historical school, Veblen remains actually a stranger to the historical method, never truly committed to placing a thorough morphology of the historical process at the center of his analytical effort. As "barbarism" becomes to Veblen the dark night in which all cats are gray, so history appears in his writings as an endless continuum in which the more things change the more they remain the same. Indeed, fascinated by what millenia apparently have in common, Veblen all but ignores the far-reaching changes and transformations that set apart century from century. For this failing he had to pay with a vengeance: it not only prevented him from adequately comprehending the mechanism of historical *development,* it robbed him even of the chance to visualize clearly some of the most important *real similarities* of consecutive historical periods.

Thus having observed correctly that since time immemorial an upper class has been in a position to appropriate a more or less sizable share of the social product, Veblen never tires of stressing that the existence of that class has been always based on exploitation, that its rich endowment with leisure and worldly goods has been always secured by fleecing the underlying population. In his morbid engrossment in this sameness of iniquity he never attempts, however, to distinguish clearly between different upper classes that at different times appropriated, on the basis of different social relations, different shares of different social outputs produced in different stages of the development of productive resources. Sparing no effort in tracing and interrelating the manifold forms in which the privileged classes have enjoyed their ill-gotten freedom from want and freedom from toil, Veblen hardly pays any attention to many much more important, and much more pernicious, aspects of the part played by the ruling classes in the course of historical development.

Nor could it be otherwise. For the counterpart, or indeed component part, of Veblen's reluctance to examine concretely the forces propelling the historical process is his thinly veiled ambivalence with regard to the significance to be assigned to the development of productive resources and productive relations. Although here too there is no shortage of remarks and allusions suggesting a strong emphasis on the evolution of society's mode of production as the factor determining the mechanism and direction of historical change, Veblen's "economic determinism" is of a peculiarly vacillating, bloodless nature. Fairly unambiguous passages that could be (and frequently were) looked upon as commitments to a somewhat crudely conceived historical materialism appear next to sentences ascribing crucially important kinks in the evolution of society to changes in "spiritual attitudes," with those changes no more explained than they are in the works of idealist historians such as Weber, Sombart, or Toynbee. Even his most famous analytic tool, the concept of "institution" so often celebrated as a sharp,

materialistic stylet cutting deeply below the surface of ideologies and appearances, turns out upon examination to be a
slippery psychological notion of "habits of thought" no more
profound than Weber's "attitude of rationality and calculations" or Sombart's "spirit of capitalism."

Like other bourgeois theorists who are unable to comprehend aspects of reality in their concrete interdependence
with all the other components of the continually changing
socioeconomic totality, Veblen has recourse to invoking *dei
ex machina* as ultimate means of interpretation. And again, as
in the case of most bourgeois historians, Veblen's wisdoms of
last resort are always of a biological or psychological nature,
have always something to do with "basic" racial characteristics of men or with the no less "fundamental" structure
of their motivation. Leaning heavily on the psychology of
William James, he conjures up a number of "instincts" con-
veniently tailored to suit his particular requirements and
treats them as permanent characteristics of the human race.

Veblen never relinquishes his biological-psychological apparatus, applies it indefatigably to the study of various aspects of social life, and decries scornfully the ever-increasing
extent to which "bad" instincts overpower the "good" ones,
and "bad" people assert their exploitative dominance over
the "good." Relentlessly confronting the actual course of
historical development with his normative yardstick, he bit-
terly denounces the shortcomings of the concrete world, the
insufficient "adjustment" of one aspect of reality to another
—and all the barbarism and all the waste that he ascribes
thereto.

This yardstick—in concrete terms—is productivity and frugality and it is this specific content of Veblen's norms as well
as the way in which he employs them that determined the
character of his work, its impressive strength and its no less
serious limitations. The ideal by which he was inspired is the
image of the artisan, mechanic, farmer—the simple com-

modity producer, in fine—who emerged as the characteristic figure of the waning Middle Ages and the waxing capitalist era. That simple commodity producer was to him the embodiment of an exceptional mode of existence that he apparently considered vastly superior to all that preceded it and to all that has come thereafter. Neither a chattel continually mutilated, depraved and degraded by slavery, nor a predatory slave driver robbed of all human dignity by basking in luxury based on the blood, sweat and toil of others—that prototype of what eventually came to be called a petty bourgeoisie seemed to have overcome the limitations of the dark ages and to have entered the road to a bright future. For at the same time his life was not yet squashed by the steamroller of capitalist development. He was still intimately related to the process and the product of his labors, still intensely experiencing the joys of a gratified "instinct of workmanship," still untouched by the pervasive mechanism of alienation that was to dominate all of the subsequent capitalist development. That honorable man consuming with genuine satisfaction the bread that he earns in the sweat of his brow and using his sparse leisure for well-deserved rest, that idealized silhouette from capitalism's glorious adolescence reappears in Veblen's vision as the no less frugal, no less productive modern factory workman and technician and serves as a standard of comparison with both the precapitalist past and the late capitalist present. And naturally enough, both are found wanting: exploitative, immoral, and profligate.

Yet he nowhere undertakes a searching inquiry into the historical ramifications and functions of those ubiquitous deviations from his basic standard, or into the particular historical circumstances and exigencies that give rise to his own "system of values" which he endows with absolute validity. Had he seriously embarked upon such an investigation, he would have found that the frugality and abstemiousness of capitalism's "founding fathers" were the indispensable accompaniment of primary accumulation of capital, were indeed enforced by its implacable requirements and by the no less implacable logic of capitalism's early competitive structure. He would have also discovered that the ethos of frugality and productivity that he so wholeheartedly embraced was no more an outgrowth of an "instinct of workmanship" than the accumulation of capital was the result of William James' "instinct of ownership." He would have seen that this glorification of both frugality and productivity constituted an ideology making a virtue of a necessity, a means of asserting the preponderance of a social class whose rise to affluence and power was inseparably bound up with austerity and hard work—at first of itself and its hired help, before too long of the hired help alone.

And looking back at the more remote past, he could also have established that the pomp and circumstance of the feudal courts, the castles, fortifications, monuments, and palaces of worship erected at the behest of worldly and ecclesiastic potentates, far from constituting an expression of a mysteriously evolving "habit of thought," reflected the hard, stubborn demands of the economic and social systems rooted in slavery and serfdom.

What applied to pre-capitalist ages or to early capitalism, applies even more patently to monopoly capitalism, the formative decades of which were observed and studied by Veblen. The display and waste of wealth on the part of the ruling class that reflect the unprecedented volume of output produced and reproduced on the basis of modern technology is wholly inevitable in a society the governing principle of which is market valuation, in which even the notions of good and evil, of beauty and justice are replaced by the concept of "values." Thus the upper stratum of a big-business-dominated social order is bound to engage in sumptuous living, to entertain and to travel on a lavish scale—in order to cultivate the necessary connections, in order to be acceptable and to belong to the exclusive circles important in terms of business, financial influence, and political power. Nor can this upper stratum be divided—as Veblen frequently suggests—into an "industrial" and a "financiering" group with the former considered to be morally superior to the latter. For neither could exist without the other: without the prince of *haute finance* there could be no captain of large-scale industry, and without the genius of production there could be no genius of enterprise-merging, amalgamating, and combining various undertakings into vast monopolistic and oligopolistic empires. At the same time, the underlying population, brought up to emulate the leaders of the Big Business world, is rendered a "captive consumer," helplessly exposed to the incessant barrage of a gigantic advertising industry hammering into the minds of the people patterns of living and structures of wants. Deprived by the process of alienation of all bases for self-esteem and security derived from accomplishments at work and from genuine, non-exploitative relations of solidarity with others, the ordinary man and woman are driven into the sphere of consumption for such a measure of confirmation and self-assurance as it may provide. A modern house with a well-groomed lawn, the newest model automobile, up-to-date kitchen appliances, and stylish clothing become the nearly exclusive means for proving to oneself and to others one's success in life, one's respectability, one's worth in the market. Veblen senses all of this, of course, but he does not see that it has very little to do with biotic and psychic "instincts" and with the "basic" nature of man. It is clearly a product of an economic and social order which is rent by the irreconcilable conflict between accumulation of capital and its very opposite: consumption of goods and services. It is the outgrowth of a system which cannot accumulate if it does not sufficiently consume, and which cannot sufficiently consume because it is compelled to accumulate. Both the nature and the measure of the resulting rationality and madness, economy and waste, profligacy and miserliness, can be adequately visualized only as the outcome of those antagonistic drives: the never-ceasing battle for maximum profits and the no-less feverish campaign against the perennially reappearing threat of underconsumption.

But unless filled with concrete, historical meaning, notions such as productivity, frugality, waste, conspicuous consumption and the like, tend to become interesting-looking but actually empty boxes. Worse still, they may easily lead astray both social analysis and social criticism. It was mentioned already that productivity and frugality, for instance, served consistently in the course of the last few centuries as an "opiate for the masses," as an apology for a socioeconomic system built upon exploitation and directed toward maximization of surplus accruing to the property-owning, neither productive nor frugal, ruling class. Accepting these slogans and lending them the dignity of universal maxims of human conduct—as was done by Veblen and is repeated in our day by various counselors of "peace of mind"—amounts to swallowing one of the principal components of bourgeois ideology and to helping to perpetuate a mentality conducive to the continuation of capitalist rule.

From this it does not follow, needless to say, that indolence and profligacy represent the battle cry of progress, and that productivity and frugality have already turned into barbaric relics of a dark age. Quite on the contrary, both productivity and frugality were enlightened and forward-moving principles at the outset of the capitalist age, and are today even more so in that part of the still economically underdeveloped world where tremendous efforts are being made to secure economic growth within the framework of a socialist society. Since the question is always and inexorably: productivity for whom? frugality for what?—the call for productivity and frugality in socialist societies has a radically different meaning and plays an altogether different role than in the advanced capitalist countries where the development of productive resources has progressed so far that meaningful leisure could be substituted for a good part of currently enforced toil and that plenty could take the place of artificially maintained want.

On the other hand, there is no more justification for considering all conspicuous consumption and luxury to be the inventions of the devil. For in the first place all consumption is, and always was, not merely (and not even primarily) private business but a *social* act. Being always in society, with society, and of society, consumption has always been *conspicuous*,—that is, shown to many, observed by many, shared by many, deriving indeed a vast share of its pleasurability from being an aspect of the individual's *social* existence. What matters, in other words, is not the conspicuousness of consumption but its concrete contents, not that it takes place in society but the kind of society in which it takes place. In fact, there is nothing unpardonable in people's vying to keep up with the Joneses! The question is "merely" who are the Joneses and what is it that people are seeking to emulate in them. There surely would be nothing to deplore if people were habitually endeavoring to excel their neighbors in reason, knowledge, appreciation of arts and sciences, devotion to the commonweal, and solidarity in collective efforts!

Equally uncritical, because representing the natural consequence of his idolization of productivity and frugality, is Veblen's treatment of all forms of unproductive resource utilization under the joint heading of waste. Lumping Egyptian pyramids, Hellenic objects of art, Gothic cathedrals, and princely castles together with gambling casinos, night clubs, and the pompous residences of the modern *nouveaux riches,* and denouncing them all as manifestations of abominable abuse of wealth, Veblen resembles an embittered shopkeeper irate about his burden of taxation and therefore decrying violently each and every kind of government spending. Yet there is good government spending and bad, there are outlays on hospitals, and roads, and TVA's, as well as expenditures on armaments, on imperialist intrigues, on the support of foreign and domestic parasites. Ranting against both types of government activity is tantamount to criticizing neither, just as attacking as waste all forms of consumption except the knife-and-fork variety destroys all possibility of exposing effectively the prevailing system of irrational and destructive employment of human and material resources.

For irrational and destructive is every use of productive resources that is not conducive to the growth, development, and happiness of men. Armament falls into this category no less than advertising, phony product differentiation no less than artificial obsolescence of durable consumer goods, crop restriction in agriculture no less than monopolistic output curtailment in industry. It should be obvious, however, that the mere fact that all of *these* forms of resource utilization (or squandering) constitute a waste of society's economic surplus (or a reduction of society's aggregate output) does not imply that *all* forms of resource utilization that draw on the economic surplus or that lead to smaller output are necessarily irrational and wasteful. Holding that would mean nothing less than viewing all of human culture as an involved and protracted process of waste and profligacy, nothing less than considering all the paintings, music, literature, architecture created in the course of millennia by the genius of mankind to be but a series of violations of the principle of productivity and frugality. Once more, what is decisive is *not* that an activity is supported out of economic surplus, that an activity detracts from the process of production, or even that an activity is rewarded in what might be considered an excessive way. What *is* decisive is the content of that activity, the nature of the performance to which it leads, the impact that its results have on the unfolding and enrichment of human potentialities. Just as living off the economic surplus does not render Leonardo or Michelangelo, Rembrandt or Picasso, Mozart or Prokofiev embodiments of "waste," so are the toil and frugality of a construction worker building a race track for a successful gambler no marks of the rationality and productivity of his employment.

Revolted and disgusted with all that goes by the name of culture in the society of monopoly capitalism—how horrified he would have been today!—Veblen neglected to draw clearly these vital distinctions. A passionate critic of capitalism, single-minded in his prodigious effort to discern, interconnect, and expose all the aspects of venality, cruelty, moral and cultural degradation that he observed on every side, he was incapable nevertheless of grasping the totality of the social order that he so profoundly and so uncompromisingly abhorred. Like a number of social critics before him and after him, he saw the existing misery without fully realizing at the same time that it is that very misery that carries in itself the objective chance of its abolition. Witnessing orgies of profligacy, idleness, and waste in the midst of squalor, disease, and exploitation, he inveighed against excess consumption and luxury and raised against them the banner of productivity and abstemiousness. He did not see that what squandering, waste, and snobbery call for is not a proscription of consumption or a condemnation of luxury but an effort to ascertain and to establish the conditions in which abundance will supersede both want and waste, in which on the basis of greatly transformed needs poverty will become a fossil of the past, and a measure of luxury will become attainable to all.

In one of his later books Veblen wrote: "The historical argument does not enjoin a return to the beginning of things, but rather an intelligent appreciation of what things are coming to." This insight, combined with his implacably critical attitude toward a perniciously organized society, render him a towering figure in American social science. Although he did not manage to attain a full understanding of the process of historical change, he frequently came close to it. Had he gone further, he would have transcended himself and taken the decisive step to materialism and to dialectic.

Theses
on Advertising

Confronted with a progressive deterioration and an increasing "Americanization" of mass media in Britain, the British Labour Party appointed a Commission under the Chairmanship of Lord Reith the assignment of which is "to consider the role of commercial advertising in present day society and to recommend whether reforms are required; if so, what?" This Advertising Commission solicited oral and written testimony from various workers in that field, submitting to them a questionnaire covering the principal points on which comments were invited. Having also been asked for our reflections on the matter, we prepared the following statement the purpose of which is not so much to answer all the questions posed in the questionnaire, as to present a more or less integrated view on this most important subject. Being inadequately informed about conditions prevailing in Great Britain, we addressed ourselves to the experience in the United States—on the assumption that much of it is relevant to problems existing in other countries.

I. Advertising and the Economy

1. Since the last quarter of the nineteenth century,

Co-authored with Paul M. Sweezy. This essay was originally published in the Winter 1964 issue of *Science & Society* and is reprinted by permission. Copyright © 1964 by Science & Society, Inc.

American industry has constituted an oligopolistic system in which small numbers of large firms have been responsible for the bulk of their industries' output. At the present time, "the one-hundred-and-thirty-odd largest manufacturing corporations account for half of manufacturing output in the United States. The five hundred largest business corporations in this country embrace nearly two-thirds of all nonagricultural economic activity."[1]

2. Except during a few comparatively brief periods of war and postwar reconstruction, American business has been plagued by a persistent shortage of effective demand in relation to its productive potential. In the words of a marketing specialist: "The problem of business used to be how to manufacture and produce goods; but the principal problem has become now how to market or sell goods."[2]

3. Under oligopolistic conditions,, *price competition* is avoided as a response to the insufficiency of demand and other forms of sales effort are substituted. "The rivalries of the business world are nowadays as keen or keener than ever. Competition with respect to the quality of products and the services associated with them has increased. However, less stress is being placed by many of our larger businesses on price competition."[3] This is, if anything, an understatement.

4. Advertising *sensu stricto* should be considered as merely one species of the large genus of non-price-competitive devices. Perhaps equally important are spurious product differentiation, artificial physical and/or "moral" obsolescence, and the like; these are, however, for the most part rendered possible by advertising. In the words of the McGraw-Hill Department of Economics: "Today, the orientation of manufacturing companies is increasingly toward the market and away from production. In fact, this change has gone so far in some cases that the General Electric Company, as one striking example, now conceives itself to

be essentially a marketing rather than a production organization. *This thinking flows back through the structure of
the company to the point that marketing needs reach back
and dictate the arrangement and grouping of production
facilities.*"[4] In the following remarks, however, we confine
attention to mass-media advertising, both in view of the
Commission's stipulated terms of reference and because
such advertising taken by itself not only plays an important
part in the non-price-competitive sales effort but also serves
as an indispensable adjunct of most other sales strategems.
"The secular rise of advertising expenditures is a sign of
secular . . . decline of price competition."[5]

5. The growing "oligopolization" of the American economy has been paralleled by a corresponding expansion of
advertising. Expenditure upon newspaper and periodicals
advertising in 1890 amounted to over $76 million, about
ten times as great as similar expenditure at the time of the
Civil War. By 1929, it had climbed to over $1,100 million
and constituted 1.38 percent of National Income as against
.59 percent in 1890. This process gained momentum with
the appearance of new advertising media (radio and particularly television), so that at the present time business outlays
for advertising and related services (advertising agencies,
market research bureaus, public relations advisors, and the
like) exceed $15 billion annually (approximately 4 percent
of national income). It should be noted that this amount
does *not* include the costs of market research, designing for
advertising purposes, and the like carried on *within* the
producing or selling concerns themselves. While reliable
estimates on the latter are not available, $10 billion per
year is considered by experts to be a not unreasonable
figure.

6. In appraising the economic effects of advertising,
economics has traditionally followed the lead of Marshall
by distinguishing between "good" and "bad," "construc-

tive" and "combative" advertisements. Those in the former category are commended as providing useful information on new products and helping "to draw the attention of people to opportunities for buying or selling of which they may be willing to avail themselves."[6] Other types of advertising are condemned as a waste of resources, doing harm by adding to the imperfections of the competitive process, causing a distribution of income different from what it would be under more perfectly competitive conditions, and manipulating (and distorting) consumers' tastes and motivations.

7. The advent of the new advertising media (radio and television) and the concomitant proliferation of advertising, although not introducing any substantially new arguments into the *economic* discussion of the subject, lend emphasis to those previously employed. The defenders are able to point to the powerful spur to spending and consumption provided by modern advertising and to stress the resulting stimulation of mass production methods, the introduction of new products, and the consequent opening up of new investment opportunities. Occasionally, they also credit advertising with furnishing the media with financial means for valuable cultural activities such as broadcasting of classical music, presentation on television of good films, plays, and educational material.[7]

8. The economists who are critical of advertising deplore the now *massive* waste of material and human resources associated with the advertising process itself as well as with other forms of the non-price-competitive sales effort which it renders possible—the increasingly fraudulent product differentiation, less and less warranted and more and more costly model changes in consumers' durable goods, propagation of ever more superfluous gadgets, etc.

9. The debate between the critics and the defenders of advertising remains of necessity inconclusive in view of self-imposed limitations on the scope of the debate. The

critics' rejection of advertising generally is predicated upon the assumption that full employemnt would prevail in the absence of advertising. Then, indeed, the resources now devoted to advertising would be more usefully employed elsewhere since, as Chamberlin puts it, "as a result [of advertising] demand for the advertised product is increased, that for other products is correspondingly diminished."[8]

10. Defenders of advertising argue that by stimulating consumption and investment it plays an indispensable role in the functioning of the capitalist economy. On this basis of American experience, this argument appears to us to be sound. There can be little doubt, we think, that the chronic underutilization of resources which has plagued the United States for more than a generation now would have been a good deal more severe if it had not been for the spectacular growth of advertising during this period. If this is correct, it follows that attempts to abolish or curtail advertising could have seriously adverse effects *unless accompanied by comprehensive and effective planning for full and socially desirable employment.* This is a point which critics of advertising consistently neglect and which should certainly be given great weight in the formulation of new policies regarding advertising.

II. Advertising and the Consumer

11. In the appraisal of the mass media's overall impact on the public, opinions differ greatly. (See Section IV below.) There is more consensus among experts on the power of advertising to influence buying on the part of the consumer, although disagreement exists on the extent of that power.

12. The critics of advertising contend that advertising campaigns if sufficiently large, persistent, and unscrupulous (availing themselves of such methods as subliminal suggestion and the like) can sell to the consumer "almost

anything." This contention is supported by some of the most authoritative experts in marketing techniques, one of the eyes of the consumers. It does not necessarily mean superior in terms of objective value or according to laboratory standards," and reports that "studies . . . conducted in the last twelve years show conclusively that individuals are influenced by advertising without being aware of that influence. An individual is motivated to buy something by an ad, but he often does not know what motivated him."[9] The most striking examples of the capacity of advertising to generate demand for worthless or even harmful products have recently been provided in the area of pharmaceuticals, cosmetic products, and the like.[10]

13. The defenders of advertising, on the other hand, maintain that no amount of advertising, however conducted, can induce the consumer to buy a product which does not represent a useful innovation or is not better or cheaper than what is otherwise available in the market. As stated by Rosser Reeves, Chairman of the Board of Ted Bates & Co., one of the largest American advertising agencies, "If the product does not meet some existing desire or need of the consumer, the advertising will ultimately fail."[11] The case most frequently cited in support of this view is the Ford Motor Company's failure to establish a market for its Edsel automobile in spite of a vast outlay on advertising.

14. It is erroneous to seek to measure the impact of advertising on consumers by studying their responses to specific advertising campaigns. That impact can only be adequately assessed if consideration is given to the totality of biotic urges and social forces which is responsible for the formation of human wants in any given historical environment. By setting standards of values, by establishing criteria of success, by molding its members' fears and aspirations, society lays the foundations from which advertising as a

whole draws its lifeblood. The outcome of *individual* advertising campaigns is determined by a multitude of more or less fortuitous circumstances particular to each case.

15. One of the functions of advertising is the *reinforcement* of the socially and/or biotically determined wants and preferences of consumers. The desire to "keep up with the Joneses," to own the largest or the newest automobile, to furnish one's house with the most recently manufactured gadgets, cannot be attributed to advertising; it stems from the general "climate" prevailing in society. Advertising, however, intensifies these propensities and facilitates their gratification. "Madison Avenue . . . serves as alarm clock for America's sleeping desires."[1][2]

16. Advertising provides the consumer with *ex post* rationalization of behavior which may be unacceptable to him on other grounds. While tobacco, liquor, profligacy may be rejected by an individual on rational grounds, the recurrent reassurances by advertising assuage his misgivings about indulging in smoking, drinking, and the like, despite his own disapproval.[1][3]

III. Advertising and the Mass Media

17. With the exception of the relatively insignificant sprinkling of non-commercial FM radio stations, *all* radio and television broadcasting stations in the United States are privately owned and depend for financial support on advertising revenue. Newspapers and periodicals, on the advertising services of which approximately 27 percent of all advertising outlay is spent, rely for more than two-thirds of their budgets on the sale of advertising space.

18. All media solicit advertising, and most provide advertisers with services of various kinds, maintaining so-called merchandising departments which collaborate with advertisers in making decisions on the timing and structure of their advertising campaigns.

19. Since the volume of advertising and the price charged for space (or time) are determined by the media's access to the public (circulation of newspapers, viewing or listening "ratings" of the stations), the need for advertising revenue compels the media to cater to as wide population strata as possible. This not only militates against too much "highbrow" or even "middlebrow" material, but provides a strong impetus to a wide coverage of sensational material such as crime, sexual deviations, and the like.

20. The influence of advertisers on the editorial policies of the media is not readily ascertained. It is important to realize, however, that there is no need to assume any nefarious collusion between advertisers and media policy-makers to explain the uniformly conservative orientation of the latter's editorial positions. This conservatism is adequately explained by the fact that the owners and executives controlling the media are in no respect different, as far as basic attitudes, mentality, and political orientation are concerned, from the owners and executives of the advertising concerns.

21. The program designs and editorial policies of the media are subject to two conflicting pressures. Advertisers, naturally seeking to reach the largest possible audience, are anxious to avoid antagonizing any prospective customers and therefore prefer the media to follow a policy of conservative and non-controversial programming and editorializing. Yet the public's interest in the media's offerings is more likely to be aroused if the programs contain new material or are rendered more absorbing by the tensions resulting from debates, contests, and rivalries. The solution habitually adopted by the media's managements is to admit such tensions in *immaterial* areas: quiz shows, sports, competitions among performers, and debates on more or less innocuous public issues or among speakers of not too widely divergent persuasions.

22. Economics of scale realized in efforts to secure *national* advertising accounts have combined with the economies of scale resulting from centralized news gathering, features buying, and newsprint procurement to advance rapidly mergers and concentration of media on a *national* scale. Strictly *local* media—primarily newspapers, catering to the needs of local business—have gone through a massive merger movement on the local level, with the result that a large and ever growing number of small and middle-sized localities in the United States have only one newspaper (sometimes with a morning and afternoon edition). The consequences of this to the formation of public opinion and to the functioning of the democratic process are self-evident.

IV. Advertising and Values

23. It is crucial to recognize that advertising and mass media programs sponsored by and related to it do not to any significant extent *create* values or *produce* attitudes but rather *reflect* existing values and *exploit* prevailing attitudes. In so doing they undoubtedly re-enforce them and contribute to their propagation, but they cannot be considered to be their taproot. There is wide consensus among specialists that advertising campaigns succeed not if they seek to *change* people's attitudes but if they manage to find, by means of motivation research and similar procedures, a way of linking up with *existing* attitudes.

24. Status-seeking and snobbery; social, racial, and sexual discrimination; egotism and unrelatedness to others; envy, gluttony, avarice, and ruthlessness in the drive for self-advancement—all of these attitudes are not *generated* by advertising but are made use of and appealed to in the contents of advertising material.

25. The debasement of cultural standards and the substitution of *Kitsch* for art in music, the plastic arts, and

literature do not *stem* from advertising, although advertising has become the chief patron and Maecenas of the *Kitsch* producers inundating the market. To the (not inconsiderable) extent to which the tastes, preferences, and needs of the patrons influence the work of the artist, the advertisers can be held responsible for the corruption of the artistic talent which they purchase.

26. Factors referred to in paragraph 21 have to be borne in mind in considering the influence of advertising and design. Although the desire to reach and influence the largest possible audiences motivates the promotion of least controversial, hackneyed, and corny productions, the drive to expand sales and to create "moral" obsolescence of products stimulates the introduction and promotion of new and sometimes esthetically valuable articles and models. The search for a compromise between those two requirements leads usually to the cheapening and "watering down" of genuine art or to an outright perversion of the effects of artistic masterworks by placing them in wholly incompatible contexts (e.g., the use of paintings by Giotto in advertisements of travel agencies or of medieval architecture in the promotion of hotels).

27. It is sometimes argued that advertising really does little harm because no one believes it any more anyway. We consider this view to be erroneous. The *greatest* damage done by advertising is precisely that it incessantly demonstrates the prostitution of men and women who lend their intellects, their voices, their artistic skills to purposes in which they themselves do not believe, and that it teaches "the essential meaninglessness of all creations of the mind: words, images, and ideas."[14] The real danger from advertising is that it helps to shatter and ultimately destroy our most precious non-material possessions: the confidence in the existence of meaningful purposes of human activity and the respect for the integrity of man.

28. The causal nexus explaining the nature of values,

prevailing standards of culture, and the quality of forth-coming artistic production cannot stop at advertising. It leads rather through advertising to the underlying structure of the market- and profit-determined economic and social order.

29. The failure to recognize the essentially instrumental, mediating part played by advertising largely accounts for the inconclusiveness of the frequently undertaken attempts to explore its effects and impact. Advertising, being a reinforcing and proliferating mechanism, can neither be held responsible nor be absolved of all responsiblity for prevailing attitudes, cultural standards, and values.

30. The trouble with advertising is *not* that it promotes conformity to certain norms of life and behavior. The trouble is that advertising of necessity promotes conformity to norms that, by any rational standard, are worthless or humanly destructive.

V. Conclusions

31. It is beyond the scope of this paper to discuss the structural changes in the economic and social order which would be required to eliminate the negative impact of advertising on the moral and cultural standards of society. It must never be lost from sight that advertising is a part of the *modus operandi* of profit-making business enterprise under present-day conditions. As Pigou clearly recognized many years ago, the only way it could be "removed altogether" would be "if conditions of monopolistic competition were destroyed."[15] America's long experience with antitrust laws has proved conclusively that this is impossible within the framework of a capitalist society. It follows that the elimination of advertising as we know it today would require the elimination of capitalism. This is a conclusion which socialists should find neither surprising nor disturbing.

32. If action is to be confined to the field of advertising

proper, it should be directed not at the enterprises which buy the advertising but at the media which carry it. The maintenance of non-commercial radio and television, strictly refusing to accept advertisements, takes care of one large aspect of the problem.

33. Controlling the contents of advertisements in newspapers and periodicals presents formidable difficulties. Any measures in that direction risk coming into conflict with principles of freedom of speech and expression. Legislation could be promulgated, however, rendering the publication of mendacious and misleading advertisements subject to serious penalties. The principal problem to be solved in this connection is the *enforcement* of such statutes.

34. American experience suggests that the most important condition for successful curbing of advertising abuses is placing the burden of proof not on the government but on the advertiser. Specifically, a government board entrusted with the supervision of advertising should be entitled to ban certain advertisements in view of their contents, unless the affected firm can prove the truthfulness of its advertised claims. The American arrangement in which the opposite procedure is followed, i.e., the advertiser is permitted to continue publicizing his unwarranted claims until the government agency involved can satisfy the courts of their groundlessness, leads to endless red tape and litigation which defeat the entire endeavor.

35. It should be possible to rule out *a priori* the advertising of certain kinds of products. Just as it is prohibited to advertise and sell narcotics, so the advertising of tobacco, liquor, and other products that are harmful could be outlawed.

Notes

1. E.S. Mason, "Introduction," in E.S. Mason, ed., *The Corporation in Modern Society* (Cambridge, Mass., 1959), p. 5.

2. Steuart Henderson Britt, *The Spenders* (New York-Toronto-London, 1960), p. 52.

3. Arthur F. Burns, *Prosperity Without Inflation* (New York, 1957), p. 83.

4. Dexter Merriam Keezer and associates, *New Forces in American Business* (New York, 1959), p. 97.

5. T. Scitovsky, *Welfare and Competition* (Chicago, 1951), p. 401 n.

6. Alfred Marshall, *Industry and Trade,* p. 305.

7. Paul A. Samuelson, *Economics* (5th ed., New York, 1961), p. 138.

8. E.H. Chamberlin, *Theory of Monopolistic Competition* (Cambridge, Mass., 1933), p. 120.

9. Louis Cheskin, *Why People Buy* (New York, 1959), pp. 54 ff.

10. James Cook, *Remedies and Rackets* (New York, 1958), *passim;* Meyer Weinberg, *TV in America* (New York, 1962), *passim.*

11. Rosser Reeves, *Reality in Advertising* (New York, 1961), p. 141.

12. James Kelly, "In Defense of Madison Avenue," *New York Times Magazine,* December 23, 1956.

13. Leon Festinger, *A Theory of Cognitive Dissonance* (Evanston, Ill., 1957), *passim.*

14. Leo Marx, "Notes on the Culture of the New Capitalism," *Monthly Review* (July-August 1959), p. 116.

15. A.C. Pigou, *Economics of Welfare* (4th ed., London, 1938), p. 199.

Social and Economic Planning

When I was invited to comment on the papers of Professors Bettelheim and Myrdal, I was instructed to pay special attention to planning in my own country. In the case of the United States, however, following this most reasonable directive runs into a major obstacle: it necessitates speaking about something that hardly exists. If I have decided, nevertheless, to be a disciplined participant in the work of the Congress and to comply as best as I can with the terms of the invitation, it is because the most tempting avenues of evasion have been effectively barred by Professors Bettelheim and Myrdal. If I should seek a way out by talking about economic and social planning where it actually takes place or where it is at least seriously attempted, I would find it difficult to add to Professor Bettelheim's admirable account of the principal problems encountered in planning for economic and social growth. At the same time, evading the terms of the invitation by *not* talking about planning where it neither takes place nor is seriously attempted has been made impossible by Professor Myrdal's provocative remarks on the advanced capitalist countries, remarks which—I think—should not be al-

This is the text of a talk delivered at the Fourth World Congress of the International Sociological Association (1959) in Stresa, Italy. It comments on papers which had been presented by Charles Bettelheim and Gunnar Myrdal. The paper was first published in the March 1965 issue of *Monthly Review*. Copyright © 1965 by Monthly Review, Inc.

lowed to pass unchallenged. What I have in mind is Professor Myrdal's contention that "in the last half-century all the rich countries have become democratic 'welfare states' with fairly explicit goals of economic development, full employment, increased social and economic equality, etc.," and that in these countries "the state is increasingly involved in regulating the national economy," albeit "planning there takes on a pragmatic and less comprehensive and programmatic character." I would like to submit, first, that this statement is applicable only partly and only with major qualifications to at least one rich country, the United States; and second, that, even to the extent that it is true, it bears little relation to the fundamental issues involved in genuine social and economic planning.

The performance of an economic system can be judged by two distinct, if closely interrelated, criteria. One is the extent to which available productive resources are utilized and, in particular, the extent to which all those who are able to work and are willing to accept employment at the going rate of pay have an opportunity to find jobs. This might be called the criterion of "fullness of employment." It is apparently Professor Myrdal's view that satisfying this criterion is an established goal of American national policy, and that the government is able to implement this goal in practice. This opinion is presumably based partly on the existence of legislation purportedly directing the administration in power to take measures necessary for the maintenance of full employment, and partly on the often reiterated claims of an influential school of economists that (a) the *theoretical* problem of an effective full employment policy has been solved and (b) the tools required for the conduct of such a policy have been created.

In my view, neither Professor Myrdal's view nor the grounds on which it rests will stand serious examination. In the first place, it must be realized that the wording of the

Employment Act of 1946—and this is the statute which is usually thought of in this connection—is, to put it mildly, ambiguous. It declares it to be a continuous responsibility of the government "to use all practicable means ... for the purpose of creating and maintaining in a manner calculated to foster and promote free competitive enterprise ... maximum employment." The level of employment to be striven for is thus clearly no higher than will "foster and promote free competitive enterprise," while "free competitive enterprise" has become the usual urbane and tactful designation for monopolistic and oligopolistic business. What has to be noted is that the Act calls for an economic policy aiming at something quite different from the starry-eyed reformer's notion of full employment. The nature of and the rationale for this policy have been stated explicitly by *Business Week* (May 17, 1952): "Unemployment remains too low for the work force to have flexibility. Anytime the jobless total is less than 2 million, even common labor is scarce. Many employers must tend to hoard skills. And certainly, the labor unions are in the driver's seat in wage negotiations. More workers can be had, to be sure. But only at considerable cost. And they probably wouldn't be of the skills most desired. There's no assurance against inflation like a pool of genuine unemployment. That is a blunt, hard-headed statement, but a fact." Thus while a case can be made for the proposition that national policy in the United States is at the present time committed to the prevention of major catastrophes like the Great Depression of the 1930's, there is nothing on the statute books or in the pronouncements of those responsible for the conduct of economic affairs to suggest that genuine and sustained full employment is to be sought, let alone maintained in practice. It would be more appropriate to say that what the government's efforts are directed at is the maintainance of a condition that is indispensable to the customary functioning of the capitalist system: the existence of a permanent and sizable "industrial reserve army."

This may indeed be the best that can be attained within the general economic and social framework of an advanced capitalist country. For theoretical solutions arrived at by abstracting from *essential* aspects of the phenomenon under consideration can hardly be expected to provide either adequate understanding or meaningful predictions of actual developments. And it *is* an essential characteristic of the American economy that it is increasingly dominated by a relatively small number of monopolistic and/or oligopolistic enterprises. This has a number of important consequences which seriously impair the applicability of Keynesian economics. Since discussing all the relevant considerations would take me too far afield, I must confine myself to drawing your attention to what I consider to be the most important.

The advancing concentration of output in the hands of a shrinking number of giant corporations enjoying vast monopoly power leads to a continual expansion of the economic surplus currently generated by the economy. Although a considerable part of this surplus is absorbed by the proliferating costs of selling, advertising, product variation, and the like, both internal and "extra-mural" investment of corporate business fails normally to attain a volume sufficiently large to utilize the "unwasted" share of the surplus that would be forthcoming under full employment conditions. Under such circumstances even the maintenance of a socially and politically indispensable level of employment calls for large (and increasing) compensatory spending on the part of the government. It is in this connection, and I may add in this regard only, that Professor Myrdal is justified in speaking about the increasing "involvement" of the state in regulating the national economy.

Even so, when confronted with the need for *increasing*

government spending, the policy prescriptions that follow from Keynesian economics run into serious difficulties. The principal reason for this is that those prescriptions refer essentially to a *competitive* capitalist economy and presuppose responses to changes in economic variables which could perhaps be reasonably expected in a competitive system, but which cannot be counted on with any degree of confidence in an economy permeated with monopoly and oligopoly. For it is an outstanding feature of monopoly that rising prices lead very slowly—if at all—to an expansion of output, be it via the establishment of additional firms in an industry or via the expansion of the existing enterprises. Consequently, an economy in which a large part of output is accounted for by monopolistic and oligopolistic producers is marked by an asymmetry which may not have been entirely absent under competitive conditions but which grows increasingly pronounced with concentration of capital: while declines of demand (unless assuming major proportions) do not lead to declines of prices but rather to reductions of output (and employment), increases in demand (unless assuming major proportions) tend to cause price increases rather than larger output (and employment). From this follows, however, that such fiscal policy measures as might be undertaken with a view to raising sagging demand to the level required for the maintenance of full employment do not necessarily lead to full employment but produce inflation instead.

For a variety of reasons, chronic or "creeping" inflation is an unacceptable state of affairs. Even if relatively harmless to a certain segment of Big Business, which is able to shift cost increases onto the consumer, it threatens the stability of the entire system, not only promoting speculation and increasing the danger of "boom and bust," but undermining the credit structure of the economy, interfering with rational calculation of business, depleting its working capital, and adversely influencing export trade. At the same time, by cutting into the real income of wide strata of the population, inflation creates sources of social unrest and endangers political equilibrium. The avoidance of inflation thus becomes a common interest of the capitalist class as a whole, and overshadows as a tenet of economic policy the concern with full employment. Not that—abstractly speaking—inflationary pressures could not be dealt with be means of various physical controls. Such controls, however, have always been anathema to business, small and large.

But in denying the ability of advanced capitalist countries to live up to the criterion of "fullness of employment," we need not rely solely on theory. The historical record speaks for itself. In the 1930's—the years of President Roosevelt's full-employment-minded New Deal administration—officially recorded (and seriously underestimated) unemployment was in only one year (1937) below nine million. After the Second World War—during what C. Wright Mills has so aptly called the years of the Great American Celebration—in at least six of the fourteen years (1948-1949, 1953-1954, 1957-1958) government-reported unemployment was in the neighborhood of five million, and according to trade union sources no less than six million.

The performance of the system is still less satisfactory when it is judged by the second standard by which it needs to be appraised. This is the composition and allocation of the social output; what I propose to call the criterion of "goodness of employment." In this respect, its wastefulness and irrationality are even more striking than is its inability to provide adequate employment opporunties. For even such levels of employment as have prevailed since the Second World War have been associated during nearly the entire period with massive government spending for military purposes. With the military budget amounting at the present time to more than $40 billion, it has been estimated that as much as $100 billion worth of output, or over 20 percent of the Gross National Product, is attributable directly and indirectly to the upkeep of the military establishment. Without this vast outlet for its overflowing economic surplus, the system would long since have bogged down in depression and severe under-employment of human and material resources.

It could, of course, be argued that these tremendous outlays on armaments cannot be taken as evidence of the irrationality and wastefulness of monopoly capitalism, since (a) these expenditures are caused by the international situation, and (b) in the absence of military spending the resources devoted to war could have found alternative, useful employment. Neither argument seems to me to be conclusive. With regard to the former, Peter F. Drucker put his finger on the nub of the matter when he wrote, "In international affairs . . . it is quite possible that it is defense technology which is causing the basic international tension rather than that the tension is responsible for our defense efforts." And the latter falls to the ground in the light of the stupendous waste in the American economy which by no stretch of imagination could be attributed to factors "exogenous" to the basic structure and the working principles of advanced capitalism.

Given available information and the choice of research projects cultivated by today's social science, it is impossible to arrive at an accurate estimate of the aggregate volume of waste taking place in the American economy. But illuminating as such a calculation would be, it is still more important to pierce the ever-thickening fog surrounding the *explanation* of the massive squandering of resources observed on every side, and to identify clearly the forces which have established and which continually reproduce the prevailing pattern of resource utilization. All the pronouncements of the witting and the unwitting apologists of the status quo notwithstanding, these forces are neither the high level of industrialization and/or "affluence" attained in the United States, nor are they to be found by superficial reflections concerning "conventional wisdom," "keeping up the with Joneses," or psychic propensities allegedly peculiar to the American race. At the bottom of the matter is the structure and *modus operandi* of the giant corporation setting the tone of economic life in the United States, its never-ceasing drive for larger profits, and the output, price, and selling policies which this drive necessitates.

I have mentioned earlier the surplus absorption by advertising outlays, selling costs, expenses of product variation, and the like. While the magnitudes at issue are impressive by themselves—over $11 billion are spent annually on advertising alone, and probably even more on other aspects of the sales effort—the cumulative effect of the processes involved defies any attempt at a short description. It reflects itself in the structure of consumers' tastes, in the state of education, in the development of human personalities and relations, in one word: in the entire cultural condition of the nation. It can be studied with all the required concreteness in the prevailing allocation and husbandry of human and material resources. While (in 1956) automobile transportation absorbed $27 billion, education (private and public) commanded $15; while $3 billion worth of resources were used for recreational goods of all kinds, $600 million were devoted to books; while basic research was assigned $500 million, the services of stockbrokers and investment counselors were valued at $900 million. And the public mentality, social consciousness, and human posture generated by this cultural condition are perhaps most strikingly revealed by the fact that the present curtailment of grain production in the United States—attained by means of administrative controls and of special bonus payments to farmers who keep down their output—has been estimated at a quantity which fairly closely approximates the caloric deficit for the entire underfed part of the world population.

Nor is this staggering waste accompanied "merely" by unspeakable misery, disease, and starvation in the under-developed countries; it coexists with massive and persistent poverty in the United States itself. In his essay on the distribution of income in 1957 (*Monthly Review*, July-August, 1959) Leo Huberman concisely describes the pre-vailing situation. It emerges from this account beyond any possible doubt that even at the present time, after two decades of relatively high employment, and after the widely heralded "income revolution," behind the glittering facade of the "affluent society" there is still one-third of the nation which is ill-fed, ill-housed, and ill-clothed. And this one-third becomes two-thirds if one considers not the entire population but only its colored component. One might add that in addition to this, all of society is ill-educated, exposed to a debilitating barrage of fraudulent politics, stupefying enter-tainment, inspirational rackets, and demoralizing press and comic books.

At the same time the notion that the government is seeking to stem this tide and is dedicated to the goal of advancing public welfare and economic and social equality is hardly more than wishful thinking. As pointed out by Paul M. Sweezy (in the same issue of *Monthly Review*), "it should never be forgotten that quantitatively the only really new feature of post-World War II capitalism [in the United States] is the vastly increased size of the arms budget. All other government spending is about the same percentage of the Gross National Product as in 1929."

What remains then but a mirage of the "democratic welfare state"? We must go further, however, and stress that even if certain welfare measures were actually to become part and parcel of government policy under capitalism, even if some of the most glaring manifestations of irrationality, waste, injus-tice, and callous indifference to human suffering were to be eradicated with a view to strengthening the basic institutions of monopoly capitalism—this would have little in common with genuine economic and social planning. For what is at issue in planning is not patchwork aiming at some improvement of the performance of the existing economic and social system, but a change in its very foundations, a reorientation of the energies and activities of society. The purpose and meaning of planning can only be attainment of a condition in which society is enabled to make *conscious* decisions about matters affecting its entire existence. Under a system of economic and social planning, the intensity of society's productive effort, the apportionment of its fruits as between present and future comsumption can no longer be left to be determined by the mechanism of profit maximization and all it implies, but are made subject to the fully considered choice of free people. Aid to poor nations, outlays on education, health, arts and sciences become no longer dependent on the tender mercies of vested interests and on the outcome of the higgling and bargaining of those who consider all devotion of resources to such ends to entail deplorable—if often unavoidable—deductions from profit, but are decided upon by society in the light of objective needs and possibilities. And the cultural life of society, the molding of the characters, propensities, tastes of men are no longer entrusted to the market and to corporate executives and their advertisers and public relations officials, but become the foremost concern of society as a whole, of its intellectual, scientific, and artistic leadership.

It would seem to me that is incumbent upon social science to devote its best energies to the clarification of these vital issues. What is required for this purpose is a resolute return of social science to its sources: the great tradition of social criticism and of unremitting search for the principles of and the road to a better social order. This calls for a systematic struggle against the fetishes, misconceptions, and superficialities which obstruct people's views of social reality and destroy their awareness of the indispensable conditions and prerequisites for their growth and development. But the successful conduct of this effort is predicated on our breaking with the routine of the so-called behavioral sciences, with the timid acceptance of the prevailing "values" as if they were eternal immutable verities. We must acknowledge that the commitment of social science is not "the recognition that actually certain people make certain evaluations"—as suggested by Professor Myrdal—but that our obligation, and indeed our sole *raison d'être*, is to comprehend the social reasons why these "evaluations" are what they are, and to do all we can to change them and to develop them in the direction of humanism and reason. If we should not undertake this task, then who should? And if it should not be done now, then when?

V
On the Political Economy of Growth

On the Political Economy of Backwardness

The capitalist mode of production and the social and political order concomitant with it provided, during the latter part of the eighteenth century, and still more during the entire nineteenth century, a framework for a continuous and, in spite of cyclical disturbances and setbacks, momentous expansion of productivity and material welfare. The relevant facts are well known and call for no elaboration. Yet this material (and cultural) progress was not only spotty in time but most unevenly distributed in space. It was confined to the Western world, and did not affect even all of this territorially and demographically relatively small sector of the inhabited globe. Germany and Austria, Britain and France, some smaller countries in Western Europe, and the United States and Canada occupied places in the neighborhood of the sun. The vast expanses and the multitude of inhabitants of Eastern Europe, Spain and Portugal, Italy and the Balkans, Latin America and Asia, not to speak of Africa, remained in the deep shadow of backwardness and squalor, of stagnation and misery.

Tardy and skimpy as the benefits of capitalism may have

This essay originally appeared in the *Manchester School of Economic and Social Studies,* Vol. XX, January 1952. It is reprinted by permission of Klaus Reprint Limited.

been with respect to the lower classes even in most of the leading industrial countries, they were all but negligible in the less privileged parts of the world. There productivity remained low, and rapid increases in population pushed living standards from bad to worse. The dreams of the prophets of capitalist harmony remained on paper. Capital either did not move from countries where its marginal productivity was low to countries where it could be expected to be high, or if it did it moved there mainly in order to extract profits from backward countries that frequently accounted for a lion's share of the increments in total output caused by the original investments. Where an increase in the aggregate national product of an underdeveloped country took place, the existing distribution of income prevented this increment from raising the living standards of the broad masses of the population. Like all general statements, this one is obviously open to criticism based on particular cases. There were, no doubt, colonies and dependencies where the populations profited from inflow of foreign capital. These benefits, however, were few and far between, while exploitation and stagnation were the prevailing rule.

But if Western capitalism failed to improve materially the lot of the peoples inhabiting most backward areas, it accomplished something that profoundly affected the social and political conditions in underdeveloped countries. It introduced there, with amazing rapidity, all the economic and social tensions inherent in the capitalist order. It effectively disrupted whatever was left of the "feudal" coherence of the backward societies. It substituted market contracts for such paternalistic relationships as still survived from century to century. It reoriented the partly or wholly self-sufficient economies of agricultural countries toward the production of marketable commodities. It linked their economic fate with the vagaries of the world market and connected it with the fever curve of international price movements.

A *complete* substitution of capitalist market rationality for the rigidities of feudal or semi-feudal servitude would have represented, in spite of all the pains of transition, an important step in the direction of progress. Yet all that happened was that the age-old exploitation of the population of underdeveloped countries by their domestic over-lords was freed of the mitigating constraints inherited from the feudal tradition. This superimposition of business mores over ancient oppression by landed gentries resulted in compounded exploitation, more outrageous corruption, and more glaring injustice.

Nor is this by any means the end of the story. Such export of capital and capitalism as has taken place had not only far-reaching implications of a social nature. It was accompanied by important physical and technical processes. Modern machines and products of advanced industries reached the poverty-stricken backyards of the world. To be sure, most, if not all, of these machines worked for their foreign owners—or at least were believed by the population to be working for no one else—and the new refined appurtenances of the good life belonged to foreign businessmen and their domestic counterparts. The bonanza that was capitalism, the fullness of things that was modern industrial civilization, were crowding the display windows—they were protected by barbed wire from the anxious grip of the starving and desperate man in the street.

But they drastically changed his outlook. Broadening and deepening his economic horizon, they aroused aspirations, envies, and hopes. Young intellectuals filled with zeal and patriotic devotion traveled from the underdeveloped lands to Berlin and London, to Paris and New York, and returned home with the "message of the possible."

Fascinated by the advances and accomplishments observed

in the centers of modern industry, they developed, and propagandized, the image of what could be attained in their home countries under a more rational economic and social order. The dissatisfaction with the stagnation (or at best, barely perceptible growth) that ripened gradually under the still-calm political and social surface was given an articulate expression. This dissatisfaction was not nurtured by a comparison of reality with a vision of a socialist society. It found sufficient fuel in the confrontation of what was actually happening with what could be accomplished under capitalist institutions of the Western type.

The establishment of such institutions was, however, beyond the reach of the tiny middle classes of most backward areas. The inherited backwardness and poverty of their countries never gave them an opportunity to gather the economic strength, the insight, and the self-confidence needed for the assumption of a leading role in society. For centuries under feudal rule they themselves assimilated the political, moral, and cultural values of the dominating class.

While in advanced countries such as France or Great Britain the economically ascending middle classes developed at an early stage a new rational world outlook, which they proudly opposed to the medieval obscurantism of the feudal age, the poor, fledgling bourgeoisie of the underdeveloped countries sought nothing but accommodation to the prevailing order. Living in societies based on privilege, they strove for a share in the existing sinecures. They made political and economic deals with their domestic feudal overlords or with powerful foreign investors, and what industry and commerce developed in backward areas in the course of the last hundred years was rapidly molded in the straitjacket of monopoly—the plutocratic partner of the aristocratic rulers. What resulted was an economic and political amalgam combining the worst features of both worlds—feudalism and capitalism—and blocking effectively all possibilities of economic growth.

It is quite conceivable that a "conservative" exit from this impasse might have been found in the course of time. A younger generation of enterprising and enlightened business-men and intellectuals allied with moderate leaders of workers and peasants—a "Young Turk" movement of some sort—might have succeeded in breaking the deadlock, in loosening the hidebound social and political structure of their countries and in creating the institutional arrange-ments indispensable for a measure of social and economic progress.

Yet in our rapid age history accorded no time for such a gradual transition. Popular pressures for an amelioration of economic and social conditions, or at least for some perceptible movement in that direction, steadily gained in intensity. To be sure, the growing restiveness of the underprivileged was not directed against the ephemeral principles of a hardly yet existing capitalist order. Its objects were parasitic feudal overlords appropriating large slices of the national product and wasting them on extravagant living; a government machinery protecting and abetting the dominant interests; wealthy businessmen reaping immense profits and not utilizing them for productive purposes; last but not least, foreign colonizers extracting or believed to be extracting vast gains from their "developmental" operations.

This popular movement had thus essentially bourgeois, democratic, anti-feudal, anti-imperialist tenets. It found outlets in agrarian egalitarianism; it incorporated "muck-raker" elements denouncing monopoly; it strove for national independence and freedom from foreign exploita-tion.

For the native capitalist middle-classes to assume the leadership of these popular forces and to direct them into the channels of bourgeois democracy—as had happened in Western Europe—they had to identify themselves with the common man. They had to break away from the political, economic, and ideological leadership of the feudal crust and the monopolists allied with it; and they had to demonstrate to the nation as a whole that they had the knowledge, the courage, and the determination to undertake and to carry to victorious conclusion the struggle for economic and social improvement.

In hardly any underdeveloped country were the middle classes capable of living up to this historical challenge. Some of the reasons for this portentous failure, reasons connected with the internal make-up of the business class itself, were briefly mentioned above. Of equal importance was, however, an "outside" factor. It was the spectacular growth of the international labor movement in Europe that offered the popular forces in backward areas ideological and political leadership that was denied to them by the native bourgeoisie. It pushed the goals and targets of the popular movements far beyond their original limited objectives.

This liaison of labor radicalism and populist revolt painted on the wall the imminent danger of a social revolution. Whether this danger was real or imaginary matters very little. What was essential is that the awareness of this threat effectively determined political and social action. It destroyed whatever chances there were of the capitalist classes joining and leading the popular anti-feudal, anti-monopolist movement. By instilling a mortal fear of expropriation and extinction in the minds of *all* property-owning groups, the rise of socialist radicalism, and in particular the Bolshevik Revolution in Russia, tended to drive all more or less privileged, more or less well-to-do elements in the society into one "counter-revolutionary" coalition. Whatever differences and antagonisms existed between large and small landowners, between monopolistic and competitive business, between liberal bourgeois and reactionary feudal overlords, between domestic and foreign interests, were largely submerged on all important occasions by the overriding *common* interest in staving off socialism.

The possibility of solving the economic and political deadlock prevailing in the underdeveloped countries on lines of a progressive capitalism all but disappeared. Entering the alliance with all other segments of the ruling class, the capitalist middle classes yielded one strategic position after another. Afraid that a quarrel with the landed gentry might be exploited by the radical populist movement, the middle classes abandoned all progressive attitudes in agrarian matters. Afraid that a conflict with the church and the military might weaken the political authority of the government, the middle classes moved away from all liberal and pacifist currents. Afraid that hostility toward foreign interests might deprive them of foreign support in a case of a revolutionary emergency, the native capitalists deserted their previous anti-imperialist, nationalist platforms.

The peculiar mechanisms of political interaction characteristic of all underdeveloped (and perhaps not only underdeveloped) countries thus operated at full speed. The aboriginal failure of the middle classes to provide inspiration and leadership to the populist masses pushed those masses into the camp of socialist radicalism. The growth of radicalism pushed the middle classes into an alliance with the aristocratic and monopolistic reaction. This alliance, cemented by common interest and common fear, pushed the populist forces still further along the road of radicalism and revolt. The outcome was a polarization of society with very little left between the poles. By permitting this polarization to develop, by abandoning the common man and resigning the task of reorganizing society on new, progressive lines, the capitalist middle classes threw away their historical chance of assuming effective control over the destinies of their nations, and of directing the gathering popular storm against the fortresses of feudalism and reaction. Its blazing fire turned thus against the entirety of existing economic and social institutions.

The economic and political order maintained by the ruling coalition of owning classes finds itself invariably at odds with all the urgent needs of the underdeveloped countries. Neither the social fabric that it embodies nor the institutions that rest upon it are conducive to progressive economic development. The only way to provide for economic growth and to prevent a continuous deterioration of living standards (apart from mass emigration unacceptable to other countries) is to assure a steady increase of total output—at least large enough to offset the rapid growth of population.

An obvious source of such an increase is the utilization of available unutilized or underutilized resources. A large part of this reservoir of dormant productive potentialities is the vast multitude of entirely unemployed or ineffectively employed manpower. There is no way of employing it usefully in agriculture, where the marginal productivity of labor tends to zero. They could be provided with opportunities for productive work only by transfer to industrial pursuits. For this to be feasible, large investments in industrial plant and facilities have to be undertaken. Under prevailing conditions such investments are not forthcoming for a number of important and interrelated reasons.

With a very uneven distribution of a very small aggregate income (and wealth), large individual incomes exceeding what could be regarded as "reasonable" requirements for current consumption accrue as a rule to a relatively small group of high-income receivers. Many of them are large landowners maintaining a feudal style of life with large outlays on housing, servants, travel, and other luxuries. Their "requirements for consumption" are so high that there is only a little room for savings. Only relatively insignificant amounts are left to be spent on improvements of agricultural estates.

Other members of the "upper crust" receiving incomes markedly surpassing "reasonable" levels of consumption are wealthy businessmen. For social reasons briefly mentioned above, their consumption too is very much larger than it would have been were they brought up in the puritan tradition of a bourgeois civilization. Their drive to accumulate and to expand their enterprises is continuously counteracted by the urgent desire to imitate in their living habits the socially dominant "old families," to prove by their conspicuous outlays on the amenities of rich life that they are socially (and therefore also politically) not inferior to their aristocratic partners in the ruling coalition.

But if this tendency curtails the volume of savings that could have been amassed by the urban high-income receivers, their will to reinvest their funds in productive enterprises is effectively curbed by a strong reluctance to damage their carefully erected monopolistic market positions through creation of additional productive capacity, and by absence of suitable investment opportunities—paradoxical as this may sound with reference to underdeveloped countries.

The deficiency of investment opportunities stems to a large extent from the structure and the limitations of the existing effective demand. With very low living standards, the bulk of the aggregate money income of the population is spent on food and relatively primitive items of clothing and household necessities. These are available at low prices, and investment of large funds in plant and facilities that could produce this type of commodity more cheaply rarely promises attractive returns. Nor does it appear profitable to develop major enterprises whose output would cater to the requirements of the rich. Large as their individual purchases of various luxuries may be, their aggregate spending on each of them is not sufficient to support the development of an elaborate luxury industry—particularly since the "snob" character of prevailing tastes renders only imported luxury articles true marks of social distinction.

Finally, the limited demand for investment goods precludes the building up of a machinery or equipment industry. Such mass consumption goods as are lacking, and such quantities of luxury goods as are purchased by the well-to-do, as well as the comparatively small quantities of investment goods needed by industry, are thus imported from abroad in exchange for domestic agricultural products and raw materials.

This leaves the expansion of exportable raw-materials output as a major outlet for investment activities. There the possibilities are greatly influenced, however, by the technology of the production of most raw materials as well as by the nature of the markets to be served. Many raw materials, in particular oil, metals, and certain industrial crops, have to be produced on a large scale if costs are to be kept low and satisfactory returns assured. Large-scale production, however, calls for large investments, so large indeed as to exceed the potentialities of the native capitalists in backward countries. Production of raw materials for a distant market entails, moreover, much larger risks than those encountered in domestic business. The difficulty of foreseeing accurately such things as receptiveness of the world markets, prices obtainable in competition with other countries, volume of output in other parts of the world, etc., sharply reduces the interest of native capitalists in these lines of business. They become to a predominant extent the domain of foreigners who, financially stronger, have at the same time much closer contacts with foreign outlets of their products.

The shortage of investible funds and the lack of investment opportunities represent two aspects of the same problem. A great number of investment projects, unprofitable under prevailing conditions, could be most promising in a general environment of economic expansion.

In backward areas a new industrial venture must frequently, if not always, break virgin ground. It has no functioning economic system to draw upon. It has to organize with its own efforts not only the productive process *within* its own confines, but it must provide in addition for all the necessary *outside* arrangements essential to its operations. It does not enjoy the benefits of "external economies."

There can be no doubt that the absence of external economies, the inadequacy of the economic milieu in underdeveloped countries, constituted everywhere an important deterrent to investment in industrial projects. There is no way of rapidly bridging the gap. Large-scale investment is predicated upon large-scale investment. Roads, electric power stations, railroads, and houses have to be built *before* businessmen find it profitable to erect factories, to invest their funds in new industrial enterprises.

Yet investing in road building, financing construction of canals and power stations, organizing large housing projects, etc., transcend by far the financial and mental horizon of capitalists in underdeveloped countries. Not only are their financial resources too small for such ambitious projects, but their background and habits militate against entering commitments of this type. Brought up in the tradition of merchandising and manufacturing consumers' goods—as is characteristic of an early phase of capitalist development— businessmen in underdeveloped countries are accustomed to rapid turnover, large but short-term risks, and correspondingly high rates of profit. Sinking funds in enterprises where profitability could manifest itself only in the course of many years is a largely unknown and unattractive departure.

The difference between social and private rationality that exists in any market and profit-determined economy is thus particularly striking in underdeveloped countries. While building of roads, harnessing of water power, or organization of housing developments may facilitate industrial growth and thus contribute to increased productivity on a national scale, the individual firms engaged in such activities may suffer losses and be unable to recover their investments. The nature of the problem involved can be easily exemplified: starting a new industrial enterprise is predicated among other things upon the availability of appropriately skilled manpower. Engaging men and training them on the job is time-consuming and expensive. They are liable to be unproductive, wasteful, and careless in the treatment of valuable tools and equipment. Accepting the losses involved may be justifiable from the standpoint of the individual firm if such a firm can count with reasonable certainty on retaining the services of those men *after* they go through training and acquire the requisite skills. However, should they leave the firm that provided the training and proceed to work for another enterprise, that new employer would reap the fruits of the first firm's outlays. In a developed industrial society this consideration is relatively unimportant. Losses and gains of individual firms generated by labor turnover may cancel out. In an underdeveloped country the chances of such cancellation are very small, if not nil. Although society as a whole would clearly benefit by the increase of skills of at least some of its members, individual businessmen cannot afford to provide the training that such an increase demands.

But could not the required increase in total output be

attained by better utilization of land—another unutilized or inadequately utilized productive factor?

There is usually no land that is both fit for agricultural purposes and at the same time readily accessible. Such terrain as could be cultivated but is actually not being tilled would usually require considerable investment before becoming suitable for settlement. In underdeveloped countries such outlays for agricultural purposes are just as unattractive to private interests as they are for industrial purposes.

On the other hand, more adequate employment of land that is already used in agriculture runs into considerable difficulties. Very few improvements that would be necessary in order to increase productivity can be carried out within the narrow confines of small-peasant holdings. Not only are the peasants in underdeveloped countries utterly unable to pay for such innovations, but the size of their lots offers no justification for their introduction.

Owners of large estates are in a sense in no better position. With limited savings at their disposal they do not have the funds to finance expensive improvements in their enterprises, nor do such projects appear profitable in view of the high prices of imported equipment in relation to prices of agricultural produce and wages of agricultural labor.

Approached thus via agriculture, an expansion of total output would also seem to be attainable only through the development of industry. Only through increase of industrial productivity could agricultural machinery, fertilizers, electric power, etc., be brought within the reach of the agricultural producer. Only through an increased demand for labor could agricultural wages be raised and a stimulus provided for a modernization of the agricultural economy. Only through the growth of industrial production could agricultural labor displaced by the machine be absorbed in productive employment.

Monopolistic market structures, shortage of savings, lack of external economies, the divergence of social and private rationalities do not exhaust, however, the list of obstacles blocking the way of privately organized industrial expansion in underdeveloped countries. Those obstacles have to be considered against the background of the general feeling of uncertainty prevailing in all backward areas. The coalition of the owning classes formed under pressure of fear, and held together by the real or imagined danger of social upheaval, continuously provokes more or less threatening rumblings under the outwardly calm political surface. The social and political tensions to which that coalition is a political response are not liquidated by the prevailing system; they are only repressed. Normal and quiet as the daily routine frequently appears, the more enlightened and understanding members of the ruling groups in underdeveloped countries sense the inherent instability of the political and social order. Occasional outbursts of popular dissatisfaction assume the form of peasant uprisings, violent strikes, or local guerrilla warfare, and serve from time to time as grim reminders of the latent crisis.

In such a climate there is no will to invest on the part of monied people; in such a climate there is no enthusiasm for long-term projects; in such a climate the motto of all participants in the privileges offered by the society is *carpe diem*.

Could not, however, an appropriate policy on the part of the governments involved change the political climate and facilitate economic growth? In our time, when faith in the manipulative omnipotence of the state has all but displaced analysis of its social structure and understanding of its political and economic functions, the tendency is obviously to answer these questions in the affirmative.

Looking at the matter purely mechanically, it would

appear indeed that much could be done by a well-advised regime in an underdeveloped country to provide for a relatively rapid increase of total output, accompanied by an improvement of the living standards of the population. There are a number of measures that the government could take in an effort to overcome backwardness. A fiscal policy could be adopted that by means of capital levies and a progressive tax system would syphon off all surplus purchasing power, and in this way eliminate non-essential consumption. The savings thus enforced could be channeled by the government into productive investment. Power stations, railroads, highways, irrigation systems, and soil improvements could be organized by the State with a view to creating an economic environment conducive to the growth of productivity. Technical schools on various levels could be set up by the public authority to furnish industrial training to young people as well as to adult workers and the unemployed. A system of scholarships could be introduced rendering acquisition of skills accessible to low-income strata.

Wherever private capital refrains from undertaking certain industrial projects, or wherever monopolistic controls block the necessary expansion of plant and facilities in particular industries, the government could step in and make the requisite investments. Where development possibilities that are rewarding in the long-run appear unprofitable during the initial period of gestation and learning, and are therefore beyond the horizon of private businessmen, the government could undertake to shoulder the short-run losses.

In addition, an entire arsenal of "preventive" devices is at the disposal of the authorities. Inflationary pressures resulting from developmental activities (private and public) could be reduced or even eliminated if outlays on investment projects could be offset by a corresponding and simultaneous contraction of spending elsewhere in the economic system. What this would call for is a taxation policy that would effectively remove from the income stream amounts sufficient to neutralize the investment-caused expansion of aggregate money income.

In the interim, and as a supplement, speculation in scarce goods and excessive profiteering in essential commodities could be suppressed by rigorous price controls. An equitable distribution of mass consumption goods in short supply could be assured by rationing. Diversion of resources in high demand to luxury purposes could be prevented by allocation and priority schemes. Strict supervision of transactions involving foreign exchanges could render capital flight, expenditure of limited foreign funds on luxury imports, pleasure trips abroad, and the like, impossible.

What the combination of these measures would accomplish is a radical change in the structure of effective demand in the underdeveloped country and a reallocation of productive resources to satisfy society's need for economic development. By curtailing consumption of the higher-income groups, the amounts of savings available for investment purposes could be markedly increased. The squandering of limited supplies of foreign exchange on capital flight, or on importation of redundant foreign goods and services, could be prevented, and the foreign funds thus saved could be used for the acquisition of foreign-made machinery needed for economic development. The reluctance of private interests to engage in enterprises that are socially necessary, but may not promise rich returns in the short run, would be prevented from determining the economic life of the backward country.

The mere listing of the steps that would have to be undertaken, in order to assure an expansion of output and income in an underdeveloped country, reveals the utter implausibility of the view that they could be carried out by the governments existing in most underdeveloped countries. The reason for this inability is only to a negligible extent the nonexistence of the competent and honest civil service needed for the administration of the program. A symptom itself of the political and social marasmus prevailing in underdeveloped countries, this lack cannot be remedied without attacking the underlying causes. Nor does it touch anything near the roots of the matter to lament the lack of satisfactory tax policies in backward countries, or to deplore the absence of tax "morale" and "discipline" among the civic virtues of their populations.

The crucial fact rendering the realization of a development program illusory is the political and social structure of the governments in power. The alliance of property-owning classes controlling the destinies of most underdeveloped countries cannot be expected to design and to execute a set of measures running counter to each and all of their immediate vested interests. If to appease the restive public, blueprints of progressive measures such as agrarian reform, equitable tax legislation, etc., are officially announced, their enforcement is willfully sabotaged. The government, representing a political compromise between landed and business interests, cannot suppress the wasteful management of landed estates and the conspicuous consumption on the part of the aristocracy; cannot suppress monopolistic abuses, profiteering, capital flights, and extravagant living on the part of businessmen. It cannot curtail or abandon its lavish appropriations for a military and police establishment, providing attractive careers to the scions of wealthy families and a profitable outlet for armaments produced by their parents—quite apart from the fact that this establishment serves as the main protection against possible popular revolt. Set up to guard and to abet the existing property rights and privileges, it cannot become the architect of a policy calculated to destroy the privileges standing in the way of economic progress and to place the property and the incomes derived from it at the service of society as a whole.

Nor is there much to be said for the "intermediate" position which, granting the essential incompatibility of a well-conceived and vigorously executed development program with the political and social institutions prevailing in most underdeveloped countries, insists that at least *some* of the requisite measures could be carried out by the existing political authorities. This school of thought overlooks entirely the weakness, if not the complete absence, of social and political forces that could induce the necessary concessions on the part of the ruling coalition. By background and political unbringing, too myopic and self-interested to permit the slightest encroachments upon their inherited positions and cherished privileges, the upper classes in underdeveloped countries resist doggedly all pressures in that direction. Every time such pressures grow in strength they succeed in cementing anew the alliance of all conservative elements by decrying all attempts at reform as assaults on the very foundations of society.

Even if measures like progressive taxation, capital levies, and foreign exchange controls could be enforced by the corrupt officials operating in the demoralized business communities of underdeveloped countries, such enforcement would to a large extent defeat its original purpose. Where businessmen do not invest, unless in expectation of lavish profits, a taxation system succeeding in confiscating large parts of these profits is bound to kill private investment. Where doing business or operating landed estates are attractive mainly because they permit luxurious living, foreign exchange controls preventing the importation of luxury goods are bound to blight enterprise. Where the only stimulus to hard work on the part of intellectuals, technicians, and civil servants is the chance of partaking in the privileges of the ruling class, a policy aiming at the reduction of inequality of social status and income is bound to smother effort.

The injection of planning into a society living in the twilight between feudalism and capitalism cannot but result in additional corruption, larger and more artful evasions of the law, and more brazen abuses of authority.

There would seem to be no exit from the impasse. The ruling coalition of interests does not abdicate of its own volition, nor does it change its character in response to incantation. Although its individual members occasionally leave the sinking ship physically or financially (or in both ways), the property-owning classes as a whole are as a rule grimly determined to hold fast to their political and economic entrenchments.

If the threat of social upheaval assumes dangerous proportions, they tighten their grip on political life and move rapidly in the direction of unbridled reaction and military dictatorship. Making use of favorable international opportunities, and of ideological and social affinities to ruling groups in other countries, they solicit foreign economic and sometimes military aid in their efforts to stave off the impending disaster.

Such aid is likely to be given to them by foreign governments regarding them as an evil less to be feared than the social revolution that would sweep them out of power. This attitude of their friends and protectors abroad is no less shortsighted than their own.

The adjustment of the social and political conditions in underdeveloped countries to the urgent needs of economic development can be postponed; it cannot be indefinitely avoided. In the past, it could have been delayed by decades or even centuries. In our age it is a matter of years. Bolstering the political system of power existing in backward countries by providing it with military support may temporarily block the eruption of the volcano; it cannot stop the subterranean gathering of explosive forces.

Economic help in the form of loans and grants given to the governments of backward countries to enable them to promote a measure of economic progress is no substitute for the domestic changes that are mandatory if economic development is to be attained.

Such help, in fact, may actually do more harm than good. Possibly the foreign assistance supplied by permitting the importation of some foreign-made machinery and equipment for government- or business-sponsored investment projects—but not accompanied by any of the steps that are needed to assure healthy economic growth—may set off an inflationary spiral increasing and aggravating the existing social and economic tensions in underdeveloped countries.

If, as is frequently the case, these loans or grants from abroad are tied to the fulfillment of certain conditions on the part of the receiving country regarding their use, the resulting investment may be directed in such channels as to conform more to the interests of the lenders than to the borrowers. Where economic advice as a form of "technical assistance" is supplied to the underdeveloped country, and its acceptance is made a prerequisite to eligibility for financial aid, this advice often pushes the governments of underdeveloped countries toward policies ideologically or otherwise attractive to the foreign experts dispensing economic counsel, but not necessarily conducive to economic development of the "benefited" countries. Nationalism and zenophobia are thus strenghtened in backward areas—additional fuel for political restiveness.

For backward countries to enter the road of economic growth and social progress, the political framework of their existence has to be drastically revamped. The alliance between feudal landlords, industrial royalists, and the capitalist middle classes has to be broken. The keepers of the past cannot be the builders of the future. Such progressive and enterprising elements as exist in backward societies have to obtain the possibility of leading their countries in the direction of economic and social growth.

What France, Britain, and America have accomplished through their own revolutions has to be attained in backward countries by a combined effort of popular forces, enlightened government, and unselfish foreign help. This combined effort must sweep away the holdover institutions of a defunct age, must change the political and social climate in the underdeveloped countries, and must imbue their nations with a new spirit of enterprise and freedom.

Should it prove too late in the historical process for the bourgeoisie to rise to its responsibilities in backward areas, should the long experience of servitude and accommodation to the feudal past have reduced the forces of progressive capitalism to impotence, the backward countries of the world will inevitably turn to economic planning and social collectivism. If the capitalist world outlook of economic and social progress, propelled by enlightened self-interest, should prove unable to triumph over the conservatism of inherited positions and traditional privileges, if the capitalist promise of advance and reward to the efficient, the industrious, the able, should not displace the feudal assurance of security and power to the well-bred, the well-connected, and the conformist—a new social ethos will become the spirit and guide of a new age. It will be the ethos of the collective effort, the creed of the predominance of the interests of society over the interests of a selected few.

The transition may be abrupt and painful. The land not given to the peasants legally may be taken by them forcibly. High incomes not confiscated through taxation may be eliminated by outright expropriation. Corrupt officials not retired in orderly fashion may be removed by violent action.

Which way the historical wheel will turn and in which way

the crisis in the backward countries will find its final solution will depend in the main on whether the capitalist middle classes in the backward areas, and the rulers of the advanced industrial nations of the world, overcome their fear and myopia. Or are they too spellbound by their narrowly conceived selfish interests, too blinded by their hatred of progress, grown so senile in these latter days of the capitalist age, as to commit suicide out of fear of death?

Economic Progress
and Economic Surplus

The spectacular economic upsurge in the socialist sector of the world, the growing pressures for economic development in the colonies and the dependencies of the advanced capitalist countries, and the dangerous lability of the economies of the advanced capitalist countries themselves place once more the inquiry into the nature and causes of the wealth of nations into the forefront of economic thought.

This "homecoming" is, however, by no means altogether joyous. Compelled by the pressure of historical events to turn to the thorny problem of economic development, economists discover with much surprise and alarm that they have to face their new task almost entirely empty-handed. The sins and omissions of the past come back to haunt the present: the analytical apparatus required for the understanding of the process of economic and social change was allowed to become neglected and rusty under the regime of "pure economics" under which static equilibrium analysis, the

---

This article originally appeared in the Fall 1953 issue of *Science & Society* and is reprinted by permission. Copyright © 1953 by Science & Society, Inc.

In a footnote, Baran noted: "I am indebted to Mrs. Joan Robinson for a most valuable discussion of this paper and to Paul M. Sweezy for comments and suggestions that convinced me of the necessity of completely reworking an earlier draft. Needless to say, such errors and confusions as may have still remained in this paper have to be blamed on no one but the author."

properties of the model of "perfect competition" and matters similarly unrelated to social and economic dynamics were accorded the pride of place on the theoretical agenda. "The economists explain to us the process of production under given conditions; what they do not explain to us, however, is how these conditions themselves are being produced, i.e., the historical movement that brings them into being."[1]

In what follows an attempt is made to submit for renewed consideration an old and simple concept that appears to be quite helpful in thinking about economic and social development.

Let economic growth be defined as increase over time in per capita output of goods and services.[2] Such an increase can be the result of one of the following developments (or a combination of them): (1) The aggregate resource utilization may expand *without changes in organization and/or technology,* i.e., previously unutilized resources (manpower, land) may be brought into the productive process; (2) The productivity per unit of resources at work may rise in view of *organizational measures,* i.e., by a transfer of workers from less productive or unproductive occupations to more productive pursuits, by a lengthening of the working day, by an improvement in nutrition and strengthening of incentives available to workers, by rationalization of production and more economic utilization of fuel, raw materials, etc; (3) *Society's "technical arm" may become stronger,* i.e., (a) the wear and tear of plant and equipment may be replaced by more efficient facilities, and/or (b) new (technologically improved or unchanged) productive facilities may be added to the previously existing stock.

The first three routes to expansion of output—(1), (2), and (3a)—are typically not associated with *net* investment.[4] There can be little doubt that the economic application of increasing technical knowledge and net investment in additional productive facilities have been the most important sources of economic growth.

Net investment can only take place, however, if society's total output *exceeds* what is used for its current consumption and for replacement of the wear and tear of its productive facilities employed during the period in question. The volume and the nature of net investment taking place in a society at any given time depends, therefore, on the *size* and the *mode of utilization* of the currently generated *economic surplus*.[5]

It is essential to differentiate in terms of "comparative statics" three variants of the concept of economic surplus:

(1) *Actual* economic surplus, i.e., the difference between society's *actual* current output and its *actual* current consumption. It is thus identical with current saving and finds its embodiment in assets of various kinds added to society's wealth during the period in question:[6] productive facilities and inventories, foreign balances, and gold hoards. Such surplus itself has been generated in all socioeconomic formations, and while its size and structure have markedly differed from one phase of development to another, its existence has characterized nearly all of recorded history. The magnitude of the actual economic surplus (saving) is at least conceptually readily established and is today regularly estimated by statistical agencies in most countries. Such difficulties as are encountered in its measurement are technical and caused by the absence or inadequacy of statistical information.

(2) *Potential* economic surplus, i.e., the difference between the output that *could* be produced in a given natural and technological environment with the help of *actually* employed productive resources and what might be regarded as *essential* consumption. In most cases, its realization would presuppose a more or less drastic reorganization of the production and distribution of social output and may imply far reaching changes in the structure of society. It exists in

three distinct forms. One is society's excess consumption (predominantly on the part of the upper income groups), the other is the output lost to society through the existence of unproductive workers, the third is the output lost because of the irrationality and wastefulness of the prevailing economic organization.[7] The identification and measurement of these three forms of the potential economic surplus run into some obstacles. These are essentially reducible to the fact that the category of the potential economic surplus itself transcends the horizon of the existing social order—relating as it does not merely to the easily observable performance of the given socioeconomic organization, but also the less readily visualized image of a more rationally ordered society.

Indeed, if looked at from the vantage point of feudalism, "essential," "productive," and "rational" was all that was compatible with and conducive to the continuity and stability of the feudal system. "Non-essential," "unproductive," and "wasteful" was all that interfered with the preservation and the normal functioning of the status quo. Accordingly, Malthus staunchly defended the "excess consumption" of the landed aristocracy, pointing to the employment-stimulating effect of such outlays. On the other hand, the economists of the ascending bourgeoisie had no compunctions about castigating the *ancien régime* for the wastefulness of its socioeconomic organization, and about pointing out the parasitic character of many of its most cherished functionaries.[8]

Yet as the capitalist order has become fully entrenched and as capitalist institutions and relationships have grown to be the institutions and relationships of society as a whole, the rubber stamp of rationality and adequacy was indiscriminately placed on all aspects of the best of all possible worlds. By elevating the dictum of the market to the role of the sole criterion of reason and efficiency, economics denies even all "respectability" to the distinction between "essential" and "non-essential" consumption, between "productive" and "unproductive" labor, between actual and potential surplus. "Non-essential" consumption is justified as providing indispensable incentives, unproductive labor is glorified as indirectly contributing to production, waste is defended as a prerequisite of "freedom."

As the dominion of capital extended, and in fact even those spheres of production not directly related to the production of material wealth became more and more dependent on it, and especially the positive sciences (natural sciences) were subordinated to it as means toward material production—second-rate sycophants of political economy thought it their duty to glory and justify every sphere of activity by demonstrating that it was "linked" with the production of material wealth, that it was a means toward it: and they honored everyone by making him a "productive worker" in the "narrowest" sense—that is a worker who works in the service of capital, is useful in one way or another to its increase . . . . [9]

Yet "capitalism creates a critical frame of mind which after having destroyed the moral authority of so many other institutions, in the end turns against its own: the bourgeois finds to his amazement that the rationalist attitude does not stop at the credentials of kings and popes but goes on to attack private property and the whole scheme of bourgeois values."[10] Thus from a standpoint located outside and beyond the capitalist frame of reference, from the standpoint of a socialist society, much of what appears to be essential, productive, rational to bourgeois economic and social thought turns out to be non-essential, unproductive, and wasteful. It may be said in general that it is only the standpoint that is intellectually *outside* the prevailing social order, that is unencumbered by its values, its superstitions, and its "self-evident truths," that permits critical insight into that social order's contradictions and hidden potentialities. The exercise of self-critique is just as onerous to a ruling class as it is to a single individual.

This is why a socialist critique of the prevailing social and economic system finds a relatively sympathetic reception on the part of orthodox economics as long as it is directed at the remnants of the feudal order. The excess-consumption of the landlords in backward countries is no less an admissible target of attack than the general wastefulness of their economic organization.[11] This critique is frowned upon, however, as soon as capitalist institutions *sensu stricto* are implicated or as soon as the imperialism of advanced capitalist countries is considered in its relation to the stagnation of the under-developed areas. Similarly, economists, socially and mentally anchored in the competitive petty-bourgeois phase (and stratum) of the capitalist society, have developed a certain degree of clairvoyance with respect to the irrationality, wastefulness, and dangers of monopoly capitalism. Oblivious to the fact that it is liberal, competitive capitalism that gives rise to monopoly, they realize some of the economic and social costs of capitalism's monopolistic phase, discern some of the most obvious manifestations of excess consumption, unproductive activities, irrationality of "economic royalism." At the same time the writers who have either liberated themselves from the shackles of an earlier age or who have grown directly into the "new era" are at times impressively perspicacious when debunking the competitive idols of the past—the sacrosanct virtues of capitalism's competitive ado-lescence.

It is this insight (and information) occasionally encountered in economic writings, in conjunction with the experience gathered in periods when the interests of the capitalist society as a whole come into conflict with those of its individual members, that permits an at least proximate assessment of the nature (and magnitude) of the potential economic surplus. With regard to large segments of the population not only of underdeveloped countries but of the advanced ones as well, what constitutes essential consump-tion is ascertainable. Where living standards are in general low—and the basket of goods available to the consumer little variegated—essential consumption can be circumscribed in terms of calories, other nutrients, quantities of clothing, fuel, dwelling space, etc. Even where the level of consumption is relatively high and involves a large variety of consumer goods and services, a judgment of the amount of real income necessary for what is socially considered a "decent livelihood" can be made.[12] This is precisely what has been done in all countries in emergency situations such as war, postwar distress, etc. What to the agnostic purist and worshipper of "consumer sovereignty" appears as an insurmountable obstacle or as a manifestation of reprehensible arbitrariness, is wholly accessible to scientific inquiry and to common sense judgment.[13]

Similarly, the classification of unproductive workers is less complicated than usually assumed. Most generally speaking these are individuals whose activities are not directly related to the process of production (or who are engaged in the production of non-essential goods) and who are maintained by a part of society's economic surplus.[14] It is entirely immaterial in the present context that many unproductive workers render services that are eminently useful to society as a whole or at least to the class dominant in it.[15] As useful as physicians or as useless as public relations experts, as socially desirable as artists or as socially harmful as narcotics peddlers, as respectable as bishops or disreputable as gamblers—the unproductive workers have still to be supported by a share of society's material output to the production of which they make no direct contribution. A large proportion of these unproductive workers can be estimated directly by consulting the occupational breakdown of the population: government officials, members of the military establishment, clergymen, etc. Others lurking in the complex spiderweb of the economic system—advertising agents, brokers, merchants, beauty parlor operators and the like—are not quite as readily identified. Nevertheless, literature abounds with references to them and much of the necessary evidence can be pieced together from some of the more useful writings on welfare economics.[16] A particularly good example is given by Schumpeter:

> A considerable part of the total work done by lawyers goes into the struggle of business with the state and its organs . . . in socialist society there would be neither need nor room for this part of legal activity. The resulting saving is not satisfactorily measured by the fees of the lawyers who are thus engaged. That is inconsiderable. But not inconsiderable is the social loss from such unproductive employment of many of the best brains. Considering how terribly rare good brains are, their shifting to other employment might be of more than infinitesimal importance.[17]

Once more: although there is no sharp dividing line between productive and unproductive work performed in capitalist society, but rather a spectrum running from wholly unproductive labor on one end to wholly productive on the other, in times of emergency this problem is more or less successfully solved. Unproductive workers are drafted into the army while productive workers are deferred. Labor exchanges move people from less essential to more essential positions. Rationing boards issue different ration cards to individuals in different occupations, with productive workers receiving preferential treatment.[18]

Conceptually no more complex, although perhaps still more difficult to measure, is the third form in which potential economic surplus is hidden in the capitalist economy. The waste and irrationality of production that fall under this category can be observed in a great number of instances. They appear as excess capacity, underutilization of economies of scale due to irrational product differentiation, inefficiency of firms shielded by monopolistic market positions, duplication of facilities called forth by competition, inadequate exploitation of technological progress caused by the desire to preserve the value of capital assets or by reluctance to expand output, and so forth.[19] Of a different nature but also constituting part of the potential economic surplus is the loss of output due to the underemployment of productive resources in small, owner-operated competitive enterprises conducted on a lower than available level of technology or the loss of agricultural output occasioned by restrictive schemes and production controls of all kinds.

While even under emergency conditions only a relatively small part of this type of potential economic surplus is actually tapped, what has been accomplished on occasions suffices to indicate at least the dimensions of the problem involved. The wartime increase in output that resulted merely from concentration of production in large-scale plants, from the elimination of the most flagrant cases of duplication, cross-hauling, and inefficiency was most impressive in the U.S. as well as in Great Britain and Germany.

(3) If the potential economic surplus is a category of considerable interest to a capitalist society under emergency conditions as well as to a nation embarking upon a program of economic development, what may be called the *planned* economic surplus is relevant only to comprehensive economic planning under socialism. It is the difference between society's "optimum" output attainable in a given technological and natural environment under conditions of planned "optimal" utilization of all available productive resources—and some chosen "optimum" volume of consumption. The conditions of its realization are in all respects different from those pertaining to both the actual and the potential economic surplus. In the first place it does *not* presuppose a maximum output that might be attainable in a country at any given time. While it *does* imply a

far-reaching *rationalization* of the productive apparatus (liquidation of inefficient units of production, maximal economies of scale, etc.), abolition of many kinds of unproductive labor (butlers and lawyers, preachers and brokers), and elimination of a large share of excess consumption, it may well be associated with a less than maximal output in view of a voluntarily shortened labor-day, of conservation of natural resources, or of conscious discarding of certain noxious types of production (coal mining, for example). Nor does the planned economic surplus call for reduction of consumption merely to what is essential; it may well go together with a level of consumption that is considerably higher than what the criterion of essentiality might suggest. What is crucial is that it would not be generated by the mechanism of profit maximization, but would be determined by a social plan and would depend on what society would *consciously* decide to produce, to consume, and to save at any given time. It may therefore be larger or smaller than the actual economic surplus under capitalism, or may even equal zero if society should choose to refrain from net investment.

As indicated above, from the standpoint of economic growth interest attaches to both the *size* and the *mode of utilization* of the economic surplus.

Under conditions of low productivity, current output tends to be absorbed by current consumption. There may never have been a stage in historical development (as distinct from pre-historic times) at which no economic surplus was generated by society's productive effort. If observations made in contemporary primitive societies provide adequate clues to the remote past, some economic surplus was embodied in durable goods (dwellings, canoes, tools, livestock, and the like) even under the most confining economic circumstances.[20] The quantity of these (simple and inexpensive) durable goods would seem to have been small and only slowly growing. While there may have been a more or less sustained replacement of the available stock of such durable goods (interrupted only by natural disasters and ravages of war) without any or with very little changes in technology, only scant "net investment" was taking place in any given period.

Whatever actual economic surplus was generated on the basis of the low total output of primitive economies was the result of the still lower standards of consumption. Not only did these standards barely reach physiological subsistence minimums, but the quantities of supplies constituting those minimums were markedly smaller than what they have come to be in later phases of history.[21]

Yet even under such circumstances the *potential* economic surplus exceeded the actual economic surplus, although the difference between them was probably small. Still, full-time priests and full-time warriors supported by a share of their communities' output are reported to have existed at the dawn of our historical experience.[22]

Subsequent history is marked by a continuous growth of the potential economic surplus with a now widening, now shrinking gap between the potential and the actual economic surplus. Output in antiquity expanded much faster than mass consumption. "It was thanks to a unique crop of technical inventions—the plough, the wheeled cart, the sailing boat, the solar calendar, the smelting of copper ores, the use of the power of oxen, and the harnessing of the winds with sails—that [the classical] civilizations had come into being."[23] At the same time the living conditions not only of the slaves but of the lower classes in general were held down to nearly primitive levels. "[The] division of society ensured that the vast masses of the [Roman] empire never tasted the fruits of their labor . . . . Because wealth was concentrated at the top, the body of society suffered from chronic underconsumption."[24]

Nevertheless, actual economic surplus was relatively small. The large difference between the potential and the actual surplus appeared in the proverbial excess consumption of the rich as well as in the equally proverbial multitude of unproductive workers. What was to become the largest single claimant of potential economic surplus—the state—began to command a growing share of total output.[25]

Nor was the situation much different during the Middle Ages. "It would be interesting, though it is impossible, to discover how much the peasants made on . . . manors which their holders did not farm for profit, after working for a whole year from one to three days a week on the lord's demesne and after paying on the customary dates the dues in kind which burdened their land. It must have been little, if anything."[26] Similarly, in cities "it was mainly for the rich, above all for the great establishments from churches to mansions maintained by bishops and princes, lesser priests, and nobles, and some municipal authorities, that craftsmen and artists produced commodities in larger quantities than before."[27]

Although the potential economic surplus appropriated by the upper classes was thus quite sizable,[28] the actual economic surplus generated in medieval societies and available for productive investment of any kind was extremely small. The difference between the potential and actual surplus was used for excess consumption of the ruling class, for the maintenance of a vast ecclesiastic organization, or for military enterprises, the objective of which was frequently to provide additional means for luxurious living and magnificent displays of the privileged few. To quote Pirenne again,

> the early centuries of the Middle Ages seem to have been completely ignorant of the power of capital. They abound in wealthy landed proprietors, in rich monasteries, and we

come upon hundreds of sanctuaries the treasure of which, supplied by the generosity of the nobles or the offerings of the faithful, crowds the altar with ornaments of gold or of solid silver. A considerable fortune is accumulated in the Church, but it is an idle fortune. The revenues which the landowners collect from their serfs or from tenants are directed toward no economic purpose. They are scattered in alms,[29] in the building of monuments, in the purchase of works of art, or of precious objects which could serve to increase the splendor of religious ceremonies. Wealth, capital, if one may so term it, is fixed motionless in the hands of an aristocracy, priestly or military.[30]

The result was lack of means for "net investment" and consequently "a system with a strong bias in favor of maintaining given methods and relations in production."[31] Combined with growth of population, this economic stagnation led to decline rather than to growth of per capita output.

The transition from feudalism to capitalism represented a radical change in both the size of the economic surplus and the mode of its utilization. Classical economists saw in fact the *raison d'etre* of the ascending bourgeois order in its providing for rapid economic progress by maximization and efficient utilization of the economic surplus. Indeed, in a well-functioning capitalist society, the classical writers implied, the actual and potential economic surplus should merge into one. Competition among enterprises would assure maximum output and eliminate all waste and irrationality from the productive process. Say's law would see to it that apart from occasional "frictional disproportionalities" full employment was continuously maintained. Competition among workers would prevent wages from rising above the subsistence minimum and from eating into profits—the source of all economic surplus.[32] The elimination of the feudal lord as owner of the land and parasitic squanderer of the rent would prevent the wastage of the economic surplus on unproductive expenditures. Nor would there be much room in a fully competitive economy for unproductive workers other than those truly essential to the functioning of the competitive capitalist order and significantly contributing to the accumulation of capital. Large selling costs, major advertising expenses, excess capacities, legal or public relations departments do not enter the model of an economy thought of as composed of relatively small firms producing at the lowest possible cost more or less homogeneous, interchangeable products. True, some unproductive workers would necessarily remain in the economic system—landlords, bankers, brokers, merchants—but the economic surplus appropriated by them would also be in its bulk accumulated rather than consumed. In fact by encroaching upon the real income of the masses to whom they would shift some of the costs of their operations they would actually contribute to capital formation rather than detract from it.[33]

Yet one more condition would need to be satisfied for the maximum economic surplus to provide for the largest attainable rates of growth. That condition is frugality and the will to invest on the part of the businessman. Once the aristocratic landlord has been deprived of sources of "unearned" income, or has himself turned into a capitalist, such frugality would remove the last pre-capitalist vestiges of excess consumption from the economic system. There appeared to be good reasons to expect this condition of economic growth to be satisfied. In the first place, the competitive mechanism would *force* businessmen to accumulate, since only by continuously plowing back their earnings in cost-reducing innovations could they hope to maintain themselves in the competitive struggle. Moreover, the maintenance of high rates of profit would provide all the necessary inducements to invest, unless diminishing returns in agriculture should continuously raise the real costs of labor's sustenance. But with this bogey removed by technological progress in agriculture, nothing should stand in the way of a harmonious expansion of capital accumulation—at least until in the remote future the stock of capital would become so large as to reduce marginal returns on it to a level insufficient to overcome the "natural" reluctance to face risks concomitant with every investment.

Secondly, the rise of the members of the business class from humble origins to affluence and power was explained by their propensity to work hard and to save. It was judged as probable—on characterological grounds—that they would retain a way of life that has led them to spectacular successes. Thirdly, the advent of what Weber and Sombart have called later the "capitalist spirit"—to which, in fact, they ascribed the genesis of modern capitalism[34] —accompanied by the prevalence of a Puritan ethic had established a system of social values in which thriftiness and the drive to accumulate were elevated to the status of supreme merit and paramount virtue.

Thus the only issue that faced society, if economic progress was to be assured, was the creation and preservation of conditions necessary for rapid accumulation of the actual economic surplus. The possibility that there should be insufficient outlets for profitable investment for the accumulated capital was hardly considered in an age in which not only ever new investment opportunities opened up at home, but the settlement of new continents appeared as a bottomless pit for investable funds.[35]

Under such circumstances the role of the government was clearly circumscribed. It was to abstain from interfering with the formation of capital by refraining from collecting unnecessary tax revenues, by giving up meddling in social affairs and subsidizing the poor, by markedly reducing the number of unproductive workers maintained by resources that otherwise would form a part of the actual economic surplus.[36] It could possibly be called upon to protect foreign markets, sources of supplies, and investments, but the need for such protection was expected to be small and in any case only sporadic.

Needless to say, this—so hastily sketched—picture of the *modus operandi* of a competitive capitalist economy is at best a rather apologetic portrayal of reality. Yet matters bear even less resemblance to it in the advanced, monopolistic phase of capitalist development.

While the growth of large-scale enterprise and monopoly has strengthened and perfected to unprecented powers the mechanisms for the generation of economic surplus, it has also seriously affected the conditions of its utilization. The attainment of a high level of industrialization in advanced capitalist countries has markedly narrowed down the opportunities for profitable investment.[37] Consequently, in the words of Alvin H. Hansen, "The problem of our generation is, above all, the problem of inadequate private investment outlets."[38]

It is hardly relevant to point to the great number of useful projects that "could" be undertaken, and the completion of which would contribute to human welfare.[39] What is crucial is that the evolution of the structure of the capitalist economy and the far-reaching changes in the nature of the investment process render their realization in the capitalist system increasingly difficult if not downright impossible.

The economic factors impeding and retarding investment under conditions of monopoly (and oligopoly) have been widely discussed in the relevant literature.[40] There is no need to go into the details of this controversy in the present context. Suffice it to say that economists of widely differing persuasions, while strongly disagreeing on the *causes* of inadequate private investment in advanced capitalist countries, generally recognize the *fact* that under monopoly capitalism such investment normally fails to utilize the currently generated economic surplus.

Nor are the "purely economic" factors the only ones that obstruct and retard investment under monopoly capitalism. One should not lose sight of the socio-political setting of private investment in the age of imperialism, wars, social and colonial revolutions. The growth of the labor movement in advanced capitalist countries combined with the spreading of "muckraking" ideologies among the middle-classes endangered in their position by the ascent of Big Business create a societal environment profoundly inimical to Big Business. What is perhaps even more important, the arrival on the historical stage of a socialist state with a well-functioning planned economy has proved beyond further dispute what socialists have been claiming for one hundred years: a modern economic system can operate, develop, and improve *without capitalists*. The result is a growing insecurity of the capitalist class, increasing consciousness of the impermanence of the existing social order, mounting fear of the social revolution. In such a "climate" the capitalist is reluctant to invest, to engage in long-run projects, to sacrifice his liquidity, to give up his ability to "run for cover" in case of emergency. This "demoralization" of the capitalist class assumes different proportions in different countries and at different times. It is at its worst where the liability of the system is most pronounced either for geographical or historical reasons.

When intended investment falls short of the volume of the actual economic surplus obtainable under conditions of full employment, depression provides the automatic "correction" by reducing aggregate output, employment, and profits and by pushing the surplus down to the level of its utilization. When intended investment absorbs a larger share or all of the actual economic surplus, the expanded productive facilities, larger output, and absolutely larger surplus in the next period recreate the problem of sufficient investment on a larger scale.[41]

If, then, intended investment fails to reach the level of the actual economic surplus that would be generated under conditions of full employment—there are the following three possibilities for averting depression and unemployment. One is to increase mass consumption (as a *ratio* of total output), and thus to reduce the proportion of output constituting actual economic surplus. This could be accomplished by an increase in *real* wages, i.e., a reduction of profits. Such a course is not open, however, to an economic system in which individual capitalists seek to maximize their profits. It is a moot problem whether mass consumption has expanded proportionately or less than proportionately to the growth of total output in the capitalist age.[42]

In any case, the individual capitalist cannot be expected to function as Santa Claus to his workers and buyers in order to increase mass consumption. What might be wholly rational from the standpoint of the capitalist economy as a whole would be suicidal if undertaken by the individual capitalist.[43]

The second possibility is shipping some of the actual economic surplus abroad. To be sure, such exports can provide an additional outlet for the overflowing economic surplus only if undertaken in exchange for gold or if the proceeds are invested abroad. If the exports are compensated for by imports, there is obviously no change in the total volume of domestically available surplus.[44] Yet, since the world's total supply of gold is rather severely limited, and since for important economic and political considerations its value cannot be indefinitely raised, investment abroad is the principal vehicle for the disposal of economic surplus in foreign countries.

But foreign investment encounters obstacles that are, if anything, more formidable than those faced by investment at home. While exceptionally attractive in terms of prospective (and actually earned) returns, they are beset by a host of political and social uncertainties that greatly impair the individual capitalist's willingness to undertake foreign ventures without help or protection from his government—particularly under conditions of general political and social instability.

Consequently, "would-be" foreign investors bring powerful pressure to bear upon the government of an advanced capitalist country to create abroad, by diplomatic and military means, political and social conditions favorable to its capitalists' investment ventures, and to exercise its power to exclude other imperialist countries from the coveted foreign markets and outlets for investment. These pressures are reinforced by business groups that do not themselves participate in capital exports but are vitally interested in foreign sales. The latter groups usually exercise their influence in favor of government loans and grants to foreign countries so as to enable those countries to buy their merchandise.

It is quite clear that foreign investment, not unlike domestic investment, represents only a temporary relief from the pressures of uninvestable economic surplus. Unless it is lost abroad as a result of commercial mishaps or of political upsets, the returns from it (as well as its possible eventual repatriation) aggravate at a later date the problem of utilization of the currently generated actual economic surplus.

The third possibility is the reduction of the *actual* economic surplus through enlarged excess consumption on the part of the capitalist class, through expansion of unproductive labor, through multiplied waste and irrationality in the production and distribution system. No individual capitalist could singly undertake such measures with the view to reducing society's actual economic surplus. This has to be imposed upon him by a general shift in institutions, mores, and values or done for him by a society as a whole, i.e., by the state.[45]

Both have taken place under monopoly capitalism. Conspicuous consumption of the capitalists,[46] lavish outlays on corporate bureaucracy, lawyers, public relations experts, etc., have become an integral part of the folklore of monopolistic capitalism. "In 1929 for every 100 engaged in commodity production in the United States, 74 were otherwise employed. In 1939, for every 100 in commodity production 87 were otherwise employed. And by 1949, for every 100 in commodity production 106 were otherwise employed."[47] Similarly, spending of vast sums for various "cultural" and political purposes on the part of giant corporations designed to bribe "public opinion" in favor of monopoly capital absorbs growing portions of corporate profits.[48]

But the most prodigious outlet for economic surplus is governmental spending. This spending has assumed various forms; the principal opportunity for its increase is offered by the development of imperialism. Regardless of the economic value or strategic significance of the territories and interests abroad that "need" to be protected, the military establishment required for such protection becomes an invaluable end in itself as a broad outlet for the economic surplus.[49] Compared with military and related spending, all other items in the government budget are of secondary importance. Neither the vastly expanded bureaucracy nor the vastly advertised welfare expenditures come even near the spending for military purposes.[50]

Two conclusions, the importance of which hardly needs stressing, emerge from this brief sketch of the mode of utilization of the economic surplus under monopolistic capitalism. *First,* greatly at variance with the historical experience and the theoretical model of capitalism's competitive youth, in its advanced monopolistic phase the capitalist economy is incapable of utilizing society's prodigious economic surplus for purposes of economic growth. A vast expansion of excess consumption on the part of the capitalist class, of unproductive labor of all kinds, of waste and irrationality becomes the indispensable prerequisite of economic and political stability. *Second,* while the power of individual firms to appropriate economic surplus has reached staggering proportions, neither the required volume of investment nor its alternatives—increase in mass consumption, capital exports, or multiplication of unproductive labor and waste— can be organized by profit maximizing individual capitalist enterprises *themselves.* Although some of the "necessary" destruction of the economic surplus is being accomplished by a purposefully manipulated accommodation of society to the "culture" of monopolistic capitalism, *the bulk of the task has to be assigned to the state.*[51] It is the paramount importance of the scope and character of the government disposal over a large share of society's economic surplus that renders it imperative to the ruling class to maintain a tight control over the policies and machinery of the state. Herefrom stems the decisive force driving toward the transformation of bourgeois democracy into fascist or semi-fascist political institutions.[52]

If the conditions of economic growth that have prevailed under competitive capitalism have largely disintegrated under advanced capitalism, they have never materialized in the countries of backward capitalism. As Lenin has stressed, capitalism has entered most underdeveloped countries the "Prussian way"—not through the growth of small, competitive business but through transfer from abroad of advanced monopolistic enterprise. Accordingly, capitalist development in these countries was not accompanied by a rise of the bourgeoisie and by an overthrow of the feudal domination of society, but rather by an accommodation between the newly arrived monopolistic business and the socially and politically firmly entrenched landed gentry.

Consequently the only "classical" requirement for growth that is fully satisfied in the underdeveloped countries is the maintenance of living standards of the population at or markedly below subsistence minimums. Yet there is neither vigorous competition of ambitious businessmen pressing for increase of output and rationalization of production, nor is there accumulation of the economic surplus in the hands of "classical" capitalists forced by the competitive process and the mores of a bourgeois society to plow back as much as possible in the expansion of their business.

The result is that output in underdeveloped countries is much below the attainable level with agriculture operating in a "antediluvian" fashion, with waste and irrationality in industry shielded by monopoly, high tariffs, and other protective devices.[53]

While thus the *potential* economic surplus is large, the *actual* economic surplus, although representing a sizable *proportion* of total output, remains rather low in absolute terms. A large share of the potential surplus goes to semi-feudal landlords who spend much of their revenue on excess consumption and the maintenance of a multitude of unproductive laborers. Another big slice is acquired by capitalists who, attempting to preserve their monopolistic positions and haunted by political insecurity, are loath to sink their funds in long-term enterprises. They prefer risky commercial operations promising large and rapid returns, or the accumulation of emergency reserves sheltered abroad from domestic and social hazards and providing lucrative hedges against inflation. Moreover, in order to be worthy partners of the politically and socially dominant coalition of the property-owning classes, and to be able to secure from it the benefits and privileges indispensable for the conduct of business, the capitalists in backward countries have to emulate the "old" and "prominent" families in their mode of living, have to engage in conspicuous consumption, erect sumptuous residences, and acquire landed estates.

Nor do the landed gentry and the capitalists in underdeveloped countries alone account for the excess consumption, the unproductive labor and waste which drastically reduce the magnitude of the actual economic surplus. Much is absorbed by the corrupt governments of the backward nations that use a substantial quantity of resources for the maintenance of elaborate and inefficient bureaucratic and military establishments. Yet while under conditions of advanced capitalism the government-organized waste and unproductive labor remove some of the *overflow* of the actual economic surplus and provide thus for a measure of economic stability, the squandering of the economic surplus on the part of the governments in backward countries represents a major drain on their scarce resources, markedly reducing their possibilities of economic development. It fulfills, however, an ·"indispensable" political function: without the sprawling government bureaucracy, without the vast military establishment, there would be no way of systematically bribing important strata of the intelligentsia, of maintaining a relatively well-paid Pretorian guard dedicated to defense of the status quo, of keeping up an apparatus of oppression assuring the continuity of the existing social order.

Of varying size, but nearly everywhere considerable, are the parts of the actual economic surplus removed abroad on account of dividends and interest collected by foreign absentee owners of industrial, agricultural, and mining enterprises in underdeveloped countries.[54]

The social and political structure of the backward capitalist countries that is responsible for the mode of utilization of their economic surplus thus determines the volume of the actual economic surplus available for net investment. The frequently registered (and deplored) lack of saving in underdeveloped countries, observable in spite of glaring inequality of income, is caused not merely by the relative smallness of aggregate output, but primarily by large excess consumption on the part of the property-owning classes, by a superabundance of unproductive labor maintained by society's meager resources, and by a staggering amount of waste and irrationality in the productive and distributive processes. Although other factors have undoubtedly much to do with the inadequacy of the volume and structure of net investment that takes place in underdeveloped areas (lack of external economies is the most conspicuous one), the waste of a large portion of economic surplus is probably the crucial cause of their economic and social stagnation.[55]

The remarkable success of the reconstruction and development effort of the countries of eastern and southeastern Europe and China that have entered the road to socialism after the war is primarily due to an effective mobilization of these countries' potential economic surplus.[56] The elimination of the excess consumption of the former ruling class, the transfer of numerous unproductive workers to socially desirable occupations, the far-reaching rationalization of the productive apparatus, the realization of economies of scale, the disappearance of capital flight, of dividend and interest transfers to foreigners, the purposeful application of the principle of comparative advantages—all placed at the disposal of a society a vast pool of resources available for useful employment.

Not that in planned economies even as relatively mature as the U.S.S.R., not to speak of the more recent arrivals in the socialist camp, the *actual* economic surplus can be fully equated with the *potential* surplus. Such an equation is neither possible nor desirable, since certain elements of the potential economic surplus are essential to the welfare and progress of society and may have to be expanded rather than contracted in a socialist society. As Marx predicted, the part of the total product ". . . which is destined for the communal satisfaction of needs such as schools, health services, etc., . . . is . . . from the outset . . . considerably increased in comparison with present-day society and it increases in proportion as the new society develops" while "the general costs of administration not belonging to production . . . will from the outset, be very considerably restricted in comparison with present-day society and it diminishes in proportion as the new society develops."[57] At the same time the devotion of a considerable volume of resources to the maintenance of a state apparatus, of a military establishment, etc., that is inevitable as long as the security of the socialist order is threatened from within and/or from without, prevents a further-reaching reallocation of the potential economic surplus either by increasing the actual economic surplus or by expanding collective or individual consumption.[58]

Only under conditions of a fully established socialist order in which both the external and internal dangers to society have disappeared and in which unproductive labor is devoted exclusively to the satisfaction of society's genuine non-material needs, in which waste and irrationality are banned from the productive and distributive process and in which the decision and the allocation of output as between current consumption and investment is made in the light of the community's requirements—only then would the actual economic surplus coincide with the planned economic surplus and correspond to society's conscious decision on the rate of the desired growth.

It should be stressed that the surplus is by no means an objective desirable per se. What is a matter of urgency for underdeveloped countries and even for advanced countries is the mobilization of the potential economic surplus for the purposes of expanded investment and/or essential consumption. The distribution of aggregate output as between consumption and surplus is determined under capitalism by the prevailing socioeconomic relations; under socialism it is "discretionary"—allowing for the time lags inevitable in the process of reallocation of resources. Where, as in many underdeveloped countries, even that economic surplus which could be obtained under conditions of maximum obtainable output and "rock-bottom" consumption is small, the course of wisdom may be to refrain from immediately increasing consumption standards. The addition to per capita consumption resulting from a distribution of what used to be potential economic surplus may be negligible, while the investment of all obtainable economic surplus in productive enterprise may lead to a large increase of total output at a later date.[59]

Yet in all countries a rational utilization of the economic surplus is an indispensable prerequisite of economic growth. The class appropriating and administering society's economic surplus that has failed to live up to its function of investing it productively and of providing thus for the development of productive resources has been sooner or later divested of this "trust" by overwhelming social forces. The feudal class that was unable to discharge the function of propelling economic development by a productive utilization of the economic surplus was supplanted by the more efficient and rational bourgeoisie. Where the capitalist class fails to make full and rational use of the prodigious economic surplus that it is in the position to appropriate, where it causes wars, destruction, and indescribable misery in its drive to dispose of the burdensome economic surplus, and where it charges for such investment activities as it performs exorbitant dues in form of excess consumption, extravagant waste, capital flights, and the like—society tends to assume the control over its economic surplus itself and to entrust its utilization to its planning organs.

Notes

1. Karl Marx, *The Poverty of Philosophy* (German ed., trans. by this writer), p. 86.

2. Colin Clark suggests a different definition: "Economic progress can be defined simply as an improvement in economic welfare. Economic welfare, following Pigou, can be defined in the first instance as an abundance of all these goods and services which are customarily exchanged for money. Leisure is an element in economic welfare and more precisely we can define economic progress as the attaining of an increasing output of these goods and services for a minimum expenditure of effort, and of other scarce resources, both natural and artificial."—*The Conditions of Economic Progress* (London, 1940), p. 1. This definition appears to me inadequate for a number of reasons: (1) The identification of economic growth with increase in welfare leaves out of account a considerable share of total output that bears no relation to welfare, however the latter may be conceived: as currently produced investment goods, armaments, net exports and the like belong into that group. (2) Regarding an increase of output of "all these goods and services which are customarily exchanged for money" as identical with "improvement in economic welfare" is untenable. Economic welfare may be greatly improved by an increased supply of goods and services that are customarily *not* exchanged for money (schools, hospitals, roads, or bridges), while on the other hand a great number of goods and services that *are* customarily exchanged for money make no contribution whatever to human welfare (patent medicines and beauty

parlors, narcotics and items of conspicuous display, etc.). (3) While it is obviously *desirable* to secure any given output with a minimum of input, even an inefficiently secured increase in output might still constitute economic growth. It would seem to be preferable, therefore, to consider economic growth as an *increase in output* of goods and services regardless of whether they make a contribution to welfare, to the available stock of producers' goods or armaments—leaving to a related but nevertheless separate examination the factors determining the composition of this output and the purposes to which it is put. It may be permissible to neglect in the present context the difficulty of comparing outputs over time, a difficulty arising whenever the outputs to be compared consist of more than one product, whenever, therefore, changes in output may affect its components unequally, and whenever certain products appear in the output of one period without appearing in the output of the other. This familiar index number problem, disturbing as it is even with regard to slow, gradual development, becomes particularly vexing when what is considered is more or less rapid economic growth, the outstanding characteristic of which is profound change not only in the magnitude but also in the composition of output. Indeed, inter-temporal comparisons threaten to be outright misleading when the periods to be compared are separated by changes in economic and social organization, by big spurts in urbanization, by increases or declines in the "marketed share" of output, and so forth. Especially troublesome is the services sector, the expansion of which would cause an increase in Gross National Product (as conventionally defined) thus suggesting "economic growth"—although in most underdeveloped countries it would be considered to be a retrograde step rather than one in the direction of economic progress. This was noted in the *United Nations Economic Survey of Europe Since the War* (Geneva, 1953): "In the Eastern European countries services not directly connected with the production and transport of goods are not regarded as productive and their value is thus excluded from national income. For a poor country which is trying to develop its industry and to reduce the underemployment common in service trades, the Marxist definition of national income has some obvious advantages over the more inclusive concept suited to wealthy industrialized economies and now commonly adopted in under-developed countries" (p. 25). Yet to the extent to which available computations are based on the "more inclusive concept" there may be no alternative to using them. It should be borne in mind, however, that for most important purposes it is the *breakdown* of the Gross National Product estimate rather than the aggregative number that is of relevance.

3. It is important to note that the higher the degree of development of a country, the more important is this factor in the process of growth. As with rising "organic composition of capital," depreciation allowances become an ever larger share of the value of total output, the mere plowing back of the depreciation allowances on a higher technological plane may cause a significant increase in productivity. While this development aggravates the instability of the advanced capitalist economies by increasing the amount of currently available surplus that has to be disposed of by investment, it also gives the advanced countries a major advantage over the underdeveloped countries where the annual amortization allowances necessarily amount to little. Cf. Karl Marx, *Theories of Surplus Value* (London, 1951), p. 354 f., where this point is stressed.

4. In actual fact some net investment may be needed for all of them: previously unused resources may be unusable without some outlays on equipment, soil improvements, and the like; organizational changes may be predicated upon the installation of conveyor belts or similar devices; technological progress yielding improved machinery to be added to or substituted for worn out equipment may be only forthcoming under conditions of large net investment. In the words of Engels: " If . . . technique largely depends on the state of science, science depends far more still on the *state* and the *requirements* of technique. If society has a technical need, that helps science forward more than ten universities. The whole of hydrostatics (Torricelli, etc.) was called forth by the necessity for regulating the mountain streams of Italy in the sixteenth and seventeenth centuries. We have only known anything reasonable about electricity since its technical applicability was discovered."—Karl Marx and Friedrich Engels, *Selected Works* (Moscow, 1950), Vol. II, p. 457. Cf. also the interesting essay by Stephen F. Mason, "Historical Roots of the Scientific Revolution," *Science & Society* (Summer 1950).

5. Strictly speaking this applies only to the world as a whole or to closed national systems, since frequently individual countries are able to supplement their own outputs with the outputs of other countries, however acquired.

6. It is a matter of definition whether *durable* consumer goods (residential dwellings, automobiles, etc.) should be treated as representing saving rather than consumption. It would seem to be

preferable to make the distinction not on the basis of the physical properties of the assets involved but in the light of their economic function, i.e., depending on whether they are acquired for consumption purposes or in order to be used as a means of production, or of commercial activity.

7. This leaves out of consideration Keynesian underemployment—the most obvious source of potential economic surplus in advanced capitalist countries, partly because attention is focused on the potential economic surplus existing even under conditions of so-called full employment, partly also because *Keynesian* underemployment is rarely of interest in the case of underdeveloped countries.

8. "The labor of some of the most respectable orders in the society, is like that of menial servants, unproductive of any value.... The sovereign, for example, with all the officers both of justice and war who serve under him, the whole army and navy, are unproductive laborers. They are the servants of the public, and are maintained by a part of the annual produce of the industry of other people.... In the same class must be ranked ... churchmen, lawyers, physicians, men of letters of all kinds: players, buffoons, musicians, opera-singers, opera-dancers, etc...."—Adam Smith, *Wealth of Nations,* p. 295.

"When the annual productions of a country more than replace its annual consumption, it is said to increase its capital; when its annual consumption is not at least replaced by its annual productions, it is said to diminish its capital. Capital may, therefore, be increased by an increased production or by a diminished unproductive consumption."—David Ricardo, *Principles of Political Economy and Taxation,* Everyman Library ed., p. 150.

9. Karl Marx, *Theories of Surplus Value,* p. 177.

10. J. A. Schumpeter, *Capitalism, Socialism, and Democracy* (New York, 1950), p. 143.

11. Although this is true with increasing reservations. At the current, imperialist stage of capitalist development, placing too much emphasis on the socio-political structure of backward countries as the main obstacle to their progress is looked at askance.

12. Food, housing, and medical requirements for various countries have been studied by the United Nations Food and Agriculture Organization and other agencies, and represent a most important field of further investigations. Cf. *Calorie Requirements,* FAO Nutritional Studies No. 5, Food and Agriculture Organization (Washington, June 1950); National Research Council, *Recommended Dietary Allowances,* Reprint and Circular Series (Washington, 1948); *Housing and Town and*

Country Planning (United Nations, 1949-1950), as well as the material referred to in these sources.

13. Where essential consumption is never defined as such, non-essential consumption is readily identified for purposes of war economic controls, excise taxation, or foreign exchange regulations.

14. "All members of society not directly engaged in reproduction, with or without labor, can obtain their share of the annual product of commodities—in other words, their articles of consumption—primarily only out of the hands of those classes who are the first to handle that product, that is to say, productive laborers, industrial capitalists, and real estate owners. To that extent their revenues are substantially derived from wages (of the productive laborers), profit, and ground rent, and appear as indirect derivations when compared to these primary sources of revenue. But, on the other hand, the recipients of these revenues, thus indirectly derived, draw them by grace of their social function, for instance, that of a King, priest, professor, prostitute, soldier, etc., and they may regard these functions as the primary sources of their revenue."—Karl Marx, *Capital* (Kerr ed.), Vol. II, p. 429.

15. This distinction would be relevant only at the point of transition to a different social order, where the former group of unproductive workers would be retained in their occupations while the latter would be shifted to other activities.

16. Cf., for instance, *Does Distribution Cost Too Much?* (New York: The Twentieth Century Fund, 1939); K.W. Kapp, *The Social Cost of Private Enterprise* (Cambridge, Mass., 1950).

17. J. A. Schumpeter, *Capitalism, Socialism, and Democracy*, p. 198.

18. To avoid misunderstanding it should be stressed that the designation of a worker as "unproductive" is *not* tantamount to his being labeled "unnecessary." Many unproductive workers are necessary, indeed essential. In the capitalist order, however, under normal non-emergency conditions the criterion of essentiality is market demand for their services, a demand determined by the class-structure, income distribution, ideology of the capitalist society. Under socialism, on the other hand, the criterion of essentiality would be altogether different, and derived from the changed structure of society, its different tastes and requirements, as well as from the working principles of a planned economy.

19. As mentioned before, these "flaws" of economic organization particularly pronounced under monopoly capitalism are usually well

brought out by the economists deriving their inspiration and categories from the competitive period of capitalist development. Yet, employing the model of "perfect competition" as their "standard of perfection" they usually forget that "... perfect competition is not only impossible, but inferior, and has no title to being set up as a model of ideal efficiency."—Schumpeter, *Capitalism, Socialism, and Democracy,* p. 106.

20. "In the primitive community saving is of minor importance ... but can be recognized as the 'natural capital' of plants and domestic animals, especially cattle."—Raymond Firth, *Primitive Polynesian Economy* (London, 1939), p. 9. The wisdom of calling the implements of production developed in a primitive economy "capital" is obviously highly dubious!

21. Cf. Raymond Firth, *Primitive Polynesian Economy,* p. 32 f. for a description of the diet and living conditions in Tikopia; as well as Melville J. Herskovits, *The Economic Life of Primitive Peoples* (New York, 1940), p. 246 f. See also the illuminating discussion of the historically changing nutritional standards in Audrey I. Richards, *Hunger and Work in a Savage Tribe* (Glencoe, Ill., 1948). It is not quite clear whether the changes in the nutritional standards reflect actual changes in physiological (and psychological) *requirements* or rather variations in the states of health, in life expectancy, etc. It is possible that nutritional *optima* for human beings are today not much different from what they were thousands of years ago, although the *size* of the human being and, therefore, its need for food would seem to have significantly increased. Cf. M. Kovalevski, *An Outline of the Origin and Development of Family and Property,* Fourth Lecture.

22. However, speaking of "barbarism" Engels observes that "war formerly waged only in revenge for injuries or to extend territory that has grown too small, is now waged simply for plunder and becomes a regular industry."—Friedrich Engels, *The Origins of the Family, Private Property, and the State* in Karl Marx and Friedrich Engels, *Selected Works,* Vol. II, p. 150. To this extent professional warriors cease to be "unproductive" workers living off their communities' output but "earn their way" by "productive" labor.

23. F. W. Walbank, *The Decline of the Roman Empire in the West* (London, 1948), p. 26.

24. *Ibid.,* p. 27.

25. "Only when the first form of the division of society into classes appeared, only when slavery appeared, when a certain class of people, by concentrating on the crudest form of agricultural labor, could

produce a certain surplus, when this surplus was not absolutely essential for the most wretched existence of the slave and passed into the hands of the slave owner, when in this way the existence of this class of slave owners took firm root—then in order that it might take firm root it was essential that a state should appear."—V.I. Lenin, *Marx, Engels, Marxism* (Moscow, 1947), pp. 430 ff.

26. Henri Pirenne, *Economic and Social History of Medieval Europe* (London, 1936), p. 65.

27. John U. Nef, *War and Human Progress* (London, 1950), p. 4.

28. "The surplus—whether small or great— is usually torn from the producers either by the government to which they are subject, or by individuals who by superior force or by availing themselves of religious or traditional feeling of subordination, have established themselves as lords of the soil."—John Stuart Mill, *Principles of Political Economy* (New York, 1888), p. 30.

29. To the extent to which alms had become an important element of mass consumption they represented "transfer payments" to be deducted from the potential economic surplus appropriated by the church. This was pointed out to me by Professor Simon Kuznets.

30. Henri Pirenne, "The Stages in the Social History of Capitalism," *Amer. Hist. Rev.* (1914), p. 500.

31. Paul M. Sweezy, "The Transition from Feudalism to Capitalism," *Science & Society* (Spring 1950), p. 137.

32. "The natural price of labor is that price which is necessary to enable the laborers, one with another to subsist and to perpetuate their race, without either increase of diminution."—David Ricardo, *Principles of Political Economy*, p. 53. Also: "If . . . wages continued the same, the profits of manufacturers would remain the same, but if . . . wages should rise . . . then their profits would necessarily fall." *Ibid.,* p. 64.

33. Similarly the bankers by providing bank credit would facilitate capital accumulation partly by centralizing smaller savings, partly by creating savings via inflation.

34. Incidentally, the development of rational calculation and accountancy so much stressed by Weber and Sombart had been pointed out as an important factor in the growth of bourgeois culture by Marx as early as 1848: "The bourgeoisie is too enlightened, it calculates too well, to share the prejudices of the feudal lord who makes a display by the brilliance of his retinue. *The conditions of existence of the bourgeoisie compel it to calculate.*"—*Wage Labor and Capital* in Karl Marx and Friedrich Engels, *Selected Works,* Vol. I, p. 91.

35. By 1900 European countries had invested *in the United States*

alone $3.5 billion, equaling the value of all equipment in American manufacturing industries and on all American farms. See Gunther Stein, *The World the Dollar Built* (London, 1952), p. 19.

36. "The clear and direct tendency of the poor laws . . . is not, as the legislature benevolently intended, to amend the condition of the poor, but to deteriorate the condition of both poor and rich; instead of making the poor rich, they are calculated to make the rich poor; and whilst the present laws are in force, it is quite in the natural order of things that the fund for the maintenance of the poor should progressively increase till it has absorbed all the net revenue of the country. . . ."—David Ricardo, *Principles of Political Economy*, p. 81. The classical bourgeoisie's distaste for militarism and military spending was stressed by Schumpeter, *Capitalism, Socialism, and Democracy*, pp. 122 ff.

37. This simple formulation is suggested in an essay by Paul M. Sweezy. Decline in the growth of population, closing of the frontier, and other factors play a prominent role in the theory of "vanishing investment opportunities." Cf. A. H. Hansen's classical formulation of the doctrine in "Economic Progress and Declining Population Growth," *Readings in Business Cycle Theory* (Philadelphia and Toronto, 1944).

38. *Ibid.,* p. 379.

39. Listing such enterprises as would be technologically indicated and socially desirable is the normal pastime of liberal technocrats and economists who are engaged in "planning" in a socio-political vacuum. The best example perhaps are the article by J. K. Galbraith in *The New York Times Magazine,* June 22, 1952, and in David Lilienthal's *Big Business, A New Era* (New York, 1952), p. 8 f.

40. Cf. Paul M. Sweezy, *The Theory of Capitalist Development,* p. 275 f.; Oskar Lange, *On the Economic Theory of Socialism* (Minneapolis, 1938), p. 114 f.; Evsey D. Domar, "Investment, Losses, and Monopolies," in *Income, Employment, and Public Policy* (New York, 1948), *passim;* J. K. Galbraith, *American Capitalism* (Boston, 1952); T. Scitovsky, *Welfare and Competition* (Homewood, Illinois, 1951), Chapter XX; and others.

41. This is, strictly speaking, only true if the investment in the first period is directed toward productive plant and equipment. Investment in residential dwellings or in inventories may have no productivity-raising effect and thus aggravate the next period's problem not by increasing the volume of investable actual surplus but by reducing the outlets for future investment.

42. Marx suggests that the latter was the case: "Although the

enjoyments of the workers have risen, the social satisfactions that they give have fallen in comparison with the increased enjoyments of the capitalists, which are inaccessible to the worker, in comparison with the state of development of society in general."—*Wage Labor and Capital* in Karl Marx and Friedrich Engels, *Selected Works,* Vol. I, p. 87. On the other hand, M. Kalecki notes that the share of national income going to manual labor was fairly constant over a period of some fifty years in Great Britain. Cf. his *Essays in the Theory of Economic Fluctuations* (London, 1939), pp. 13-41. Needless to say that wages do not fully account for mass consumption; they may serve, however, as a satisfactory index of it.

43. In that sense labor organizations that by means of economic and political struggle succed in *increasing* labor's share in total income or in shortening the labor day, thus reducing total output, perform a *stabilizing* function under monopoly capitalism, even if their endeavors are meeting with embittered resistance on the part of individual members or groups of the capitalist class, acting in accordance with their particular interests.

44. However, even mere exchange of exports for imports may be of considerable importance to the capitalist economy. It may provide the indispensable *physical assortment* of consumption and investment goods; it may diversify the basket of consumer goods and thus increase consumption of those groups in society that are in the position to save; it may finally open outlets for new products and sources of cheaper (or better) raw materials and thus create opportunities for new investment. Nor should it be overlooked that the mere exchange of exports for imports, regardless of its significance for the economy as a whole, represents usually a source of large profits to the capitalists engaged in international trade and may, therefore, be energetically pushed by them.

45. As Marx foresaw, "Bourgeois society reproduces in its own form everything against which it has fought in feudal or absolutist form."—*Theories of Surplus Value,* p. 176.

46. "At the historical dawn of capitalist production—and every capitalist upstart has personally to go through this historical stage—avarice and the desire to get rich are the ruling passion. . . . When a certain stage of development has been reached, a conventional degree of prodigality, which is also an exhibition of wealth, and consequently a source of credit, becomes a business necessity to the 'unfortunate' capitalist. Luxury enters into capital's expenses of representation. . . . Although, therefore, the prodigality of the capitalist never possesses the

bona fide character of the open-handed feudal lord's prodigality, but on the contrary has always lurking behind it the most sordid avarice and the most anxious calculation, yet his expenditure grows with his accumulation. . . ."—Karl Marx, *Capital,* Vol. I, p. 650. Paul M. Sweezy in his *Theory of Capitalist Development,* p. 81, rightly draws attention to the fact that in this statment Marx has anticipated much of what was later expounded by Thorstein Veblen.

47. Victor Perlo, *American Imperialism* (New York, 1951), p. 226. A note on the same page explains that "engaged in commodity production" includes employees in agriculture, mining, construction, manufacturing, transportation, communication, public utilities, as well as farm operators.

48. Cf. J. A. Hobson, *Imperialism: A Study* (London, 1948), p. 96.

49. C.F. J.A. Hobson, *Imperialism: A Study,* Chapter VII.

50. For the reasons preventing the government in a capitalist society from channeling the economic surplus into investment in productive enterprise or into mass consumption. Cf. Paul M. Sweezy, *The Theory of Capitalist Development,* p. 348 f., and Paul A. Baran, "National Economic Planning" in *A Survey of Contempory Economics,* B.F. Halcy, ed. (Homewood, Illinois, 1952), Vol. II, p. 355 f.

51. The "New Economics" developed by J. M. Keynes—the Ricardo of monopoly capitalism—is essentially a brilliant theoretic rationalization of this new function of the state under conditions of advanced capitalism.

52. For a somewhat more expanded treatment of this point cf. "Fascism in America," in *Monthly Review* (October 1952).

53. Many "infant industry" tariffs, eminently rational and useful under conditions of growth, have turned in underdeveloped countries into "senile industry" crutches protecting monopolistic business from the sharp winds of foreign competition that might force them to modernize and rationalize their methods of production.

54. The payments to foreign investors are in most cases out of proportion to the original increase of investable funds provided by capital imports. "For example, the average rate of return on United States foreign investments in 1949 was about 17 percent. . . . Many underdeveloped countries feel that this is too high a price to pay for capital."—*Measures for the Economic Development of Underdeveloped Countries* (United Nations, 1951), par. 255.

55. Cf. *Measures for the Economic Development of Underdeveloped Countries, passim;* also Paul Baran, *Amer. Econ. Rev.* (May 1951, Suppl.), p. 355 f. and *Manchester School* (January 1952).

56. Cf. Doreen Warriner, *Revolution in Eastern Europe* (London, 1950).

57. Karl Marx, *Critique of the Gotha Program* in Karl Marx and Friedrich Engels, *Selected Works,* Vol. II, p. 20 f.

58. On the problem of the "withering away" of the state in a communist society, cf. Joseph Stalin, *Problems of Leninism* (11th ed., Moscow, 1939), p. 606.

59. Such a policy will probably be indicated everywhere where rapid population growth tends to reduce continuously the *per capita* share of aggregate output, where, in other words, total output has to grow very fast if it is to overcompensate the increase in the population.

Reflections on Planning of the Economic Development of India

The objective of planning for the economic development of India should be the maximal possible increase of current output, and such allocation of it as will insure the largest attainable rates of growth of output for the period encompassed by the planning horizon: twenty to thirty years. In the light of this general goal, the immediate task facing economic policy is as complete as possible utilization of the country's *available* productive resources.

Although this basic goal is in conflict with a program of maximization of gainful employment in the short run, this conflict is only partial. For unemployment consists of two segments that must be sharply distinguished. On the one hand there are the unemployed who are *urban* dwellers and have no jobs although there are available the plant and facilities required for their productive employment. On the other hand there are the fully or partly unemployed who inhabit the villages and who subsist—if ever so precariously—by drawing on their families.

It is clear that the limitations on the productive employability of the latter group (the "disguised" unem-

This article originally appeared in *The Economic Weekly* (Bombay) on February 18, 1956, and is reprinted by permission. Baran was working at the Indian Statistical Institute in Calcutta at the time.

ployed) are set by the speed of the accumulation of additional plant and equipment. Those limitations cannot be removed in the short run; they can be overcome only by a major investment effort. The limitation on the productive employability of the former group of unemployed (the "Keynesian" unemployed) are of an altogether different type: they are the result of an insufficient effective demand and of prevailing monopolistic controls over the existing means of production. They *can* be removed by appropriate economic policies. The existence of limitations on output and employment stemming from the inadequacy of effective demand and from monopolistic controls is intolerable in advanced countries. It constitutes a veritable disgrace in the case of a poor country.

In an excellent study by Messrs. Lobel and Das (prepared for the Indian Statistical Institute) it is shown that the underutilization of existing productive capacity in India reaches as much as 40 percent. The situation is even worse in some individual industries. To be sure, this unutilized capacity is unevenly distributed, and an attempt at its full utilization is bound to run into bottlenecks of various kinds. It is the primary, and indeed the most urgent, task of economic planning at the present stage of India's economic development to examine carefully the structure of the available unutilized capacities and to identify the bottlenecks that are likely to obstruct the full utilization of the available excess capacities. Such bottlenecks may appear in various areas; the measures needed to deal with them have to be selected accordingly. Broadly speaking they will fall into the following groups:

(1) Deficit financing of the planned investment program to create the effective demand for additional output.

(2) Investment in such plant and facilities as may be needed to overcome possible shortage, and to assure the

necessary composition (proportionality) of output. The productivity of such (supplementary) investment would be necessarily very high.

(3) Where the output that would be produced at full capacity utilization is of such a physical nature as to exceed the (increasing) effective demand, shifts in production may be necessary. Where such shifts are impossible—for technical reasons—government purchases with a view to exporting the resulting surpluses must be organized.

(4) Where existing monopolistic controls are such as to prevent expansion of output in response to rising effective demand, nationalization of the relevant plants and facilities is called for.

(5) If balance of payments complications should arise, severe economies of foreign exchange as well as purposeful borrowing abroad must be instituted.

Until the investment program in *new* plants and facilities has begun absorbing a growing number of "disguised" unemployed—that is, as long as those unemployed are compelled to remain in their villages—all measures must be taken to improve their lot in the countryside. Such measures include first and foremost an agrarian reform that will provide for a more equitable distribution of *that share of agricultural output that is currently consumed in the villages,* and, second, the provision of a stable market for both agricultural and handicraft outputs that are marketed by the rural population. A government purchasing agency for the products of cottage industries, thus removing the limitations of effective demand on their output, would be urgently required. Such an agency could either market that output at home, if there is sufficient demand for it (at lower prices), or export it—absorbing, if need be, such losses as may occur. This amount of subsidy to the rural population would constitute a social relief payment warranted by the distressed state of the rural population and by the desirability of preserving the skills of rural craftsmen.

Of the maximum attainable current output, a maximum possible share must be mobilized for productive investment. Possible foreign assistance apart, the resources required for an investment program are provided by the *economic surplus* that is currently generated in the economy. The *actual* economic surplus is equal to the actually observed saving (and investment). In poor countries this actual surplus is small, both absolutely and in relation to national income. The actual economic surplus does not delineate, however, the volume of resources that *could be* mobilized for investment in productive plant and facilites. It is the *potential economic surplus* hidden in the country's economic structure that has to be tapped if a concentrated effort to promote economic development is to be undertaken.

This potential economic surplus appears under a number of headings. In addition to the output that can be secured by full utilization of available productive capacities, the most important categories are the following:

(1) *Excess consumption on the part of upper income groups.* This is reflected in the high standard of living of those groups, in the large number of servants maintained by them, in trips abroad, in the acquisition of jewels, foreign luxuries, and the like. It appears in the construction of lavish residences (Bombay), in the acquisition of land, and in other forms. The exact magnitude of the amount that could be saved by the suppression of this form of resource utilization is not readily calculated; such tentative estimates as I have been able to make suggest that it might reach as much as 500 crores[1] per year. It would be an urgent task of economic research to secure as precise information as

possible on this crucially important portion of the national income. It should be a matter of the utmost importance to those concerned with economic planning to scrutinize closely all possible measures (fiscal as well as administrative) that might enable the government to secure that slice of the national product for the purposes of economic development.

(2) *Unproductive workers* who absorb a considerable share of national income. They are first and foremost absentee landowners and money-lenders; also superabundant merchants, traders, agents, and commission-men as well as redundant civil servants, lawyers, and advertising agents. Their total revenue might be estimated to be close to 2000 crores per year. It would be imperative to study this problem carefully to estimate the amount of possible savings and to examine the possibility of a planned transfer of the individuals involved to socially useful occupations.

(3) Losses suffered by the economy as a result of *fluctuations of business activity.* To the extent to which such fluctuations are attributable to domestic causes, suitable countercyclical measures have to be considered and adequately prepared. To the extent to which such fluctuations may be caused by changes in world market conditions, the government should stand ready to insulate the economy against sudden declines in the demand for and the prices of Indian exports. Here again, economic planning calls for timely arrangements that would be able to cope with the problem.

(4) The drain on national resources caused by *capital flight* and by *transfer of profits abroad.* Strict controls on capital movements and the blocking of transfers abroad of profits earned in India by foreign companies are indispensable. Profits thus blocked will find their way into investment in India. In view of the smallness and frequently undesirable allocation of foreign private investment in India, the disincentive effect of such measures with regard to

further private foreign investment may be safely disregarded.

It is my considered opinion that given a determined effort to eliminate waste in the Indian economy, and to mobilize at least a part of its potential economic surplus, the ratio of investment to national income could be rapidly raised to 15 percent.

No planning for the economic development of an underdeveloped country can be considered to represent a wholehearted undertaking as long as the prevailing low ratio of investment to national income is accepted as a datum, and until all possibilities for its increase have not been fully explored and realized. It is of crucial importance, however, to secure the indispensable increase in the investment ratio *not* by an encroachment upon the desperately low levels of mass consumption, but by a systematic mobilization of the potential economic surplus. Whether from the standpoint of economic rationality—the effect on the health and efficiency of the working population—or whether from the standpoint of elementary canons of social equity—a program of financing the necessary investment by increased indirect taxes is wholly inadmissible. It would be most undesirable even if the entire potential economic surplus were already mobilized. It is altogether reprehensible as long as *nothing has been undertaken to utilize the potential economic surplus for development purposes.*

Little need be said about the *mode of utilization* of the economic surplus. Under the prevailing conditions, a considerable part of investment in the so-called private sector is undertaken in the wrong areas. Therefore, a system of strict investment controls is necessary to assure the proper allocation of investment funds. Licensing of imports, of new construction, etc., represent some of the requisite tools.

The division of the proposed investment between the

public and private sectors as envisaged in the Second Five Year Plan is subject to doubt. It leaves to the government all the projects that by their very nature are bound to be most difficult and most seriously hampered by lack of skilled manpower, of industrial tradition, etc. It reserves at the same time to private business such enterprises as are more readily established and operated. The result will be a "socialization of losses" accompanied by private appropriation of rising profits. Such a situation will be readily exploited by those who are interested in discrediting the idea of economic planning with a view to forcing the "re-privatization" of inefficient and unprofitable government enterprises. It is mandatory, therefore, that the public sector should contain not merely the "tough" subjects, but also a sufficient number of ventures that in the present state of the economy will yield satisfactory profits and display the advantages of planned economy.

The division of the entire investment outlay provided for by the Second Five Year Plan as between producer goods industries and consumer goods industries is inadequate. Given full utilization of the existing capacity of the consumer goods industries, a much larger allocation to producer goods industries is possible. Such a larger allocation, combined with a considerable increase of the investment total, could yield much more impressive rates of growth and permit a much earlier liquidation of "hidden" unemployment.

The problems referred to above offer a rich field of work for economists and statisticians concerned with actual economic planning. The development of economic thought and research has always been closely related to the needs of society at various stages of its development. Where this relation has been torn apart, economics has been condemned to sterility or has even played a negative, reactionary role in the process of social advancement. What is needed in India today is undivided attention to the central issues of the mobilization and correct allocation of investment funds.

Notes

1. A crore equals 10 million rupees. A rupee exchanges at about seven or eight to the dollar.

Comments on
The Political Economy of Growth

On looking over this book again with a view to writing a foreward for the French and German translations as well as for the new American printing, I have a strong feeling of ambivalence. There is first the thought that it may not be too immodest on my part to submit this work once more to the reader in its original form. Neither historical events which have taken place since it was written, nor subsequent reflection and study, partly stimulated by the criticism to which it has been subjected, have changed my conviction that *taken as a whole* the view which it presents and the argument which it advances are still entirely valid. But then there are other considerations—referring not to the whole but to parts—which are less comforting. For were I at this time to write the book afresh, I would try to eliminate what strike me now as weaknesses and to develop several of its themes in a more comprehensive and convincing manner. However, since the pressure of other, not unrelated, work renders such a major undertaking impossible, I must reluctantly adopt the principle of "letting bygones be bygones," and attempt to resolve the conflict between the whole and the parts by means of this prefatory note dealing briefly with those aspects of the book which are most in need of reconsideration and supplementation. The

---

These comments were written as a foreword to the 1962 edition of *The Political Economy of Growth* (Monthly Review Press).

order in which the topics are taken up is determined not so much by their general importance as by the sequence in which they appear in the book itself.

Hard as I tried to clarify the prevailing confusion about a central concept of economic theory, that of *consumer sovereignty*, the success attained was anything but spectacular. There are few other areas where the limitations of the conventional economist are as obvious and as damaging to insight as in the treatment of this subject. Irrevocably committed to taking the existing economic and social order for granted, and thinking exclusively in categories reflecting capitalist relations of production, even the ablest academic economist is inexorably trapped by the basic predicament of all bourgeois thought: the compulsion to choose continually between equally pernicious alternatives. Like the man condemned to death who was granted "freedom of choice" between being hanged and being shot, bourgeois economics is eternally plagued by the problem whether the irrationality of monopoly is better than the anarchy of competition; whether the cumulation of means of destruction is better than unemployment; whether inequality of income and wealth leading to saving and investment on the part of the rich is better than fair shares and greatly reduced saving and investment. In the same way the problem of consumers sovereignty is viewed as the question whether the consumer—however much exposed to the barrage of advertising and high-pressure salesmanship—should be left free to spend his income in any way he pleases or be forced to accept a basket of goods which a "commissar" would judge to be best for him. It can be readily seen that placed before *this* dilemma, the economist is indeed confronted by a Hobson's choice. Kneeling awestricken before the absolute truth of the consumer's "revealed preferences" places him in the disturbing position of having to refuse to make any judgments on the resulting composition of output and hence on all the waste and cultural degradation which so obviously characterize our society. On the other hand, rejecting the consumer's revealed preferences as the *ultima ratio* in favor of a set of decisions imposed by government would be equally distressing, implying as it would the repudiation of all the teachings of welfare economics and—more importantly—of all the principles of individual freedom which the economist rightly strives to uphold.

The conservative reaction to this perplexity appears in two variants. One school of thought deals with the problem by denying its existence. This school holds that the molding of consumers' tastes and preferences by the advertising and high-pressure sales efforts of corporate business is nothing but a bogey, because in the long run no amount of persuasion and no ingenuity of salesmanship can change "human nature," can force upon the consumer what he does not want.[1] Furthermore—so the argument runs—the revealed preferences of consumers yield results which are quite adequate and call for no particular improvements.[2]

Another conservative current of thought takes a different tack. It freely acknowledges that the consumer's revealed preferences have nothing in common with the traditional notion of consumer *sovereignty*, that the power of the giant corporations is such as to mold consumers' tastes and preferences for the benefit of corporate interests, and that all of this has a deleterious effect on both our economy and our society. As Professor Carl Kaysen puts it:

> One aspect of [its] broad power . . . is the position that corporate management occupies as taste setter or style leader for the society as a whole. Business influence on taste ranges from the direct effects through the design of material goods to the indirect and more subtle effects of the style of language and thought purveyed through the mass media—the school of style at which all of us are in

attendance every day . . . . This, more shortly stated, is the familiar proposition that we are a business society, and that the giant corporation is the "characteristic," if not the statistically typical, institution of our society . . . . [3]

Yet skeptical and realistic as the writers of this orientation are, they place the utmost emphasis on the fact that these irrationalities and calamities are *inherent* in the order of things, which they identify with the economic and social system of monopoly capitalism. "To touch the corporation deeply," remarks Professor Mason, "is to touch much else."[4] And in our day touching "much else" is definitely not on the economist's agenda.

This is not the stance of the so-called liberal. Considering the consumer's revealed preferences to be the source of our society's irrational allocation of resources, of its distressing moral and cultural condition, the liberal is exercised about the pernicious impact of advertising, about fraudulent product differentiation and artificial product obsolescence; he inveighs against the quality of culture purveyed by the educational system, Hollywood, the newspapers, the radio and TV networks; and, driven by this indignation, he arrives at the conclusion that "the choice is not whether consumers or a central planner should exercise sovereignty but whether and how the producer's power to ignore some consumers and influence the preferences of others should be curbed, modified, or shared in some ways."[5] To accomplish this curbing, modifying, and sharing, he recommends a list of "remedies and policies" ranging from regulatory measures such as those taken by the Food and Drug Administration, through government support for opera houses and theaters, to the formation of Distinguished Citizens Committees whose task would be to influence public opinion in the direction of rational choices and better taste.

Disappointing as it may be to many, there can be little

doubt that at the present stage of capitalist development
the conservative "realist" often comes nearer to the truth
than the liberal meliorist. Just as it makes no sense to
deplore war casualties without attacking their cause, war, so
it is meaningless to sound the alarm about advertising and
all that accompanies it without clearly identifying the locus
from which the pestilence emanates: the monopolistic and
oligopolistic corporation and the non-price-competitive
business practices which constitute an integral component
of its *modus operandi*. Since this locus itself is never
approached, is indeed treated as strictly out of bounds by
Galbraith, Scitovsky, and other liberal critics, since nothing
is further from their minds (or at least their public
utterances) than "touching deeply" the giant corporation,
what can be expected from their recommending various
regulatory boards and even their possible appointment to
Distinguished Citizens' Committees? One would think that
the record of already existing regulatory agencies is sufficiently eloquent in showing that it is Big Business that does
the regulating rather than vice versa. And is more evidence
needed on the ineffectuality of the Food and Drug Administration, the Federal Trade Commission, and the Federal
Communications Commission than has already been assembled thus far?[6] Nor is there any need to elaborate on the
profound impact on society exercised by the recent activities
and reports of the President's most distinguished Commission
on National Goals.[7] But the liberal meliorists ignore all this.
Treating the state as an entity which presides over society but
does not form a part of it, which sets society's goals and
reshuffles its output and income but remains unaffected by
the prevailing relations of production and impervious to the
dominant interests, they fall prey to a naive rationalism
which, by nurturing illusions, merely contributes to the
maintenance of the status quo.[8] Compared with this, the

"contracting out" dictum—"we have . . . reached the frontier between economic and political theory; and we shall not cross it"—with which Professor Scitovsky a decade ago concluded his *magnum opus*,[9] formulates a relatively tenable position.

For the crux of the problem is not even approached by the liberal critic. In the first place, he of all people, being a good Keynesian, cannot avoid inconsistency when he recommends the interference with or curtailment of corporate advertising and other sales activities. In this regard *The Wall Street Journal* and the "realistic" economists who share its views are surely on firmer ground. For all these "undesirable" business practices *do* in fact promote and increase sales, and *do* actually directly and indirectly help in propping up the level of income and employment.[10] So also does the sale of ever more motor cars, even if they do strangle our cities and poison our atmosphere; and the production of armaments and the digging of shelters. None of these activities can be regarded as promoting the progress and happiness of the human race, although all of them constitute remedies against sagging production and increasing unemployment.[11] And yet such is the dialectic of the historical process that *within the framework of monopoly capitalism* the most abominable, the most destructive features of the capitalist order become the very foundations of its continuing existence—just as slavery was the *conditio sine qua non* of its emergence.

The "realistic" conservative scores also over the liberal "do-gooder" in his general comprehension of the problem of consumer sovereignty. For in warning against exaggerating the impact of advertising, high-pressure salesmanship, and the like, on the preferences and choices of consumers, they occupy a position of formidable strength. Their statements that consumers like only what they care for and buy only what they wish to spend money on are obviously tautologies, but, being tautologies, they are equally obviously correct. From this, to be sure, it does not follow, as some business economists like to assert, that the barrage of advertising and salesmanship to which the consumer is continually exposed has *no* influence on the formation of his wants. But neither is it true that these business practices constitute *the* decisive factor in making the consumer want what he wants. Professor Henry C. Wallich comes closest to the spot where the dog is buried in his shrewd observation that "to argue that wants created by advertising are synthetic, are not genuine consumer wants is beside the point—it could be argued of all aspects of civilized existence."[12] This, to be sure, is overstating the case. Human wants are not *all* wholly "synthetic," created by an almighty Madison Avenue (or "purified" and "ennobled" by a Madison Avenue "in reverse": government regulatory boards and/or Distinguished Citizens Committees for the Promotion of Good Taste): that view reflects the spirit of limitless manipulability of man which is so characteristic of the "men in gray flannel suits" who dominate the executive offices of corporations and the important bureaus of the government. But neither do *all* wants stem from man's biotic urges or from a mythical eternally unchanging "human nature": that concept is metaphysical obscurantism which flies in the face of all historical knowledge and experience. The truth is that wants of people are complex historical phenomena reflecting the dialectic interaction of their physiological requirements on the one hand, and the prevailing social and economic order on the other.[13] The physiological requirements sometimes must be abstracted from for analytical purposes because they are *relatively constant.* And once this abstraction is explicitly made and firmly borne in mind, the make-up of human wants can (and must) be legitimately thought of as being "synthetic," i.e., determined by the nature of the economic and social order under which people live. What Professor Wallich apparently fails to see is that the issue is *not* whether the prevailing social and economic order plays a prominent part in molding people's "values," volitions, and preferences. On this—Robinson Crusoe having finally departed from economics textbooks to his proper insular habitat—there is nearly unanimous consensus among serious students of the problem. The issue is rather *the kind of social and economic order* that does the molding, the kind of "values," volitions, and preferences which it instills into the people under its sway. What renders the social and economic order of monopoly capitalism so irrational and destructive, so crippling to the individual's growth and happiness, is *not* that it influences, shapes, "synthesizes" the individual—as Professor Wallich suggests, every social and economic order does this—but rather the *kind* of influencing, shaping, and "synthesizing" which it perpetrates on its victims.

A clear understanding of this permits a further insight. The cancerous malaise of monopoly capitalism is not that it "happens" to squander a large part of its resources on the production of means of destruction, that it "happens" to allow corporations to engage in liminal and subliminal advertising, in peddling adulterated products, and in inundating human life with moronizing entertainment, commercialized religion, and debased "culture." The cancerous malaise of the system which renders it a formidable obstacle to human advancement is that all this is not an assortment of fortuitously appearing attributes of the capitalist order, but the very basis of its existence and viability. And such being the case, bigger and better Food and Drug Administrations, a comprehensive network of Distinguished Citizens Committees, and the like can merely spread a veil over the existing mess rather than clean up the mess itself. To use an earlier comparison once more: building sumptuous cemeteries and expensive monuments for the victims of war does not reduce their number. The best—and the worst—that such seemingly humanitarian efforts can accomplish is to dull people's sensitivity to brutality and cruelty, to reduce their horror of war.

But to return to the starting point of this argument. Neither I nor any other Marxist writers with whose works I am familiar, have ever advocated the abolition of consumer sovereignty and its replacement by the orders of a commissar. The attribution of such an advocacy to socialists is simply one aspect of the ignorance and misrepresentation of Marxian thought that are studiously cultivated by the powers that be. The real problem is an entirely different one, namely, whether an economic and social order should be tolerated in which the individual, from the very cradle on, is so shaped, molded, and "adjusted" as to become an easy prey of profit-greedy capitalist enterprise and a smoothly functioning object of capitalist exploitation and degradation. The Marxian social-ist is in no doubt about the answer. Holding that mankind has now reached a level of productivity and knowledge which make it possible to transcend this system and replace it by a better one, he believes that a society can be developed in which the individual would be formed, influenced, and educated not by a profit- and market-determined economy, not by the "values" of corporate presidents and the outpouring of their hired scribes, but by a system of rationally planned production for use, by a universe of human relations determined by and oriented toward solidarity, cooperation, and freedom. Indeed, only in such a society can there be sovereignty of the individual *human being*—not of the "consumer" or the "producer," terms which in themselves reflect the lethal fragmentation of the human personality under capitalism. Only in such a society can the individual freely co-determine the amount of work done, the composition of output consumed, the nature of leisure activities engaged in—free from all the open and hidden persuaders whose motives are preservation of their privileges and maximization of their profits.

And to those of my critics who skeptically or "realistically" sneer and condescendingly remark that the image of such a society is nothing but a utopia, all I can answer is that if they are right, all of us—my critics and myself—are utopians. They because they believe that a social and economic order which they wish to preserve can be made to last forever by means of manipulative tricks and superficial reforms that fail even to touch its increasingly manifest irrationality, destructiveness, and inhumanity; I because I trust that mankind, which has already managed to sweep capitalism off the face of one third of the globe, will in the fullness of time complete this Herculean task and succeed in establishing a genuinely human society. Having to choose between these two utopias, I prefer the second, subscribing to the beautiful words of Simone de Beauvoir: "Socialist Europe, there are moments when I ask myself whether it is not a utopia. But each idea not yet realized curiously resembles a utopia; one would never do anything if one thought that nothing is possible except that which exists already."[14]

Chapters Three and Four, dealing with monopoly capitalism, call for a clarification of the argument. The required modifications are not far-reaching, but may add—I hope—to its consistency and persuasiveness. My views on this vast subject have crystallized in the course of extensive work undertaken jointly with Paul M. Sweezy; the results of our studies and discussions will be presented in a book which we hope to complete in the near future. What follows in this section is confined therefore to only two points which the reader should bear in mind when turning to the relevant part of this volume.

I have argued above that it is necessary to probe deeper than the readily observable surface with regard to the problem of consumer sovereignty. This is at least equally true when it comes to what I consider to be the key to the understanding of the general working principles of capitalism: the concept of the "economic surplus." That I was unable to explain it sufficiently well is apparent from the fact that a critic as eminent as Nicholas Kaldor failed to grasp its meaning and significance.[15]

The root of the trouble is that Mr. Kaldor, like all other economists spellbound by the surface appearances of the capitalist economy, insists on identifying the economic surplus with statistically observable profits. If such an identification were legitimate, there would be no need to introduce the term "economic surplus," and—what is obviously more important—there might be no justification for speaking about *rising* surplus. The crux of the matter is, however, that profits are *not* identical with the economic surplus, but constitute—to use what has become now a hackneyed metaphor—merely the visible part of the iceberg with the rest of it hidden from the naked eye. Let us recall that at an early stage of the development of political economy (and capitalism) the relevant relations were seen much more clearly than they are at the present time. An intense theoretical struggle was fought, in face, to establish that the rent of land (and interest on money capital) are not necessary costs of production but components of the economic surplus. At a later phase, however, when the feudal landlord and moneylender were replaced by the capitalist entrepreneur and banker, *their* returns were "purged" of the surplus "stigma" and became promoted to the status of necessary prices of scarce resources or of indispensable rewards for "waiting," "abstinence," or "risk-taking." In fact, the very notion of "economic surplus," still prominent in the writings of John Stuart Mill, was declared *non grata* by the new economic science which proclaimed any and every outlay as "necessary" as long as it received the stamp of approval from the revealed preferences of consumers operating in a competitive market.

The situation became more complicated with the proliferation of monopoly; and a number of economists—beginning with Marshall but later on inspired primarily by the work of Pigou—who conducted their investigations from the vantage point of competitive capitalism found it impossible to treat *monopoly* profits as necessary costs of production.[16] This was undoubtedly an important step forward; it constitutes, however, only the beginning of what needs to be understood. For monopoly capitalism generates not only profits, rent, and interest as elements of the economic surplus, but conceals an important share of the surplus under the rubric of costs. This is due to the ever widening gap between the productivity of the *necessary productive workers* and the share of national income accruing to them as wages.

A simple numerical illustration may be helpful here. Assume that in period I, 100 bakers produce 200 loaves of bread, with 100 loaves constituting their wages (one loaf per man), and 100 loaves being appropriated by the capitalist as surplus (the source of his profit and his payment of rent and interest). The productivity of the baker is two loaves per man; the share of surplus in national income is 50 percent, and so is the share of labor. Now consider period II in which the productivity of the baker has increased by 525 percent to 12.5 loaves and his wage has risen by 400 percent to five loaves per man. Assume further that now only 80 bakers are employed in baking, producing altogether 1,000 loaves while the remaining 20 are engaged as follows: five men are commissioned to change continually the shapes of the loaves; one man is given the task of admixing with the dough a chemical substance that accelerates the perishability of bread; four men are hired to make up new wrappers for the bread; five men are employed in composing advertising copy for bread and broadcasting same over the available mass media; one man is appointed to watch carefully the activities of other baking companies; two men are to keep abreast of legal developments in the antitrust field; and finally two men are placed in charge of the baking corporation's public relations. All of these individuals receive also a wage of five loaves per man. Under these new circumstances, the total output of 80 bakers is 1,000 loaves, the aggregate wage of the 100 members of the corporation's labor force is 500 loaves, and profit plus rent plus interest are 500 loaves.[17] It might seem at first that nothing has changed between period I and period II except for the increase of the total volume of output. The share of labor in national income has remained constant at 50 percent, and the share of surplus does not appear to have varied either. Yet such a conclusion, though self-evident from the inspection of customary statistics, would be wholly unwarranted and in fact would merely serve to demonstrate how misleading such statistical inferences can be. For the statistical fact that the shares of labor and capital have not changed from period I to period II is irrelevant so far as our problem is concerned. What has happened, as can be readily seen, is that a share of the economic surplus, all of which in the earlier period was available to the capitalist as profit and for payment of land rent and interest, is now used to support the costs of a non-price-competitive sales effort, is—in other words—*wasted*.[18]

In the light of this, it should be clear that Mr. Kaldor's

and other critics' contention that my admission of the validity of the thesis that the share of wages in income remained more or less constant over a number of decades is wholly incompatible with my maintaining the theory of the *rising surplus*—that this contention reflects merely their own failure to understand the surplus concept. A constant, and indeed a rising, share of labor in national income can coexist with rising surplus simply because the increment of surplus assumes the form of an increment of *waste*. And since the "production" of waste involves labor, the share of labor may well grow if the share of waste in national output is increasing. Treating productive and unproductive labor indiscriminately as *labor* and equating profits with surplus obviously obscure this very simple proposition.

Several objections to the above could be raised. In the first place, it could be (and is being) asserted that there is no point in distinguishing between productive and unproductive labor or between socially desirable output and waste since there is no possibility of making these distinctions "objective" and precise. The correctness of the latter assertion can be readily granted. But that brandy and water mixed in a bottle cannot be separated, and that it may be impossible to establish accurately the proportions in which the two liquids are combined, does not alter the *fact* that the bottle contains both brandy and water and that the two beverages are present in the bottle in some definite quantities. What is more, to whatever extent the bottle may be filled, it can be safely asserted that in the absence of one or the other ingredient of the mix, it would be less full than in its presence. That we cannot at the present time neatly separate the wheat from the chaff, i.e., identify unequivocally the dimensions of the socially desirable output and of the economic surplus in our economy, is in itself an important aspect of the economic and social order of monopoly capitalism. Just as the problem of consumer sovereignty is *not* whether a commissar should

screen existing consumers' wants and *impose* on them standards of good taste, but rather how to attain a social and
economic order which will lead to the emergence of a
differently oriented individual with different wants and
different tastes, so it reflects a complete misunderstanding of
the issue to demand from the critical economist that he
present a comprehensive compilation of the existing number
of unproductive workers and the existing volume and forms
of waste. Apart from the, by no means trivial, fact that under
prevailing conditions there is not (and cannot be) available
the amount and kind of information and knowledge that
would permit the drawing up of such a "catalogue," no
economist, however ingenious, could presume to set himself
up as a sort of tsar empowered to lay down the criteria by
which the "sorting out" process should be carried out. For it
can only be a socialist society itself—in which people are not
governed by the profit motive and in which the individual is
steeped not in the "values" and mores of the market place
but in the consciousness emerging from the new, socialist
relations of production—which will give rise to a new structure of individual preferences and to a new pattern of
allocation of human and material resources. All that the
social scientist can do in this regard is to serve as Hegel's "owl
of Minerva which commences its flight in the onset of dusk,"
and signal *orbi et urbi* that a social order is fatally ill and
dying. The concrete forms and working principles of what is
moving to take its place and the exact specification of the
changes which the new society will carry in its train, can be
broadly visualized but not precisely established by economists and statisticians, however skillful they may be. This
must be left to the social *practice* of those who will struggle
for and succeed in achieving a socialist order.

Of a different nature is another argument advanced against
the theory of the rising surplus. Its burden is that
the distinction between socially desirable output and

economic surplus is irrelevant, even if it could be made with all the required exactness. For since a satisfactory level of income and employment depends on an adequate amount of aggregate spending *regardless of what the spending is on*, the question whether it evokes useful output or waste, employs productive or unproductive labor is brushed aside as having no bearing on "business conditions," and on the extent to which the society of monopoly capitalism provides for "fullness" of employment. This reasoning, cogent as it is, resembles all Keynesian short-run analysis in being desperately myopic. It is undoubtedly true that investment in productive equipment and investment in submarines, consumption of books and "consumption" of advertising, incomes of physicians and incomes of drug peddlers, all enter aggregate effective demand and help to maintain income and employment. It is equally clear, however, that the resulting structure of output, consumption, and investment exercises a profound impact not merely on the quality of society and the welfare of its members but also on its further growth and developmental possibilities. Moreover, while a few decades ago it might have been possible to argue that, given a shortage of *rational* employment, any employment—as irrational as digging holes in the ground, for example—is better than *no* employment, even this cold comfort is no longer available in our day when the alternative to unemployment is no longer relatively innocent digging but the all but innocent stockpiling of means of destruction.[19]

A further objection has been voiced that while all the above may be correct, it should not be forgotten that it is precisely owing to all the irrationality and waste that characterize monopoly capitalism that high levels of income and employment are maintained, considerable amounts of rational investment are induced, and certain—if admittedly low—rates of economic growth are achieved. This argument is very much akin to the counsel to burn the house in order to roast the pig. But the worst of it is that it is not even true that in the process "the pig gets roasted," that—to paraphrase J. K. Galbraith[20]—such increases in wealth as have taken place under monopoly capitalism in the United States go far to render the irrationality of the system "inconsequential." It surely is not "inconsequential" that even after World War II—during what C. Wright Mills has so aptly called the years of the "Great American Celebration"—in at least one half of the period (1948-1949, 1953-1954, 1957-1958, 1960 to date) government-reported unemployment has been in the neighborhood of five million, and according to trade union sources no less (and probably more) than six million.

Nor can it be shrugged off as "inconsequential" that in what has come to be referred to as the affluent society, approximately one-third of the people live under conditions of abject poverty, and at least one-fifth of all American families (and twice as large a proportion of non-white American families) subsist in miserable substandard and slum dwellings. And if cold statistical aggregates are left aside and concrete conditions are examined in specific areas, the human tragedy encountered defies description. "In a slum section composed almost entirely of Negroes in one of our largest cities," writes a former president of Harvard University, James Bryant Conant, "the following situation was found: A total of 59 percent of the male youth between the ages of sixteen and twenty-one were out of school and unemployed. They were roaming the streets . . ."[21]

All that can be said for the objection now under discussion is that the development of capitalism in general and of its last phase—monopoly capitalism—in particular, while nowhere near creating anything resembling a good society,[22] has produced the objective potentialities for the emergence of such a society. The prodigious expansion of the forces of production which has taken place during the period of imperialism, although a by-product of war, exploitation, and waste, has indeed laid the foundations for the truly affluent society of the future. But such a society cannot evolve under the rule of an oligarchy administering society's vast resources for the benefit of a few hundred giant corporations and with the all-controlling purpose of the preservation of the status quo. Such a society can become reality only when its abundant resources will be administered by a human "association in which the free development of each is the condition for the free development of all."

This brings me to the second comment which I should like to make in connection with the monopoly capitalism chapters of this book. This comment refers to the view of innovation and technological progress under monopoly capitalism which is there advanced. Although I still believe in the basic soundness of Steindl's contention, to which I subscribed, that technological progress and innovation are a function of investment rather than vice versa, I have devoted insufficient space to the undeniable dialectical interaction of the two processes. Not only do the institutionalized research and development staffs of giant corporations operate, to some extent at least, with a momentum of their own, and grind out inventions and technical improvements as a matter of normal routine,[23] but what is perhaps even more important, the military establishment which has become a permanent and vast component of the economy of monopoly capitalism, has turned into a continuously operating "external stimulus" to both investment and scientific and technological progress. As the demand of the military has to a considerable extent replaced the demand of the would-be investor, so the sequence of Soviet Sputniks and Luniks has taken over some of the functions of the "perennial gale" of competition. This does not call for regressing to the position of Schumpeter to whom technological progress was a *deus cum machina*—autonomous and inexplicable. Nor does it imply that technological progress *determines* investment, so that forthcoming increments to knowledge tend to be regularly translated into additional productive facilities. What it does suggest, however, is that the consolidation of research and development activities within the framework of giant corporations *combined with a steady flow of military demand* creates certain investment opportunities when there otherwise would be fewer or none. And the importance of the military nature of demand as well as of the monopolistic and oligopolistic nature of supply expresses itself most precisely in the *selection* of the technological potentialities which are made use of as well as in the rejection of those which remain in the files of scientists and engineers. Both the slow progress made in the economic application of atomic energy as well as the very uneven advances in automation would seem to justify the proposition that only that technical progress is acceptable to monopolistic and oligopolistic business which is either required by the military or sharply reduces costs without at the same time unduly expanding output.

We turn now to the underdeveloped countries. To Chapters Five, Six, and Seven, dealing with one of the three dominant themes of our age (the other two being the vicissitudes of monopoly capitalism during its current period of decline and fall, and the outlook for the nascent socialist societies in Europe and Asia),[24] I would like to add a qualification and a reaffirmation. The former has to do with the applicability of the general theory advanced in this book to some highly populated areas with what Marx called the "Asiatic mode of production"—notably India and

Pakistan. In such parts of the underdeveloped world, several critics have contended, it might well be feasible to ascertain with some degree of accuracy the *magnitude* of the economic surplus appropriated by landowners, usurers, and commercial intermediaries of all kinds, but it would be wholly impossible to channel that segment of the surplus into productive investment even after these parasitic strata had been swept aside by a social revolution. This view is based on two sets of considerations. First, it is argued, a revolutionary government which would carry out the necessary expropriation measures could not possibly substitute itself for the blood-sucking rent collectors, money lenders, and greedy traders who were eliminated by the very revolution that put it into power. With such a switch in the destination of the surplus thus politically precluded, the nationalization and confiscation measures would not lead to an accumulation of an investible surplus in the hands of the revolutionary government but to its lapsing into the peasants' desperately skimpy consumption basket. The second point is that in an underdeveloped country in which the economic surplus accrues to a numerically insignifcant group of exploiters. (as was and is the case in countries with a "classic" feudal system and/or those dominated by a handful of domestic and foreign monopolists) the situation is quite different from that prevailing in a society in which a multi-million-strong stratum of kulaks, village bosses lending money on the side, small traders, dealers, and brokers, appropriate altogether an amount of economic surplus constituting a large slice of total national income but providing only low per capita incomes to its recipients. In the former case the expropriators can be relatively easily expropriated, and their fate after the expropriation does not present a major social problem; their number being small, they either find alternative employment, emigrate, or retire to live on some remnants of their fortunes. In the latter case, however, the surplus recipients, being many, constitute an important social and political force; and, once deprived of their revenues, present a serious problem in social welfare. In fact, supporting them on even a minimum level by means of relief or artificially created jobs could annul much of the advantage derived from the expropriation itself.

These are serious problems, and although I was by no means oblivious of their existence when writing this book,[25] they may not have received sufficient attention and emphasis. I do not believe, however, that recognizing their importance vitiates the basic approach to the issues confronting the underdeveloped countries which is outlined here. It undoubtedly implies that in some countries the breakthrough to the open road of economic and social growth is more difficult than in others, and that the obstacles that need to be overcome are in some places more formidable than elsewhere. It may well be, indeed, that in countries which are particularly plagued by the structural malaise just described, the strategy of development may have to be different from the one suitable to societies more favorably structured. Lenin's famous law of uneven development suggests obviously not only that the historical *process* is different in different societies, but also that the stage reached at any given time differs from country to country. There is thus no general formula applicable to all situations regardless of time and place, and nothing was ever further from my mind than an intention to assert the existence of such a magic wand.

Consider for instance a country in which there exists a certain nucleus of an industrial economy and where the peasantry, whether exploited by kulaks, or held in servitude by feudal landlords, is intensely land-hungry, and longs for nothing but individually owned plots of land. In such a country it may be possible to generate a sizable amount of economic surplus via the economy's industrial sector. If, in addition, the country is relatively small so that whatever aid it may receive from abroad can materially influence the volume of its capital accumulation, it may well be able to afford to allow its peasants to "sit it out" for a while, and to learn by observation and experience the advantages of a rational and modern organization of agricultural production. Such has apparently been the broad perspective of some socialist countries in eastern and southeastern Europe.

Take, on the other hand, a large country with a small industrial oasis in a vast sea of subsistence farming. Here the industrially generated surplus is of necessity small, and the practically accessible foreign assistance can constitute at best only a drop in the bucket of development requirements. If in such a country, the peasants' craving for *individually* owned plots is for any number of economic or cultural reasons not urgent or even absent, its agricultural economy can be shifted onto new tracks based on cooperative farming or even on a system of state-operated, large-scale, and increasingly productive "factories in the field." The gentry, rich peasants, village storekeepers, and moneylenders displaced in the process may either be integrated into the new agricultural economy or find employment in the expanding industrial and distributive sectors. And the surplus which they used to appropriate may become available for purposes of economic development. This would seem to be—in a nutshell— the model of the Chinese strategy of economic development.

And visualize finally a banana or sugar republic—if that flattering designation is considered applicable to the semi-colonial dictatorships involved—where the bulk of agricultural output is produced in plantations, and where the agricultural population consists predominantly or in large part not of peasants but of agricultural workers. In such countries the expropriation of the peasant was so

thoroughly completed by the domestic and foreign plantation owners that even the image of individual land holdings
has all but evaporated from the mentality of the rural
proletariat. There mass parcelling of land is not on the
agenda at all, and the nationalization of the plantations
places immediately at the disposal of society as a whole the
surplus that was previously appropriated by foreign and
domestic corporations. This is not to say that all of the
surplus so released can be used to raise immediately the
wretched living conditions of the working population. Also
complications and frictions in the process of the reorganization of the economy, difficulties in securing new sources
of essential supplies, as well as in finding new markets for
customary exports—all largely due to the sabotage and
obstruction on the part of the former ruling class at home
and its allies and protectors abroad—may temporarily
reduce aggregate output and accordingly also the volume of
available surplus. In such a situation the possibility of
overcoming all these hurdles is to such an extent dependent
on various economic and political factors at home and
abroad that there can hardly be a generalization that would
fit the individual case. The obvious example of what I
mean is the dramatic experience of Cuba since its great
revolution.[26]

Thus each and every one of the underdeveloped countries
presents a wide spectrum of economic, social, cultural, and
political configurations; and nothing could be more futile
than to seek to force them into a rigid mold of a "universal
prescription." But as the intellectual gratification derived
from the discovery of a broad generalization should not be
permitted to deflect attention from the specificity of
concrete reality, so fixation on detail must not be allowed
to bar the insights which can only be gained through
generalizing—i.e., theoretical—thought. And this brings me
to what I referred to earlier as a reaffirmation of my views

on the basic problem confronting the underdeveloped countries. The principal insights which must not be obscured by matters of secondary or tertiary importance, are two.

The first is that, if what is sought is *rapid* economic development, comprehensive economic planning is indispensable. Small and gradual changes taking place, as it were, on the margin may well be expected to come about by a spontaneous process of trial and error. A few percent increase of output of any product already being produced can usually be obtained without any major planning effort, by raising somewhat its price and by letting the necessary adjustments "work themselves out." However, if the increase in a country's aggregate output is to attain the magnitude of, say, 8 to 10 percent per annum; if in order to achieve it, the mode of utilization of a nation's human and material resources is to be radically changed, with certain less productive lines of economic activity abandoned and other more rewarding ones taken up; then only a deliberate, long-range planning effort can assure the attainment of the goal. On this there is actually hardly any disagreement among serious students of the subject.[27] What is perhaps even more important, on this there is no ambiguity in the historical record. While the most conservatively estimated per capita rates of economic growth in the socialist countries have been in the order of 10 percent per annum, in capitalist countries—advanced and underdeveloped alike—they rarely exceed 3 percent, except for extraordinary circumstances of war booms and postwar reconstruction.

The second insight of crucial importance is that no planning worth the name is possible in a society in which the means of production remain under the control of private interests which administer them with a view to their owners' maximum profits (or security or other private advantage). For it is of the very essence of comprehensive planning for economic development—what renders it, indeed, indispensable—that the pattern of allocation and utilization of resources which it must impose if it is to accomplish its purpose, is *necessarily* different from the pattern prevailing under the status quo. Since, however, the prevailing pattern of resource allocation and utilization corresponds, at least approximately, to the best interests of the dominant class, it is inevitable that any serious planning endeavor should come into sharp conflict with that dominant class and its allies at home and abroad. This conflict can be resolved in one of three ways: the Planning Board, if one is created by a capitalist government, can be taken over—like the government itself—by the dominant interests, its activites turned into a sham, and its existence used to nurture the illusion in the underlying population that "something constructive is being done" about economic development. The second possibility is that the Planning Board established by a reform government remains more or less impervious to the influences, pressures, and bribes of powerful interests, is staffed by honest reformers who believe in the independence and omnipotence of the state in the capitalist society and set out to introduce far-reaching changes in the national economy. In that case the Board is bound to run into tenacious resistance and sabotage on the part of the ruling class, achieves very little if anything, and ends up in a state of frustration and impotence with the fatal by-product of discrediting the very idea of planning in the eyes of large strata of the population. The third alternative is that planning becomes the battle cry of a broad popular movement, is fought for relentlessly against the entrenched beneficiaries of the *ancien régime*, and is turned into the basic organizational principle of the economy by a victorious social revolution sweeping aside the former ruling class together with the institution of private property in the means of production on which its very existence rests.

It may be objected that all this may well be true if the fundamental premise is granted: that what is needed is *rapid* economic development. But why the hurry? Why this "obsession" with economic growth, to use an expression of a recent writer on the Soviet economy? The mere asking of these questions reflects the intellectual distance of Western observers from the living conditions in the underdeveloped countries and the mood of the people who have to endure them. Ours is an age in which misery, starvation, and disease are no longer accepted as ineluctable fate, and ours is the century in which socialist construction has moved from the realm of theory into the realm of practice. The peoples of the backward areas now *know* that economic and social progress *can* be organized, given the will, determination, and courage to declare a war against underdevelopment and given the unbreakable resolution to wage that war in the face of the most ruthless resistance on the part of domestic and foreign exploiters.

From such historical experience as we have, it is abundantly clear that the struggle is protracted, hard, and cruel. The victory of the social revolution, although decisive, is merely a success "in the first round." The establishment of the capitalist mode of production and of bourgeois rule, where it was fully attained, took centuries of cataclysmic developments. It can hardly be expected, even in our much faster moving time, that the greatest social transformation of all—the abolition of private property in the means of production and therefore of exploitation of man by man—should be fully achieved within a few short decades. It is quite understandable that to many the ascent appears sometimes to be prohibitively steep and the uphill movement hopelessly difficult. Since it is impossible to attempt here a comprehensive analysis of the hurdles and problems encountered in the process of socialist construction, I shall limit myself to a few brief remarks on some areas where the roadblocks have been particularly conspicuous in the recent past.

First and foremost among them is the international arena where social revolutions, regardless of where and how they unfold, meet with the implacable hostility of the ruling class of the United States—the most powerful citadel of reaction in the world today. No regime is too corrupt, no government too criminally negligent of the vital interests of its people, no dictatorship too retrograde and cruel to be denied the economic, military, and moral support of the leading power of the "free world"—as long as it proves its allegiance to the anti-socialist Holy Alliance. At the same time, no popular movement, however inclusive and however heroic, no socialist government, however democratically elected and however dedicated to the advancement of its people, can count on as much as non-intervention on the part of those who never tire of hypocritical professions of their devotion to social progress and to the democratic process. The unabating aggressiveness of the imperialist powers—large and small—immeasurably obstructs the economic and social progress in the countries which have entered the road of socialist construction.[28] Looking at the matter in purely economic terms and considering the burden of defense expenditures imposed on the socialist countries by the ever present threat of imperialist aggression, it is obvious how large the costs are that the nascent socialist societies are forced by their class enemy to bear.[29]

The massive diversion of resources from investment, residential construction, and production of consumer goods that is necessitated by the maintenance of the indispensable defense establishment, slows down the rates of economic growth of the socialist countries, prevents a more rapid increase in the living standards of their peoples, and creates and recreates frictions and bottlenecks in their economies. This heavy load will have to be carried by the socialist societies as long as the threat of imperialism exists; its burden will not decline until the socialist economies have grown—in spite of it—so strong as to greatly reduce its *relative* weight.

The second area in which the difficulties of the socialist countries have been most marked is that of agricultural production. There the sources of trouble are manifold. The process of industrialization, accompanied of necessity by a population shift from rural to urban areas, and the maintenance of a military establishment which eats but does not produce, have significantly raised the aggregate demand for food and other products of agriculture. This increase of demand has been, on the whole, nowhere accompanied by a sufficient expansion of supply. This is primarily due to the fact that while in countries with considerable underemployment in the villages, the productivity *per man at work* could be raised *relatively* fast, the increase of productivity *per acre* has proved to be an extremely slow process. Thus what might be called the mechanical revolution in agriculture brought about by the introduction of electricity, tractors, combines, and the like accomplished its purpose by freeing millions of peasants for nonagricultural employment; it did *not* lead to the spectacular increases of agricultural output per acre of land that was expected by many economic theorists—Marxist and non-Marxist alike. The increase of productivity per acre depends apparently much more than was anticipated on the *chemical* revolution in agriculture: on the application of synthetic and other fertilizers, on seed selection, the adoption of improved methods of livestock breeding, and so forth. This is, inevitably, a slow process: 2 to 3 percent increases of output per acre per year are considered by agronomists to constitute a respectable performance. The achievement of such a rate of growth is predicated on the availability of the necessary supplies (fertilizers, choice seeds, breeding animals, etc.), but also on the skill, diligence, and patience of the cultivators.[30]

This in turn points to another complication which has arisen in the Soviet Union as well as in other industrializing socialist countries. It stems from the fact that the industrialization of an agricultural country, particularly in its early phases, involves quite naturally the "glamorization" of industrial work, its acquiring greatly enhanced prestige and attractiveness. Large new industrial plants, tremendous power developments revolutionizing the lives of entire regions, thrilling technological achievements move into the center of national (and international) attention, become objects of intense—and justified—pride, and are allotted a preponderant proportion of publicity, of the government's political and organizational effort, and of scarce administrative and scientific talent. By comparison, the plodding day-to-day drudgery of agricultural work recedes into the gray and dull background of social existence. A young man or woman of ambition, ability, and energy no longer wishes to remain "stuck in the mud" of the agricultural backwaters, to stay confined to the "idiocy of rural life" and be limited in his or her growth and development to what can be achieved even in the most progressive agricultural community. The lure of the city, of its opportunities for material and social advancement, education, participation in cultural activities and plain fun, as well as the desire to become a member of the industrial working class—the most respected stratum of society— exercise an all but irresistible pull on the younger generation. The result is that agriculture becomes increasingly abandoned by its best potential workers, and left to elderly people or to those who do not have the imagination, the enterprise, and the drive to move into the "big, wide world."[31]

This in turn contributes seriously to the persistent lag in the growth of productivity in agriculture. Nor is it easy to compensate for the relative weakness of the agricultural labor force by the employment of technical devices. Work in industry gives rise to discipline and standards of performance by a specific momentum of its own. The collective nature of the activity involved, its structuring and timing by conveyor belts and similar arrangements, the interdependence and indispensability of specific operations—all impose on the industrial worker a certain rhythm of work which sets its tone, determines its tempo, and largely accounts for its outcome. The situation in agriculture is quite different—such modernization of agricultural methods of production as has taken place notwithstanding. Apart from certain collective functions, the individual worker is to a large extent on his own. Whether in plowing a field or in tending to an animal, it is his (or her) initiative, conscientiousness, and exertion which markedly influence the degree of success attained. And where hidebound conservatism, irresponsibility, and aversion to hard work characterize those working in agriculture, aggregate agricultural output is bound to be seriously affected.

Under capitalist conditions the tendency of the cream of agricultural manpower to migrate to the cities has usually been kept in check by the slowness of the capital accumulation process and by the more or less chronic shortage of urban jobs resulting therefrom. Accordingly, agriculture remained overcrowded, competition in it fierce, and productivity and real income per man increased much more slowly than productivity per acre. In the socialist society matters had to take a different course. The collective, large-scale organization of agriculture which, by doing away with the unviable dwarfholdings of the peasantry, creates the indispensable conditions for the long-term, sustained growth of agricultural production, transforms the peasant into an industrial worker working in agriculture. In this way it insulates him from the ruinous impact of the capitalist market, immunizes him against the sticks and carrots of the competitive struggle, *without putting him at the same time into the framework of integration, coordination, and discipline characteristic of a large-scale modern industrial enterprise.* And what is even more paradoxical and economically serious: by advancing him to the status of a full-fledged working member of a socialist society, it accords him automatically a claim to a share of aggregate social output, to real income, which is at least approximately equal to the shares of other, more productive workers.

This amounts in effect to a reversal of the earlier relation: agriculture becomes subsidized by industry. This is exactly as it should be, except that these subsidies do not lead to an adequate expansion of agricultural output. In the longer run this problem can, and undoubtedly will, be solved. Once a considerably higher stage of economic development is reached, the living and working conditions in city and countryside will be more nearly equalized and it will become possible to provide for the movement of skilled, educated, and socially conscious and responsible workers not only from the village to the city but also from the city to the village, with both of these movements turning into a general means of enhancing the variety, stimulation, and gratification derived from productive work in industry as well as in agriculture. Before that situation is reached, however, there is still a long way to go. In the meantime, in different socialist countries reliance is placed on different palliatives. In some countries the collectivization of agriculture was halted (or even reversed) with a regulated exchange between city and village taking the place of an immediate socialization of agriculture. In another socialist country, China, a solution has been sought in the opposite direction, through a more rapid transformation of the peasant economy into a system of socially operated, disciplined, large-scale agricultural enterprises. In the Soviet Union an in-between course has been followed: agricultural work is being "re-glamorized," investment in agriculture is being increased as much as possible, and incentives to collective farmers raised by shifting relative prices in favor of agriculture. Much of this puts an additional strain on the industrial economy, cuts into real wages of industrial workers, and reduces the volume of surplus investible outside of agriculture, thus slowing down the overall rate of economic growth. Even so, the agricultural difficulties, not insuperable but seriously hampering and retarding the development of the socialist societies, represent only a fraction of the tremendous price which the socialist societies have to pay for having first emerged in underdeveloped countries.

It is against the background of this economic stringency—the insufficiency of agricultural output to keep pace with the rising living standards of the people, and the shortage of industrial output in the face of rapidly growing demands from within and without the individual socialist countries—as well as of the intensified class struggle in the international arena that one must consider the *political* troubles within the socialist camp. Under this heading, there is in the first place the all-important problem of retention of popular support by the socialist government during the most trying effort to initiate the "steep ascent." What has come to be called the "revolution of rising expectations" which is sweeping the world's underdeveloped countries confronts not only reactionary and corrupt regimes seeking to stem it by all available means, but also revolutionary governments dedicated to economic development and socialism. Since a rational plan of economic advancement calls not for the shot-in-the-arm policy of an immediate increase of popular consumption, but for a well-considered strategy of assuring maximum possible rates of growth over a planning horizon of, say, ten to twenty years, it is not only possible but most likely that during the early phase of the effort mass consumption should rise very slowly, if at all. Only after the foundations of a progressive economy have been laid, and the "hump" overcome, can the system begin to yield fruits in the form of an expanding supply of consumer goods, housing, and the like.

Yet the masses who have just been through a revolution, who have fought and suffered in the bitter struggles against their class enemies and exploiters at home and abroad, seek and feel entitled to immediate improvements in the daily lives of their cities and villages. The fledgling socialist government cannot conjure such improvements out of the ground. Still engaged in the "uninterrupted revolution," it must demand "blood, sweat, and toil" without being able to offer commensurable rewards *hic et nunc*. Only the most class-conscious and insightful groups in society recognize and comprehend the momentous issues involved. Broad strata of the population, unaccustomed to thinking in terms of economic necessities and longer-run perspectives, can easily become disaffected, can fall prey to enemy propaganda which seeks to capitalize on their age-old superstitions and ignorance, can lose their faith in the revolution. They do not grasp that the suffering under the *ancien régime* was suffering for the benefit of their domestic overlords and their imperialist exploiters, that the misery which they had to endure in the past was misery without hope and prospect—while the privations accompanying the revolution are the birth pangs of a new and better society. And ignoring this fundamental difference, they frequently became apathetic or even hostile to the revolution itself. This inevitably gives rise to a more or less acute conflict between socialism and democracy, between people's long-run *needs* and their short-run *wants*. Under such circumstances the socialist government's unwavering and uncompromising commitment to the overriding interests of society as a whole, its unquestionable duty to defend these interests against their foreign and domestic enemies no less than against opportunists and traitors among its adherents, creates the need for political repression, for curtailment of civil liberties, for limitation of individual freedom. This need can only recede and eventually disappear when the objective hurdles are at least approximately mastered, when the most burning economic problems are at least approximately solved, and when the socialist government has attained a measure of stability and equilibrium.[32]

Stemming from the same basic cause, in one word poverty, is the second category of troubles besetting the socialist camp: the relations among socialist countries. These relations have obviously not been as harmonious as a socialist would have liked them to be; but while giving rise to legitimate concern, they must be subjected to a dispassionate analysis and put into a proper historical perspective. Although nothing that might resemble adequate information is at my disposal, from what little I have been able to learn it would seem that the causes of the existing tensions relate to several closely interdependent issues.

One has to do with the allocation of economic resources within the socialist camp, and stems essentially from the vast differences in the degree of economic development attained by the individual socialist countries. To put it in its simplest terms, the question is, how much aid should the economically most advanced members of the socialist camp—primarily the Soviet Union but also Czechoslovakia, the German Democratic Republic, and Poland—give other less (and very much less) developed socialist countries? Clearly, no such problem would exist if all socialist societies were about equally rich or if all were about equally poor. It should also be clear that at the present time an even proximate *equalization* of per capita incomes between the haves and the have-nots in the socialist camp is entirely impossible. It would drastically reduce the living standards of the, say, 250 million people living in the better-off parts of the socialist world, and even if such a move could substantially accelerate the growth of the worse-off parts inhabited by over 700 million people, it would be politically and socially wholly unfeasible, would be, indeed, suicidal to socialism in the more fortunate nations.

This issue was obviously not on the agenda as long as the Soviet Union and other European socialist countries were in the throes of reconstruction from the economic catastrophe caused by the war, and could furnish no more than symbolic assistance to the worst situated arrivals in the socialist camp. It became more urgent in the middle 1950's, by which time the Soviet Union had made major strides in its economic reconstruction and advancement, and embarked—after the death of Stalin—on a course of a far-reaching economic and political liberalization. In the economic realm this implied a shift from the earlier policy of austerity and limitation of current consumption for the sake of the highest attainable rates of investment and growth, to a marked increase in the supply of housing, manufactured consumer goods, and food to the Soviet people who had suffered grievous privations during the prewar era of industrialization and were forced to make even more enormous sacrifices during the shattering years of the war. In the area of politics it meant a drastic change in the general atmosphere prevailing in Soviet society, the elimination of political repressions, and a break with the rigid dogmatism which affected all aspects of Soviet life during the rule of Stalin. As far as international relations are concerned, the new course involved a major effort to arrive at some accommodation with the United States with a view to the preservation of peace, to a reduction of the burden of armaments, and to securing a relaxation of international tensions necessary for the consolidation and progress of socialist societies in the Soviet Union as well as in the countries which entered the road to socialism after the Second World War. Indeed, the advancement and increasing welfare of these socialist societies were pronounced to be one of the most important leverages for the further expansion of socialism in the world. In what appeared to be a repudiation or at least an important modification of the conventional theory of imperialism, the new Soviet leadership declared such an accommodation to be not impossible in view of the radical shift in the world's balance of power caused by the rapidly mounting strength of the socialist bloc and the progressive disintegration of the imperialist control over colonial and dependent countries. In fact, the latter process was to be accelerated by the extension of economic and political aid to the newly emerging nations.

Various aspects of this new course were met with skepticism in China and other socialist countries still struggling desperately with the initial, most formidable, hurdles on the road to economic development. The disagreement involved the timeliness and wisdom of the liberalization program in the Soviet Union in the light of the needs of the *entire* socialist camp, the appraisal of the "appeasibility" of the imperialist powers, and the judgment on what constitutes the best strategy in the struggle against imperialism and for peace and socialism.[33]

But while increasingly pronounced in the course of the last few years, it was not until the Twenty-second Congress of the Communist Party of the Soviet Union in the autumn of 1961 that the controversy erupted into a publicly acknowledged major conflict. Although still retaining its original roots, the dispute became acerbated by a number of developments. In the last couple of years, for reasons which it would take us too far afield to discuss, the economic development of China has suffered a serious setback,[34] and accordingly its need for large-scale economic assistance from the Soviet Union has greatly increased. Soviet policy at the same time remains committed to continuing on the road to further liberalization. This was solemnly proclaimed in the program of socialist construction in the Soviet Union adopted by the Congress, which provides for spectacular increases not only of the Gross National Product of the U.S.S.R. in the next twenty years, but also for a significant reduction of the number of working hours of Soviet workers and for a vast improvement of the general living standard of the Soviet people. The question naturally arises whether it is necessary to set the Soviet welfare targets as high as they are fixed in the new Program, whether the policy adopted with regard to the rates of growth of the entire economy combined with somewhat less ambitious goals in terms of *consumption* would not leave more room for a program of large-scale assistance to other socialist countries. In other words, does not the Soviet Party leadership take a too narrow, "nationalist" view of the needs and requirements of the *entire* socialist camp and focus too much on the rapid betterment of the economic situation of the Soviet people? And would not more rapid progress of the Chinese, North Korean, North Vietnamese, and other underdeveloped socialist economies have a larger impact on the world as a whole, and on the peoples in the non-socialist under-developed countries in particular, than the Soviet Union's "attaining and surpassing American standards of living" in twenty years, as envisaged by the new Program, rather than in, say, the thirty years that it would take if a larger slice of its national product were devoted to the advancement of other socialist societies?

These questions translate themselves into political terms. As mentioned earlier, the Soviet Union's departure from the policies of austerity and curtailment of consumption for the sake of rapid growth goes hand in hand with the accelerated drive of "de-Stalinization," with the reduction and progressive abolition of the system of political repression which was largely due to the earlier regime of belt-tightening and maximal exertion. It goes without saying that nothing could be more welcome to a socialist than the evolution of the Soviet Union into a socialist democracy with the highest attainable levels of welfare and enjoying an ever wider degree of individual freedom. Neither the Chinese, who remained remarkably free of Stalin's abuses of power, nor any other socialists to my knowledge, have objected to the elimination and drastic suppression of all the aberrations and crimes committed by Stalin and his henchmen. What is at issue therefore is not "de-Stalinization" per se, but the abandonment of the policy of "forced marches" which is so prominently associated with the name of Stalin. Neither China nor some other socialist countries are as yet *economically ready* for the "thaw"; and, not being economically ready, they cannot afford the liberalization, the relaxation of the pressures on consumption, and all that goes with them which in the Soviet Union are at the present time not only feasible but constitute major steps toward the economic, political, and cultural advancement of Soviet society. In explaining to their peoples their policy of rapid industrialization, collectivization of agriculture, and ineluctable limitation of consumption, the socialist governments of China and some other socialist countries made extensive use of the Soviet example and of the authority of Stalin who was universally considered to be the chief architect of the Soviet successes. The dramatic overthrow of that image of Stalin at a time when the policies which he symbolized cannot yet be discarded, constitutes undoubtedly a severe political shock to those socialist governments which are still confronted with the kind of obstacles which the Soviet Union by now has been able to overcome.

Similarly, in their international relations, China and other socialist countries of Asia find themselves in a position quite different from that of the Soviet Union and the European socialist countries. With important parts of their countries still under the control of the enemy, politically discriminated against, militarily threatened, and economically blockaded by the imperialist powers, the socialist countries of Asia are much less able and willing to accept a detente on the basis of the prevailing status quo than the socialist countries of Europe. While in Europe the settlement of the German question is the only major issue standing in the way of an at least temporary accommodation, the issues in Asia are many and complex and their solution appears even less likely that an acceptable compromise over Germany. This difference in the objective situation obviously contributes to the crystallization in the Soviet Union and in China of different appraisals of the international situation.

And yet, taking the risks which always attach to prophecy, I would venture the opinion that in spite of all the heat generated in the current debate and all the sharp arrows flying back and forth between the protagonists, the conflict will not inflict irreparable harm on the cause of socialism. In the longer run the fundamental identity of the relations of production prevailing in the socialist countries will prove to be a more powerful factor than the temporary divergencies among their leaderships on short-run strategy and tactics. Just as the socialist mode of production survived all the abhorrent doings of Stalin, so the socialist revolutions in China and elsewhere remain irreversible historical facts which cannot be altered, let alone annulled, by whatever frictions and disagreements may temporarily shake their political superstructures. Compromises are possible and will probably be arrived at. But even should the socialist governments of the countries involved fail to arrive at a mutually acceptable *modus vivendi*, the resulting estrangement need neither prevent the continuous progress of the individual countries on the road to socialism, nor preclude their cohesion and solidarity in the fullness of time.

To conclude: the dominant fact of our time is that the institution of private property in the means of production—once a powerful engine of progress—has now come into irreconcilable contradiction with the economic and social advancement of the people in the underdeveloped countries and with the growth, development, and liberation of people in advanced countries. That the existence and nature of this conflict have not yet everywhere been recognized and fully understood by the majority of people is one of the most important, if not the decisive, aspect of this conflict itself. It reflects the powerful hold on the minds of men exercised by a set of creeds, superstitions, and fetishes stemming from the very institution of private property in the means of production which now desperately needs to be overthrown. The argument, now most prominent in bourgeois thought, that the "adjustment" of people to a pernicious social order and their inability and unwillingness to rise up against it *prove* that this social order caters adequately to human needs, demonstrates merely that bourgeois thought is guilty of rank betrayal of all its finest traditions of humanism and reason. One may well wonder what would have been the reaction of the great philosophers of the Enlightenment if they were told that the existence of God is adequately *proved* by the fact that many people believe in it? Substituting ignorance and "revealed preferences" for truth and reason, gloating over all manifestations of irrationality and backwardness, whether in advanced or underdeveloped countries, as proving the impossibility of a more rational social order, bourgeois thought in our day has negated itself and has returned to the condition which in its glorious youth it set out to conquer: agnosticism and obscurantism. Thus it exchanges the great commitments of all intellectual endeavor—the search for and the clarification of truth, the guidance and support of man in his struggle for a better society—for the contemptible functions of rationalizing irrationality, inventing arguments in defense of madness, serving as a source of an ideology of vested interest, and recognizing as a genuine human *need* merely the interests of those whose sole concern is the preservation of the status quo.

Notes

1. *"The consumer is king today. . . .* Business has no choice but to discover what he wants and to serve his wishes, even his whims."— Steuart Henderson Britt, *The Spenders* (New York-Toronto-London, 1960), p. 36 (italics in the original). Also: *"If the product does not meet some existing desire or need of the consumer, the advertising will ultimately fail."*—Rosser Reeves, *Reality in Advertising* (New York, 1961), p. 141 (italics in the original).

2. "The so-called waste in our private economy happens to be the way people make a living and in so doing spread well-being among all. It happens to be the way we get our gleaming schools and hospitals and

highways and other 'public' facilities."—*The Wall Street Journal,* October 7, 1960, p. 16.

3. "The Corporation: How Much Power? What Scope?" in Edward S. Mason, ed., *The Corporation in Modern Society* (Cambridge, Mass., 1959), p. 101.

4. *Ibid.,* p. 2.

5. Tibor Scitovsky, "On the Principle of Consumers' Sovereignty," *Amer. Econ. Rev.* (May 1962). I am indebted to Professor Scitovsky for letting me see a copy of this paper prior to publication.

6. Cf. for example, James Cook, *Remedies and Rackets* (New York, 1958), *passim;* and "Behind the FCC Scandal," *Monthly Review* (April 1958).

7. Cf. *Goals for Americans: The Report of the President's Commission on National Goals* (New York, 1960), *passim.*

8. For a lucid exposition of the Marxist theory of the state, cf. Stanley W. Moore, *The Critique of Capitalist Democracy: An Introduction to the Theory of the State in Marx, Engels, and Lenin* (New York, 1957).

9. *Welfare and Competition: The Economics of a Fully Employed Economy* (Chicago, 1951), p. 450.

10. This point was made for the first time to my knowledge in the excellent paper by K. W. Rothschild, "A Note on Advertising," *Economic Journal* (1942).

11. "Right now, officials incline toward a new round of military ordering in preference to either massive public works or a cut in taxes, if they decide the economy needs another push."—*Business Week,* December 9, 1961. And it is not only "right now" that this is the "official inclination." For "some advisers like the idea of shelters, but want to push it at a time when the economy needs a stimulant."—*Ibid.,* November 4, 1961. Thus the shelters are not to protect the people against radioactive fallout but against depression and unemployment.

12. Quoted in Steuart Henderson Britt, *The Spenders,* p. 31.

13. For a more extended discussion of this, cf. *Marxism and Psychoanalysis* in this volume.

14. *Les Mandarins* (Paris, 1954), p. 193. I have translated this passage from the French.

15. Cf. his review of the present book in *Amer. Econ. Rev.* (March, 1958), pp. 164 ff.

16. It was reserved for Schumpeter (to be followed eventually by Berle, Galbraith, and others) to make an effort to save the "honor" of monopoly profits by proclaiming even them to be "necessary costs of

production." This *tour de force* was accomplished by pointing out that technological innovations were predicated upon monopoly gains on the part of the innovators, that it is monopoly profit that enables corporations to maintain costly research laboratories, etc. Thus static vice was made into dynamic virtue and the last attempt of economic theory to retain some minimum standards for the rational appraisal of the functioning of the capitalist system was swept aside by the comprehensive endorsement of the status quo.

17. Clearly, if the wage of the twenty unproductive workers is higher than five loaves per man—as it would be realistic to assume it would be—then either the real wage of the bakers would have to be lower or the profits would be encroached upon, or both. In the former case, the surplus is larger; in the case of reduced profits, it remains the same; and if both the productive workers' wages *and* profits are lower, the surplus is increased by the amount of the wage reduction.

18. Incidentally, a couple of other interesting things can be learned from this very simple illustration: first, customary statistics would usually tend to suggest that the productivity per man engaged in the bakery business has increased less than it actually did: with 100 men employed in the bakery concern in period I as well as in period II, and with output rising from 200 loaves to 1,000 loaves, productivity would appear to have gone up by 400 percent rather than by 525 percent as was actually the case. To be sure, a careful "sorting out" of the labor force denominator used for the computation, with a view to limiting it to *productive workers* only, could remedy this deficiency, but the statistical information which is usually supplied renders such an adjustment impossible. Secondly, statistics commonly compiled would show that wages have increased in exactly the same proportion as productivity (from one to five loaves), while in reality the wages of the *productive workers* lagged considerably behind the rise of *their* productivity. That the official statistics convey such garbled impressions is obviously not fortuitous; it is due to the concepts which govern their organization. With the notion "economic surplus" denied official recognition, and with the all but meaningless distinction between "production" and "non-production" workers substituted for the all-important difference between *productive* and *unproductive* workers, available statistics hide rather than illuminate a most important aspect of capitalist reality.

19. An extension of this discussion can be found in "Reflections on Underconsumption" in this volume.

20. *American Capitalism: The Concept of Countervailing Power*

(Boston, 1952), p. 103.

21. *Slums and Suburbs: A Commentary on Schools in Metropolitan Areas* (New York-Toronto-London, 1961), pp. 33 ff.

22. This is not the place to go into a more detailed description and analysis of the quality of the monopoly capitalist society; for this the interested reader is referred to *Monopoly Capital*.

23. Cf. Paul M. Sweezy, "Has Capitalism Changed?" in Shigeto Tsuru, ed., *Has Capitalism Changed? An International Symposium on the Nature of Contemporary Capitalism* (Tokyo, 1961), pp. 83 ff.

24. Since this book was first published, Latin America has joined the regions of socialist beginnings.

25. Cf. pp. 167 ff. as well as pp. 262 ff.

26. A comprehensive account of the developments in Cuba will be found in Leo Huberman and Paul M. Sweezy, *Cuba: Anatomy of a Revolution* (2nd ed., New York, 1961), and an elaboration of the remarks above in *"Reflections on the Cuban Revolution"* in this volume.

27. This is not the place for a survey of the relevant literature; suffice it to mention the writings of H. B. Chenery, E. S. Mason, T. Scitovsky, and J. Tinbergen, the principal burden of which is the demonstration of the necessity of coordination and synchronization of investment if the rapid economic development of underdeveloped (or, for that matter, developed) countries is to be effectively advanced.

28. The grave harm done to the magnificent revolutionary effort of the Cuban people by the "starving out" strategy of American imperialism is the most striking and the most distressing case in point.

29. Those who are so influenced by the mendacious propaganda of imperialism as to believe that the vast armaments buildup in the United States is governed by the fear of aggression on the part of the socialist countries *must* read the monumental work of Professor D. F. Fleming, *The Cold War and Its Origins,* 2 vols. (New York, 1961), as well as the revealing account of the *actual* course of disarmament negotiations in recent years by Professor J. P. Morray, *From Yalta to Disarmament: Cold War Debate* (New York, 1961). It is hard to believe that anyone who is *willing* to recognize the truth can fail to be impressed by the incontrovertible evidence assembled in these extraordinary studies.

30. The situation is obviously somewhat different in parts of the world where the underemployment of manpower in agriculture is matched by underutilization of arable land—as in the case of Cuba. Under such circumstances, aggregate agricultural output can be, at any rate in the early stages, rapidly increased by taking into cultivation

previously uncultivated areas, although even in such cases major difficulties are caused by lack of agricultural implements, fertilizers, and livestock.

31. After the Second World War the situation in the Soviet Union in particular was seriously aggravated by the casualties suffered by the agricultural male population to a larger extent than by the industrial proletariat, who were more frequently exempted from military service.

32. The Soviet experience during the last decade provides an excellent illustration of this development.

33. In Albania, and possibly elsewhere, it was apparently also held that Soviet grants and credits to non-socialist underdeveloped countries reflect nothing but an illusion that the non-socialist governments of those countries could be genuinely won over to the cause of peace and socialism. In a decisive moment, regardless of what benefits they may derive from the Soviet Union and other socialist countries, these governments would betray their benefactors and join the imperialist camp. Therefore—it was argued—all resources allocated to such uncertain friends are wasted and could and should be more usefully employed in helping socialist countries. This is reported in an article by F. Konstantinov, the editor-in-chief of the offical theoretical organ of the Central Committee of the Communist Party of the Soviet Union, *Kommunist:* "Raskolnicheskaya, antimarksistskaya deyatelnost albanskikh rukovoditeley." ("The divisive, anti-Marxian activity of the Albanian leaders.")—*Kommunist* (November, 1969), p. 48.

34. Albania has apparently fared even worse, although there, according to some reports, the fault lies chiefly with highly inefficient management on the part of the party leadership.

VI
On Socialism

On Soviet
Themes

That the present is but a fleeting moment between the past
and the future was never so vividly clear to me as in the
five weeks that I spent in Moscow early in 1956. During
that time I spoke to many people: to ordinary citizens, the
proverbial "man in the street," students, university teachers, scientific workers, and writers, to both members and
non-members of the Communist Party. Some of them I
have known for as long as thirty years, others I just
encountered. Some of them knew that I was a foreigner,
others did not. Some of them spoke freely, with abandon,
"letting their hair down," behaving as if this was the
long-awaited opportunity for talking about things they
could not discuss before, for saying all that they had on
their minds. Others were formal, restrained, weighing every
word and studiously avoiding any "ticklish" subjects, anything that might be interpreted as an indiscretion. Yet all
of them, those who talked much and those who talked
little, those who treated me as an old friend and those who
acted as if they were representatives of one power talking
to an ambassador of another—all of them without exception stressed one point: the paramount, indeed, the sole

This article originally appeared in the July-August 1956 issue of
Monthly Review. Copyright © 1956 by Monthly Review, Inc.

purpose of the current analysis of the past is to derive lessons for the future. And the principal lesson for the future that all of them draw, that all of them consider to be of overriding importance, is that what has happened in the last twenty years of the Stalin era must not, and—what is most significant—*need* not, happen again. It is the ability to look at things in historical perspective, the capacity for comprehending current events as aspects of the historical process, that is most striking about Soviet people today, about old and young, about the highly educated ones and those with only rudimentary knowledge. For regardless of the primitivized, vulgarized, and distorted form in which it was frequently presented to them—it was after all Marxian thought in which they were steeped, it was the philosophy of historical materialism in which they were brought up. In their profound conviction that the tragic and sordid aspects of the Stalin regime will not reappear, they are by no means naively optimistic or guided merely by wishful thinking. It has escaped them no more than many foreign observers that the present men on top were all members of the Stalin team, for the most part selected and appointed by him, and thus to a large extent co-responsible for his policies. If they feel nevertheless that the Stalin system is now a thing of the past, that what has occurred need not occur again—their strong sense of history gives them good reasons for their confidence.

One of these reasons has to do with the specific circumstances that gave rise to the Stalin dictatorship. When so many people talk in Moscow today about the return to Leninist principles, they realize fully that what is at issue is not merely the *desirability* of such a return but the *applicability* of those principles to Soviet reality. Indeed, the period of Lenin's leadership in the Soviet state differed in a crucially important respect from the time in which Stalin was at its helm. Lenin led a revolutionary movement that in the critical months of 1917 was carried by massive popular support. Having written on its banners "Peace," it had the enthusiastic backing of a huge army that was exhausted and bled white by a senseless and disastrous war. Having associated itself with the peasants' age-old craving for land, it could rely on the sympathy and cooperation of a large stratum of the rural masses. In nationalizing capitalist enterprise that was swollen with war profits, it was fulfilling the aspirations of the majority of urban workers. Accordingly, there was little terror during the first phase of the Revolution. It assumed major proportions only considerably later when foreign intervention and the formation of White Armies resulted in a Civil War, and it was directed exclusively against the resistance of the former ruling classes, against attempts to overthrow the revolutionary government. By 1921 political repression was greatly reduced, the activities of the Cheka were markedly curbed, and life in the country was essentially normalized.

The situation was altogether different when Stalin undertook his "revolution from above"—the forced collectivization of Russian agriculture. For that drive—carried out with terrifying speed and ruthlessness—there was no popular support. There was undoubtedly enthusiàsm among parts of the urban population for the program of industrialization, for the construction of industrial enterprises and power stations; there was none when it came to the collectivization of agriculture. Indeed, if the 1917 Revolution gave land to the peasants, the 1929-1930 "revolution from above" was interpreted as taking it away from them. While in 1917 the objective conditions and the outlook of the Russian peasantry were "ripe" for a bourgeois agrarian revolution, in 1929 neither the material prerequisites nor the attitude of the peasantry were "ripe" for a socialist transformation of the village. There was not even much sympathy for such a transformation among industrial workers, most of whom were freshly recruited from the villages and were strongly influenced by the sentiment prevailing in the countryside.

Under such circumstances the collectivization—if it was to be carried out at all—*could* be carried out only *against* the people; that is, only with the help of massive political repression. The secret police turned from an administrative *instrument* of the regime into its principal *political* foundation. As the deportations and terror in the countryside assumed major proportions, as the food crisis associated with the industrialization effort and accentuated by the upheavals caused by collectivization contributed to the spreading and deepening of general discontent, the role of the OGPU became increasingly prominent. It supplanted the Party organizations which to a larger or lesser degree reflected grass-root opinion, and rapidly developed a vested interest in its own preservation and aggrandizement. Its apparatus and power became all-pervasive, and it continued its expansion at a time when the original need for repression all but disappeared. In fact—and this is crucially important—it was precisely at the time when the political and economic development in the country rendered the maintenance of police terror increasingly redundant and harmful, that the OGPU undertook everything in its (prodigious) power to strengthen and to perpetuate its sway over the nation. It was not fortuitous that it was at the end of 1934 when the overall economic and political situation had markedly improved, when both industrialization and collectivization had achieved considerable successes, that Kirov was murdered in Leningrad, and that that murder was seized upon as a signal for mass extermination of all elements of the Party that might have stood in the way of the OGPU dictatorship.

Two factors were primarily responsible for its ability to accomplish that end. One was that Stalin, who had commenced by *using* the OGPU in enforcing the policy of industrialization and collectivization, became rapidly identified with its apparatus, became indeed its leader and its exponent. Having never had much popularity and status *within the Party*, having received strong indications of mounting intraparty opposition toward his authoritarian rule at the Seventeenth Party Congress (January-February 1934) where, as I learned in Moscow, a very large number of delegates voted against him in a secret ballot, Stalin sought support outside of the Party and found in the OGPU the mechanism that enabled him to establish his position of paramount power. Stalin's profound distrust of the Party and his hostility toward its leading echelons where he was always outclassed and outranked in the past led him to a complete amalgamation with the OGPU, an amalgamation upon the stability of which both became wholly dependent. It made it possible for Stalin incrasingly to disregard the Party and to have the OGPU organize his elevation to the status of an infallible leader; it made it possible for the OGPU to be powerfully backed and protected by Stalin. This system could, however, prevail for any length of time only in an atmosphere of acute danger. Such an atmosphere was continuously created and recreated by the OGPU with the connivance and, indeed, instructions of Stalin.

And this brings us to the second factor that played a tremendous role in the consolidation of the Stalin-OGPU regime. This was Hitler's rise to power in Germany. Representing from the very beginning a *real* threat to the security of the Soviet Union, German fascism was incessantly and most successfully used by Stalin and the OGPU as a reason for an intensified campaign against all potential opposition to their absolute rule. This campaign reached altogether macabre proportions in the late 1930's; it was explained by the necessity of suppressing all elements of a possible "Fifth Column" in the country—an explanation that was widely accepted both inside and outside of the Soviet Union. The sense of emergency justifying maximum "vigilance" and serving as a rationalization for incessant application of political repression could obviously be easily driven to a pitch in the years of war. Its maintenance after the war became facilitated by the internal difficulties that had to be overcome in the first years of post-war reconstruction, and later by the stresses and strains of the "Cold War." When, by 1952, the rationalization of the OGPU terror by the existence of emergency and external danger was wearing increasingly thin, the "doctors plot" was manufactured by the OGPU and Stalin to give the philosophy of "vigilance" a new lease on life.

But if the need for a repressive regime for the success of the industrialization and collectivization program was becoming highly questionable as early as 1934, and manifestly absent in 1937—the year of the greatest triumph of Soviet industrial and agricultural construction—in the 1950's the Stalin-OGPU reign of terror lost all conceivable *raison d'être*. The economy had been making rapid strides, the foundations of a socialist order were firmly laid, popular loyalty toward the principles of socialism was unquestionable, the basic structure of the Soviet society was securely grounded in broad popular support. In that setting, the Stalin-OGPU tyranny became not only politically superfluous but a formidable threat to the further development of the Soviet Union. It imposed untold suffering on millions of people, it stifled the intellectual life of the country, it jeopardized the efficient functioning of the economy, it affected adversely the evolution of other socialist countries, and it increased the danger of war. Its abolition became desperately overdue; the death of Stalin was not the *cause* of its liquidation. This kind of government would have been liquidated sooner or later in any case. The death of Stalin made its liquidation possible at the time at which it actually began.

This poses a question of overriding importance to the theory of socialism in general and to us, Western socialists, in particular. I raised it with many people in Moscow, and the resulting discussion was most illuminating. Broadly speaking, the problem is the relation of socialism to democracy. Can socialism be attained by the socialist party's securing the approval of the majority of the people in any given country with that approval resulting from a process of systematic persuasion and enlightenment, or can socialism become a reality only by being imposed upon society by a more or less sizeable minority hoping to be *eventually* borne out by popular support? Furthermore, can socialism be attained so as to fully safeguard the interests of the opposing minority, or are the interests of that minority to be sacrificed whichever way the transition to socialism may take place? Indeed, does not the argument of the previous section imply that the Stalin-OGPU regime, the mass ruination of the so-called kulaks, and the terrorization of the nation *during* the collectivization campaign were essentially justified? Does not that line of reasoning accept the position suggested in Khrushchev's first report to the Twentieth Party Congress and in Mikoyan's speech delivered in the debate of this report, that Stalin's terror was wholly damnable during the *last twenty years of his life* (that is since the murder of Kirov in 1934) without being reprehensible during the preceding five years, when millions of people were destroyed in the course of the collectivization campaign? And does not this position in turn mean that terror is being "sorted out," with terror applied (in this case) to peasants condoned, but with terror directed against outstanding Party members condemned? Putting it differently, is the terroristic enforcement of collectivization upon an unwilling peasantry for the sake of industrialization and construction of socialism to be considered legitimate, while the massacre of Communists who were possibly to some extent expressing the sentiment of the masses to be treated as a crime?

Looking at the problem from a somewhat different angle, it may be asked whether—given the costs of collectivization and industrialization—the original decisions to undertake both were justified? And there can hardly be any doubt that in assessing those costs one has to take into account not only the terroristic activities of the Stalin-OGPU regime *during* the collectivization drive proper, but everything that has happened in the course of the subsequent years. For it is only on the basis of and with the help of the power that Stalin gained in 1929-1934 that he was able to do what he did in 1934-1953.

These questions were hotly debated in Moscow in various circles, and the answers to them that I heard suggested little of the uniformity and streamlining of opinion that some travellers discover after one week's stay in Moscow's Hotel Metropole. There were some people who expressed themselves unequivocally to the effect that Stalin's (*and* the Communist Party's) policy of industrialization and collectivization was a tremendous, tragic blunder, and that the correct course would have been to move slowly along the lines suggested by the right-wing opposition, aiming at a gradual improvement of living conditions in the village and a "cotton-goods industrialization" in the cities. The number of people holding this view was, however, conspicuously small— even after the terrible revelations contained in Khrushchev's second (secret) report to the Twentieth Party Congress became widely known.

Most of those to whom I talked, as well as those who talked among themselves in my presence, argued that the basic policy of the Soviet government in the course of the industrialization and collectivization campaigns was essentially correct, that it was fully borne out by subsequent experience, that in its absence Russia would have lost the war, with the suffering resulting therefrom greatly surpassing all the misery that was endured under Stalin. They were convinced that both industrialization and collectivization were indispensable if the country was to move forward, that under the specific conditions prevailing in Russia in those days there was no way of achieving that end without compulsion—even if the compulsion actually employed was excessive. What was most remarkable, nearly all the people whom I saw, whether roundly condemning Stalin and everything associated with him or recognizing his achievements and deploring his excesses, stressed with great pride and emotion that in striking the balance of the Stalin era, one must not forget to give full weight to the role that the sacrifices of the Soviet people and their spectacular successes in socialist construction have played in the advancement of socialism in the world. It is on the basis of those sacrifices and those successes—they stressed—that other countries in the socialist camp, but in particular China, are able today to avoid many of the pitfalls and hardships that would have been otherwise inevitable.

And in any case—I was told in a discussion that I had with a group of students—the questions that I asked could not be treated in an abstract, unhistorical way. They could be approached only with reference to concrete situations. For the Soviet Union today—all of them agreed—the issues no longer exist. For *now* future progress is *not* predicated upon the methods adopted by Stalin. Now the Soviet Union is in a position to continue and to widen its advance toward socialism with the full consent and indeed enthusiastic cooperation of the people.

This points to another reason for the generally prevailing belief that terror and compulsion need not reappear in Soviet life. It is the breathtaking change that has taken place in the structure of Soviet society in the course of the last thirty years. For the country is dominated now by a new generation which, tempered by the struggle for industrialization and hardened by the ordeals of the war, is unique in its moral strength, its patriotism, and the level of its knowledge and insight. This generation that is now everywhere in the driver's seat displays in every aspect of national life its craving for education, for opportunity for unhampered development, for freedom, and for justice. This generation reads voraciously the best in the world's literature, overflows the universities, concentrates in the most difficult areas of science, mobs lecture halls, and responds with spontaneous ovations to the Comédie Française, to David Oistrakh, to Emil Gilels, to "Porgy and Bess," and to a good paper on the "Relation of Dialectical Logic to Formal Logic." This generation is impatient with the "old-timers" who fill their books and articles with stale citations, who have lost the ability of thinking for themselves, who cover their intellectual indolence by reference to authority. The mental frame of reference of Soviet youth was not drawn by the OGPU; it was drawn by the writings of Marx and Engels, of Pushkin and Tolstoy, of Shakespeare and Goethe, which were printed and reprinted in the Soviet Union in millions of copies. Its ideas were not shaped by Stalin's hangmen assassinating innocent people, nor were they formed by comic books extolling rape and murder. Its ideas were molded in schools and youth organizations where socialism, humanism, and devotion to the commonweal never ceased to be the content of education.

It is here where the fundamental difference lies between the fascist despotism of a Hitler or a Franco and the no less repulsive oriental tyranny of a Stalin. The difference is the *content* of the historical development that those dictatorships were able to enforce. If in the case of Hitler it was the unleashing of the most destructive, most bloody war in human history, if in the case of Franco it is continual misery and degradation of a great people—in the case of Stalin it is the creation of all the prerequisites for the development of a prosperous and free society. In the process of building the foundations of socialism in Russia, vast quantities of filth and refuse were flying in all directions and were obscuring the contours of what was being accomplished. Yet at the same time a generation was being brought up whose most pronounced characteristic is the urge to clean out the Augean stables, tear down the gallows, break up the concentration camps, get rid of the executioners and their apologists, and proceed from what has been attained to what still remains to be achieved. I am convinced that it was the irresistible pressure of Soviet youth that has transformed the slow, gradual "de-Stalinization" of 1953-1955 into the mighty eruption of 1956. And I am no less convinced that this pressure which gains momentum with every success that it attains will sweep before itself whatever may come into its way. It is the pressure of a great and irreversible awakened people that will transform Russia—perhaps more rapidly than frequently assumed—into a free, socialist democracy.

A Few Thoughts
on the Great Debate

In briefest terms, the central issue brought to the fore by
the Twenty-second Congress and the new Program of the
Communist Party of the Soviet Union seems to me to be
the following: Does the formal and irreversible break with,
and the uncompromising condemnation of, the entire
complex of repression, violence, and dogmatism which
constituted a prominent feature of Stalin's domination in
the socialist part of the world call also for an equally
decisive change in the strategy of socialist construction
adopted under his leadership?

Although, to my knowledge, *all* socialists—on the right
wing and on the left wing of the movement, in the Soviet
Union and in Italy, in China and in France—recognize the
necessity and desirability of the break, there are several
countries where there is no such consensus regarding the
advisability of a change in the strategy of socialist
construction. The right, or, as it is now called, "revisionist"
wing uses the universal revulsion against the misdeeds of

This article was written as a contribution to a symposium on the
Twenty-second Congress of the Communist Party of the Soviet Union
arranged by the left-wing Italian magazine *Nuovi Argomenti* (edited by
Alberto Moravia and Alberto Carocci) in conjunction with the
publishing house of Einaudi. The article was first published in the May
1962 issue of *Monthly Review*. Copyright © 1962 by Monthly Review,
Inc.

Stalin to demand a more or less radical abandonment of *basic policies* associated with his name. Apart from whatever specific arguments against these policies they may advance, their case rests heavily on the contention that all the abuses and excesses of Stalin's rule represent an inevitable outgrowth of the basic policies for which it stood. The left, or "orthodox" group, on the other side, insists on preserving more or less intact these basic policies, even at the cost of soft-pedalling the drive against the "cult of the personality." Its argument is essentially that Stalin's "general line" was on the whole correct, that such crimes and excesses as were committed represented not an integral part but a more or less fortuitous and therefore avoidable accompaniment of what was otherwise a wise course. In warning against "throwing out the baby with the bath-water," this current of opinion is able to adduce as powerful supporting evidence the undeniable fact that in China where a left-wing, Stalinist course has been followed, Stalinist terrorism and aberrations are conspicuously absent.

This is obviously anything but a purely doctrinal dispute; what it reflects are, rather, two fundamental and closely interrelated problems confronting the world's socialist camp. First, it must be clearly recognized that the different countries constituting the socialist part of the world find themselves at the present time in radically different stages of economic development. At one end of the spectrum stand the Soviet Union, Czechoslovakia, the German Democratic Republic, and also Poland and Hungary where levels of industrialization and productivity have been attained (or, in part, have been inherited) which make it possible to shift gears and to move forward along the road of balanced economic progress. In these countries there is—occasional bottlenecks and temporary shortages of various kinds notwithstanding—no need for a stern policy of austerity, no longer any necessity for severe curtailment of the production of consumer goods, housing, and the like. Settling down to high but not breakneck rates of investment and expansion of output, these countries are able not only to afford the abandonment of the policy of "forced marches" that was characteristic of the Stalin era; they *must* greatly liberalize the economic and social conditions prevailing in their societies if further economic, cultural, and political advancement is to be assured. For here, as elsewhere, there is a powerful dialectic at work: the very system of extreme pressure on consumption, of unquestioned subordination to authority, and of rigidly dogmatic concentration on principal targets, which was imposed by Stalin and which enabled the Soviet Union to get over the "hump" of initial industrialization—this very system has turned, in the current phase of history, into a prohibitive obstacle to further economic and social growth. This was visible on every side. The utmost centralization in the administration of industry—to take one example—was not only possible as long as the size of the industrial sector was small, but was altogether indispensable in a period of relative industrial inexperience, shortage of qualified managerial personnel, and minimal choice in the rational utilization of industrial output. The same degree of centralization in the organizational structure of a vast industrial economy, disposing of able and skilled administrators at all levels and with a relatively wide choice in the utilization of output, leads to time-consuming and energy-wasting bureaucratic procedures, undermines the initiative of industrial managers and their responsiveness to new methods of production and to changing demands on the part of consumers—in a word, causes an irrational allocation of resources. Similarly, severe limitation of consumption, of construction of housing and other facilities, while inevitable at a time when the principal task is "primary accumulation," reduces incentives to work and to strive for higher qualifications, and not only imposes avoidable sacrifices and suffering on working people but becomes an impediment to efficient production. And finally, in a different area, if iron-fisted insistence on discipline and on the assignment of absolute priority to the immediate tasks of economic development in all intellectual, artistic, and cultural activity may have been conducive at a certain stage to the generation of an unwavering single-mindedness of purpose among broad popular masses, the continuation of such unbending dogmatism at the present time perpetuates a narrow-minded incapacity to comprehend new historical developments and becomes a formidable fetter on creativity and freedom in all areas of national life.

All this is indisputable, and as far as the Soviet Union and other similarly situated socialist countries are concern-ed there is no room for disagreement with the view that—to paraphrase a line from Schiller—"Stalin has done his duty and Stalin must go." That he did much more (or rather much less) than his duty—that he permitted himself and others to usurp vast powers and to abuse them for purposes of self-aggrandizement, nepotism, and arbitrariness, for the sake of vengeance and persecution directed against personal enemies—made it imperative that his departure assume the dimensions of a major political upheaval. Stalin's henchmen and satraps had to be uprooted everywhere, the methods of government which had become established under his direction had to be thoroughly revamped, the entire prevailing atmosphere had to be drastically changed if the vitally necessary and unpostponable liberalization and rejuve-nation were to be accomplished.

But one man's meat is another man's poison, and what constitutes a necessary and positive development in the Soviet Union's advance to a socialist democracy is wholly premature for China, which still has a long way to go until it reaches the Soviet Union's level of industrialization and

per capita output. Indeed, China is still in the throes of the
most difficult initial phase of economic development, and
the problems which it faces are in many respects even more
complex than those which confronted the Soviet Union
during the first two Five Year Plans. Under such
conditions—aggravated as they have been by a series of
natural disasters in agriculture and possibly by certain
errors committed by the leadership—liquidation of austerity, relaxation of pressure on consumption, and a measure
of "demobilization" of national effort are certainly not on
the immediate agenda. Having reached at best only the first
encampment on the long and arduous ascent to a richer
society, the Chinese "people throughout the country must
determine to work hard for several more years to fulfill this
glorious task in the spirit of uninterrupted revolution."[1]

And having systematically inspired the people of China by
invoking the glowing example of Soviet successes, linked
inseparably for twenty-five years with the stewardship of
Stalin, having explained their strategy of development to
the Chinese masses largely in terms evolved in the Soviet
Union under the influence of Stalin, the Chinese leadership
feels at the present time less than ever inclined to demolish
wholesale an ideological structure that has come to play a
crucial role in China's as yet "uninterrupted revolution."
For not only would such a wrecking operation tend to
undermine popular confidence in the leadership itself; it
would hardly meet with much understanding and approval
among the rank and file of the party and the broad popular
masses who themselves were never subjected to Stalin's
reign of terror. Thus to the Chinese, "de-Stalinization" is
anything but an urgent issue. Little as they actually ever
cared for Stalin himself—and for that dislike they have
weighty historical reasons—as far as they are concerned, the
condemnation of Stalin's *basic policies* and the destruction

of his commanding prestige could hardly come at a less propitious time.

To be sure, abstractly speaking, there might have been a possibility of significantly changing the general situation and of rendering the more underdeveloped parts of the socialist world more amenable to a broadly gauged program of de-Stalinization and liberalization. This might have been more nearly feasible if the advanced socialist countries, in the first place obviously the Soviet Union, had been able and willing to alleviate markedly the difficulties experienced at the present time in China by furnishing *massive* economic assistance. Needless to say, to make a major impact on the economic situation of a country as vast and populous as China, such aid would have to assume truly gigantic proportions. And it is equally obvious that rendering economic aid on such a scale would soon exceed the capabilities of the Soviet Union and of the better-off socialist countries in Europe. Further, an attempt to squeeze as much aid as possible out of the economies of the advanced socialist countries would not merely preclude all the liberalization and belt-loosening which have been undertaken, but would also jeopardize the political stability of these countries themselves, as was clearly shown in the "Kronstadts" of Berlin, Budapest, and Poznan.

In any case, this course of denying or slowing down the long awaited improvement of the wretched living conditions which the Soviet, German, and Polish peoples have had to endure now for many years, was flatly rejected by their present leadership. The relevant passages of the new Program of the Communist Party of the Soviet Union leave little doubt about the nature of this decision. Although stressing the commitment of the CPSU to international socialist solidarity and proffering brotherly help to other socialist countries, the document states that the CPSU and the Communist Parties of the other socialist countries consider their tasks to be: In the economic field, expansion of trade between the socialist countries, development of the socialist international division of labor, increasing coordination of long-range economic plans among the socialist countries envisaging a maximum saving of social labor and an accelerated development of the world socialist economy, and the promotion of scientific and technical cooperation.[2]

Khrushchev was even more explicit in his Report to the Twenty-second Congress where he observed that "by a common effort of fraternal parties were found and are being perfected new forms of inter-state relations—relations of economic, political, and cultural cooperation based on principles of equality, *mutual advantage*, and brotherly *mutual* help."[3]

But deeds and concrete blueprints are more eloquent than words and ringing declarations. And while it goes without saying that it is completely impossible to equalize per capita incomes in socialist countries in so widely divergent stages of economic development—particularly when the populations of the low income countries so vastly outnumber those of the relatively advanced ones—it is easy to understand that the majestic edifice of a society of plenty projected at the Twenty-second Congress has produced mixed reactions in the Chinese and some other Communist parties struggling desperately to overcome abysmal poverty in their countries. Reassured and strengthened as they may feel by the tremendous successes of the Soviet Union, and proud as they may be in the magnificent vistas opened up by the new Program, they can hardly fail to experience the strong sense of estrangement which "have nots" usually develop toward "haves." Considering that the Program envisages an increase of Soviet national product by 500 percent in twenty years, that real per capita income is expected to grow in the same period by 350 percent, and that at the end of this time span the Soviet people are to enjoy the *highest* standard of living in the world, the shortest work week, and the most comprehensive social welfare arrangements, the question naturally arises whether *such* a momentous expansion of consumption and welfare is wholly compatible with socialist solidarity and fraternal mutual help. With the gap between the Soviet output and that of other socialist countries as large as it is, wouldn't there be something to be said for the Soviet Union's seeking to "reach and overtake" the American per capita income, say, in thirty years rather than in the twenty years prescribed in the Program, and for its gaining in this way the possibility of providing more generous support to other members of the socialist camp? Further, wouldn't signficant Soviet aid to the underdeveloped socialist countries in Asia, greatly accelerating and facilitating their socialist construction, enhance the prestige of socialism in the rest of the underdeveloped world even more than glittering prosperity in the Soviet Union alone?

These are terribly difficult questions whose answers are of necessity matters of judgment which can only be properly arrived at by taking into account the specific conditions prevailing in the individual countries as well as the overall strategy of the world's socialist movement. And wherever such is the case, there is ample room for differences of opinion and for more or less violent controversy. What renders the situation particularly complex, moreover, is that the elbow room available to the present Soviet leadership is much narrower than it would be to a regime of Stalin's type. With the liberalization and democratization of national life already having made considerable progress, it becomes increasingly hard for those who preside over the country and the Party today to make decisions which are likely to be unpopular, to allocate resources to purposes which, however worthy in themselves, are remote from the daily needs and aspirations of the Soviet "man in the street," who longs to have at last decent housing, decent food, and decent clothing.

This economic tension rending the world's socialist camp has its counterpart in a no less serious political strain, which constitutes the *second* question that has to be considered. For the circumstances of the individual socialist countries are not only most uneven in economic terms; they are no less so in the political realm, and in particular in the now all-important area of international relations. At the present time, the chief concern of the Soviet Union and of a number of European socialist countries—politically stable and embarked on long-range programs of economic and social advancement— is the alleviation of the threat of war, and, if possible, some reduction of the burden of armaments, both crucial to the realization of their ambitious goals. Just as in 1924, after the failure of the Hamburg uprising, a "right-wing" Soviet leadership took the view that the capitalist world had entered a period of "relative stabilization," and oriented its foreign policy under Litvinov toward relaxation of international tensions and collective security, so it is now held—for different reasons—that the current period demands "peaceful coexistence," and some accommodation with the imperialist powers. Then the reorientation took place because it was clear that the revolutionary storm following World War I had drawn to its close; now it is considered to be imperative because of the catastrophic consequences of a possible war, and because only under conditions of peace can the respite be won that is necessary to render the world's socialist camp wholly invincible and thus to win decisively the historic struggle for socialism on a global scale.

Thus what is involved here are the foremost problems of

international revolutionary strategy. Which issues constitute the "program minimum" of today, the issues that *must* be settled before an accommodation with the Western powers can be accepted? Is it sufficient to arrive at some *modus vivendi* which would guarantee, say, an undisturbed development of the German Democratic Republic, as appears sometimes to be the Soviet view, or should a comprehensive settlement of the much more complex problems in Asia be considered to be a *conditio sine qua non* of any detente? And this in turn raises the question of how to assess the power and the capacity to fight of the imperialist bloc. Is imperialism now, in the age of atomic equilibrium and universal uprising of colonial and dependent peoples, merely a "paper tiger" which would collapse if put on trial, or is there still enough life and vigor in the beast to destroy the world if cornered and driven to desperation?

If is easy to see that the answers of Asian Communists to these questions must tend to be quite different from those of the Soviet Communist Party. China and several other Asian countries are still in the grip of civil war. Nearly everywhere guerrilla fighters are waging heroic battles against reactionary, hateful dictatorships imposed and maintained in power by the military might of the United States. Frustrated in their most elementary aspirations, as in the case of China and Taiwan, or split in the middle like Korea, Vietnam, and Laos; denied their indisputable rights in international political bodies; subjected to economic discrimination and boycott, the socialist countries of Asia obviously regard the return of Taiwan to the homeland, the liberation of South Korea and South Vietnam, their admission to the United Nations, and so forth, as being no less urgent than the settlement of the conflict over Berlin.

This does not mean, as is frequently asserted in Western newspapers—maliciously, ignorantly, or both—that China wants to go to war over those issues or even is advocating that the foreign policy of the socialist camp should be one of taking reckless risks. Nothing could be further from the truth. What it does mean, however, is that the Chinese consider a more intransigent attitude toward the West to be imperative, believe that the "Spirit of Camp David" and most of what goes with it harms the morale of revolutionaries in Asia and elsewhere, and insist that at the present historical juncture a hard, uncompromising stand against imperialism would greatly contribute to the awakening and radicalization of the masses in the underdeveloped countries and thus to the strengthening of their socialist movements. The Soviet Union's taking at the same time the opposite tack, attempting to attain at least a measure of relaxation in the international atmosphere and to find some compromises on various, if only secondary issues, gives rise to the dark suspicion that the present Soviet leadership may be willing to come to terms with the United States if not at the expense, then at least without due regard to the interests, of China and the other socialist countries of Asia. It may be noted in passing that, ironically enough, there was more *concrete* evidence to support this suspicion in the case of Stalin than in the case of Khrushchev. It was the former and not the latter who was prepared to make a deal with President Roosevelt's emissary—Harry Hopkins—and to discourage the Chinese Communists' seizure of power in exchange for admittedly desperately needed American help to the Soviet Union. That nothing came of that deal is certainly more the "fault" of the Chinese and of the United States than of Stalin.

What this raises is the far-reaching question whether the *short-run* interests of the Soviet people are not now coming into a *genuine* contradiction not only with those of the underprivileged socialist countries but also with those of other backward nations striving for independence and socialism. For, wanting above all to prevent war and determined to attain its goals of socialist construction, the Soviet leadership is certainly continuously exposed to the danger of a "nationalist aberration." It may, indeed, come to feel less than enthusiastic about "premature" revolutionary upheavals in various parts of the world, not only in view of the danger of a military conflagration which they may entail, but also because, if successful, they may place the Soviet Union before the terrible dilemma of either providing large-scale economic aid or losing face in the underdeveloped world and in the international socialist movement. We are confronted here with a problem which is not altogether new. It may have been wholly appropriate for the Soviet leadership in the days of Stalin to put brakes on revolutionary movements on a number of historical occasions—when the Soviet Union was not in a position to weather the possible military consequences of a socialist revolution in another country, and when it was unable to give such a revolution the necessary economic support. But would such a policy of breaking and "going slow" be equally justified if adopted *now*, when the military and economic might of the Soviet Union is incomparably larger?

As usual, one thing leads to another. Major problems, if unsolved, produce minor irritations, and the latter frequently overshadow the former. The number of such frictions and irritations in Sino-Soviet relations is apparently at the present time legion; their significance ranges from the withdrawal of Soviet technicians from China so as to stop their indoctrination with the Chinese appraisal of Soviet politics and Soviet leadership, to such symbolic acts as Chou En-lai's early departure from the Twenty-second Congress or the Chinese press's giving only limited space and attention to the proceedings of the Congress and to the new Program which it adopted. There can be little doubt that these relatively minor, derivative conflicts could be ironed out without too much trouble—say, in a summit conference between Khrushchev and Mao Tse-tung—provided that the truly serious differences which lie behind them could be amicably composed. But it is by no means certain that this is possible *in the short run*. In practice, they may only be alleviated by a change in the objective conditions: when the progressive development of China and other socialist countries of Asia will have greatly narrowed the economic gap between them and the Soviet Union; when the international balance of power will have so changed as to improve greatly the international position of the Asian socialist countries; and when the threat of war recedes because of the rapidly growing military might of the socialist camp and the increasing resistance to military adventures in the Western world.

Meanwhile, if the considerations advanced above come anywhere near to encompassing the essence of the Great Debate, they suggest that it is by no means impossible that in the present phase of the world's revolutionary movement, the center of moral gravity and the seat of political leadership may move from Moscow to Peking, all the military strength and economic achievements of the Soviet Union notwithstanding. This need not preclude by any means the individual socialist countries' forward movement toward socialism, nor does it render it impossible that reconciliation and harmony among them will be achieved in the fullness of time. But to try to speculate on all the manifold short-run and long-run ramifications of such a momentous development would transcend by far the limits of this short note.

Notes

1. *National Program for Agricultural Development, 1956-1967* (Peking, 1960), p. 57.

2. *Program of the Communist Party of the Soviet Union (Draft),*

Part II, sec. 6, para. 14. It is characteristic of the generally noticeable compromise nature of the program that this clear statement is followed (in para. 16 of the same section) by the rather vague promise that "the CPSU and the Soviet people will do everything in their power to support all the peoples of the Socialist community in their construction of socialism and Communism."

3. *Pravda,* October 18, 1961 (italics added). This position was apparently spelled out and strongly stressed in an article in *Mezhdunarodnava Zhisn* (March 1962), which is reported to have declared that unilateral sacrifices on the part of the Soviet people are entirely out of order. Cf. *New York Times,* March 26, 1962. See also "Answers to Readers' Inquiries Concerning the functions of the Committee for Mutual Economic Aid (*Comecon*)," published in the theoretical organ of the Central Committee of the CPSU, *Kommunist* (February 1961), where the "trade versus aid" principle is strongly emphasized. Of great interest are also the remarks of F. Konstantinov, editor-in-chief of that journal, concerning the admittedly quite separate case of the Albanian leadership which is accused by the Russians as well as by other socialist countries of seeking to perpetuate itself in spite of its inefficiency and inadequacies by becoming a permanent "pensioner" of the socialist camp.—*Kommunist* (November 1961).

Reflections
on the Cuban Revolution

The three weeks which I recently [September - October 1960] spent in Cuba were an unforgettable experience. We drove through districts of Havana where sprawling army barracks are being transformed by the soldiers of the Revolutionary Army into spacious school and dormitory buildings for thousands of university students. We walked through abysmal quarters in Santiago de Cuba where hovels, the horror and sordidness and misery of which are beyond my power of description, are being torn down and replaced by entire streets of light, clean, colorful little houses. We went through parts of Cuba's subtropical countryside (in the provinces of Oriente and of Pinar del Río) where new dwellings, vegetable gardens, barns, chicken hatcheries, dairy farms, cattle and pig breeding farms, schools, hospitals, and stores are popping up on every side like big mushrooms after an ample rainfall. We watched on both sides of the highway bulldozers and tractors clearing virgin land for cultivation, and we saw field after field only a few weeks earlier thickly covered by age-old underbrush now checkered by furrows of rice and corn and cotton.

While viewing all this, I suddenly relived a childhood joy

This essay appeared in the January 1961 issue of *Monthly Review*. Copyright © 1961 by Monthly Review, Inc. Sections XI and XII were talks given over radio station KPFA in Berkeley, California, on April 21 and May 4, 1961.

of seeing the warm April sun usher in the spring and liberate as if by a magic wand the earth, the rivers, the flowers, the animals from the heavy, oppressive burden of frost, ice, and snow. Just as in those distant days it was the poor people, the people with too little bread, fuel, shelter, and clothing to brave the cold long winter who rejoiced most over the arrival of spring, so now in Cuba it is the poor people, the people who never had all-year-round employment, never had enough food, enough medical care, enough shoes and schools for their children who are celebrating the miraculous burst of life, the dramatic resurrection of their nation. And I could not help thinking of another wonderful island and of another wonderful city where last year I was shown around by my good friend Danilo Dolci. There is perhaps even more poverty, even more misery in the villages of Sicily, and the narrow streets and courtyards behind the Cathedral of Palermo are perhaps even more terrifying, even more heartrending than anything I saw in Havana or Santiago. But the striking difference between Cardinal Ruffini's Sicily and Fidel Castro's Cuba can be seen in the human faces. There they expressed squalor, fear, and hopelessness. Here, wherever we went in the countryside and with whomever we talked on the farms and on construction jobs, we saw black faces and white faces and brown faces radiating enthusiasm and pride about what has been accomplished in the less than two years since the triumph of the Revolution, and hope and confidence about what is still to be achieved in the future.

I

Cuban intellectuals and members of the revolutionary movement—and we talked with many on various levels and in various fields of work—frequently insisted on the uniqueness, the peculiarity of the Cuban Revolution. They stressed with visible pride that the Cuban Revolution has followed no preconceived scheme, has not been governed by any "bookish" theory. Their revolution, they said, has grown spontaneously, owing its methods, its direction, and its triumph to specific conditions in Cuba as well as to the genius of Fidel Castro. There is not the slightest reason to doubt these statements, and I am convinced that this is precisely how the Cuban Revolution is seen and thought of by most, if not by all, of those who made it. And yet, just as it would be wrong to judge an individual's actions solely on the basis of what he himself thinks of them, so it would be an error to consider the Cuban Revolution merely in the light of what is or has been thought about it by the Cuban revolutionaries themselves. For while it certainly would be sterile doctrinairism to try to squeeze Cuba's history of the last few years into textbook categories of political theory, or to interpret the Cuban Revolution primarily in terms of the revolutionary experience at other times and in other places, it would be irrational to overlook certain broad similarities, certain important common features displayed by all revolutions, the Cuban included.

Indeed, it is the presence of such similarities and common features which has made it possible to arrive at a theory of revolutions, however fragmentary, that has enabled all great revolutionary leaders to learn from a careful study of earlier revolutionary experience. What follows makes no pretense to being a systematic analysis of the Cuban Revolution. It is rather a hasty attempt to put together what seem to me to be some of the salient considerations that have to be borne in mind in seeking to understand the momentous developments taking place in Cuba today.

II

It must be clearly realized that the Cuban Revolution is

not merely a *political* revolution. Political revolutions which have taken place repeatedly in nearly all countries of the world have usually overthrown one government in favor of another, changing the personal composition and sometimes even the ideological or social make-up of the political group in power. These changes may have been purely nominal (as in the case of many political upsets in Latin American countries) or quite consequential not only to the countries involved but to the world at large (as for instance de Gaulle's *coup d'état* in 1958, or of the farthest reaching impact upon the country in question and the world as a whole (as for instance the ascent of Hitler in 1933). And yet all of these changes in political institutions, radical and dramatic as they may have often appeared, did not affect to any appreciable degree the basic economic and social structure of the respective countries. The fundamental relations of production and of ownership of land, industrial facilities, and other means of production remained essentially undisturbed. The acid test of the purely political rather than social nature of any such upheaval is its *reversability*. After more than twenty years of Mussolini's rule, Italy returned without too much trouble to the institutions of a bourgeois democracy. Western Germany after Hitler (and the most devastating war in its history) resembles closely the Weimar Republic preceding the Nazi era, and the cancellation of the de Gaulle constitution and the re-establishment of the Fourth Republic in France is not only conceivable but entirely possible.

All this is quite different in the case of a social revolution, the outstanding characteristic of which is that it drastically alters the country's socioeconomic structure. The basic economic relations, the ownership of the principal means of production, the economic and political status of entire social classes, all undergo a sweeping transformation. Such transformations have been accompanied in the course of history by much violence. And attempts to reverse such a complete revamping of society usually lead to civil wars. Big estates appropriated by land-hungry peasants are not easily taken back. Factories nationalized or seized by revolutionary workers are not readily restored to their former owners. And social classes that have fought their way to power cannot be thrown back without a bitter struggle. Social revolutions thus tend to create *faits accomplis* and after relatively short periods of time those *faits accomplis* can no longer be undone.

III

Although it began as a *political* movement directed against the Batista dictatorship, the Cuban Revolution evolved early and rapidly into a *social* revolution. This raises a host of important questions: Who made the Revolution? What has been its course thus far? Whose interests did it advance? Who are its friends and who are its enemies? What social order is emerging from it? On all of these questions there is a great deal of misapprehension in various quarters, and most of this misapprehension is deliberately created by a biased network of communication.

A number of foreign students of the Cuban Revolution have stressed the leading part played by young intellectuals, and some have even considered the Cuban Revolution to be an outstanding manifestation of the worldwide "revolt on the campuses"—similar to what has taken place in Turkey, South Korea, Japan, and elsewhere. This view has deep theoretical roots, and relates to two propositions which are central to both political theory and a general interpretation of the historical process. One is an implied rejection of the principal tenet of historical materialism according to which it is social *classes* that are the prime agents on the historical scene, with both the composition of these classes and their broad political and ideological outlook determined chiefly by their position in the economic structure. The other, closely connected with the first, is the assertion that the *intellectuals* constitute a separate social stratum, an "elite" above classes which plays an independent and indeed a decisive role in history. This doctrine, the most influential recent exponent of which was the late German sociologist Karl Mannheim, is held, not unnaturally, in great esteem by many intellectuals on both sides of the Atlantic, and has been strongly advanced in this country by C. Wright Mills.

There are many reasons for this hypostatization of the intellectuals. Leaving aside the obvious, but therefore by no means irrelevant, one that the glorification of intellectuals is most flattering to the intellectuals themselves, four considerations must be primarily borne in mind. In the first place, the assignment of a crucially important role to the intellectuals is a sociological derivative of an idealistic philosophical position. If intellectuals are the salt of the earth, responsible for the nature and direction of social development, then clearly it is *ideas* that run history. There is the further implication that these ideas are not mere reflections of processes in the material world (tensions between forces and relations of production, struggles among social classes, and so forth) but rather unfold in and emanate from the pensive heads of the "freely floating intellectual elite" (Mannheim). Secondly, the leadership of nearly all major social movements in history (with the exception of the most primitive peasant rebellions) has consisted of or included intellectuals by upbringing or individuals turned intellectuals in the course of their political careers. What is then simpler than to conclude that since there were always intellectuals prominently associated with revolutionary movements, the intellectuals were their cause and their engine? Thirdly, the growing awareness among intellectuals of the irrationality, inhumanity, and degeneration of capitalism has been accompanied in many Western countries by an increasing disillusionment with the labor movement and a sharpened disappointment with its lack of political dynamism and its widespread capitulation before the capitalist order. Under such circumstances the faith in the awakening of the intellectuals remains the only bright spot on the horizon for those who seek a way out of the impasse of the status quo. And finally, in many countries, treating the intellectuals as the yeast of history, counting upon them to move things off dead center serves many intellectuals as a convenient rationalization for staying in their academic or literary ivory towers, for refraining from participating actively in such political and social struggles as are being actually fought in their societies.

But if all of these factors help explain why intellectuals assign to intellectuals such a vastly inflated role in the historical process, one should avoid the error of denying their influence or indeed, in certain situations, decisive impact on the speed, direction, and outcome of social movements. For the question is really not whether intellectuals have taken part in, and often made major contributions to, social movements. On that there can be no reasonable doubt. The problem is rather under what historical circumstances do intellectuals become drawn into such movements, under what conditions are they capable of affecting the course of events in any particular way, and what forces determine the specific part which they play. And this problem is certainly not solved but merely evaded by profound-sounding discourses about the independence of the intellectuals, about their unflagging devotion to truth, or about their selfless dedication to progress and to the commonwealth. None of these theories explains in the least the fact that in certain countries and at certain times some intellectuals become highly effective leaders of popular movements while in other countries at other times they are either entirely stymied or become active or passive supporters of the status quo.

The issue was highlighted in a short conversation between Fidel Castro and the able French journalist Claude Bourdet. Replying to Bourdet's remark that the Cuban Revolution is a segment of a movement sweeping the entire world, of the "revolution of the youth," Castro put his finger on the nub of the matter: "Certainly the youth," he said, "but above all, the workers, the peasants, the victims of colonialism, all the exploited . . ." (*France-Observateur*, September 29, 1960, p. 7). And yet, this penetrating observation by one whose knowledge of the matter is surely unequaled, calls, I think, for a qualification. It not only reflects Castro's characteristic modesty, it also refers less to the earlier than to the later part of the Revolution, not to the question of who *made* it, but to the question of whose basic interests it has primarily served in the course of its short history. For the transformations which have taken place in the mass basis of the Revolution undoubtedly constitute one of its most significant aspects; and while they come as no surprise to a student, they deserve most careful analysis, offering as they do an experimental verification of a general theory.

IV

The class that made the Revolution is the rural population, the Cuban *campesinos*. This class was driven to revolt by the increasingly insufferable state of poverty, exploitation, and backwardness to which it was condemned by the old order. Its success in making the Revolution and the direction it gave the Revolution were largely determined by its economic, social, and ideological structure.

Only a relatively small proportion (about a fourth) of

those who work on the land were individual cultivators of all kinds. Of these individual cultivators, only a fraction held title to the plots they tilled; the rest of them were sharecroppers and tenants, subtenants, or squatters. The overwhelming majority of the *campesinos*, on the other hand, was composed of agricultural laborers working on sugar, tobacco, and coffee plantations, earning a bare subsistence wage in the few busy months of the harvest season and reduced to unemployment and extreme privation during the remaining months of the *tiempo muerte*. Consequently, the land population of Cuba differs very markedly from what might be called the "classical" peasantry of pre-revolutionary Eastern Europe, some Mediterranean countries, Japan, China, and some parts of Latin America. It depends for its livelihood not on individual plots of land but on employment on plantations. It is not a stratum of owners and tenants but of agricultural laborers. And accordingly, it has no proprietary or would-be proprietary relations to the land, but consists primarily of proletarians wholly alienated from their means of production (and subsistence) and having nothing to sell but their labor power. This accounts also for relatively little social differentiation and for relatively great cohesion among the *campesinos*: the wealthy peasant, the "kulak," and the "middle peasant" aspiring to become wealthier—the dominant economic and political figures in the villages of many other countries—were relatively unimportant in the Cuban countryside. All this stems from one fundamental fact: for historical reasons that need not be traced here, the better part of Cuba's agriculture had *not* evolved into a feudal system but became at an early stage an appendage of monopoly capital. The prevalent form of proprietary unit—the *latifundium*—was not typically a feudal estate operated by serfs, but a plantation run by a corporation with the help of hired labor. This decisively affected the economic status as well as the basic attitudes of the Cuban land population. Living off their labor and not off what they might have considered if ever so tenuously to be their land, dependent upon large-scale "factories in the field" and not upon subsistence farms, exploited by vast capitalist firms and not by time-honored feudal relations, the Cuban *campesinos* longed and fought not for the ownership of the soil they tilled, but for essentially working class objectives: steady employment, more human working conditions, and more adequate wages.

Not being inhabited by a petty bourgeois stratum of small peasant proprietors, the Cuban countryside thus never became a "breeding ground of bourgeois ideology." Although there is no shortage of superstitions and mystical creeds—particularly in the more desolate and destitute mountain regions of the island—they have not assumed the form of organized religions and have little if any influence on the social, economic, and political consciousness of the rural masses. Nor did the Catholic Church ever develop into a powerful factor in Cuban life. While the ruling class was traditionally too greedy and too disdainful of the *campesinos* to bother to proselytize him into the Catholic faith, the Church itself did nothing to become identified with the vital needs and aspirations of the Cuban people. Prior to Cuba's gaining its independence, the Church sided with the Spanish overlords; later on, it supported one dictator after another; it belatedly hinted at rather than openly expressed antipathy toward the most brutal and abusive of them—Batista—could not change the popular image of the Catholic Church as the religious organization not of the poor but of the rich, not of working people but of the ruling class. As pointed out in an incisive article by James N. Wallace, "Castro vs. Catholicism" (*Wall Street Journal*, October 26, 1960), Catholicism, a mighty pillar of the status quo in most Latin American and many European countries, could not even approximately fulfill that function in Cuba. As I was told by a number of eyewitnesses: when pastoral letters condemning the Revolution were recently read in Catholic churches, congregations rose and left the building singing the national anthem.

V

It is quite clear, however, that what has been said thus far about the economic, social, and ideological condition of the rural population in Cuba is not sufficient to explain its having successfully made the Revolution. There are other underdeveloped countries where the underprivileged are even worse off than they were in Cuba, and there are other backward areas where the possibilities of liberation are even more propitious than they were in Cuba. What, then, were the specific circumstances which facilitated the breakthrough of the Cuban *campesino*, and how did they influence the course of the Cuban Revolution?

Three sets of considerations provide, I think, at least a partial answer to these questions. First, just as the economic situation of the *campesinos* accounted for the previously noted absence of a pronounced social differentiation and a high degree of cohesion in the Cuban countryside, so did the economic status of Cuba as a whole create a strong sense of *national* solidarity among Cubans in various walks of life. For in the slightly more than fifty years of its formal political independence, Cuba has never emerged from its dependency on the United States. Cuba's essentially colonial status manifested itself on all sides. Its most conspicuous symbol is the United States' naval base in Guantánamo, and it reflected itself in the vast proportion of Cuba's productive resources owned and controlled by United States capital. The principal industry, sugar, was largely operated by United States corporations and depended nearly exclusively on United States markets. Telephone and telegraph services, electric power, gasoline, radio and television sets, consumer durable goods, and a large proportion of the country's food were all supplied by United States business. Gangsters, gamblers, and shady operators of all kinds invaded Havana from New York, Chicago, and Miami and turned it into a preserve and amusement park of the American underworld. Consecutive dictators closely connected with United States business interests, participating directly or through stooges in a multitude of crooked deals promoted by Yankee speculators, acted as United States *Gauleiters* in Cuba and were at the beck and call of the American Ambassador. As Mr. Kennedy nostalgically remarked in his last TV debate with Mr. Nixon, the Ambassador holding office in Havana in 1957 told him during his visit that he, the Ambassador, was "the second most powerful man in Cuba." The Ambassador understated his position.

Small wonder that under such circumstances anti-Yankee sentiment was rife in the broad masses of the Cuban people who watched American corporations derive immense profits from their Cuban investments, who observed American executives and their retainers live in indescribable luxury in air-conditioned palaces, and who could not help attributing the prevailing poverty and underutilization of human and material resources to the country's colonial position. And it was inevitable that the hatred of Yankee domination was not confined to the lower classes but made deep inroads into the ranks of the middle and upper bourgeoisie, which—if not directly or indirectly in the service of American capital—had to bear the brunt of United States economic competition, and had to suffer the chronic humiliation of being second class citizens in their own country. To be sure, this spirit of *national* indignation was far from being a spirit of revolt. As is usual with most bourgeois nationalism, it was ambivalent. On the one hand, it was dampened by the fear of the neighboring American colossus and a strong sense of helplessness in dealing with the United States. On the other hand, it was crippled by the apprehension that the masses, once aroused by an anti-imperialist, nationalist action might "overshoot the mark," and turn it into a *social* revolution directed not merely against foreign, but also against native exploiters.

The flood of American anti-Communist propaganda in the years of the Cold War has greatly contributed to strengthening this apprehension in the circles of the national bourgeoisie. The result was an amalgam of hatred, fear, and frustration leading in turn to an attitude favoring both sporadic encouragement of the opposition as well as meek compromises on all essential issues. That nothing in Cuba could be done without, let alone against, Washington, was as much the ultimate wisdom of the "mature" spokesmen of the bourgeoisie, as the insistence that "something *must* be done" was characteristic of its so-called liberal wing.

The situation changed to some extent during the later years of the Batista dictatorship, and this brings us to the second factor accounting for the success of the Cuban revolutionary movement. For the criminality, corruption, and cruelty of that regime, exceptional even by Latin American standards, greatly strengthened the oppositional tendencies even among the most conservative elements of the Cuban bourgeoisie. That Washington did nothing to curb, let alone remove, Batista, that as high-ranking an American dignitary as Vice-President Nixon on a visit to Havana commended his administration's "stability and efficiency," added fuel to the fire of anti-Yankee sentiment. Thus nationalism, merging with the acute and nearly universal revulsion against the increasingly terroristic and increasingly predatory Batista tyranny, gave rise to a general political atmosphere of tolerance and even sympathy toward all attempts to rid the country of the insufferable yoke.

This consensus on the urgency of a political change led to the *neutralization* of large segments of the Cuban middle class during the early phases of the revolutionary struggle. And there can hardly be any doubt, I think, that this neutralization played a decisive role in the success of the revolution. It provided the revolutionary movement with invaluable support of various kinds: money, contacts, information, places of refuge from Batista's persecution. It greatly facilitated the recruitment of students and professional people for the revolutionary cause. What is probably most important, it created a climate in the country in which the morale of the Batista army became increasingly shaky and eventually collapsed. It was the breakdown of the morale of Batista's army that enabled hundreds of partisans to score victories over thousands of heavily armed government soldiers and to capture (and distribute among the *campesinos*) their arms and their supplies.

It is against this background of the economic, political, and moral bankruptcy of the *ancien régime* that one has to view the emergence of the third factor that determined the success and the subsequent course of the Cuban Revolution. That factor is the leadership given it by Fidel Castro. And while it is impossible to say what road a man as extraordinary, as complex, and as gifted as Castro would have traveled under other historical circumstances, it is quite certain that it was the particular condition of his country as well as the complete disorientation within his own class that pushed that scion of a wealthy land-owning family in the direction of revolutionary struggle. The state of Cuban society under the reign of Batista, however, explains only Castro's first steps in the revolutionary movement and accounts for his general philosophy during that first phase. For at the outset, the horizon of the

Castro movement coincided on the whole with the horizon of the broad liberal wing of the Cuban bourgeoisie, with the view that a *political* turnover could no longer be postponed, with the insight that *some* economic reforms were indispensable if the people of Cuba were to emerge from their misery. Yet if Castro's heroism and dedication played a crucial role in the initiation of the 26th of July Movement, it was his genius, his integrity, and his miraculous intuition which enabled the Movement to transcend the *political* objectives of a bourgeois *coup d'état,* and to carry the revolution to its ultimate goal—a *social* transformation of the country. Indeed, Castro's greatness has been his complete identification with the Revolution, his capacity to grow with it, his ability to grasp its inner logic, his power of visualizing its next step, and his masterly skill in interpreting and clarifying it to the masses of the Cuban people. And while he thus fulfilled the true task of political leadership, it was the greatness of the Revolution, the cohesion, dedication, and courage of the Cuban *campesinos* which turned Castro's torch into a blazing fire which consumed Batista, imperialism, and capitalism in Cuba.

VI

No mention has been made thus far of the urban workers. Indeed, the role played by them in fighting and winning the revolutionary battles was small. It would seem that on the whole the employed segment of the industrial working class remained passive throughout the revolutionary period. Forming the "aristocratic" layer of the Cuban proletariat, these workers partook of the profits of monopolistic business (foreign and domestic), were well paid by Latin American standards, and enjoyed a standard of living considerably higher than that of the masses of the Cuban people. The fairly strong trade union movement was dominated by "business unionism" United States style, and was thoroughly permeated by racketeering and gangsterism. The Communist Party, although influential among the rank and file, was numerically weak, outlawed, and subjected to persecution, terror, and assassinations on the part of Batista's police and Batista's strongmen in the trade union organizations. The CP's policy was therefore extremely cautious. Anxious not to expose its meager cadres to physical annihilation, the Party was reluctant to engage in overt actions and confined itself for the most part to political education and direct trade union activity. Anchored primarily in the urban working class and having few roots in the countryside, it took almost no part in Castro's *campesino* movement; only a handful of Communist Party members joined the rebels in the Sierra Maestra.

This "wait and see" attitude of the working class toward the 26th of July Movement continued during the first months after the Revolution. It was not until the revolutionary government embarked upon nationalization of industrial enterprises that industrial workers began giving really active support to the Revolution, began to realize its socialist character. Since then, as the Revolution moved ever more pronouncedly beyond its original political objectives, and toward the realization of a socialist society in Cuba, the labor movement has identified itself to an ever increasing extent with Fidel Castro. To be sure, the trade unions reproduced on a smaller scale the tensions and differentiations besetting the nation as a whole. Some right-wing labor leaders who at first joined the Revolution have since defected, just as have middle class politicians for whom the Revolution was "going to far." On the other side, "ultra-left" labor politicians have been grumbling about insufficient benefits accruing to labor at the present time, and, imbued by an old syndicalist tradition, have threatened or even organized strikes against government-owned enterprises.

The situation was somewhat different in what might be called the *declassé* part of the working class: the unemployed in the cities and the large numbers of those more or less steadily engaged in service trades, the tourist industry, and the economy's distributive sector. In these groups there was apparently a considerable amount of sympathy for the 26th of July Movement, which, however, was more akin to the sentiments of the middle class than to the enthusiasm for the Revolution on the part of the *campesinos*. Finding no organized expression, it contributed nevertheless to the spread of the general atmosphere favorable to the revolutionary movement, thus facilitating the activities of its underground network and broadening Castro's popular base on the day after the Revolution.

VII

And so it came about that Cuba's Great Revolution followed the pattern of a "permanent revolution," passing rapidly from one stage of revolutionary struggle to the next, compressing more than a century of historical development into the narrow span of less than a year, and solving within weeks problems which elsewhere and earlier have occupied entire decades. Having started as a national, anti-imperialist, political revolution it had immediately to cope with the desperate animosity and bitter resistance of American imperialism, and was thus forced within a few months to enter the next phase and to turn into a social revolution. And the social revolution, by its very nature, could not but begin immediately to assume a proletarian, socialist character. Propelled by rural workers and led by a political group deriving its inspirations and its program from the economic and social conditions of the *campesinos*, the Revolution instead of parcelling out land and thus creating *more* private property in the means of production—the characteristic and essential feature of a bourgeois revolution—organized at the outset producers' cooperatives in agriculture and thus drastically *reduced* the sphere of private property in the countryside. Carrying out the universally approved mandate to destroy Batista's tyranny, it confiscated the property of the most notorious and most offensive members of the Batista gang, and thus broke the back of the narrow but powerfully entrenched comprador stratum of the Cuban bourgeoisie.

And yet, even with the help of hindsight, it cannot be safely assumed that the Revolution would have run its full course toward the abolition of private property in all the important means of production, if it had not been for the powerful catalyst provided by the hostility and intransigence of the United States. In spite of a hatred of imperialism shared by almost the entire nation, it was not until the refusal by American-owned oil companies to process Soviet oil that the properties of those companies were first "intervened" and then nationalized. Nor was it before the unilateral abrogation of the Cuban sugar quota by the American government that further American enterprises were taken over. And it was not until the recent general embargo on most United States exports to Cuba, that the remainder of American business in Cuba was turned into social property. In sum, it was the firm, unwavering reaction to American challenges, the courageous and uncompromising prosecution of the anti-imperialist struggle which ripened, hothouse fashion, the fledgling Cuban Revolution and pushed it in the direction of economic planning and socialism.

All this was not "realization of an idea" or execution of a previously conceived plan. Quite on the contrary, the Revolution groped its way from step to step, moving in response to the challenges and necessities of the historical situation, teaching the leadership and the masses the categorical imperatives of its own development, overcoming all obstacles to its progress, and destroying in the process its enemies as well as its false friends, the counter-revolutionaries as well as the traitors and the weaklings. By its experience it confirmed, however, a number of most important tenets of the theory of economic and social development. It demonstrated once more that in the present age all genuine efforts at liberation and economic and social advancement of colonial and dependent countries grow necessarily into political revolutions and that these political revolutions equally necessarily transcend themselves and evolve into social revolutions are nc longer *intra*-national revolutions the outcome of which is determined by the class struggle on the international arena, by the relative strength of the world's socialist and imperialist camps.

VIII

The international setting of the Cuban Revolution has had a profound influence on its course. The sharp and undisguised hostility of the American ruling class toward the social transformation in Cuba has accentuated the anti-imperialist character of the Revolution and added to its scope and momentum. At the same time it markedly affected the class struggle within Cuba itself. The dialectic of the process involved is remarkable and deserves careful attention. Having administered a crushing defeat to the Batista-comprador sector of the Cuban ruling class during the winter of 1958-1959, the 26th of July Movement took over the government of a nearly united nation. With the *campesinos* and the industrial workers on its side, with most of the bourgeoisie allied or neutralized, the revolutionary government of Cuba faced practically no opposition. That the honeymoon would not last forever was foreseeable from the very outset. At every step going beyond its political, bourgeois-democratic phase the Revolution necessarily lost some of the bourgeoisie's sympathy and support. And every time a further number of so-called middle-of-the-road politicians, intellectuals, and ordinary bourgeois turned their backs on Fidel Castro, some of his old friends and comrades-in-arms defected, withdrew into private life, or joined the counter-revolutionaries in Miami and in Guatemala. Such losses of marginal supporters, of vacillating fellow-travellers are inevitable in every revolution that is running its full course. Many leaves fall off before the heart of the artichoke is reached. But what has greatly accelerated and sharpened the process of differentiation and polarization within an all but unanimous people in arms is the incessantly present American influence. For without the prospect (or hope) of an American intervention, the Cuban counter-revolutionaries would not have the slightest chance of success. Completely isolated from the people, out of step with its aspirations, its struggles, and its achievements, these "former people" would have to have thrown in the sponge, reconciled themselves to living in a new society, or emigrated to more congenial parts. Only the ever-present prospect of American Marines descending from Guantanamo or of a contingent made up of American-trained, American-equipped, and American-transported Cubans invading the island from their American-maintained bases in Guatemala and Florida has upheld the spirit of the counter-revolutionaries, has given them reason to bide their time and to look forward to an opportunity to put the clock back, to have an Iran, a Spain, a Guatemala, in Cuba.

There can be no doubt that this continual "re-fueling" of the counter-revolutionaries' morale has done much harm to the Cuban Revolution. Without it there would have been no guerrillas in the Escambray; without it there would be no need for political repression; without it 200,000 worker and *campesino* militiamen would not need to spend a good part of their time in armed vigils in the towns and on the beaches of the country; and without it the overworked, overstrained leaders of the Revolution could devote themselves singlemindedly to the burning task of organizing the national economy rather than live in a permanent state of emergency, coping all the time with genuine or imaginary threats to national security. To be sure, even the ever present danger of an American-promoted counter-revolution has been of some advantage to the Cuban Revolution. Although it has led some to abandon or to betray it, it has at the same time cemented more firmly than would have otherwise been possible the cohesion, the devotion, and the determination of all the popular, anti-imperialist forces in the country. That the words inscribed on the banner of the Cuban Revolution are not only "Cuba sí, Yanquí no" but also "Patria o Muerte," is the contribution of the American ruling class to the cause of Cuban liberation.

The international setting of the Cuban Revolution has also another side to it. It is generally sensed in Cuba, and for this there is much incontrovertible evidence, that in the absence of a powerful bloc of socialist countries, the Cuban Revolution would have been crushed long ago by the forces of imperialism. Indeed, the help provided Cuba by the Soviet Union, by China, and by the socialist countries of Eastern Europe is immeasurable. Politically and morally it assumed vast significance by giving the Cubans the strong sense of not being alone, of reassuring them in their desperate, unequal struggle with the American giant. Economically, it tided them over what would undoubtedly have developed into a fatal crisis. By supplying them with oil, the Soviet Union prevented their being left suddenly without any kind of fuel. By opening their markets to Cuban sugar, the socialist countries saved Cuba's most important single industry. By granting Cuba credits and shipping to Cuba industrial and agricultural equipment as well as by dispatching to Cuba experts and technicians, they enabled the country to maintain and to begin developing its agricultural and industrial economy.

And this corroborates the crucially important proposition that every new arrival in the socialist camp finds the going easier than the country which preceded it, that the strength of socialism in the world is cumulative, that socialist "dividends" will become more frequent and more ample as the number and the power of the socialist countries increase. Just as the cost of modern industry and technology was paid for during the Industrial Revolution by the lives and health and happiness of generations of English and Indian and Irish workers and peasants, so the sweep of socialism in our time is the fruit of the heroism, endurance, and toil of the Russian workers and peasants in the era of the Five Year Plans.

IX

The Cuban Revolution was born with a silver spoon in its mouth. The solidarity and dedication of its people, the isolation, political bankruptcy, and moral despicability of its adversaries saved the country the administrative chaos and economic turmoil that might have resulted from a long and destructive civil war. The island is nothing short of a paradisiac garden where the fertility of the soil is such that it is almost possible to harvest without sowing. The world-renowned French agronomist René Dumont has estimated that if cultivated as intensively as South China, Cuba could feed fifty million people. Under the reign of American corporations, it provided a miserable livelihood for a small fraction of that number. Many advocates of capitalism, while granting the inhumanity and injustice of the capitalist system, like to boast about its supreme efficiency. Only a little study and reflection is needed to see that this claim has no foundation even in the most advanced capitalist countries. When it comes to Cuba (and other underdeveloped countries), its monstrous absurdity is visible to the naked eye.

What I have termed [in *The Political Economy of Growth*, Chapter 2] "potential economic surplus" assumes in Cuba gigantic proportions. Sugar cane grows like a weed, and its output could be easily multiplied at minimal cost above the low level enforced by the limitations of the world market. Vast areas of virgin land ideally suited for agriculture can be taken into cultivation by investment of moderate amounts of capital in bulldozers, tractors, and rural housing. Much of the perennial scourge of the Cuban countryside—mass unemployment during the *tiempo muerte*—can be broken up and eventually abolished by diversifying and staggering crops, by using idle manpower on construction jobs, by developing processing plants for agricultural products and other industries.

In nearly all the other countries that have gone through a socialist revolution and embarked upon a program of rapid economic development, shortage of food has been the principal obstacle to progress. New industrial enterprises could be more or less rapidly established. Some foreign exchange could be found to import indispensable machinery. Existing energy sources could be made to carry heavier loads. Even unskilled manpower could be taught to operate and to service complicated new equipment. When it came to agriculture, however, the situation was quite different. In the absence of unutilized land, increases of agricultural output were hard to come by. Technological improvements are difficult and sometimes impossible to introduce in the framework of subsistence farming and against frequently encountered opposition of superstitious and ignorant peasants. And even when and where small increases of output were achieved against exasperating odds, it often proved impossible to obtain those increments for urban consumption. In the absence of an adequate supply of manufactured consumer goods—itself depending on a measure of industrial development or availability of foreign exchange—the peasants, barely eking out a physiological subsistence minimum, consumed rather than brought to market whatever extra output they were able to produce.

Cuba miraculously escapes this vicious circle. In a short time it can radically increase and diversify its agricultural output. It can not only maintain and, if need be, expand its principal export crops—sugar, tobacco, coffee—but it can readily produce at home the staples which it used to import—rice, corn, cotton, vegetable oils, and animal fats. Becoming thus self-sufficient with regard to food, it can devote the foreign exchange proceeds of its exports to the acquisition of machinery, oil, and those raw materials and consumer goods which it is impossible, or at least at the present time uneconomical, to produce at home. Being produced in large-scale agricultural enterprises and not by a multitude of subsistence farmers, Cuba's agricultural product comes naturally to market and is available for export and for urban consumption and processing. It serves thus directly as a base for a program of industrialization, housing, education, and health.

Enabled in this way to organize an immediate improvement of the wretched living conditions of the masses, the Cuban Revolution is spared the excruciating but ineluctable compulsion that has beset all preceding socialist revolutions: the necessity to force a tightening of people's belts today in order to lay the foundations for a better tomorrow. Conveying to the people right away the benefits of a more rational organization of the social economy, giving people now what they crave most—more food, more housing, more schools, and more hospitals—the Cuban revolutionary government can retain more easily than any previous revolutionary regime the loyalty and the support of broad popular masses. It can therefore carry out the most far-reaching transformation ever accomplished in human history—the transition from capitalism to social-ism—with a minimum of repression and with a minimum of violence, in an atmosphere of freedom and enthusiastic participation of a resurrected nation.

X

Thus far the government of Fidel Castro has fulfilled its historical mandate and has fully grasped and lived up to its unique opportunity. It has initiated an unprecedented burst of creative activity in agriculture and got under way a vast program of expansion and diversification of agricultural output. It has brilliantly perceived the peculiarities and the necessities of Cuba's road to socialism, and proceeded at an early stage to organize producers' cooperatives and large state farms in the countryside. Sensitive and responsive to the vital needs of the people, it has embarked on a comprehensive campaign of housing construction, slum clearance, and school building. Inspired by and inspiring a tremendous outburst of dormant popular energies, it has put the army, the slum-dwellers, the unemployed on the job of building houses, schools, cities, farms, roads, and hospitals.

It certainly cannot be said as yet that the Revolution has completed its task, that everything is now under control and that Cuba from now on can advance undisturbed on its way to a better and richer society. Such might have been and still might be the case in the absence of harassment and threat from the United States. As matters stand, however, the situation is most precarious, and the difficulties and dangers confronting the Cuban Revolution are numerous and serious. First and foremost, there is obviously the possibility of direct or indirect military action on the part of the United States. The dilemma faced by the policy-makers in Washington is genuine and serious. The Cuban Revolution exercises an irresistible magnetism and consti-tutes a source of encouragement and hope to all the peoples of Latin America, whose economic, social, and political condition is the same as or worse than that prevailing in Cuba before the Revolution. Too much is at stake for American corporations, too important are the interests involved, to tolerate a victory of the Cuban people. And yet simply to use the iron fist and to crush the Cuban Revolution is a very risky course of action at the present time. Not only must the power of the Soviet Union and the socialist bloc be reckoned with but also the intrinsic brittleness of all American alliances and dependencies in the so-called free world. What is more, who is to say whether the wave of revulsion and hostility against the United States that would inevitably sweep all of Latin America in the event of American aggression against Cuba would not do even more harm to American corporate interests than the survival of the Cuban Revolution? The "compromise" apparently arrived at in Washington seems to be an attempt to strangle the Cuban Revolution economically, combined with a systematic build-up in Guatemala and elsewhere of a Cuban counter-revolutionary force for an eventual invasion of Cuba. I think that the first part of this program—economic sanctions culminating in a *de facto* suppression of all American-Cuban trade—is doomed to failure. No doubt is is causing and will cause in the future many frictions and dislocations in the Cuban economy, but none of these difficulties threatens to be such that it could not be overcome by the Cuban government in cooperation with the socialist bloc. Yet the slimmer the chances of Cuba's succumbing under economic pressures, the larger the danger of an accelerated realization of the second part of the scheme: armed invasion aiming at the establishment of a "free" Cuban administration on Cuban soil and the overthrow of the revolutionary government. It would be idle to speculate on the purely military problems involved; but it is quite certain that what was feasible in Iran and in Guatemala would prove impossible in Cuba. There is neither an army holding effective power and ready at any time to stab in the back the civilian government, nor is there a subdued helpless population forced to accept passively whatever happens around the presidential palace. Two hundred thousand workers and *campesinos* under arms would turn such an invasion into a civil war, and it hardly needs adding that a repetition of Spain today could easily bring about a global holocaust.

By comparison with this life-and-death question, all the other problems facing the Cuban government seem to be almost trivial. On the social and political side there is the big open problem of Cuba's future political life, and of the mechanism assuring both a socialist and a democratic evolution of Cuban society. Having successfully smashed the principal pillar of the *ancien régime*—its military establishment—the Revolution has also disposed of the phony parliamentary institutions which for years have been covering up the dictatorship of American capital and its Cuban retainers. There can be no doubt about the wisdom of the revolutionary government's refusal to call a parliamentary election at the present time. Such an election would serve not merely to revive what has become a defunct and compromised institution, but also to enable the counter-revolutionary forces to integrate and to organize themselves under the guise of a political party operating *within* the framework of the new, socialist Cuba. Social revolutions are never carried out by elections, and it is to Fidel Castro's everlasting credit that he has escaped the pitfall of "parliamentary cretinism." Equally wise and timely was the decision of the revolutionary government to reorganize drastically the judiciary and to substitute judges accepting the Revolution for the guardians of the old order.

But while all this is based at the present time on direct democracy in action, on the people's unlimited confidence in and affection for Fidel Castro, the time is not too distant when it will become indispensable to create and develop institutions essential to the normal functioning of a democratic, socialist society. Whether such institutions will be direct popular assemblies of the Swiss cantonal type (which would not be impossible in a country as small as Cuba) or whether they will assume the form of *campesinos'* and workers' councils resembling the Soviet pattern is immaterial. What is important is that some system of democratic representation and control should evolve in the near future. Nor will it be possible to maintain indefinitely the loose, amorphous constitution of the 26th of July Movement. That will have to crystallize itself into a cohesive, closely knit organization serving as the regularly functioning link between the broad masses of the working people and their socialist government.

On the economic side there is the necessity to streamline the government's economic administration and to work out and carry through a well-considered plan of economic development. There is the urgent need to recruit and train suitable cadres for industry, agriculture, and the civil service—to replace those who have left the country, as well as to satisfy the economy's new and ever growing requirements. In conjunction with this there is the huge task of reorganizing the country's system of higher education, of finding a sufficient number of competent instructors to produce a new generation of physicists, chemists, agronomists, engineers, physicians, statisticians, and school teachers. There are the pressing claims of the unemployed and of those who have been losing their livelihood as a result of the disappearance of American tourism and of a vast shift in the country's foreign trade.

But all of these are manageable problems and all of them can be dealt with rationally, given peace and given time—in particular if the government is permitted to concentrate on their solution. Given peace and given time! Whether the Cuban people will have the good fortune of getting both or whether they will have to go through an ordeal of a devastating civil war no one, I am afraid, can safely predict. All that can be hoped for is that the American ruling class will be able to avoid the crime and the folly of another Suez, perhaps to be followed by the agonies of another Algeria, and that the heroic workers and *campesinos* of Cuba will be able to continue their magnificent forward movement guided by the courage, the wisdom, and the genius of Fidel Castro.

XI

During the last few days [the Bay of Pigs invasion], the hearts and minds of all those to whom the cause of progress and freedom is not a matter of lip service but a deep commitment have been going out in anguish, concern, and sympathy to the heroic workers and *campesinos* of Cuba. During the last few days, the dagger which has been held in the hands of counter-revolutionary gangs assembled and trained in Louisiana and Florida, in Guatemala and Nicaragua—that dagger was thrust into the flesh of the Cuban people. This operation was preceded by a number of other operations: bombers flew over Cuba, dropping bombs on civilians, killing men, women, and children, destroying factories and dwellings, blowing up bridges, and setting afire vital supplies. Acts of arson were perpetrated in which hundreds of thousands of tons of sugar were burned, in which stocks of other commodities were wrecked, in which fruits of Cuban labor were ruined. This sequence of operations was sponsored, promoted, and rendered possible by the government of the United States. The dagger was supplied by the American government, the bombers were supplied by the American government, and so were the bombs. This has been recognized everywhere, in this country and in the rest of the world, and to quote one of many sources, I shall refer to *Business Week* (April 15, 1961) where it is explicitly stated:

President Kennedy has decided to give active U.S. support to Cuban insurgents in their mounting effort to topple the Communist-dominated regime of Fidel Castro. The President made a firm decision to do this about a month ago. His decision is marked departure from the previous policy of relying on economic sanctions and diplomatic encirclement to bring about the collapse of Castro.

Whatever one may think about this policy adopted by President Kennedy in terms of political wisdom, there cannot be the slightest doubt that the sequence of operations undertaken from American soil with the help of the United States government constitutes a criminal offense under international law—however interpreted or construed. The government of the United States, which makes so much of its adherence to international law and which never misses an occasion to admonish other governments to respect the canons of that law, has broken it in the most flagrant fashion. Article 15 of the Charter of the Organization of American States to which the United States government has subscribed, with the advice and consent of the Senate, reads as follows: "No state or group of states has the right to intervene, directly or indirectly, for any reason whatever, in the internal or external affairs of any other state. The foregoing principle prohibits not only armed force but also any other form of interference or attempted threat against the personality of the state or against its political, economic and cultural elements." The wording of the Neutrality Act which is on the statute books of the United States is different. What it stipulates, however, is exactly the same.

The question naturally arises, why were these crimes committed? The answer is given in a White Paper of the United States Department of State—released on April 4 and published in full in *The New York Times*. This paper, written by Professor Arthur M. Schlesinger, Jr., of Harvard University, in close collaboration with President Kennedy, gives the reason for our policy toward revolutionary Cuba. And this reason boils down to a very simple proposition: the United States is committed to resist by all means at its disposal any revolution in Latin America, and presumably elsewhere, which transcends the limits of a bourgeois revolution. Any revolution which goes beyond certain political reforms, which goes beyond certain institutional changes that might strengthen parliamentary government or something resembling parliamentary government, any revolution which goes further—toward socialism—is a revolution which the United States sets itself up to fight to the bitter end.

Mr. Schlesinger commends certain accomplishments of the Cuban Revolution such as schools built, medical clinics established, new housing, the opening up of beaches and resorts to the people, the elimination of graft and corruption in the government; but he very carefully omits all reference to such reforms as the nationalization of factories, the formation of collective farms, the organization of a planned economy, the great effort to free the country from its pernicious dependence on one crop, sugar—all measures which are indispensable to genuine progress and genuine development of Cuba's economy and society. He states that Castro has interfered with the middle classes in Cuba, and that after having suppressed the middle classes, he has struck down elements in organized labor. How could he have nationalized the means of production and started to organize a socialist planned economy without harming the interests of the bourgeoisie? And those who know what elements in organized labor were struck down in Cuba, know also that these elements of gangsterism, elements of so-called business unionism that were infesting the body of Cuba's organized labor. These were elements which any healthy labor movement would wish to be rid of at the earliest possible opportunity.

In the entire White Paper, which is full of solicitude for the Cuban people's freedom and advancement, there is nowhere a reference to the workers and *campesinos* of Cuba. There is nowhere a reference to the immense progress that has been achieved in only two years in living and working conditions, in the elimination of unemployment, in the struggle against illiteracy, in all aspects of life—not of the Cuban middle class, but of the vast majority of the Cuban people. President Kennedy in his reply to Mr. Khrushchev considers the fact that 100,000 Cubans have left Cuba since the Revolution to be one of the most telling indictments of the Cuban Revolution. Has there ever been a revolution in which certain elements were not dispossessed, in which certain groups did not choose to emigrate, in which certain strata of the population did not turn into counter-revolutionaries? What is the meaning of the word "revolution" if no one is dethroned, if no one is thrown out of power and wealth and status? If none of these things occur, why speak of revolution? The United States Department of State has proclaimed itself to be the supreme judge of what kind of revolution is conducive to a country's welfare and what kind is not. The Department of State is to decide from now on which revolution is good and which is bad. And any revolutions that are bad—bad because harmful to American national interests as they are interpreted by the Department of State—the government of the United States is determined to suppress.

It would be worthwhile for those who are not accustomed to thinking in historical terms to take a glance at some history books and to realize what the reaction was to the American Revolution at the time it took place. Let me present to you a few references on that subject:

> The Revolution had been stirred up by a few crafty men who had played upon the ignorance and the passions of the mob; by a handful of conspirators was the "draught designed to cheat the crowd and fascinate mankind." And these conspirators were "an infernal, dark-designing group of men . . . obscure, pettifogging attorneys, bankrupt shop-keepers, outlawed smugglers . . . wretched banditti . . . the refuse and dregs of mankind." (Charles A. and Mary R. Beard, *The Rise of American Civilization*, 1937, p. 269.)

This is what was said about George Washington and his friends and combatants at the time of the American Revolution. How does this compare with what Messrs. Berle, Schlesinger & Company, even the President of the United States, have to say about Fidel Castro?

But the main accusation which is made against the Cuban Revolution is that it is an "alien product," that it receives support from abroad. Professor Schlesinger makes a lot of the fact that the Cuban Revolution represents an inroad of forces which are "alien to the inter-American system." Let me submit to you another passage from the standard work of the Beards: "It is difficult to believe that the Congress could have staggered through the Revolution, if it hadn't procured such generous financial assistance from the government at Paris." This statement referring to the

American Revolution can be found on p. 242 of *The Rise of American Civilization*.

This, however, does not exhaust Professor Schlesinger's mighty assault on the Cuban Revolution. The Cuban Revolution is something which he is determined to see destroyed because it has not been carried out by a process of free elections. Quite a historian he who believes that revolutions are carried out by elections! For a revolution is precisely an upset in the existing constitutional or governmental process, an upset which—by definition—cannot be carried out within the framework of the constitutional or governmental process which it sets out to destroy. And with reference to this point I would like to mention a further passage from the Beard's work (p. 257): "It would be conservative to say that, as far as balloting was a measure of popular support, not more than one third of the adult white males in America ever set the seal of their approval on the Revolution by voting for its committeemen and delegates."

Let us put it bluntly: the White Paper is disingenuous. The White Paper is an absolutely hopeless attempt to disguise a very simple proposition. And this proposition is that what our government is setting out to defend, cost what it may, is not the process of free elections, not democratic freedom, not civil liberties of any kind. What our government is setting out to defend is private property in the means of production. What our government is setting out to defend in this hemisphere, under the name of the inter-American system, is the American empire exploited by American corporations. If we want historical evidence for this proposition, such evidence is amply available. The United States government has never gone out of its way to overthrow any Latin American dictators, nor has it made any efforts to upset Mr. Franco in Spain, Mr. Salazar in Portugal, or any of the tyrannical sheikhs maintaining slavery in the Near East. But remember what happened when a few years ago the Republic of Guatemala put Mr. Arbenz into power—by means of a most democratic, most orderly, parliamentary election. Mr. Arbenz began transcending the limits of a bourgeois regime, he began tampering with bourgeois institutions. Mr. Arbenz proceeded to enact a genuine agrarian reform. And in the process of so doing he interfered with the interests of the United Fruit Corporation. At that point he was declared to be "subversive," at that point the United States government went into action to overthrow Mr. Arbenz's democratically elected administration, at that point the CIA "elected" a new government for Guatemala which promptly canceled all of Mr. Arbenz's reforms. A similar fate befell Dr. Mossadegh in Iran, about whose massive popular support there has never been any doubt, as soon as he dared to tackle Western oil interests.

Of course none of this has been or is being done in the name of private property. It would be hard to arouse much enthusiasm that way. All this has been and is being done in the name of democracy and free elections. And to this end an assumption is tacitly smuggled in that the only expression of democracy is a free election, that democracy and free elections are one and the same. In this way, what is actually only one aspect of democracy is turned into a fetish; although in many countries and on many occasions, free election has meant nothing but plain and unadulterated swindle. What does free election mean in the American South, and what is the precise content of a free election when the people—as is more and more the case in this country in general—are given the choice between six and half-a-dozen? What is the significance of a free election in countries where opinion is shaped by a corrupt press and corrupt radio and television, where the freedom of the people is in the hands of a corrupt police force, and where the nation as a whole lives under the weight of omnipotent vested interests? As if the decision of people cannot be expressed by other means than free elections—and in certain historical situations, *only* by other means! The Cuban people have, indeed, exercised their privilege of freely electing: by fighting and dying in the mountains of the Sierra Maestra they have elected a revolutionary, democratic, progressive government and have overthrown the bloody tyranny of Batista.

What is more, it so happens that in the last few days the Cuban people had another occasion for a free election. For the entire invasion enterprise was based on one fundamental assumption, that the Cuban people are seething with unrest under their "oppressor" Fidel Castro, that the Cuban people want nothing more than an opportunity to rise up in arms against their new tyrant. To quote *Business Week* once more, "the main hope of an anti-Castro victory depends upon massive defections from Castro's armed forces and militia which number about 300,000" (April 15, 1961). These 300,000 militia men and women are armed, according to reports published in our press, with the most modern weapons; they control the entire country. Why didn't they, workers and *campesinos* of Cuba, supposedly oppressed and miserable under their present regime, turn their weapons against their oppressors and exploiters? The torch of "freedom" was brought to them, the cry of revolt was sounded by the ex-Batista men who landed on the soil of Cuba, the liberators arrived in the middle of the island. The Cuban people were given the historic opportunity of a truly free election. They were given the possibility of making a choice between Miro Cardona and Fidel Castro. All of us know what the Cuban people decided. All of us know how they voted. Making use of this opportunity for a free election, they rallied as one man behind their democratic, socialist government and threw the invaders where they belonged: into the garbage can of history.

The question which arises now is what policy Washington will henceforth adopt with regard to Cuba. To this there is as yet no obvious answer. I heard over the radio President Kennedy's speech today. I haven't been able to read it as yet. The speech seems to be full of ambiguity and vagueness. But one thing is apparently decided on in administration quarters and that is that the fight against the Cuban people should be continued, that everything possible should be done to destroy the Cuban Revolution. The reason which is now given for this decision, a reason which is an addition to those advanced in the White Paper, is that Cuba constitutes a threat to the national security of the United States. The utter ludicrousness of this proposition is so obvious that it hardly calls for comment. The six million people who live in Cuba are supposed to represent a threat to the security of this mightiest nation in the world! On the island of Cuba, in Guantánamo, the United States has a naval base. This naval base undisputedly controls all of Cuba. Where then is the threat to American security? Has it been claimed anywhere that the Soviet Union or any other country within or without the hemisphere has been using Cuba as a military base? No such claims have come to my attention. Was Premier Castro ever asked to commit himself not to allow any power to use Cuba as a military base? No such request was ever made to my knowledge, although I am convinced that such an assurance would be given by Castro for the asking. Is there a threat to United States security in the 300,000 Cuban militiamen armed with rifles and machine guns? Is there a threat to the security of the United States in the fifty or eighty or whatever the number may be of fighter planes which are supposedly reaching Cuba from Czechoslovakia or some other country in the socialist part of the world? Apart from the fact that fighter planes are weapons of defense and not of offense, is the military potential of the United States such that eighty planes could jeopardize the safety of our shores? I don't think that anyone could honestly maintain any of this. I think that to all the other shams this sham is a fitting addition.

But what is and has been an issue all along is the example of *Fidelismo*. The staggering, magnificent success of the Cuban Revolution is a source of hope and inspiration to the Latin American people everywhere. What is threatened by Cuba is not American security. What is threatened by Cuba is what President Kennedy and Professor Schlesinger refer to as the inter-American system. And the inter-American system is only a thinly veiled euphemism for the control of Latin America by United States corporations. What is threatened by Cuba is a continual exploitation of Latin American peoples. And these peoples, inspired by the shining example of Cuba, may decide to substitute for President Kennedy's inter-American system another system. A system of freedom, of progress, of socialism.

This is why *Fidelismo* has to be crushed. This is why no means are considered to be too dirty to be used in the effort to strangle the Cuban Revolution. In the light of this, what effrontery it is to accuse Fidel Castro and his government of procuring weapons from wherever they may be able to get them in order to defend their people and their Revolution against undisguised aggression! What effrontery it is to cite their attempt to defend themselves as a reason for our seeking to rape Cuba! Over 100 years ago Karl Marx wrote in his little book *The Civil War in France* the following magnificent sentence: "All this only proves that the bourgeois of our day considers himself the legitimate successor of the baron of old who thought every weapon in his own hand fair against the plebeian, while in the hands of the plebeian a weapon of any kind constituted in itself a crime." This is the spirit of our present government. This is the spirit of the New Frontier. And it is to a policy in this spirit that people who consider themselves intellectuals—Messrs. Berle, Schlesinger, Rostow and the like—lend their support and their talents.

XII

A major fiasco in the life of an individual or in the history of a nation may have a redeeming aspect. It may offer an opportunity for a re-evaluation of the philosophy which underlay the course that led to the disaster, an occasion for a re-examination of the fallacies that were believed, and for a study of the mistakes and errors that were committed. Looked at from this standpoint, the news that has been forthcoming from Washington in the course of the last couple of weeks sounds anything but encouraging. The process of soul-searching that is reported to be taking place in the White House and in other government agencies doesn't seem to refer to the basic philosophy of the Kennedy Administration. It refers, rather, to the methods by which those policies were implemented, to the technicalities which were employed in their execution. In actual fact, the President himself announced in a major speech, which he delivered immediately after the Cuban debacle, that the Cold War will be conducted henceforth with increased vigor; and in making this declaration, he proclaimed that the struggle will be carried on "regardless of the cost and regardless of the peril." So belligerent, so aggressive were the statements made by Mr. Kennedy that *The Wall Street Journal* felt prompted to remark that the President "has laid down a line which bears a remarkable resemblance to the foreign philosophy of Senator Barry Goldwater, the Arizona arch-conservative." What is more, the President went out of his way to rally behind that "line" the support of General MacArthur and former President Hoover, of Mr. Truman and General Eisenhower, not to speak of Mr. Nixon. In this way Mr. Kennedy seeks to create an impression of national unity behind his policy of an intensified Cold War, of a more vigorous, more brutal struggle against socialism.

I cannot now go into the major question of the rationale of the Cold War, nor can I discuss the vital problem whether this drummed-up national unity in the struggle against socialism corresponds to the interests of the American people. Much as I would like to, I cannot now examine the proposition that it is the mission of the American people to serve as the world's gendarme, guarding private property wherever it may be threatened by social revolution. It is equally impossible to deal with the very serious doubt that should arise in everybody's mind as to what contribution we make to human development and advancement by turning every social revolution into a civil war, by making every social revolution a violent one, by provoking repression and terror where repression and terror had been conspicuously absent—as in the case of Cuba. All of these major points must be left aside. What I would like to draw to your attention now are two issues which are as important as they are specific and immediate.

The first one is, what will be the policy of the United States government toward Cuba in the immediate future? Even before April 17, President Kennedy announced that under no circumstances would American military forces be employed against Cuba or would American soil be used as a jumping-off place for an invasion of Cuba. We know now that those words were nothing but a legalistic smoke screen behind which the invasion of Cuba was being prepared, behind which the invaders were being trained, supplied, and equipped by American government agencies. As the London *Economist* states in its April 29 issue, "It is admitted that this was an American operation over which the President had control." His statement, therefore, that under no circumstances would American forces be employed was, to put it mildly, disingenuous—a statement that covered up rather than illuminated what was actually going on. Now Secretary of State Rusk has made a statement before the Latin American Subcommittee of the Senate of which Senator Morse is the chairman, in which he repeated the earlier announcement of the President reiterating that American forces would not be employed against Cuba. In his words: "No direct intervention in Cuba is being contemplated." The question that obviously arises is, what *is* being contemplated with regard to Cuba.

One thing has apparently been decided, that Operation Cuba should from now on be conducted not as a private United States venture but as a joint enterprise of all American states. The Organization of American States is to be mobilized and made the father of a renewed assault against Cuba. Its members are to be bribed and cajoled and frightened into accepting Washington's "leadership." The President threatened that should the Latin American countries refuse to cooperate in an effort to suppress Castro in Cuba, the United States will "go it alone." Meanwhile the Latin American governments are to be worked on to assure their compliance. Their participation at the present time is apparently most doubtful. The conference of the foreign ministers of the American states, scheduled time and again, has been canceled once more, because the Latin American governments are not in line with what Mr. Kennedy wants them to do.

The reason for this reluctance of the Latin American governments to get involved in a Cuban adventure is very simple: the opposition to an anti-Castro campaign is very strong all over Latin America—very much stronger than our press would lead us to believe. It has to be pointed out at this stage that the Kennedy Administration is in very serious danger of repeating all over Latin America an error which may be as disastrous as the one which led to the invasion of Cuba. Even if Mr. Kennedy's ambassadors should succeed by hook or crook in aligning the Latin American governments behind his policy against Castro, it should be seriously considered whether such an alignment would be worth the paper on which it might be recorded. The only assumption on which the adventure in Cuba made any sense at all was that the Cuban people were opposed to Castro and were ready to rise on the first available occasion to overthrow his "tyranny." This assumption has proved to be fallacious as all of those who knew anything about Cuba have predicted. Whether it was C. Wright Mills, or whether it was Paul Sweezy and Leo Huberman, or whether it was myself—all of those who have visited Cuba and studied the Cuban Revolution have been writing and saying on many occasions that the people of Cuba were enthusiastic supporters of their revolutionary government. Now this finding has been empirically verified by the CIA and its agents, and the opposite stories fabricated by the Cuban refugees have been proven to be nothing but figments of their wishful imaginations.

Is the government in Washington now going to repeat its earlier error, as it were, in reverse? Is it going to take the word of its various Latin American client governments to be the expression of the will of their peoples? Mr. Kennedy should know better than that by now; he should know enough to take the words of Latin American rulers for what they are—expressions of their class interests, of their mortal fear of their own nations. This warning should be heeded, because if it is disregarded, as the warnings concerning Cuba were, the policy of the United States is headed for an even larger disaster than the Bay of Pigs.

Regardless of what CIA operatives and Messrs. Berle,

Schlesinger, and Rostow pick up in the cocktail lounges of Latin American capitals, President Kennedy would be well advised to try to comprehend the real situation in Latin America. This real situation is the abysmal misery prevailing in those countires, the complete fiasco of all the "development" programs that have been undertaken thus far, and the utter bankruptcy of their ruling classes in dealing with the burning problems confronting their own peoples. And what Mr. Kennedy would understand is that *Fidelismo* is indeed the first ray of hope which has entered the horizon of the Latin American peoples, a ray of hope in an otherwise hopeless world. In fighting *Fidelismo* our government fights against the future, fights all that the Latin American masses live and strive for. The sooner the United States abandons this ignominious struggle, the sooner the United States accepts the fact that with all other colonial empires, the American empire is bound to collapse in this century of national liberation, the greater are the chances of the world's and this country's survival. Obstinacy on this issue would inescapably lead to catastrophe.

And this brings me to the other point I wanted to discuss with you tonight. The President took the position in his speech to the newspaper editors that in its struggle against world socialism the United States will not feel bound by international treaties and obligations. Mr. Nixon put the matter in very simple terms by saying that some legal pretext has to be found for doing whatever is required. Mr. Kennedy announced that treaty obligations should not be treated as an excuse for inaction, and *Business Week* (of April 29), explains that "in the process, the U.S. could run afoul of the legal niceties of the United Nations and inter-American pledges against nonintervention." Now if this position should actually become the official line of our government, if Washington should adopt the view that the

United Nations Charter, the statute of the Organization of the American States, and all the international commitments that go with them, that all of these are nothing but scraps of paper to be torn into pieces as soon as what the administration considers to be in the national interest demands it—then I submit that the United States government is officially renouncing foreign policy in favor of the law of the jungle. How can we conceivably expect with this attitude to arrive at *any* settlement of international problems, at *any* agreements which would reduce the threat of a thermonuclear holocaust? How can we conceivably expect to succeed in the present negotiations concerning an atom test ban and disarmament, if we say in advance that whatever "legal niceties" such treaties may contain, will be of no relevance to us if and when we decide that our national interest demands their disregard and repudiation? If this course should be followed, if international policy should be given up in favor of unilateral power politics, then it should be entirely clear that what we are moving toward is not an intensified Cold War but an inevitable world war.

In other words, the issue now is not whether the Cold War should be continued. The issue now is not whether the defense of capitalist institutions against the advance of socialism should remain the paramount principle of American foreign policy. The issue which Cuba has brought to the fore is whether the defense of these institutions, and the struggle against socialism are to be driven to the point of a world war with all the consequences that such a war would inevitably entail. The United States government has continually insisted, and the American press has continually reiterated, that the foreign policy of the United States is based on respect for international law. What is to become of this assertion? Is it to be proven to be another link in the long chain of shams that make up the ideology of the ruling class? Now that the class struggle has moved on to the arena of international relations and is no longer merely an internal struggle within nations, international law is apparently following the fate of all law: it becomes merely a tool in the hands of the dominant class to be used and to be thrown away at its convenience. The only difference, but a difference which ought to be seriously pondered, is that in the case of disregard of *domestic* law, the consequences may be relatively minor. Domestic riots, unrest, and even revolutions can be and often have been suppressed—at least temporarily—by the armed forces of the Establishment. In the case of disregard of *international* law, particularly at the present time when the capitalist class is not the only one to wield power, the consequences may be fatal, may be nothing short of an international atomic conflagration.

The decision which the Washington administration has to make at the present time is either to face the realities of the world in the process of national and social revolution or to adopt, perhaps irrevocably, the policy of the iron fist. If the latter course is chosen then, indeed, all of Latin America has to be *forced* to do whatever the State Department wants it to do, then each and every country on the face of the earth has to be put on notice that the United States will carry out its designs regardless of the will of the rest of the world, that the United States is prepared to fight wherever capitalism is threatened—"regardless of the cost and regardless of the peril."

Is there any chance that such a policy could succeed? In my opinion the chance is exactly zero. We are undoubtedly able to intervene militarily in Cuba, to bomb that island out of existence, destroy Castro, and ruin all the achievements of the Cuban people. But in return we are going to get another Algeria, another decade of bitter guerrilla warfare in which we won't be any more able to win than the French were able to win in Africa, or were able to win in Indo-China. And what we are going to get in the rest of Latin America is exactly the same. Guerrillas fighting in the mountains and in the hills, thousands and hundreds of thousands of casualties with no conceivable hope for an ultimate "stabilization" of an order that flies in the face of all the needs and all the aspirations of the people. The only answer that the learned pundits in Washington have come up with thus far is to train our own guerrillas, to match the revolutionary fighters with our specialists in counter-revolution. If all this weren't so tragic, it would be truly comical. Our guerrillas are supposed to fight armed peasants and workers who enjoy immense popular support, who speak the language of their peoples, who express their peoples' innermost wants and hopes! Our guerrillas are supposed to hide in villages and hamlets—on instructions from Washington and in order to prevent the peasants living in those villages and hamlets from seizing the land which they have been coveting for generations! Whoever thought up this brilliant idea, how much less could he have understood the nature, the internal make-up, the motives and the driving forces of a revolution?

But it could be asked here, what is our alternative? Our alternative is undoubtedly an extremely difficult one to swallow for all those who cannot develop the slightest sense of historical perspective, who cannot comprehend at all the basic characteristic of the present epoch. This basic characteristic is that our century is the century of the liberation of the oppressed peoples. This is the century in which colonialism is being liquidated and in which economic development of underdeveloped countries is proceeding by leaps and bounds—everywhere it is breaking through the stranglehold, the fetters and constraints imposed by the existence of the capitalist system. For one fact, I think, is undeniable: capitalism has dismally failed as a possible framework for a rapid development of under-developed countries. And the peoples of those countries recognize this fact with ever increasing clarity. From all the reports which one gets from Latin America as well as from other countries—including India—it becomes abundantly clear that the capitalist system cannot produce in those countries the type of growth and the rates of growth which are required if they are to emerge from their state of misery and backwardness. Are we going to insist on their sticking to the system of capitalist institutions and on their sacrificing all possibilities of growth on the altar of private property? If we do, we are undoubtedly going to have allies—the ruling classes of the backward countries that oppose all change and fear nothing more than the social revolution. In insisting on this—regardless of cost and regardless of peril—we will share the fate of those allies and become hated and despised by the masses of people everywhere. And in the end we will suffer, again together with those allies, the same kind of fiasco that befell us in Cuba in the company of our puppet Miro Cardona. Are we to go from one place to another, trying to stamp out popular revolutions here, there, and everywhere, seeking to shore up a bankrupt, corrupt, and retrograde system?

It could be objected at this point that it is impossible to expect an American government, a government which is dedicated to the preservation of capitalism and which is dominated by capitalist interests, to do anything but struggle for the preservation of capitalism, to do anything but fight the development of socialism. This is undoubtedly true, and I have never been one of those who believe that one can induce a government of a capitalist country to aid, abet—or, for that matter, not to oppose—socialism. And I do not consider it to be my function to advise a capitalist government how best to obstruct the advancement of socialism. But what I do consider to be my function, as well as the function of every decent person today, is to do everything possible to prevent such a government from committing the ultimate crime of plunging the world into the catastrophe of global war for the sake of the preservation of the capitalist system.

Such a world catastrophe can be, must be, and will be avoided if the government of the United States begins to comprehend that in addition to breaking there is also the possibility of bending; that in addition to standing still like a rock, there is also the possibility of trying to find some accommodation to the great landslide that is sweeping the world. Britain has, after all, been able to relinquish a great deal of its empire, and as a result—paradoxically enough— the British capitalists have been able to salvage a great deal of their colonial possessions and investments. What the British ruling class has understood is that it is a wiser course to leave five minutes before one is thrown out, rather than to insist on the ultimate showdown the outcome of which is beyond doubt. The comparison between the conduct of the British ruling class in India and the conduct of the French ruling class in Indo-China and Africa is as striking as it should be instructive. This comparison indicates not that the British government has turned socialist—far from it!—it indicates merely that the British ruling class has developed a sense of what cannot be helped, that the British ruling class would rather survive as long as possible than go under in the flames of a catastrophic conflict.

Though powerful forces determine the broad, general course of history, at each individual junction there is a measure of freedom for those who happen to sit at the steering wheel. There is a range of choice between the position taken by the Portuguese in Angola, the whites in the Union of South Africa, the Belgians in the Congo, and what could be done by a sensible, decent government even if it is also a strictly capitalist government. Must we now assume that the United States government, led by Mr. Kennedy and standing at the New Frontier, will follow the example of the Portuguese rather than the example of the British? I cannot accept this as inevitable. There is, there *must* be a possibility for the American people—in spite of the image of national unity that has been contrived in Washington—to make their government see the light, adopt a policy of reason, a policy of peace. There is no way of writing an insurance policy for the capitalist system for an indefinite period of time, either in this country or anywhere else in the world. There may be, however, a way of assuring the world's survival provided the "furies of private property" can be—if only partly—tamed, if the ruling class of this country can be prevented from committing suicide out of fear of death.

There is the frightful danger that American capitalism, cornered, threatened, and frightened, may be incapable of leaving the rest of the world alone without so slamming the door that the entire building collapses. It is this act of despair that has to be prevented by all available means. It may very well be that our only hope today is that the allies of the United States in Western Europe will be able to stay the hands of our jingoists. But all of us, and particularly those of us who had anything to do with putting Mr. Kennedy into power, have the supreme responsibility of leaving no stone unturned to impress upon the Washington Administration that the issue now is not more or less Cold War, that the issue now is not even capitalism or socialism, that the issue now is world survival or a world catastrophe.

Index

Modern Reader Paperbacks